Version Control with Git

Powerful Tools and Techniques for
Collaborative Software Development

Prem Kumar Ponuthorai and Jon Loeliger

Beijing · Boston · Farnham · Sebastopol · Tokyo

Version Control with Git

by Prem Kumar Ponuthorai and Jon Loeliger

Published by O'Reilly Media, Inc., 1005 Gravenstein Highway North, Sebastopol, CA 95472.

O'Reilly books may be purchased for educational, business, or sales promotional use. Online editions are also available for most titles (*http://oreilly.com*). For more information, contact our corporate/institutional sales department: 800-998-9938 or *corporate@oreilly.com*.

Acquisitions Editor: Melissa Duffield
Development Editors: Virginia Wilson and Shira Evans
Production Editor: Beth Kelly
Copyeditor: Audrey Doyle

Proofreader: Piper Editorial Consulting, LLC
Indexer: Sue Klefstad
Interior Designer: David Futato
Cover Designer: Karen Montgomery
Illustrator: Kate Dullea

May 2009:   First Edition
August 2012:   Second Edition
November 2022:   Third Edition

Revision History for the Third Edition
2022-10-21: First Release
2022-11-04: Second Release
2023-02-03: Third Release

See *http://oreilly.com/catalog/errata.csp?isbn=9781492091196* for release details.

978-1-492-09119-6

[LSI]

Table of Contents

Part II.   Fundamentals of Git

Part III.   Intermediate Skills

Part IV. Advanced Skills

Preface

Git is a free, open source, distributed version control system created by Linus Torvalds. Git requires low operational overhead, yet is flexible and powerful enough to support the demands of complex, large-scale, distributed software development projects.

Our goal in this book is to show you how to get the most out of Git and how to manage a Git repository with ease. By the end, you will have learned Git's philosophy, fundamental concepts, and intermediate to advanced skills for tracking content, collaborating, and managing your projects across teams.

Who This Book Is For

We wrote this book with software engineers (developers, infrastructure engineers, DevOps, etc.) in mind as our primary audience. As such, most of the concepts and examples we use relate to the daily routines and tasks of folks in the software development industry. However, Git is robust enough to track content in areas as varied as data science, graphic design, and book authoring, just to name a few. (Case in point: we used Git as our underlying versioning system to keep track of reviews and edits while writing this book!) Regardless of your title or level of proficiency, if you are using Git as your version control system, you will find value in these pages.

Essential Know-How

Prior experience with any version control system, its aims, and its goals will be a helpful foundation to understand how Git works and to build upon your knowledge as you read this book. You should have some familiarity with using any command-line tool, such as the Unix shell, along with basic knowledge of shell commands, because we use a lot of command-line instructions in the examples and discussions in the book. A general understanding of programming concepts is also a plus.

We developed the examples on the macOS and Ubuntu environments. The examples should work under other platforms such as Debian, Solaris, and Windows (using Git-installed command-line tools, such as Git for Windows), but you can expect slight variations.

Some exercises in the examples may require system-level operations that need root access on machines. Naturally, in such situations you should have a clear understanding of the responsibilities of operations that need root access.

New in This Revision

In this third edition, we take an entirely new, modular approach to the topics by breaking down the concepts of Git. We start by introducing you to the basics and the fundamental philosophy of Git, then gradually build upon intermediate commands to help you efficiently supplement your daily development workflow, and finally conclude with advanced `git` commands and concepts to help you become proficient in understanding the inner mechanics of how Git works under the hood.

Another change we made in this edition was adding more illustrations to explain complex Git concepts to give you a mental model for easier comprehension. We also highlight features from the latest release of Git and provide you with examples and tips that can help improve your current distributed development workflow.

Navigating the Book

We organized this edition into categories according to the reader's familiarity and experience using Git. While we categorize the sections to get progressively more advanced to incrementally build your proficiency with Git, we designed the chapters within each section so that you can leverage the content either as standalone topics or as a series of topics building on one another sequentially.

We strove to apply a consistent structure and a consistent approach to teaching concepts in every chapter. We encourage you to take a moment to internalize this format. This will help you leverage and navigate the book as a handy reference at any point in the future.

If you have picked up the book amid juggling other responsibilities and are wondering what would be the best order to hit the ground running, fret not. Table P-1 will help guide you toward the chapters we feel will help you gain the most knowledge in the least amount of time.

Table P-1. Categories matrix

	Thinking in Git	Fundamentals of Git	Intermediate skills	Advanced skills	Tips and tricks
Software engineering	X	X	X	X	X
Data scientist	X	X	X		X
Graphic designers	X	X			X
Academia	X	X			X
Content authors	X	X			X

Installing Git

To reinforce the lessons taught in the book, we highly encourage you to practice the example code snippets on your development machine. To follow along with the examples, you will need Git installed on your platform of choice. Because the steps to install Git vary according to the version of your operating system, we've provided instructions on how to install Git in Appendix B accordingly.

A Note on Inclusive Language

Another important point we would like to highlight about the examples is that we feel strongly about diversity and inclusion in tech, and raising awareness is a responsibility we take seriously. As a start, we will be using the word *main* to indicate the default branch name.

Omissions

Due to its active community base, Git is constantly evolving. Even as we write this edition, another new version of Git was published for commercial use: version 2.37.1, to be precise. It was not our intention to leave information out of this book; it's simply the inevitable reality when writing about an ever-changing technology.

We deliberately chose not to cover all of Git's own core commands and options so that we could instead focus on common and frequently used commands. We also do not cover every Git-related tool available, simply because there are too many.

Despite these omissions, we feel confident that this book will equip you with a strong foundation and prepare you to dive deeper into the realms of Git if the need arises. For a detailed list of release changes, you can look up the Release Notes documentation (*https://oreil.ly/R2nn4*) for Git.

Conventions Used in This Book

The following typographical conventions are used in this book:

Italic
> Indicates new terms, URLs, email addresses, filenames, and file extensions.

`Constant width`
> Used for program listings as well as within paragraphs to refer to program elements such as variable or function names, databases, data types, environment variables, statements, and keywords.

`Constant width bold`
> Shows commands or other text that should be typed literally by the user.

`Constant width italic`
> Shows text that should be replaced with user-supplied values or by values determined by context.

This icon signifies a useful hint or a tip.

This icon indicates a warning or caution.

This icon indicates a general note.

Furthermore, you should be familiar with basic shell commands to manipulate files and directories. Many examples will contain commands such as these to add or remove directories, copy files, or create simple files:

```
# Command to create a new directory
$ mkdir newdirectory


# Command to write content into a file
$ echo "Test line" > file.txt

# Command to append content at the end of a file
$ echo "Another line" >> file.txt
```

```
# Command to make a copy of a file
$ cp file.txt copy-of-file.txt


# Command to remove a file
$ rm newdirectory/file

# Command to remove a file
$ rmdir newdirectory
```

Commands, root permissions, and commands that need to be executed with root permissions appear as a `sudo` operation:

```
# Install the Git core package
$ sudo apt-get install git-core
```

How you edit files or effect changes within your working directory is pretty much up to you. You should be familiar with a text editor. In this book, we'll denote the process of editing a file by either a direct comment or a pseudocommand:

```
# edit file.c to have some new text
$ edit file.c
```

O'Reilly Online Learning

 For more than 40 years, *O'Reilly Media* has provided technology and business training, knowledge, and insight to help companies succeed.

Our unique network of experts and innovators share their knowledge and expertise through books, articles, and our online learning platform. O'Reilly's online learning platform gives you on-demand access to live training courses, in-depth learning paths, interactive coding environments, and a vast collection of text and video from O'Reilly and 200+ other publishers. For more information, visit *https://oreilly.com*.

How to Contact Us

Please address comments and questions concerning this book to the publisher:

O'Reilly Media, Inc.
1005 Gravenstein Highway North
Sebastopol, CA 95472
800-998-9938 (in the United States or Canada)
707-829-0515 (international or local)
707-829-0104 (fax)

We have a web page for this book, where we list errata, examples, and any additional information. You can access this page at *https://oreil.ly/VCG3e*.

Email *bookquestions@oreilly.com* to comment or ask technical questions about this book.

For news and information about our books and courses, visit *https://oreilly.com*.

Find us on LinkedIn: *https://linkedin.com/company/oreilly-media*.

Follow us on Twitter: *https://twitter.com/oreillymedia*.

Watch us on YouTube: *https://youtube.com/oreillymedia*.

Acknowledgments

The collective sum of the knowledge of many outweighs the sum of one. In light of that, this project is made possible with the help of many people. I personally owe a huge thank-you to Matthew McCullough, who provided me the opportunity to continue to teach the world about Git and GitHub in this edition of the book. I also thank Jon Loeliger, the main author of the book, who's work provided a great reference to dig deep into the weeds of Git knowledge in earlier editions of the book.

I would like to thank my tech reviewers, Jeff King, Jess Males, Aaron Sumner, Donald Ellis, and Mislav Marohnić, who had to read through the raw writings of the book and provided immense feedback to ensure that the chapters took shape in a way that was comprehensible for everyone.

Also, I'd like to thank Taylor Blau, who provided early guidance and valuable feedback in earlier chapters of the book, which helped me approach the overall structure for later parts of the book. Lars Schneider developed the idea and concept for the section "Git LFS" on page 426, which was based on a talk he prepared; for this, I thank him deeply. The works of Elijah Newren, Derrick Stolee, and Vincent Driessen are referenced with permission, and I am grateful for their contribution. I would also like to thank Peter Murray; our talks about the structure of the book provided me assurance and guidance that I was on the right track with the changes being introduced for this third edition.

To my editors and to the staff at O'Reilly—especially Shira Evans, Virginia Wilson, Beth Kelly, Audrey Doyle, Kim Sandoval, Sue Klefstad, David Futato, Karen Montgomery, Kate Dullea, Suzanne Huston, and Melissa Duffield—I extend a heartfelt thank-you for your patience, motivation, and cheering to ensure that we would get this across the finish line.

Finally, I want to thank my wife, Tejirl, and my daughter, Temyksciraa, for providing unconditional moral support and patience; for sacrificing family dinners, date nights, and holidays; and most of all, for believing in me. Thanks also to my parents, Ponuthorai and Jayaletchmy, who taught me perseverance. And a special thank-you to

Raksha, my sweet White Swiss Shepherd, who patiently waited by my side throughout the entire writing process.

Attributions

The Git Trademark Policy (*https://oreil.ly/YU0BU*) is available online.

Linux® is the registered trademark of Linus Torvalds in the United States and other countries.

PowerPC® is a trademark of International Business Machines Corporation in the United States, other countries, or both.

Unix® is a registered trademark of The Open Group in the United States and other countries.

Thinking in Git

The chapters in this first part of the book introduce you to Git and its foundations. We start by providing you with an overarching view of the Git ecosystem, followed by a look at Git's characteristics so that you can learn what makes Git unique and how it operates. Following this, we share examples of what it looks like to work with Git via the command-line interface and some code examples.

In the second part of the book, we dive into the technicalities of how Git works internally. We start by explaining repositories before discussing the Git object store, further solidifying the notion that Git under the hood is really a content-addressable database. We made the decision to discuss Git internals early in the book because we believe it will help you prepare for later chapters.

In a nutshell, the first two chapters of Part I aim to put you in a Git mindset. Git is perceived to have a steep learning curve, but it really has to do with the way you understand how files and projects are being version-controlled, especially if you are transitioning from a traditional centralized version control system to Git, which is distributed in its implementation. It is this transition that may make understanding Git complex early on. You can rest assured that once you learn to think in Git, the rest of the technical skill will flow.

## CHAPTER 1

Introduction to Git

Simply put, Git is a content tracker. Given that notion, Git shares common principles of most version control systems. However, the distinct feature that makes Git unique among the variety of tools available today is that it is a distributed version control system. This distinction means Git is fast and scalable, has a rich collection of command sets that provide access to both high-level and low-level operations, and is optimized for local operations.

In this chapter you will learn the fundamental principles of Git, its characteristics, and basic `git` commands, and you'll receive some quick guidance on creating and adding changes to a repository.

We highly recommend that you take time to grasp the important concepts explained here. These topics are the building blocks of Git and will help you understand the intermediate and advanced techniques for managing a Git repository as part of your daily work. These foundational concepts will also help you ramp up your learning when we break down the inner workings of Git in chapters grouped in Part II, "Fundamentals of Git", Part III, "Intermediate Skills", and Part IV, "Advanced Skills".

Git Components

Before we dive into the world of `git` commands, let's take a step back and visualize an overview of the components that make up the Git ecosystem. Figure 1-1 shows how the components work together.

Git GUI tools act as a frontend for the Git command line, and some tools have extensions that integrate with popular Git hosting platforms. The Git client tools mostly work on the local copy of your repository.

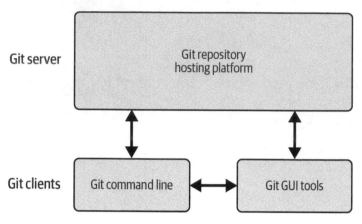

Git server

Git clients

Figure 1-1. Overview of Git components

When you are working with Git, a typical setup includes a Git server and Git clients. You can possibly forgo a server, but that would add complexity to how you maintain and manage repositories when sharing revision changes in a collaborative setup and would make consistency more difficult (we will revisit this in Chapter 11). The Git server and clients work as follows:

Git server

A Git server enables you to collaborate more easily because it ensures the availability of a central and reliable source of truth for the repositories you will be working on. A Git server is also where your remote Git repositories are stored; as common practice goes, the repository has the most up-to-date and stable source of your projects. You have the option to install and configure your own Git server, or you can forgo the overhead and opt to host your Git repositories on reliable third-party hosting sites such as GitHub, GitLab, and Bitbucket.

Git clients

Git clients interact with your local repositories, and you are able to interact with Git clients via the Git command line or the Git GUI tools. When you install and configure a Git client, you will be able to access the remote repositories, work on a local copy of the repository, and push changes back to the Git server. If you are new to Git, we recommend starting out using the Git command line; familiarize yourself with the common subset of `git` commands required for your day-to-day operations and then progress to a Git GUI tool of your choice.

The reason for this approach is that to some extent, Git GUI tools tend to provide terminologies that represent a desired outcome that may not be part of Git's standard commands. An example would be a tool with an option called `sync`, which masks the underlying chaining of two or more `git` commands to achieve a desired outcome. If for some reason you were to enter the sync subcommand on the command line, you might get this confusing output:

```
$ git sync

git: 'sync' is not a git command. See 'git --help'.

The most similar command is
        svn
```

 git sync is not a valid git subcommand. To ensure that your local working copy of the repository is in sync with changes from the remote Git repository, you will need to run a combination of these commands: git fetch, git merge, git pull, or git push.

There are a plethora of tools available at your disposal. Some Git GUI tools are fancy and extensible via a plug-in model that provides you the option to connect and leverage features made available on popular third-party Git hosting sites. As convenient as it may be to learn Git via a GUI tool, we will be focusing on the Git command-line tool for examples and code discussions, since this builds a good foundational knowledge that will lead to Git dexterity.

Git Characteristics

Now that we have given an overview of the Git components, let's learn about the characteristics of Git. Understanding these distinct traits of Git enables you to effortlessly switch from a centralized version control mindset to a distributed version control mentality. We like to refer to this as "Thinking in Git":

Git stores revision changes as snapshots
> The very first concept to unlearn is the way Git stores multiple revisions of a file that you are working on. Unlike other version control systems, Git does not track revision changes as a series of modifications, commonly known as *deltas*; instead, it takes a snapshot of changes made to the state of your repository at a specific point in time. In Git terminology this is known as a *commit*. Think of this as capturing a moment in time, as through a photograph.

Git is enhanced for local development
> In Git, you work on a copy of the repository on your local development machine. This is known as a *local repository*, or a clone of the remote repository on a Git server. Your local repository will have the resources and the snapshots of the revision changes made on those resources all in one location. Git terms these collections of linked snapshots *repository commit history*, or *repo history* for short. This allows you to work in a disconnected environment since Git does not need a constant connection to the Git server to version-control your changes. As a

natural consequence, you are able to work on large, complex projects across distributed teams without compromising efficiency and performance for version control operations.

Git is definitive

Definitive means the `git` commands are explicit. Git waits for you to provide instructions on what to do and when to do it. For example, Git does not automatically sync changes from your local repository to the remote repository, nor does it automatically save a snapshot of a revision to your local repo history. Every action requires your explicit command or instruction to tell Git what is required, including adding new commits, fixing existing commits, pushing changes from your local repository to the remote repository, and even retrieving new changes from the remote repository. In short, you need to be intentional with your actions. This also includes letting Git know which files you intend to track, since Git does not automatically add new files to be version-controlled.

Git is designed to bolster nonlinear development

Git allows you to ideate and experiment with various implementations of features for viable solutions to your project by enabling you to diverge and work in parallel along the main, stable codebase of your project. This methodology, called *branching*, is a very common practice and ensures the integrity of the main development line, preventiing any accidental changes that may break it.

In Git, the concept of branching is considered lightweight and inexpensive because a branch in Git is just a pointer to the latest commit in a series of linked commits. For every branch you create, Git keeps track of the series of commits for that branch. You can switch between branches locally. Git then restores the state of the project to the most recent moment when the snapshot of the specified branch was created. When you decide to merge the changes from any branch into the main development line, Git is able to combine those series of commits by applying techniques that we will discuss in Chapter 6.

 Since Git offers many novelties, keep in mind that the concepts and practices of other version control systems may work differently or may not be applicable at all in Git.

The Git Command Line

Git's command-line interface is simple to use. It is designed to put full control of your repository into your hands. As such, there are many ways to do the same thing. By focusing on which commands are important for your day-to-day work, we can simplify and learn them in more depth.

As a starting point, just type **git version** or **git --version** to determine whether your machine has already been preloaded with Git. You should see output similar to the following:

```
$ git --version
git version 2.37.0
```

If you do not have Git installed on your machine, please refer to Appendix B to learn how you can install Git according to your operating system platform before continuing with the next section.

Upon installation, type **git** without any arguments. Git will then list its options and the most common subcommands:

```
$ git

usage: git [-v | --version] [-h | --help] [-C <path>] [-c <name>=<value>]
           [--exec-path[=<path>]] [--html-path] [--man-path] [--info-path]
           [-p | --paginate | -P | --no-pager] [--no-replace-objects] [--bare]
           [--git-dir=<path>] [--work-tree=<path>] [--namespace=<name>]
           [--super-prefix=<path>] [--config-env=<name>=<envvar>]
           <command> [<args>]

These are common Git commands used in various situations:

start a working area (see also: git help tutorial)
   clone     Clone a repository into a new directory
   init      Create an empty Git repository or reinitialize an existing one

work on the current change (see also: git help everyday)
   add       Add file contents to the index
   mv        Move or rename a file, a directory, or a symlink
   restore   Restore working tree files
   rm        Remove files from the working tree and from the index

examine the history and state (see also: git help revisions)
   bisect    Use binary search to find the commit that introduced a bug
   diff      Show changes between commits, commit and working tree, etc
   grep      Print lines matching a pattern
   log       Show commit logs
   show      Show various types of objects
   status    Show the working tree status

grow, mark and tweak your common history
   branch    List, create, or delete branches
   commit    Record changes to the repository
   merge     Join two or more development histories together
   rebase    Reapply commits on top of another base tip
   reset     Reset current HEAD to the specified state
   switch    Switch branches
   tag       Create, list, delete or verify a tag object signed with GPG

collaborate (see also: git help workflows)
   fetch     Download objects and refs from another repository
   pull      Fetch from and integrate with another repository or a local branch
   push      Update remote refs along with associated objects

'git help -a' and 'git help -g' list available subcommands and some((("git help command")))
concept guides. See 'git help <command>' or 'git help <concept>'
to read about a specific subcommand or concept.
See 'git help git' for an overview of the system.
```

For a complete list of `git` subcommands, type **`git help --all`**.

As you can see from the usage hint, a small handful of options apply to `git`. Most options, shown as `[ARGS]` in the hint, apply to specific subcommands.

For example, the option `--version` affects the `git` command and produces a version number:

```
$ git --version
git version 2.37.0
```

In contrast, `--amend` is an example of an option specific to the `git` subcommand `commit`:

```
$ git commit --amend
```

Some invocations require both forms of options (here, the extra spaces in the command line merely serve to visually separate the subcommand from the base command and are not required):

```
$ git --git-dir=project.git    repack -d
```

For convenience, documentation for each `git` subcommand is available using `git help subcommand`, `git --help subcommand`, `git subcommand --help`, or `man git-subcommand`.

The complete Git documentation (*https://oreil.ly/7njp8*) is online.

Historically, Git was provided as a suite of many simple, distinct, standalone commands developed according to the Unix philosophy: build small, interoperable tools. Each command sported a hyphenated name, such as `git-commit` and `git-log`. However, modern Git installations no longer support the hyphenated command forms and instead use a single `git` executable with a subcommand.

The `git` commands understand both "short" and "long" options. For example, the `git commit` command treats the following examples equivalently:

```
$ git commit -m "Fix a typo."
$ git commit --message="Fix a typo."
```

The short form, -m, uses one hyphen, whereas the long form, --message, uses two. (This is consistent with the GNU long options extension.) Some options exist in only one form.

 You can create a commit summary and detailed message for the summary by using the -m option multiple times:

```
$ git commit -m "Summary" -m "Detail of Summary"
```

Finally, you can separate options from a list of arguments via the *bare double dash* convention. For instance, use the double dash to contrast the control portion of the command line from a list of operands, such as filenames:

```
$ git diff -w main origin -- tools/Makefile
```

You may need to use the double dash to separate and explicitly identify filenames so that they are not mistaken for another part of the command. For example, if you happened to have both a file and a tag named *main.c*, then you will need to be intentional with your operations:

```
# Checkout the tag named "main.c"
$ git checkout main.c

# Checkout the file named "main.c"
$ git checkout -- main.c
```

Quick Introduction to Using Git

To see Git in action, you can create a new repository, add some content, and track a few revisions. You can create a repository in two ways: either create a repository from scratch and populate it with some content, or work with an existing repository by *cloning* it from a remote Git server.

Preparing to Work with Git

Whether you are creating a new repository or working with an existing repository, there are basic prerequisite configurations that you need to complete after installing Git on your local development machine. This is akin to setting up the correct date, time zone, and language on a new camera before taking your first snapshot.

At a bare minimum, Git requires your name and email address before you make your first commit in your repository. The identity you supply then shows as the commit *author*, baked in with other snapshot metadata. You can save your identity in a configuration file using the `git config` command:

```
$ git config user.name "Jon Loeliger"
$ git config user.email "jdl@example.com"
```

If you decide not to include your identity in a configuration file, you will have to specify your identity for every `git commit` subcommand by appending the argument `--author` at the end of the command:

```
$ git commit -m "log message" --author="Jon Loeliger <jdl@example.com>"
```

Keep in mind that this is the hard way, and it can quickly become tedious.

You can also specify your identity by supplying your name and email address to the `GIT_AUTHOR_NAME` and `GIT_AUTHOR_EMAIL` environment variables, respectively. If set, these variables will override all configuration settings. However, for specifications set on the command line, Git will override the values supplied in the configuration file and environment variable.

Working with a Local Repository

Now that you have configured your identity, you are ready to start working with a repository. Start by creating a new empty repository on your local development machine. We will start simple and work our way toward techniques for working with a shared repository on a Git server.

Creating an initial repository

We will model a typical situation by creating a repository for your personal website. Let's assume you're starting from scratch and you are going to add content for your project in the local directory ~/my_website, which you place in a Git repository.

Type in the following commands to create the directory, and place some basic content in a file called *index.html*:

```
$ mkdir ~/my_website
$ cd ~/my_website
$ echo 'My awesome website!' > index.html
```

To convert ~/my_website into a Git repository, run `git init`. Here we provide the option `-b` followed by a default branch named `main`:

```
$ git init -b main

Initialized empty Git repository in ../my_website/.git/
```

If you prefer to initialize an empty Git repository first and then add files to it, you can do so by running the following commands:

```
$ git init -b main ~/my_website

Initialized empty Git repository in ../my_website/.git/

$ cd ~/my_website
$ echo 'My awesome website!' > index.html
```

You can initialize a completely empty directory or an existing directory full of files. In either case, the process of converting the directory into a Git repository is the same.

The `git init` command creates a hidden directory called *.git* at the root level of your project. All revision information along with supporting metadata and Git extensions are stored in this top-level, hidden *.git* folder.

Git considers *~/my_website* to be the *working directory*. This directory contains the current version of files for your website. When you make changes to existing files or add new files to your project, Git records those changes in the hidden *.git* folder.

For the purpose of learning, we will reference two virtual directories that we call *Local History* and *Index* to illustrate the concept of initializing a new Git repository. We will discuss the *Local History* and *Index* in Chapters 4 and 5, respectively.

Figure 1-2 depicts what we have just explained:

```
.
└── my_website
    ├── .git/
    │   └── Hidden git objects
    └── index.html
```

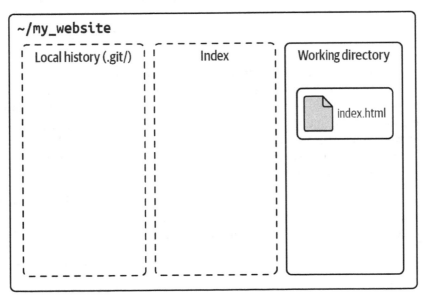

Figure 1-2. Initial repository

The dotted lines surrounding the *Local History* and *Index* represent the hidden directories within the *.git* folder.

Adding a file to your repository

Up to this point, you have only *created* a new Git repository. In other words, this Git repository is empty. Although the file *index.html* exists in the directory *~/my_website*, to Git, this is the *working directory*, a representation of a scratch pad or directory where you frequently alter your files.

When you have finalized changes to the files and want to deposit those changes into the Git repository, you need to explicitly do so by using the `git add` *file* command:

```
$ git add index.html
```

 Although you can let Git add all the files in the directory and all subdirectories using the `git add .` command, this stages everything, and we advise you to be intentional with what you are planning to stage, mainly to prevent sensitive information or unwanted files from being included when commits are made. To avoid including such information, you can use the *.gitignore* file, which is covered in Chapter 5.

The argument `.`, the single period or *dot* in Unix parlance, is shorthand for the current directory.

With the `git add` command, Git understands that you intend to include the final iteration of the modification on *index.html* as a revision in the repository. However, so far Git has merely staged the file, an interim step before taking a snapshot via a commit.

Git separates the `add` and `commit` steps to avoid volatility while providing flexibility and granularity in how you record changes. Imagine how disruptive, confusing, and time-consuming it would be to update the repository each time you add, remove, or change a file. Instead, multiple provisional and related steps, such as an add, can be *batched*, thereby keeping the repository in a stable, consistent state. This method also allows us to craft a narrative of why we are changing the code. In Chapter 4 we will dive deeper into this concept.

We recommend that you strive to group logical change batches before making a commit. This is called an *atomic* commit and will help you in situations where you'll need to do some advanced Git operations in later chapters.

Running the `git status` command reveals this in-between state of *index.html*:

```
$ git status

On branch main

No commits yet

Changes to be committed:
```

```
      (use "git rm --cached <file>..." to unstage)
            new file:   index.html
```

The command reports that the new file *index.html* will be added to the repository during the next commit.

After staging the file, the next logical step is to commit the file to the repository. Once you commit the file, it becomes part of the *repository commit history*; for brevity, we will refer to this as the *repo history*. Every time you make a commit, Git records several other pieces of metadata along with it, most notably the commit log message and the author of the change.

A fully qualified `git commit` command should supply a terse and meaningful log message using active language to denote the change that is being introduced by the commit. This is very helpful when you need to traverse the repo history to track down a specific change or quickly identify changes of a commit without having to dig deeper into the change details. We dive in deeper on this topic in Chapters 4 and 8.

Let's commit the staged *index.html* file for your website:

```
$ git commit -m "Initial contents of my_website"

[main (root-commit) c149e12] initial contents of my_website
 1 file changed, 1 insertion(+)
 create mode 100644 index.html
```

 The details of the author who is making the commit are retrieved from the Git configuration we set up earlier.

In the code example, we supplied the `-m` argument to be able to provide the log message directly on the command line. If you prefer to provide a detailed log message via an interactive editor session, you can do so as well. You will need to configure Git to launch your favorite editor during a `git commit` (leave out the `-m` argument); if it isn't set already, you can set the `$GIT_EDITOR` environment variable as follows:

```
# In bash or zsh
$ export GIT_EDITOR=vim

# In tcsh
$ setenv GIT_EDITOR emacs
```

 Git will honor the default text editor configured in the shell environment variables `VISUAL` and `EDITOR`. If neither is configured, it falls back to using the `vi` editor.

After you commit the *index.html* file into the repository, run `git status` to get an update on the current state of your repository. In our example, running `git status` should indicate that there are no outstanding changes to be committed:

```
$ git status

On branch main
nothing to commit, working tree clean
```

Git also tells you that your *working directory* is clean, which means the working directory has no new or modified files that differ from what is in the repository.

Figure 1-3 will help you visualize all the steps you just learned.

The difference between `git add` and `git commit` is much like you organizing a group of schoolchildren in a preferred order to get the perfect classroom photograph: `git add` does the organizing, whereas `git commit` takes the snapshot.

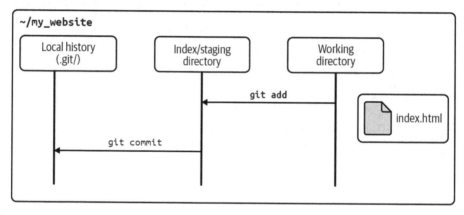

Figure 1-3. Staging and adding a file to a repository

Making another commit

Next, let's make a few modifications to *index.html* and create a repo history within the repository.

Convert *index.html* into a proper HTML file, and commit the alteration to it:

```
$ cd ~/my_website

# edit the index.html file.

$ cat index.html
<html>
<body>
My website is awesome!
</body>
</html>

$ git commit index.html -m 'Convert to HTML'
```

```
[main 521edbe] Convert to HTML
 1 file changed, 5 insertions(+), 1 deletion(-)
```

If you are already familiar with Git, you may be wondering why we skipped the `git add index.html` step before we committed the file. It is because the content to be committed may be specified in more than one way in Git.

Type **git commit --help** to learn more about these options:

```
$ git commit --help

NAME
    git-commit - Record changes to the repository

SYNOPSIS
    git commit [-a | --interactive | --patch] [-s] [-v] [-u<mode>] [--amend]
               [--dry-run] [(-c | -C | --squash) <commit> | --fixup [(amend|reword):]<commit>)]
               [-F <file> | -m <msg>] [--reset-author] [--allow-empty]
               [--allow-empty-message] [--no-verify] [-e] [--author=<author>]
               [--date=<date>] [--cleanup=<mode>] [--[no-]status]
               [-i | -o] [--pathspec-from-file=<file> [--pathspec-file-nul]]
               [(--trailer <token>[(=|:)<value>])...] [-S[<keyid>]]
               [--] [<pathspec>...]

...
```

Detailed explanations of the various commit methods are also explained in the `git commit --help` manual pages.

In our example, we decided to commit the *index.html* file with an additional argument, the `-m` switch, which supplied a message explaining the changes in the commit: `'Convert to HTML'`. Figure 1-4 explains the method we just discussed.

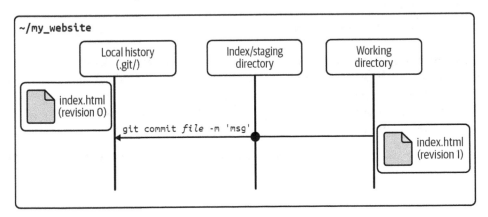

Figure 1-4. Staging and adding changes to a tracked file in a repository

Note that our usage of `git commit index.html -m 'Convert to HTML'` does not skip the staging of the file; Git handles it automatically as part of the commit action.

Viewing your commits

Now that you have more commits in the repo history, you can inspect them in a variety of ways. Some `git` commands show the sequence of individual commits, others show the summary of an individual commit, and still others show the full details of any commit you specify in the repository.

The `git log` command yields a sequential history of the individual commits within the repository:

```
$ git log

commit 521edbe1dd2ec9c6f959c504d12615a751b5218f (HEAD -> main)
Author: Jon Loeliger <jdl@example.com>
Date:   Mon Jul 4 12:01:54 2022 +0200

    Convert to HTML

commit c149e12e89a9c035b9240e057b592ebfc9c88ea4
Author: Jon Loeliger <jdl@example.com>
Date:   Mon Jul 4 11:58:36 2022 +0200

    Initial contents of my_website
```

In the preceding output, the `git log` command prints out detailed log information for every commit in the repository. At this point you have only two commits in your repo history, which makes it easier to read the output. For repositories with many commit histories, this standard view may not help you traverse a long list of detailed commit information with ease; in such situations you can provide the `--oneline` switch to list a summarized commit ID number along with the commit message:

```
$ git log --oneline

521edbe (HEAD -> main) Convert to HTML
c149e12 Initial contents of my_website
```

The commit log entries are listed, in order, from most recent to oldest[1] (the original file); each entry shows the commit author's name and email address, the date of the commit, the log message for the change, and the internal identification number of the commit. The commit ID number is explained in "Content-Addressable Database" on page 29. We will discuss commits in more detail in Chapter 4.

If you want to see more detail about a particular commit, use the `git show` command with a commit ID number:

---

1 Strictly speaking, they are not in *chronological* order but rather are a *topological* sort of the commits.

```
$ git show c149e12e89a9c035b9240e057b592ebfc9c88ea4

commit c149e12e89a9c035b9240e057b592ebfc9c88ea4
Author: Jon Loeliger <jdl@example.com>
Date:   Mon Jul 4 11:58:36 2022 +0200

Initial contents of my_website

diff --git a/index.html b/index.html
new file mode 100644
index 0000000..6331c71
--- /dev/null
+++ b/index.html
@@ -0,0 +1 @@
+My awesome website!
```

 If you run `git show` without an explicit commit number, it simply shows the details of the HEAD commit, in our case, the most recent one.

The `git log` command shows the commit logs for how changes for each commit are included in the repo history. If you want to see concise, one-line summaries for the current development branch without supplying additional filter options to the `git log --oneline` command, an alternative approach is to use the `git show-branch` command:

```
$ git show-branch --more=10

[main] Convert to HTML
[main^] Initial contents of my_website
```

The phrase `--more=10` reveals up to an additional 10 versions, but only two exist so far and so both are shown. (The default in this case would list only the most recent commit.) The name `main` is the default branch name.

We will discuss branches and revisit the `git show-branch` command in more detail in Chapter 3.

Viewing commit differences

With the repo history in place from the addition of commits, you can now see the differences between the two revisions of *index.html*. You will need to recall the commit ID numbers and run the `git diff` command:

```
$ git diff c149e12e89a9c035b9240e057b592ebfc9c88ea4 \
         521edbe1dd2ec9c6f959c504d12615a751b5218f

diff --git a/index.html b/index.html
index 6331c71..8cfcb90 100644
--- a/index.html
+++ b/index.html
@@ -1 +1,5 @@
-My awesome website!
```

```
+<html>
+<body>
 My website is awesome!
+</body>
+</html>
```

The output resembles what the `git diff` command produces. As per convention, the first revision commit, `9da581d910c9c4ac93557ca4859e767f5caf5169`, is the earlier of the content for *index.html*, and the second revision commit, `ec232cddfb94e0dfd5b5855af8ded7f5eb5c90d6`, is the latest content of *index.html*. Thus, a plus sign (+) precedes each line of new content after the minus sign (-), which indicates removed content.

 Do not be intimidated by the long hex numbers. Git provides many shorter, easier ways to run similar commands so that you can avoid large, complicated commit IDs. Usually the first seven characters of the hex numbers, as shown in the `git log --oneline` example earlier, are sufficient. We elaborate on this in "Content-Addressable Database" on page 29.

Removing and renaming files in your repository

Now that you have learned how to add files to a Git repository, let's look at how to remove a file from one. Removing a file from a Git repository is analogous to adding a file but uses the `git rm` command. Suppose you have the file *adverts.html* in your website content and plan to remove it. You can do so as follows:

```
$ cd ~/my_website
$ ls
index.html  adverts.html

$ git rm adverts.html
rm  'adverts.html'

$ git commit -m "Remove adverts html"
[main 97ff70a] Remove adverts html
 1 file changed, 0 insertions(+), 0 deletions(-)
 delete mode 100644 adverts.html
```

Similar to an addition, a deletion also requires two steps: express your intent to remove the file using `git rm`, which also *stages* the file you intend to remove. Realize the change in the repository with a `git commit`.

 Just as with `git add`, with `git rm` we are not directly deleting the file; instead, we are changing what is tracked: the deletion or addition of a file.

You can rename a file indirectly by using a combination of the `git rm` and `git add` commands, or you can rename the file more quickly and directly with the command `git mv`. Here's an example of the former:

```
$ mv foo.html bar.html
$ git rm foo.html
rm 'foo.html'

$ git add bar.html
```

In this sequence, you must execute `mv foo.html bar.html` at the onset to prevent `git rm` from permanently deleting the *foo.html* file from the filesystem.

Here's the same operation performed with `git mv`:

```
$ git mv foo.html bar.html
```

In either case, the staged changes must subsequently be committed:

```
$ git commit -m "Moved foo to bar"
[main d1e37c8] Moved foo to bar
 1 file changed, 0 insertions(+), 0 deletions(-)
 rename foo.html => bar.html (100%)
```

Git handles file move operations differently than most similar systems, employing a mechanism based on the similarity of the content between two file versions. The specifics are described in Chapter 5.

Working with a Shared Repository

By now you have initialized a new repository and have been making changes to it. All the changes are only available to your local development machine. This is a good example of how you can manage a project that is only available to you. But how can you work collaboratively on a repository that is hosted on a Git server? Let's discuss how you can achieve this.

Making a local copy of the repository

You can create a complete copy, or a *clone*, of a repository using the `git clone` command. This is how you collaborate with other people, making changes on the same files and keeping in sync with changes from other versions of the same repository.

For the purposes of this tutorial, let's start simple by creating a copy of your existing repository; then we can contrast the same example as if it were on a remote Git server:

```
$ cd ~
$ git clone my_website new_website
```

Although these two Git repositories now contain exactly the same objects, files, and directories, there are some subtle differences. You may want to explore those differences with commands such as the following:

```
$ ls -lsa my_website new_website
...
$ diff -r my_website new_website
...
```

On a local filesystem like this, using `git clone` to make a copy of a repository is quite similar to using `cp -a` or `rsync`. In contrast, if you were to *clone* the same repository from a Git server, the syntax would be as follows:

```
$ cd ~

$ git clone https://git-hosted-server.com/some-dir/my_website.git new_website
Cloning into 'new_website'...
remote: Enumerating objects: 2, done.
remote: Counting objects: 100% (2/2), done.
remote: Compressing objects: 100% (103/103), done.
remote: Total 125 (delta 45), reused 65 (delta 18), pack-reused 0
Receiving objects: 100% (125/125), 1.67 MiB | 4.03 MiB/s, done.
Resolving deltas: 100% (45/45), done.
```

Once you clone a repository, you can modify the cloned version, make new commits, inspect its logs and history, and so on. It is a complete repository with a full history. Remember that the changes you make to the cloned repository will not be automatically pushed to the original copy on the repository.

Figure 1-5 depicts this concept.

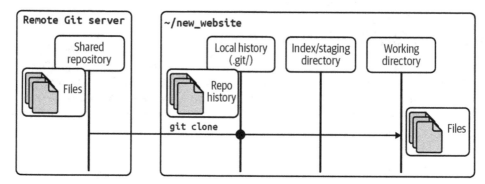

Figure 1-5. Cloning a shared repository

Try not to be distracted by some of the terms you see in the output. Git supports a richer set of repository sources, including network names, for naming the repository to be cloned. We will explain these forms and usage in Chapter 11.

Configuration Files

Git configuration files are all simple text files in the style of *.ini* files. The configuration files are used to store preferences and settings used by multiple `git` commands. Some of the settings represent personal preferences (e.g., should a `color.pager` be used?), others are important for a repository to function correctly (e.g., `core` repositoryformatversion), and still others tweak git command behavior a bit (e.g., gc.auto). Like other tools, Git supports a hierarchy of configuration files.

Hierarchy of configuration files

Figure 1-6 represents the Git configuration files hierarchy in decreasing precedence:

.git/config
> Repository-specific configuration settings manipulated with the --file option or by default. You can also write to this file with the --local option. These settings have the highest precedence.

~/.gitconfig
> User-specific configuration settings manipulated with the --global option.

/etc/gitconfig
> System-wide configuration settings manipulated with the --system option if you have proper Unix file write permissions on the *gitconfig* file. These settings have the lowest precedence. Depending on your installation, the system settings file might be somewhere else (perhaps in */usr/local/etc gitconfig*) or may be absent entirely.

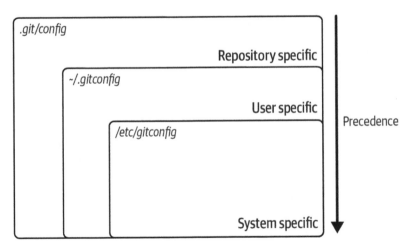

Figure 1-6. Git configuration files hierarchy

For example, to store an author name and email address that will be used on all the commits you make for all of your repositories, configure values for user name and user.email in your *$HOME/.gitconfig* file using git config --global:

```
$ git config --global user.name "Jon Loeliger"
$ git config --global user.email "jdl@example.com"
```

If you need to set a repository-specific name and email address that would override a --global setting, simply omit the --global flag or use the --local flag to be explicit:

```
$ git config user.name "Jon Loeliger"
$ git config user.email "jdl@special-project.example.org"
```

You can use git config -l (or the long form --list) to list the settings of all the variables collectively found in the complete set of configuration files:

```
# Make a brand-new, empty repository
$ mkdir /tmp/new
$ cd /tmp/new
$ git init

# Set some config values
$ git config --global user.name "Jon Loeliger"
$ git config --global user.email "jdl@example.com"
$ git config user.email "jdl@special-project.example.org"

$ git config -l
user.name=Jon Loeliger
user.email=jdl@example.com
core.repositoryformatversion=0
core.filemode=true
core.bare=false
core.logallrefupdates=true
user.email=jdl@special-project.example.org
```

When specifying the command git config -l, adding the options --show-scope and --show-origin will help to print the various sources for the configurations! Try this out with git config -l --show-scope --show-origin in your terminal.

Because the configuration files are simple text files, you can view their contents with cat and edit them with your favorite text editor too:

```
# Look at just the repository-specific settings

$ cat .git/config
[core]
    repositoryformatversion = 0
    filemode = true
    bare = false
    logallrefupdates = true
ignorecase = true
    precomposeunicode = true

[user]
    email = jdl@special-project.example.org
```

The content of the configuration text file may be presented with some slight differences according to your operating system type. Many of these differences allow for different filesystem characteristics.

If you need to remove a setting from the configuration files, use the `--unset` option together with the correct configuration files flag:

```
$ git config --unset --global user.email
```

Git provides you with many configuration options and environment variables that frequently exist for the same purpose. For example, you can set a value for the editor to be used when composing a commit log message. Based on the configuration, invocation follows these steps:

1. `GIT_EDITOR` environment variable

2. `core.editor` configuration option

3. `VISUAL` environment variable

4. `EDITOR` environment variable

5. The `vi` command

There are more than a few hundred configuration parameters. We will not bore you with them but will point out important ones as we go along. A more extensive (yet still incomplete) list can be found on the `git config` manual page.

 A complete list of all `git` commands (*https://oreil.ly/Gj2zg*) is online.

Configuring an alias

Git aliases allow you to substitute common but complex `git` commands that you type frequently with simple and easy-to-remember aliases. This also saves you the hassle of remembering or typing out those long commands, and it saves you from the frustration of running into typos:

```
$ git config --global alias.show-graph \
        'log --graph --abbrev-commit --pretty=oneline'
```

In this example, we created the `show-graph` alias and made it available for use in any repository we create. When we use the command `git show-graph`, it will give us the same output we got when we typed that long `git log` command with all those options.

Summary

You will surely have a lot of unanswered questions about how Git works, even after everything you've learned so far. For instance, how does Git store each version of a file? What really makes up a commit? Where did those funny commit numbers come from? Why the name "main"? And is a "branch" what I *think* it is? These are good questions. What we covered gives you a glimpse of the operations you will commonly use in your projects. The answer to your questions will be explained in detail in Part II.

The next chapter defines some terminology, introduces some Git concepts, and establishes a foundation for the lessons found in the rest of the book.

## CHAPTER 2

Foundational Concepts

In the previous chapter, you learned the foundations of Git, its characteristics, and typical applications of version control. It probably sparked your curiosity and left you with a good number of questions. For instance, how does Git keep track of revisions of the same file at every commit on your local development machine? What are the contents of the hidden *.git* directory, and what is their significance? How is a commit ID generated, why does it look like gibberish, and should you take note of it?

If you have used another version control system, such as SVN or CVS, you may notice that some of the commands described in the preceding chapter seemed familiar. Although Git serves the same function and provides all the operations you expect from a modern version control system, an exception to this notion is that the inner workings and principles of Git differ in some fundamental and surprising ways.

In this chapter, we explore why and how Git differs by examining the key components of its architecture and some important concepts. We will focus on the basics, common terminology, and the relationship between Git objects and how they are utilized, all through the lens of a single repository. The fundamentals you'll learn in this chapter also apply when you're working with multiple interconnected repositories.

Repositories

A Git repository is simply a key–value pair database containing all the information needed to retain and manage the revisions and history of files in a project. A Git repository retains a complete copy of the entire project throughout its lifetime. However, unlike most other version control systems, the Git repository provides not only a complete working copy of all the files stored in the project but also a copy of the repository (key–value pair database) itself with which to work.

Figure 2-1 illustrates this explanation.

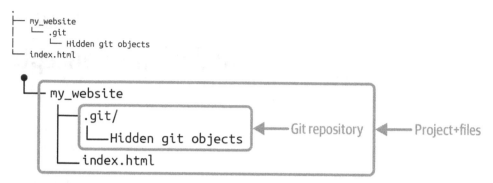

Figure 2-1. Git repository

 We use the term *repository* to describe the entire project and its key–value pair database as a single unit.

Besides file data and repository metadata, Git also maintains a set of configuration values within each repository. We already worked with some of these in the previous chapter, specifically, the repository user's name and email address. These configuration settings are not propagated from one repository to another during a clone or duplicating operation. Instead, Git manages and inspects configuration and setup information on a per-environment, per-user, and per-repository basis.

Within a repository, Git maintains two primary data structures: the object store and the index. All of this repository data is stored at the root of your working directory in the hidden subdirectory named *.git*.

The object store is designed to be efficiently copied during a clone operation as part of the mechanism that supports a fully distributed version control system. The index is transitory information, is private to a repository, and can be created or modified on demand as needed.

The next two sections describe the object store and index in more detail.

Git Object Store

At the heart of Git's repository implementation is the object store. It contains your original data files and all the log messages, author information, dates, and other information required to rebuild or restore any version or branch of the project to a specific state in time.

Git places only four types of objects in the object store: blobs, trees, commits, and tags. These four atomic objects form the foundation of Git's higher-level data structures:

Blobs

Each version of a file is represented as a blob. *Blob*, a contraction of "binary large object," is a term that's commonly used in computing to refer to some variable or file that can contain any data and whose internal structure is ignored by the program. A blob is treated as being opaque. A blob holds a file's data but does not contain any metadata about the file or even its name.

Trees

A tree object represents one level of directory information. It records blob identifiers, pathnames, and a bit of metadata for all the files in one directory. It can also recursively reference other (sub)tree objects and thus build a complete hierarchy of files and subdirectories. In simple terms, a tree records the contents of a single level in the directory hierarchy. It lists files and subtrees by including their name and an identifier for the Git object they represent (either a blob OID or another tree for subdirectories).

Commits

A commit object holds metadata for each change introduced into the repository, including the author, committer, commit date, and log message. Each commit points to a tree object that captures, in one complete snapshot, the state of the repository at the time the commit was performed. The initial commit, or root commit, has no parent. Most commits have one commit parent, although later in the book we explain how a commit can reference more than one parent.

Tags

A tag object assigns a presumably human-readable name to a specific object, usually a commit. `9da581d910c9c4ac93557ca4859e767f5caf5169` refers to an exact, well-defined commit, but a more familiar tag name like `Ver-1.0-Alpha` might make more sense!

 The four objects in the object store are immutable. Note that only an *annotated tag* is immutable. A *lightweight tag* is not an immutable object, since it can be used as a reference that we can update directly.

Over time, all the information in the object store changes and grows, tracking and modeling your project edits, additions, and deletions. To use disk space and network bandwidth efficiently, Git compresses and stores the objects in *packfiles*, which are also placed in the object store.

Index

The index stores binary data and is private to your repository. The content of the index is temporary and describes the structure of the entire repository at a specific moment in time. More specifically, it provides a cached representation of all the blob objects that reflects the current state of the project you are working on.

The information in the index is *transitory*, meaning it's a dynamic stage between your project's working directory (filesystem) and the repository's object store (repository commit history). As such, the index is also called the *staging directory*.

Figure 2-2 provides a visual representation of this concept:

```
.
└─ repository
   ├─ .git/
   │  └─ Index
```

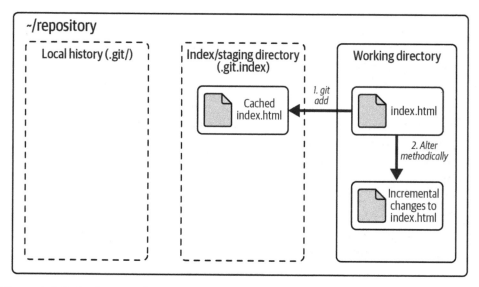

Figure 2-2. Index/staging directory

The index is one of the key distinguishing features of Git. This is because you are able to alter the content of the index methodically, allowing you to have finer control over what content will be stored in the next commit. In short, the index allows a separation between incremental development steps and the committal of those changes.

Here's how it works. As a software engineer, you usually add, delete, or edit a file or a set of files. These are changes that affect the current state of the repository. Next, you will need to execute the `git add` command to stage these changes in the index. Then the index keeps records of those changes and keeps them safe until you are ready to commit them. Git also allows you to remove changes recorded in the index. Thus the index allows a gradual transition of the repository (curated by you) from an older version to a newer, updated version.

As you'll see in Chapter 6, the index also plays an important role in a merge operation, allowing multiple versions of the same file to be managed, inspected, and manipulated simultaneously.

Content-Addressable Database

Git is also described as a content-addressable storage system. This is because the object store is organized and implemented to store key–value pairs of each object it generates under the hood when you are version-controlling your project. Each object in the object store is associated with a unique name produced by applying SHA1 to the content of the object, yielding a SHA1 hash value.

Git uses the complete content of an object to generate the SHA1 hash value. This hash value is believed to be effectively unique to that particular content at a specific state in time, thus the SHA1 hash is used as a sufficient index or name for that object in Git's object store. Any tiny change to a file causes the SHA1 hash to change, causing the new version of the file to be indexed separately.

SHA1 values are 160-bit values that are usually represented as a 40-digit hexadecimal number, such as `9da581d910c9c4ac93557ca4859e767f5caf5169`. Sometimes, during display, SHA1 values are abbreviated to a smaller, easier-to-reference prefix. Git users use the terms *SHA1*, *hash*, and sometimes *object ID* interchangeably.

Globally Unique Identifiers

An important characteristic of the SHA1 hash computation is that it always computes the same ID for identical content, regardless of *where* that content is. In other words, the same file content in different directories and even on different machines yields the exact same SHA1 hash ID. Thus the SHA1 hash ID of a file is an effective globally unique identifier.

A powerful corollary is that files or blobs of arbitrary size can be compared for equality across the internet by merely comparing their SHA1 identifiers.

We will explore this property in a little more detail in the next section.

Git Tracks Content

Git is much more than a version control system. Based on what we learned earlier, it will help you understand the inner mechanics of Git if you think of Git as a *content tracking system*.

This distinction, however subtle, guides much of the design principle of Git and is perhaps the key reason it can perform internal data manipulations with relative ease, and without compromising performance when done right. Yet this is also perhaps one of the most difficult concepts for new users of Git to grasp, so some exposition is worthwhile.

Git's content tracking is manifested in two critical ways that differ fundamentally from almost all other version control systems:[1]

- First, Git's object store is based on the hashed computation of the *contents* of its objects, not on the file or directory names from the user's original file layout.
- Second, Git's internal database efficiently stores every version of every file, not their differences as files go from one revision to the next.

Let's explore this a little more. When Git places a file into the object store, it does so based on the hash of the data (file content) and not on the name of the file (file metadata). In fact, Git does not track file or directory names, which are associated with files in secondary ways. The data is stored as a blob object in the object store. Again, Git tracks content instead of files.

If two separate files have exactly the same content, whether in the same or different directories, Git stores only a single copy of that content as a blob within the object store. Git computes the hash code of each file only according to its content, determines that the files have the same SHA1 values and thus the same content, and places the blob object in the object store indexed by that SHA1 value. Both files in the project, regardless of where they are located in the user's directory structure, use that same object for content.

Because Git uses the hash of a file's complete content as the name for that file, it must operate on each complete copy of the file. It cannot base its work or its object store entries on only part of the file's content or on the differences between two revisions of that file. Using the earlier example of two separate files having exactly the same content, if one of those files changes, Git computes a new SHA1 for it, determines that it is now a different blob object, and adds the new blob to the object store. The original blob remains in the object store for the unchanged file to use.

For this reason, your typical view of a file that has revisions and appears to progress from one revision to another revision is simply an artifact. Git computes this history as a set of changes between different blobs with varying hashes, rather than storing a filename and a set of differences directly. It may seem odd, but this feature allows Git to perform certain tasks with ease.

---

1 Monotone, Mercurial, OpenCMS, and Venti are notable exceptions here.

Figure 2-3 provides a visual representation of this concept.

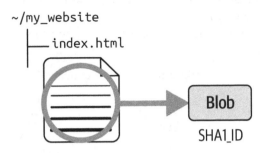

Figure 2-3. Blob object

Pathname Versus Content

As with many other version control systems, Git needs to maintain an explicit list of files that form the content of the repository. However, this need not require that Git's manifest be based on filenames. Indeed, Git treats the name of a file as a piece of data that is distinct from the contents of that file. In this way, it separates index from data in the traditional database sense. It may help to look at Table 2-1, which roughly compares Git to other familiar systems.

Table 2-1. Database comparison

System	Index mechanism	Data store
Relational database	Indexed Sequential Access Method (ISAM)	Data records
Unix filesystem	Directories (/path/to/file)	Blocks of data
Git	.git/objects/`hash`, tree object contents	Blob objects, tree objects

The names of files and directories come from the underlying filesystem, but Git does not really care about the names. Git merely records each pathname and makes sure it can accurately reproduce the files and directories from its content, which is indexed by a hash value. This set of information is stored in the Git object store as the *tree* object.

Git's physical data layout isn't modeled after the user's file directory structure. Instead, it has a completely different structure that can nonetheless reproduce the user's original file and directory layout in a project. Git's internal structure is a more efficient data structure for its own operations and storage considerations.

When Git needs to create a working directory, it says to the filesystem, "Hey! I have this big blob of data that is supposed to be placed at pathname *path/to/directory/file*. Does that make sense to you?" The filesystem is responsible for saying, "Ah, yes, I recognize that string as a set of subdirectory names, and I know where to place your blob of data! Thanks!"

Figure 2-4 provides a visual representation of this concept.

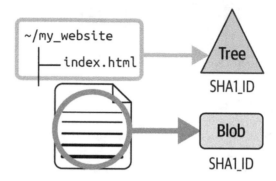

Figure 2-4. Tree object

Packfiles

Next, let's look at how Git stores the blob and tree objects in its object store. If you're following closely, you might think that Git is implementing an inefficient method to store the complete content of every version of every file directly in its object store. Even if Git compresses the files, it is still inefficient to have the complete content of different versions of the same file. For instance, what if we only add, say, one line to a file? Git will still store the complete content of both versions.

Luckily, that's not how Git internally stores the objects in its database. Instead, Git uses a more efficient storage mechanism called *packfiles*. Git uses zlib (*https:// zlib.net*), a free software library that implements the DEFLATE algorithm (*https:// oreil.ly/GD3OL*) to compress each object prior to storing it in its object store. We will dive deeper into packfiles in Chapter 11.

For efficiency, Git's algorithm by design generates deltas against larger objects to be mindful of the space required to save a compressed file. This size optimization is also true for many other delta algorithms because removing data is considered cheaper than adding data in a delta object.

Take note that packfiles are stored in the object store alongside the other objects. They are also used for efficient data transfer of repositories across a network.

Visualizing the Git Object Store

Now that we know how Git efficiently stores its objects, let's discuss how Git objects fit and work together to form a complete system:

- The blob object is at the "bottom" of the data structure; it references no other Git objects and is referenced only by tree objects. It can be considered a leaf node in relation to the tree object. In the figures that follow, each blob is represented by a rectangle.

- Tree objects point to blobs and possibly to other trees as well. Any given tree object might be pointed at by many different commit objects. Each tree is represented by a triangle. In Chapter 15, we will learn how a tree object can also point to a commit object, but for now, we will keep it simple.

- A circle represents a commit. A commit points to one particular tree that is introduced into the repository by the commit.

- Each tag is represented by a parallelogram. Each tag can point to, at most, one commit.

The branch is not a fundamental Git object, yet it plays a crucial role in naming commits. Each branch is pictured as a rectangle:

```
.
└── ~/project
    ├── .git
    │   └── .git/objects/*
    ├── file dead23
    └── file feeb1e
```

Figure 2-5 captures how all the pieces fit together. This diagram shows the state of a repository after a single, initial commit added two files. Both files are in the top-level directory. Both the main branch and a tag named V1.0 point to the commit with ID 1492.

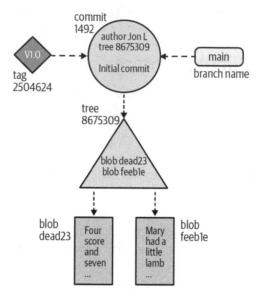

Figure 2-5. Git objects

Now let's make things a bit more complicated. Let's leave the original two files as is, adding a new subdirectory with one file in it. The resulting object store looks like Figure 2-6:

```
.
└── ~/project
    ├── .git
    │   └── .git/objects/*
    ├── file dead23
    ├── file feeb1e
    └── newsubdir
        └── file 1010b
```

As in Figure 2-5, the new commit has added one associated tree object to represent the total state of the directory and file structure. Because the top-level directory is changed by the addition of the new subdirectory, the *content* of the top-level tree object has changed as well, so Git introduces a new tree, `cafed00d`.

However, the blobs `dead23` and `feeb1e` didn't change from the first commit to the second commit. Git realizes that the IDs haven't changed and thus they can be directly referenced and shared by the new `cafed00d` tree.

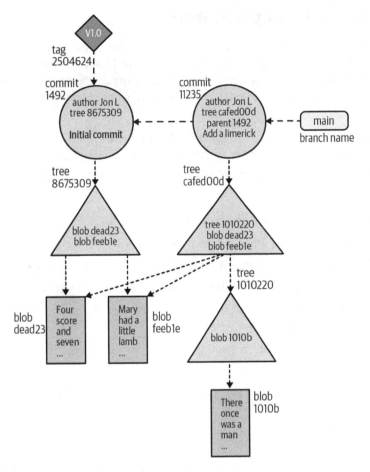

Figure 2-6. Git objects after a second commit

Pay attention to the direction of the arrows between commits. The parent commit or commits come earlier in time. Think of it as a *DAG diagram*: a directed acyclic graph where each node is directed from an earlier node in a single direction to form its topological ordering of the graph.

Therefore, in Git's implementation, each commit points back to its parent or parents. Many people get confused by this because the state of a repository is conventionally portrayed in the opposite direction: as a dataflow *from* the parent commit *to* child commits. In other words, ordered from left to right, the rightmost commit in a DAG diagram represents the latest state of a repository.

In Chapter 4, we extend these pictures to show how the history of a repository is built up and manipulated by various commands.

Git Internals: Concepts at Work

With some tenets out of the way, let's peek under the hood and see how all these concepts fit together in a Git repository. We will start by creating a new repository and inspecting the internal files and object store in much greater detail. We'll do this by starting at the bottom of Git's data structure and working our way up in the object store.

Before we go any further, it is important to know that Git has a few categories of commands to implement its inner mechanics. To get a detailed, categorized list of all the commands, type `git help -a` in your terminal. Git commands are categorized as follows:

- Main porcelain commands (high-level commands for routine Git operations)
- Ancillary commands (commands that help query Git's internal data store)
- Low-level commands (plumbing commands for internal Git operations)
- External commands (commands that extend the standard Git operations)
- Commands that act as a bridge with a selected version control tool (interacting with other commands)
- Command aliases (custom aliases created by users to mask complex Git commands)

Typically, for our daily use and interaction with Git, we will mostly use a subset of the main porcelain commands. In this section, we will be using some low-level or plumbing commands to better understand Git internals.

Again, typing `git help -a` on your terminal will give you a full list of the command and the category it belongs to.

Inside the .git Directory

To begin, initialize an empty repository using `git init`, and then run the `tree .git` command to reveal what's created:

```
$ mkdir /tmp/hello
$ cd /tmp/hello
$ git init -b main
Initialized empty Git repository in /tmp/hello/.git/

# List all the files in the current directory
$ tree .git
    .git
├── HEAD
```

```
├── config
├── description
├── hooks
│   ├── applypatch-msg.sample
│   ├── commit-msg.sample
│   ├── fsmonitor-watchman.sample
│   ├── post-update.sample
│   ├── pre-applypatch.sample
│   ├── pre-commit.sample
│   ├── pre-merge-commit.sample
│   ├── pre-push.sample
│   ├── pre-rebase.sample
│   ├── pre-receive.sample
│   ├── prepare-commit-msg.sample
│   ├── push-to-checkout.sample
│   └── update.sample
├── info
│   └── exclude
├── objects
│   ├── info
│   └── pack
└── refs
    ├── heads
    └── tags

8 directories, 17 files
```

As you can see, *.git* contains a lot of stuff. The files are displayed based on a template directory that you can adjust if desired by passing in the `--template=tem`
`plate_directory` option. For example, if you prefer to create a new repository that implements custom Git hooks, you can point to a template that is preconfigured with a custom directory structure and Git hook files. We will discuss Git hooks in Chapter 14.

 Depending on the version of Git you are using, your actual manifest may look a little different. For example, older versions of Git do not use a *.sample* suffix on the *.git/hooks* files. You can learn more about the command by running `man git-init` in the command line.

In general, you don't have to view or manipulate the files in the *.git* directory. These "hidden" files are considered part of Git's plumbing or configuration commands.

Initially, the *.git/objects* directory (the directory for all of Git's objects) is empty, except for a few placeholders:

```
$ find .git/objects

.git/objects
.git/objects/pack
.git/objects/info
```

Let's now carefully create a simple object:

```
$ echo "hello world" > hello.txt
$ git add hello.txt
```

If you typed "hello world" exactly as it appears here (with no changes to spacing or capitalization), then your *objects* directory should now look like this:

```
$ find .git/objects
.git/objects
.git/objects/3b
.git/objects/3b/18e512dba79e4c8300dd08aeb37f8e728b8dad
.git/objects/pack
.git/objects/info
```

Note that there is only one object at this point in time: the blob object with a SHA1 ID generated based on the content of the file *hello.txt*. All of this looks pretty mysterious. But it's not, as the following sections explain.

Blob Objects and Hashes

When we created the file *hello.txt* and staged it in the *index* directory using `git add`, Git internally created a blob object. At this point, Git doesn't care that the filename is *hello.txt*. Git cares only about what's inside the file: the sequence of 12 bytes that represent "hello world" and the terminating newline (the same blob created earlier). Git performs a few operations on this blob, calculates its SHA1 hash, and enters it into the object store as a file named after the hexadecimal representation of the hash. The hash in this case is `3b18e512dba79e4c8300dd08aeb37f8e728b8dad`. The 160 bits of a SHA1 hash correspond to 20 bytes, which takes 40 bytes of hexadecimal to display, so the content is stored as *.git/objects/3b/18e512dba79e4c8300dd08aeb37f8e728b8dad*.

Git inserts a / after the first two digits to improve filesystem efficiency. (Some filesystems slow down if you put too many files in the same directory; making the first byte of the SHA1 into a directory is an easy way to create a fixed, 256-way partitioning of the namespace for all possible objects with an even distribution.)

You can verify that the content in the file is not changed by Git (it's still the same comforting "hello world") by using the generated hash value to extract the content from the object store, utilizing a low-level plumbing command:

```
# Using the git cat-file command
$ git cat-file -p 3b18e512dba79e4c8300dd08aeb37f8e728b8dad
hello world
```

or

```
# Using the git hash-object command
$ echo "hello world" | git hash-object --stdin
3b18e512dba79e4c8300dd08aeb37f8e728b8dad
```

Git also knows that 40 characters is a bit chancy to type by hand, so it provides a command to look up objects by a unique prefix of the object hash:

```
$ git rev-parse 3b18e512d
3b18e512dba79e4c8300dd08aeb37f8e728b8dad
```

How Do We Know a SHA1 Hash Is Unique?

There is an extremely slim chance that two different blobs will yield the same SHA1 hash. When this happens, it is called a *collision*. However, a SHA1 collision is so unlikely that you can safely bank on it never interfering with your use of Git. But could a collision happen at random? Let's see.

With 160 bits, you have 2^{160} or about 10^{48} (1 with 48 zeros after it) possible SHA1 hashes. That number is just incomprehensibly huge. Even if you hired a trillion people to produce a trillion new unique blobs per second for a trillion years, you would still only have about 10^{43} blobs.

If you hashed 2^{80} random blobs, you might find a collision. Don't take our word for it; read Bruce Schneier's blog post "Cryptanalysis of SHA-1" (*https://oreil.ly/BtN34*).

SHA1 has traditionally been known to be a cryptographically secure hash. That is, until recently, when security researchers were able to point out flaws in the integrity of the SHA1 hash function. They published their findings on their website, Shattered (*https://shattered.io*).

Starting with version 2.13.0, Git began implementing logic to detect and reject the kind of attacks described in the SHAttered paper. The probability of such an attack vector being repeated is not something that can be guaranteed in the future. For this reason, Git introduced a new repository format extension that enables the use of SHA256 instead of SHA1. It is described in detail in the Git technical documentation (*https://oreil.ly/RW7eA*).

Now let's move up the data structure to understand how pathnames and filenames are stored by Git.

Tree Object and Files

Now that the "hello world" blob is safely ensconced in the object store, let's take a look at how it is associated with a filename. Git wouldn't be very useful if it couldn't find files by name.

As mentioned before, Git tracks the pathnames of files through another kind of object, called a *tree*. When you use `git add`, Git creates an object for the contents of each file you add, but it doesn't create an object for your tree right away. Instead, it updates the index. The index is found in *.git/index* and keeps track of file pathnames and corresponding blobs. Each time you run commands such as `git add`, `git rm`, or `git mv`, Git updates the index with the new pathname and blob information.

Whenever you want, you can create a tree object from your current index by capturing a snapshot of its current information with the low-level `git write-tree` command (an action you will rarely execute in your typical daily work).

At the moment, the index contains exactly one file, *hello.txt*:

```
$ git ls-files -s
100644 3b18e512dba79e4c8300dd08aeb37f8e728b8dad 0       hello.txt
```

Here you can see the association of the file, *hello.txt*, and the 3b18e5... blob.

Next, let's capture the index state and save it to a tree object:

```
$ git write-tree
68aba62e560c0ebc3396e8ae9335232cd93a3f60

$ find .git/objects
.git/objects
.git/objects/68
.git/objects/68/aba62e560c0ebc3396e8ae9335232cd93a3f60
.git/objects/pack
.git/objects/3b
.git/objects/3b/18e512dba79e4c8300dd08aeb37f8e728b8dad
.git/objects/info
```

Now there are two objects: the "hello world" blob object at 3b18e5 and a new one, the tree object, at 68aba6. As you can see, the SHA1 object name corresponds exactly to the subdirectory and filename in *.git/objects*.

But what does a tree look like? Because it's an object, just like blob, you can use the same low-level plumbing command to view it:

```
$ git cat-file -p 68aba6
100644 blob 3b18e512dba79e4c8300dd08aeb37f8e728b8dad    hello.txt
```

The contents of the object should be easy to interpret. The first number, 100644, represents the file attributes of the object in octal, which should be familiar to anyone who has used the Unix `chmod` command. Here, 3b18e5 is the object name of the *hello world* blob, and *hello.txt* is the name associated with that blob.

It is now easy to see that the *tree* object has captured the information that was in the index when you ran `git ls-files -s`.

A Note on Git's Use of SHA1

Before inspecting the contents of the tree object in more detail, let's reemphasize an important feature of SHA1 hashes:

```
$ git write-tree
68aba62e560c0ebc3396e8ae9335232cd93a3f60

$ git write-tree
68aba62e560c0ebc3396e8ae9335232cd93a3f60

$ git write-tree
68aba62e560c0ebc3396e8ae9335232cd93a3f60
```

In the preceding example, every time you compute another tree object for the same index (no adding or removing of files), the SHA1 hash remains exactly the same. Git doesn't need to re-create a new tree object. If you're following these steps on your computer, you should be seeing *exactly the same SHA1 hashes* as the ones published in this book.

In this sense, the hash function is a true function in the mathematical sense: for a given input, it always produces the same output. Such a hash function is sometimes called a *digest* to emphasize that it serves as a sort of summary of the hashed object. This is also true for any hash function; even the lowly parity bit has this property.

For example, if you create the exact same content as another developer, regardless of where or when or how both of you work, an identical hash is proof enough that the full content is identical too. In fact, Git treats them as identical, and this notion is extremely important.

But hold on a second—aren't SHA1 hashes unique? What happened to the trillions of people with trillions of blobs per second that never produce a single collision? This is a common source of confusion among new Git users. So read on carefully, because if you can understand this distinction, then everything else in this chapter will be easy.

Identical SHA1 hashes in this case *do not count as a collision*. It would be a collision only if two *different* objects produced the same hash. Here, you created two separate instances of the very same content, and the same content always has the same hash.

Git depends on another consequence of the SHA1 hash function: it doesn't matter *how* you got a tree called `68aba62e560c0ebc3396e8ae9335232cd93a3f60`. If you have it, you can be extremely confident that it is the same tree object that, say, another reader of this book has. Consider the following:

Scenario 1
> Bob might have created the tree by combining commits A and B from Jennie and commit C from Sergey on a shared repository.

Scenario 2

Working in that same shared repository, you might have created the same tree but via a different path. You might have gotten commit A from Sue and an update from Lakshmi that combines commits B and C.

The results are the same for the generated tree object in both scenarios. This facilitates distributed development with Git.

If you're asked to look for object `68aba62e560c0ebc3396e8ae9335232cd93a3f60` and find such an object, then since SHA1 is a cryptographic hash, you can be confident that you're looking at precisely the same data from which the hash was created.

The converse is also true: if you don't find an object with a specific hash in your object store, then you can be confident that you do not hold a copy of that exact object. To summarize, you can determine whether your object store does or does not have a particular object even though you know nothing about its (potentially very large) contents. The hash thus serves as a reliable label or name for the object.

Tree Hierarchies

In our examples from the previous section, we only have information regarding a single file, but in actuality, projects contain complex, deeply nested directories that are refactored and moved around over time. In this section, we will be creating a new subdirectory that contains an identical copy of the *hello.txt* file to see how Git handles this scenario:

```
$ pwd
/tmp/hello
$ mkdir subdir
$ cp hello.txt subdir/
$ git add subdir/hello.txt
$ git write-tree
492413269336d21fac079d4a4672e55d5d2147ac

$ git cat-file -p 4924132693
100644 blob 3b18e512dba79e4c8300dd08aeb37f8e728b8dad    hello.txt
040000 tree 68aba62e560c0ebc3396e8ae9335232cd93a3f60    subdir
```

The new top-level tree contains two items: the original *hello.txt* file as well as the new *subdir* directory, which is of type `tree` instead of `blob`.

Look more closely at the object name `subdir`. Do you notice anything unusual? Indeed, it's our old friend, the SHA1 `68aba62e560c0ebc3396e8ae9335232cd93a3f60`!

How can this be, you ask? Well, the new tree for *subdir* contains only one file, *hello.txt*, and that file contains the same old "hello world" content. So the *subdir* tree is exactly the same as the older, top-level tree! And yes, you are correct if you pointed out that it is for this reason alone that it has the same SHA1 object name as before: traits of a *true function* in the mathematical sense.

Let's look at the *.git/objects* directory and see what this most recent change affected:

```
$ find .git/objects
.git/objects
.git/objects/49
.git/objects/49/2413269336d21fac079d4a4672e55d5d2147ac
.git/objects/68
.git/objects/68/aba62e560c0ebc3396e8ae9335232cd93a3f60
.git/objects/pack
.git/objects/3b
.git/objects/3b/18e512dba79e4c8300dd08aeb37f8e728b8dad
.git/objects/info
```

There are still only three *unique* objects: a blob containing "hello world"; one tree containing *hello.txt*, which contains the text "hello world" plus a newline; and a second tree that contains *another* reference to *hello.txt* along with the first tree.

Figure 2-7 illustrates this concept.

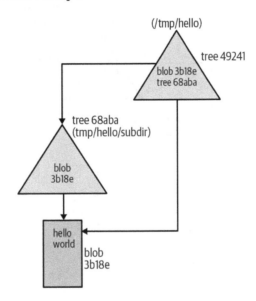

Figure 2-7. Tree hierarchies

Commit Objects

The next object to discuss is the commit. Now that *hello.txt* has been added with the `git add` command and the tree object has been produced with `git write-tree`, we can create a commit object using low-level plumbing commands like this:

```
$ echo -n "Commit a file that says hello\n"
| git commit-tree 492413269336d21fac079d4a4672e55d5d2147ac
3ede4622cc241bcb09683af36360e7413b9ddf6c
```

The result will look something like this:

```
$ git cat-file -p 3ede462
tree 492413269336d21fac079d4a4672e55d5d2147ac
author Jon Loeliger <jdl@example.com> 1656932750 +0200
committer Jon Loeliger <jdl@example.com> 1656932750 +0200

Commit a file that says hello
```

Figure 2-8 illustrates this concept.

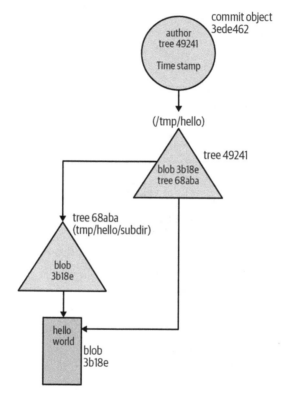

Figure 2-8. Commit object

If you're following along on your computer, you probably found that the commit object you generated does *not* have the exact same value as the one in this example. If you've understood everything so far, the reason for that should be obvious: our commit object is not the same as your commit object.

Your commit object contains your name and the time you made the commit, whereas our commit object contains a different timestamp and author name, so of course it is different.

On the other hand, your commit does have the same tree. This is why commit objects are separate from their tree objects: different commits often refer to exactly the same tree. When that happens, Git is smart enough to transfer around only the new commit object, which is tiny, instead of the entire tree and blob objects, which are probably much larger.

In real life, you can (and should!) pass over the low-level plumbing commands `git write-tree` and `git commit-tree` used in the examples. You can just use the *porcelain* `git commit` command. You don't need to remember all those plumbing commands to be a perfectly happy Git user.

In essence, a basic commit object is fairly simple, and it's the last ingredient required for a real version control system. The commit object just shown is the simplest possible one, containing the following:

- The name of a tree object that actually identifies the associated files
- The name of the person who composed the new version (the author) and the time when it was composed
- The name of the person who placed the new version into the repository (the committer) and the time when it was committed
- A description of the reason for this revision (the commit message)

By default, the author and committer are the same; there are a few situations where they're different.

 You can use the command `git show --pretty=fuller` to see additional details about a given commit.

A use case closer to home is when a project contains multiple commits. In such a situation, when you make a new commit in the project you can give it one or more parent commits. Given this context, consider the most recent commit (or its associated tree object) in the project. Because it contains, as part of its content, the hash of its parent commits and of its tree, and *that* in turn contains the hash of all of its subtrees and blobs recursively through the whole data structure, it follows by induction that the hash of the original commit uniquely identifies the state of the whole data structure rooted at that commit.

By following back through the chain of parents, you can discover the history of your project, thus the term *commit history*. Commit objects are also stored in a graph structure, although it's completely different from the structures used by tree objects. More details about commits and the commit graph are given in Chapter 4.

Tag Objects

Finally, the last object Git manages is the tag. Although Git implements only one kind of tag object in its object store, it supports two basic tag types, usually called a lightweight tag and an annotated tag.

Lightweight tags are simply references to a commit object and are usually considered private to a repository. Lightweight tags are not stored as permanent objects in the object store.

An *annotated tag* creates an object. It contains a message, supplied by you, and can be digitally signed using a GnuPG key according to RFC 4880.

Git treats both lightweight and annotated tag names equivalently for the purposes of associating a commit with a meaningful, human-readable name.

 A typical use case for an annotated tag is when you're creating a specific release version for your projects. A typical use case for a lightweight tag is when you need a temporary label attached to a commit object.

You create an annotated, unsigned tag with a message on a commit using the `git tag` command:

```
$ git tag -a V1.0 3ede462
```

Git will launch your configured default editor after the command is issued, and you can provide a tag message to complete the operation.

You can view the newly created tag object via the `git cat-file -p` command, but what is the SHA1 of the tag object? To find it, use the tip in "Blob Objects and Hashes" on page 38:

```
$ git rev-parse V1.0
6b608c1093943939ae78348117dd18b1ba151c6a

$ git cat-file -p 6b608c
object 3ede4622cc241bcb09683af36360e7413b9ddf6c
type commit
tag V1.0
tagger Jon Loeliger <jdl@example.com> 1656932858 +0200

Tag version 1.0
```

In addition to the log message and author information, the tag refers to the commit object 3ede462.

Git usually tags a commit object, which points to a tree object, which encompasses the total state of the entire hierarchy of files and directories within your repository.

Recall from Figure 2-5 that the V1.0 tag points to the commit named 1492, which in turn points to a tree (8675309) that spans multiple files. Thus the tag simultaneously applies to all files of that tree.

This is unlike CVS, for example, which will apply a tag to each individual file and then rely on the collection of all those tagged files to reconstitute a whole tagged revision. And whereas CVS lets you move the tag on an individual file, Git requires a new commit, encompassing the file state change onto which the tag will be moved.

Summary

We have discussed the inner workings of Git to an elaborate extent, so let's now recap the key takeaways from this chapter. We started with a high-level discussion of the repository, where we learned about the various working directories Git replies upon, mainly the index, working directory, and local history. We continued with the Git object store and analyzed each of the immutable Git objects. We also learned how to interact with those internal objects directly using low-level git commands that you would rarely use on a daily basis. Grasping this concept should highlight the fact that Git as a concept is merely a simple content-addressable database whereby its inner mechanics are somewhat direct, yet may at times be difficult to comprehend. We also described visually the relationship between the objects in Git's object store to help establish a good foundation for the chapters in Part II of the book.

## PART II

Fundamentals of Git

The following chapters highlight how Git manages files, explain the importance of the index and how it relates to this process, and take a detailed look at the commit object and the important role that branches play in a Git repository.

Before we proceed, we would like to explain why we chose to discuss these topics in this order.

In "Git Internals: Concepts at Work" on page 36, we dissected the available objects within the Git object store. Let's look at how the objects are created and when they establish links with each other.

First we will create an empty directory and inspect the content using the `tree` command:

```
$ mkdir myrepo && cd myrepo

$ git status
fatal: not a git repository (or any of the parent directories): .git

$ tree .git
.git [error opening dir]

0 directories, 0 files
```

Since this is not a Git repository, there is no *.git* directory. Next, we will initialize an empty Git repository and reinspect the directory content:

```
$ git init -b main
Initialized empty Git repository in /myrepo/.git/

$ tree .git
.git
```

```
├── HEAD
├── config
├── description
├── hooks
│   ├── applypatch-msg.sample
│   ├── commit-msg.sample
│   ├── fsmonitor-watchman.sample
│   ├── post-update.sample
│   ├── pre-applypatch.sample
│   ├── pre-commit.sample
│   ├── pre-merge-commit.sample
│   ├── pre-push.sample
│   ├── pre-rebase.sample
│   ├── pre-receive.sample
│   ├── prepare-commit-msg.sample
│   ├── push-to-checkout.sample
│   └── update.sample
├── info
│   └── exclude
├── objects
│   ├── info
│   └── pack
└── refs
    ├── heads
    └── tags

8 directories, 17 files
```

Here we see that the *.git* folder is created; this is where the `git` objects will be stored in their respective folders.

When initializing, we created a branch named `main`. In Chapter 3, we will learn that branches are just pointers to commit objects, specifically, to the `HEAD` or tip commit of the current branch. Let's examine the content of the *HEAD* directory from the tree output:

```
$ cat .git/HEAD
ref: refs/heads/main
```

It points to the name of the branch we created earlier. Let's further examine what it contains:

```
$ cat .git/refs/heads/main
cat: .git/refs/heads/main: No such file or directory
```

Interestingly, we have a branch, but the content is empty. We will circle back to this later.

We will now create a file and run the `tree` `.git` command again:

```
$ echo "Hello Git" > file
$ tree .git
.git
├── HEAD
├── config
├── description
├── hooks
```

```
│   ├── applypatch-msg.sample
│   ├── commit-msg.sample
│   ├── fsmonitor-watchman.sample
│   ├── post-update.sample
│   ├── pre-applypatch.sample
│   ├── pre-commit.sample
│   ├── pre-merge-commit.sample
│   ├── pre-push.sample
│   ├── pre-rebase.sample
│   ├── pre-receive.sample
│   ├── prepare-commit-msg.sample
│   ├── push-to-checkout.sample
│   └── update.sample
├── info
│   └── exclude
├── objects
│   ├── info
│   └── pack
└── refs
    ├── heads
    └── tags

8 directories, 17 files
```

Notice that there is no *index* directory created yet. Next, we mark the file to be tracked by Git:

```
$ git add file
$ tree .git
.git
├── HEAD
├── config
├── description
├── hooks
│   ├── applypatch-msg.sample
│   ├── commit-msg.sample
│   ├── fsmonitor-watchman.sample
│   ├── post-update.sample
│   ├── pre-applypatch.sample
│   ├── pre-commit.sample
│   ├── pre-merge-commit.sample
│   ├── pre-push.sample
│   ├── pre-rebase.sample
│   ├── pre-receive.sample
│   ├── prepare-commit-msg.sample
│   ├── push-to-checkout.sample
│   └── update.sample
├── index
├── info
│   └── exclude
├── objects
│   ├── 9f
│   │   └── 4d96d5b00d98959ea9960f069585ce42b1349a
│   ├── info
│   └── pack
└── refs
    ├── heads
    └── tags

9 directories, 19 files
```

Once the file is tracked, running the `tree .git` command will reveal two changes. One, we now have an *index* directory that is of the type binary, and two, we have some new content in the *object* directory; we will discuss this in more detail in Chapter 5:

```
$ cat .git/index
DIRCb◆Fx◆◆
b◆Fx◆◆

◆◆I◆◆◆
◆◆◆◆◆◆◆◆B◆4◆file◆◆(◆◆◆[◆o+◆fu◆◆◆\%
```

Let's examine the content of the *object* directory using some low-level `git` commands:

```
# check the type of object
$ git cat-file -t 9f4d96
blob

# check the content of object
$ git cat-file -p 9f4d96
Hello Git
```

Here you can see that the content is of type `blob` and is what we supplied.

We will now make our first commit:

```
$ git commit -m "Initial commit"
[main (root-commit) 75f501d] Initial commit
 1 file changed, 1 insertion(+)
 create mode 100644 file


# run tree .git to investigate changes in the git object store
$ tree .git
.git
├── COMMIT_EDITMSG
├── HEAD
├── config
├── description
├── hooks
│   ├── applypatch-msg.sample
│   ├── commit-msg.sample
│   ├── fsmonitor-watchman.sample
│   ├── post-update.sample
│   ├── pre-applypatch.sample
│   ├── pre-commit.sample
│   ├── pre-merge-commit.sample
│   ├── pre-push.sample
│   ├── pre-rebase.sample
│   ├── pre-receive.sample
│   ├── prepare-commit-msg.sample
│   ├── push-to-checkout.sample
│   └── update.sample
├── index
├── info
│   └── exclude
├── logs
│   ├── HEAD
│   └── refs
│       └── heads
│
```

```
|             └── main
├── objects
│   ├── 16
│   │   └── b2356b798a3bfa903c9a54dc608282f4394e2b
│   ├── 9f
│   │   └── 4d96d5b00d98959ea9960f069585ce42b1349a
│   ├── 75
│   │   └── f501da811525b594f2240e015eeebeed388042
│   ├── info
│   └── pack
└── refs
    ├── heads
    │   └── main
    └── tags

14 directories, 25 files
```

Observe the changes. When the first commit is created, you get the SHA summary with the label (root commit). This same abbreviated SHA shows up in full length in the *object* directory. We can validate this using the following:

```
# check the content of the commit object
$ git cat-file -p 75f501
tree 16b2356b798a3bfa903c9a54dc608282f4394e2b
author Prem Kumar Ponuthorai <ppremk@gmail.com> 1658662758 +0200
committer Prem Kumar Ponuthorai <ppremk@gmail.com> 1658662758 +0200

Initial commit
```

We also see that the commit object contains the tree object. Looking into the tree object further reveals that it is linked to the blob object we created earlier. We will discuss this in more detail in Chapter 4:

```
# check the content of the tree object
$ git cat-file -p 16b23
100644 blob 9f4d96d5b00d98959ea9960f069585ce42b1349a readme.md
```

Since we have a commit object, let's go back and look in the *.git/refs/heads/main* directory:

```
$ cat .git/refs/heads/main
75f501da811525b594f2240e015eeebeed388042
```

This time we have some content, and that content is the commit object SHA. We've come full circle now. This relationship is illustrated briefly in Figure II-1.

These examples showcase the Git internals and how they are intricately linked, which made it challenging for us to determine the best possible way to order the chapters. In the end we decided to stick to an outside-in, top-down approach whereby we start by explaining what branches are, followed by commits, and finally how files are managed along with their relation to the index within a Git repository. Our rationale was that we wanted to approach these topics in the order in which you would be implementing them in your daily routine. In other words, we start at the surface and then peek under the hood to show you the inner mechanics of Git.

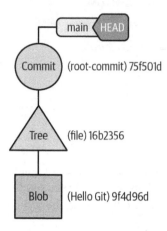

Figure II-1. Git objects relationship

So what does this mean to you? You may encounter some concepts or verbiage along the way that aren't fully explained immediately, which may be confusing or might raise even more questions. When you are feeling this, just note it and keep going. At the end of this part of the book, it will all make sense.

## CHAPTER 3

Branches

A branch allows the user to launch a separate line of development within a software project. When you create a branch, you are creating a fork from a specific state of the project's timeline. This allows development to progress in multiple directions simultaneously. Think of it as time travel, where you have the ability to create alternate parallel timelines from a single starting point. A branch also gives you the ability to create different versions of a project. Often, a branch can be reconciled and merged with other branches to combine divergent efforts.

Creating branches in Git is considered a lightweight and inexpensive operation. This is because a branch is just a pointer to a specific commit object in a Git repository. Git allows many branches, and thus many different lines of development within a repository can exist simultaneously at any given moment. Moreover, Git has first-rate support for merges between branches. As a result, most Git users make routine use of branches and are naturally encouraged to do so frequently.

In this chapter, we will take a top-down approach to thinking about how branches function in Git by looking at how developers maintain multiple lines of development within a project. The concept discussed in this chapter will complement the key takeaways we learned in Chapter 2.

We will show you how to list, view, select, create, and discard branches. We will also provide some best practices so that your branches don't disrupt the fabric of time and the existence of parallel timelines.[1]

---

[1] We are aware of the time travel paradox and the complications that can arise, so we shall stick to only imagining the timelines and not do the actual time travel yet.

Motivation for Using Branches in Git

In a Git repository, a branch can be created for a countless number of technical, philosophical, managerial, and even social reasons. The distributed nature of Git, combined with a well-thought-out branching strategy, enables the existence of various development workflows that provide a structured way of working on projects among diverse teams. Here are some common rationales:

- A branch can reflect the stages of your project development lifecycle—for example, the stable, development, release candidate, and production release stages. This can provide clarity and streamline the workflow among teams in a systematic and coordinated manner.

- More often than not, a branch is also used to represent a specific product release. If you want to start a new-release version of your project but you know that some of your customers may want to stick with an older-release version, you have the option to maintain the older-release version as a separate branch for backward compatibility.

- A branch provides you an option to iterate and work on a specific feature or to research a fix for a bug in your project in an isolated development environment. This enables you to create multiple feature branches that encapsulate well-defined concepts or ideas that you can consolidate via a merge prior to cutting a release. Git's branching system is robust yet inexpensive; thus this approach is encouraged and is not considered overkill when working with small changes in each branch you create. The word *feature* simply indicates that each branch in the repository has a particular purpose.

- An individual branch in a large and complex project can represent the work of an individual developer. This method of working enables teams with complicated project development requirements to segregate the implementation of different moving parts of a project independently, before creating a new branch to integrate and unify the multiple moving parts into a final product for specific releases.

Git also has the notion of a *tracking branch*, or a branch to keep clones of a repository in sync. Chapter 11 explains how to use a tracking branch.

Branching Guidelines

Establishing best practices and clear practical guidelines in your projects ensures their success and provides a pleasant experience for everyone involved. Working with branches in a Git repository is no exception. In this section, we will elaborate on some common practices and guidelines when you are working with branches in Git.

Branch Names

The name you assign to a branch is essentially arbitrary, though there are some imposed limitations. When you initialize a new repository, Git assigns a default branch name. As of Git version 2.37.1, the default branch name is `master`, but this is subject to change in an effort to be respectful and inclusive in naming conventions. The default branch in Git is used by developers to maintain their projects' robust and stable codebase. Git allows you to rename or even delete the default branch. If you are initializing a new repository, you can change the default branch name as follows:

```
$ git init --initial-branch=branch-name
```

or

```
$ git init -b branch-name
```

Alternatively, you can edit the Git configuration file to include the `init.default Branch` attribute to always use a specified default branch name of your choice:

```
$ git config --global init.defaultBranch branch-name
```

If you plan to rename a Git repository's branch name while preserving the repository's commit history, you can easily do so like this:

```
$ git branch -m old-branch-name new-branch-name
```

To support scalability and categorical organization, you can create a hierarchical branch name that resembles a Unix pathname. As an example, suppose you want to easily identify, via branch name, various feature implementations and bug fixes or represent changes contributed by you as an individual (if your contribution will be picked up and merged by an integration manager): you can create a hierarchical structure on separate branches named something like *features/feature-A*, *bug/ticket-no-x*, and *ppremk/feature-B*.

An advantage when using hierarchical branch names is that Git, just like the Unix shell, supports wildcards. For instance, given the naming scheme *bug/ticket-no-x* and *bug/ticket-no-y*, you can select all *bug* branches at once with a clever and familiar shorthand:

```
git show-branch 'bug/*'
```

Dos and Don'ts in Branch Names

Branch names must conform to a few simple rules:

- You can use the forward slash (/) to create a hierarchical name scheme. However, the name cannot end with a slash.

- No slash-separated component can begin with a dot (.). A branch name such as `feature/.new` is invalid.

- The name cannot start with a minus sign (–).
- The name cannot contain two consecutive dots (..) anywhere.
- The name cannot include any spaces or other whitespace characters.
- The name cannot include a character that has special meaning to Git, including the tilde (~), caret (^), colon (:), question mark (?), asterisk (*), and open square bracket ([).
- The name cannot include an ASCII control character, which is any byte with a value lower than \040 octal, or the DEL character (\177 octal).

These branch name rules are enforced by the `git check-ref-format` plumbing command, and they are designed to ensure that each branch name is easily typed and usable as a filename within the *.git* directory and scripts.

Managing Branches

Other than the default branch, a repository may have many different branches during a project's lifespan; however, you will naturally work in only a single branch at a time, which is the current or active branch. The active branch helps determine which files are checked out in your *working directory*: in other words, it reflects the state of a file currently in development.

Furthermore, the current branch is often an implicit operand in Git commands, such as the target of the merge operation. By default, every time you initialize a new Git repository, `main` is the active branch, but you can create additional branches and make any branch the current branch.

Figure 3-1 presents a commit graph containing two branches. Notice how the HEAD points to the branch name and stays updated, pointing to the latest commit in the branch. Keep this graph structure in mind when you manipulate branches because it reinforces your understanding of the elegant and simple object model underlying Git's branches. We will explore commits in detail in Chapter 4.

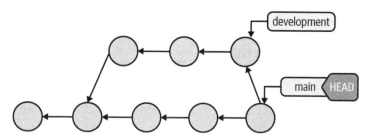

Figure 3-1. Commit graph with branches

Working in Branches

Creating a branch in your repository allows the content of the repository to split in multiple directions, with each direction representing a branch. Let's assume you have two branches in your repository: a default branch and a divergent line of development. Every commit you create will be applied to only one of the branches—that is, whichever branch is marked as active.

Adhering to the branch naming rules and guidelines, it will help if your branch name is terse and reflects the context of its purpose. The branch name will always refer to the most recent commit on the branch, also called the *tip* or *HEAD* of the branch. By technical definition, a branch name is a simple pointer to a specific commit; thus the branch name moves forward incrementally as you add new commits to the active branch you are developing on. Figure 3-2 illustrates this concept.

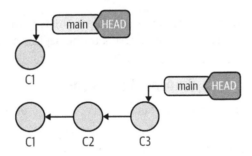

Figure 3-2. Branch name as a dynamic pointer

Since a branch name is dynamic and points to the tip or HEAD commit in the series of commits on the branch, Git doesn't keep track of where or from which specific commit a branch originated. If you need to refer to an older commit in the branch, you will need to provide an explicit commit object ID or a relative name such as dev~5 (which means move the branch name pointer back by five commits, starting from the current commit). If you need a static reference point of a particular commit in a branch, because the branch represents a stable point in the project, you can explicitly assign either a lightweight or an annotated tag name. Figure 3-3 illustrates this concept.

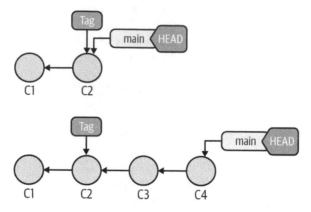

Figure 3-3. Branch name versus tag name

A branch includes sufficient commits to rebuild the history of the project along the branch from which it diverged, all the way back to the beginning of the project.

Branches Versus Tags

A branch and a tag may seem similar, but they serve different purposes.

A tag can be used as a temporary bookmark (lightweight tag) or as a fixed reference point (annotated tag) to delineate when a specific version of a product was released. Thus tags are static and always point to a specific commit object in a Git repository.

A branch points to and moves with each commit made during development. Each reference to the branch (branch name) will follow every diverging line of development within your repository. Thus branches are dynamic.

So when should you use a tag, and when should you use a branch? The decision is ultimately up to you and your project development policies. However, you should consider the key differentiating characteristic: is the reference static and immutable, or is it dynamic? If it's the former, you should use a tag. If it's the latter, you should use a branch.

You can name a branch and a tag with the same name. If you do, you will have to use their full ref names to distinguish them. For example, you could use `refs/tags/v1.0` and `refs/heads/v1.0`. We recommend that you simply avoid using the same name for both a branch and a tag, unless you have a compelling reason to do so. The sequence Git uses to determine which reference to use is based on the rule explained in the gitrevisions documentation (*https://oreil.ly/Mvm6S*).

In Figure 3-4, the `development` branch points to the tip or `HEAD` commit Z, the most recent commit in that branch. If you want to reproduce the state of the repository as it was at Z, then all the commits reachable from Z back to the original commit, A, are needed. The reachable portion of the graph is highlighted with wide lines and covers every commit except S, G, H, J, K, and L. Do note that the arrows from commit W to F and commit X to R represent a merge operation between the respective branches. We will revisit what a merge operation is in Chapter 6.

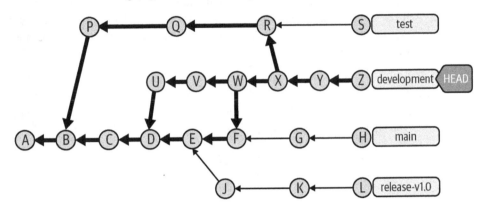

Figure 3-4. Commits reachable from development

Each of your branch names, as well as the committed content on each branch, is local to your repository. However, when making your repository available to others, you can publish or elect to make one or any number of branches and the associated commits available too. Publishing a branch must be done explicitly; we will elaborate on this in Chapter 11. Also, if your repository is cloned, your branch names and the development on those branches will all be part of the newly cloned repository copy.

Creating Branches

Git is built to support an arbitrarily complex branching structure. This includes creating new branches from existing branches and creating forks diverging into multiple branches from the same commit.

When you create a new branch, it is always based upon an existing commit within the repository. This can be the current tip or `HEAD` commit, or it can be a different commit that you reference explicitly using its commit SHA (commit object ID).

A branch may be short lived or long lived; its lifetime is, again, your decision. Within the span of its lifetime, a given branch name may be added and deleted multiple times as you see fit for your development needs.

The basic form of the command to create a new branch is as follows:

```
$ git branch branchname start-point
```

If you do not specify a *start-point*, the default start point will be the tip or HEAD commit on the currently active branch. In other words, the default is to start a new branch at the point where you're working right now.

Note that the `git branch` command merely introduces the name of a branch into the repository. It does not change your working directory to *use* the new branch. The command simply creates a new named branch at the given commit. This also means that there will be no changes to the files in your working directory, nor will there be implicit changes to the branch context. And, of course, no new commits will be made when the command is executed.

You can't actually start working on the branch until you switch to it, as we will show in "Switching (Checking Out) Branches" on page 66. The main reason for this is because the tip or HEAD is still pointing to the active branch from when you created the new branch. Figure 3-5 helps illustrate this concept.

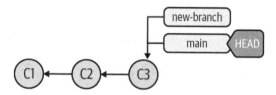

Figure 3-5. The HEAD, active branch, and new branch

Suppose that your project's branching strategy reflects its production release versions, and you are tasked with fixing a bug in a certain release. It may be convenient to use the *start-point* parameter to create a new bug-fix branch from the most recent commit of the specified release branch. This enables you to switch your working directory to reflect the project's state at the point that represents the release.

For instance, you might specify a branch named `rel-2.3` to represent Production Version 2.3 of your project. You can make a bug fix on a separate branch for the specified version as follows:

```
$ git branch bugs/fix-1311 rel-2.3
```

> The *start-point* parameter accepts a branch name, a commit SHA, or a tag name. Using the commit SHA gives you the freedom to point to any commits in a series of commits within the development line of any branch. In other words, it allows you to fork in multiple directions from a single commit to explore alternate solutions from a common starting point:
>
> ```
> $ git branch bugs/fix-1311 e69de29bb2d1d6434b8b29ae775ad8c2e48c5391
> ```

Listing Branch Names

The `git branch` command lists branch names found in the repository:

```
$ git branch
bugs/pr-1311
development
* main
```

In this example, three branches are shown. The active branch currently checked into your working directory is identified by the asterisk. This example also shows two other branches, `bugs/pr-1311` and `development`.

Without additional parameters, only branches in the local repository are listed. As you'll see in Chapter 11, there may be additional remote tracking branches in your repository. You can list those branches by providing the `git branch` command with the `-r` parameter option. You can list both *local* and *remote* branches with the `-a` parameter.

Viewing Branches and Their Commits

The `git show-branch` command provides more detailed output than the `git branch` command. It lists the commits that contribute to one or more branches in roughly reverse chronological order. As with the `git branch` command, when no option parameter is provided, the `git show-branch` command will list the *local* branches. When you use the `git show-branch` command with the option `-r`, it shows the remote tracking branches; with the option `-a`, it shows all *local* and *remote* branches.

The `git show-branch` command output is divided into two parts, separated by a line of dashes (`---`).

The section above the separator lists the following:

- The names of branches enclosed in square brackets, one per line
- Each branch name prefixed with special characters: an asterisk (*) to denote the current branch and an exclamation point (!) to reference *feature* branches
- Each branch name with its one-line commit message from the most recent commit in that branch, which can be helpful as a quick reference

The section below the separator lists each commit together with its branch name, adhering to the following conventions:

- As an output in a matrix format, stating which commits are present in each listed branch's respective columns.

- Prefixed with special characters. A plus sign (+) indicates that the commit is present in the listed branch, an asterisk (*) indicates that the commit is present in the current branch, and a minus sign (−) denotes that the commit is a *merge commit* on the branch.

- With its one-line commit message. As mentioned earlier, Git assigns the branch name to the most recent commit; thus previous commits on the same branch will have the same branch name with a special trailing character: a caret (^).

Let's look at an output from the git show-branch command:

```
$ git show-branch
  ! [bugs/pr-1] Fix Problem Report 1    ❶
   * [dev] Improve the new development  ❷
    ! [main] Added Bob's fixes.         ❸
  ---
   *   [dev] Improve the new development.
   *   [dev﹏] Start some new development.
  +    [bugs/pr-1] Fix Problem Report 1.
  +*+ [main] Add Bob's fixes.
```

❶ Commits within the branch bugs/pr-1 start in the first column.

❷ Commits within the current branch dev start in the second column.

❸ Commits within the branch main start in the third column.

 Use the separator dashes as columns and the branch names as column headers. This helps in reading the matrix output.

For example, both of the following commits are identified by asterisks and are present in the dev branch:

```
  ! ...
   * [dev] Improve the new development
    ! ...
  ---
   *   [dev] Improve the new development
   *   [dev&#x2038;] Start some new development.
   ...
   ...
```

These two commits are not present in any other branch. They are listed in reverse chronological order: the most recent commit is at the top, and the oldest commit is at the bottom. We will discuss in Chapter 4 why branch names are suffixed with carets (^`) to represent a penultimate commit. Similarly, dev and dev^ are the two most recent commits on the branch dev.

Although the commits within a branch are ordered, branches themselves are listed in an arbitrary order. This is because all branches have equal status; there is no rule stating that one branch is more important than another.

If the same commit is present in multiple branches, it will have a plus sign or an asterisk indicator for each branch. Thus the last commit shown in the previous output is present in all three branches:

```
! [bugs/pr-1] Fix Problem Report 1
 * [dev] Improve the new development
  ! [main] Added Bob's fixes.
---
 ...
 ...

+*+ [main] Added Bob's fixes.
```

The first plus sign means the commit is in `bugs/pr-1`, the asterisk means the same commit is in the current branch `dev`, and the second plus sign means the commit is also in the `main` branch.

When invoked, the `git show-branch` command traverses all the commits on all branches being shown, stopping the listing on the most recent common commit present on all of them. In the earlier example, Git listed four commits before it found one common to all three branches (`Added Bob's fixes.`), at which point it stopped.

Stopping at the first common commit is the default heuristic for reasonable behavior. It is presumed that reaching such a common point yields sufficient context to understand how the branches relate to each other. If for some reason you actually want more commit history, use the `--more=num` option, specifying the number of additional commits you want to see going back in time along the common branch.

The `git show-branch` command's output displays a maximum number of 29 branches and commits at a time.

If you want to limit the history shown for the `git show-branch` command, you can pass in the *branch names* as parameters. For example, if a new branch named `bugs/pr-2` is added starting at the `main` commit, it would look like this:

```
$ git branch bugs/pr-2 main
$ git show-branch
! [bugs/pr-1] Fix Problem Report 1
 ! [bugs/pr-2] Added Bob's fixes.
  * [dev] Improve the new development
   ! [main] Added Bob's fixes.
----
  *   [dev] Improve the new development
  *   [dev,] Start some new development.
  +   [bugs/pr-1] Fix Problem Report 1
++*+ [bugs/pr-2] Added Bob's fixes.
```

If you want to see the commit history for just the bugs/pr-1 and bugs/pr-2 branches, you could use the following:

```
$ git show-branch bugs/pr-1 bugs/pr-2
! [bugs/pr-1] Fix Problem Report 1
 ! [bugs/pr-2] Added Bob's fixes.
--
+  [bugs/pr-1] Fix Problem Report 1
++ [bugs/pr-2] Added Bob's fixes.
```

Fortunately, in our examples we used a well-structured naming convention for our branches; thus we can use wildcard matching of branch names as well. The same results can be achieved using the simpler bugs/* branch wildcard name:

```
$ git show-branch bugs/*
! [bugs/pr-1] Fix Problem Report 1
 ! [bugs/pr-2] Added Bob's fixes.
--
+  [bugs/pr-1] Fix Problem Report 1
++ [bugs/pr-2] Added Bob's fixes.
```

Switching (Checking Out) Branches

As we mentioned earlier, you can only work on one branch at a time; this reflects the state of the files in your working directory. When you need to work on a different branch, you will need to use the git checkout command:

```
$ git checkout branch
```

When you specify a branch name to the git checkout command, it makes that branch the new, current working branch. Consequently, it changes your working directory file and directory structure to match the state of the given branch. Git also has a built-in mechanism to safeguard any uncommitted changes in your current working directory when you are checking out to another branch, to keep you from losing data during the process.

The git checkout command can be used to not only get a specific branch state but also to give you access to all the states of the repository going back from the tip of the branch to the beginning of the project.

A basic example of checking out a branch

Let's use the previous section's example to better understand the state of the working directory before and after changing branches using the `git checkout` command. Suppose we want to shift gears from the `dev` branch to the `bugs/pr-1` branch to provide a solution to the problem. We can do so as follows:

```
$ git branch
  bugs/pr-1
  bugs/pr-2
* dev
  main

$ git checkout bugs/pr-1
Switched to branch "bugs/pr-1"

$ git branch
* bugs/pr-1
  bugs/pr-2
  dev
  main
```

The files and the directory structure of your working directory will be updated to reflect the state and contents of the new branch, `bugs/pr-1`. Naturally, the extent of that change depends on the differences between your now current branch, `bugs/pr-1`, and the previous branch, `dev`. The effects of changing branches can be generalized as follows:

- Files and directories present in the branch being checked out but not in the current branch are checked out of the object store and placed into your working directory. If there were files in the `bugs/pr-1` branch that were not present in the `dev` branch, you will see those new files appearing in your working directory.

- Files and directories present in your current branch but absent in the branch being checked out will be removed from your working directory. Any files that were present in the `dev` branch but were not part of the `bugs/pr-1` branch will disappear from your working directory.

- Files common to both branches are modified to reflect the content present in the checked-out branch. If there is a file that is common to both the `dev` and `bugs/pr-1` branches, the content of the file will be modified to match the state it was in when the commit was made in the `bugs/pr-1` branch.

 The checkout or switching branches operation happens almost instantaneously. This is one of the features of Git that truly and strongly differentiates it from many other version control systems. Git is also good at determining the minimum set of files and directories that actually need to change during a checkout operation.

Checking out when you have uncommitted changes

In the previous example, we demonstrated checking out to a branch when your working directory was clean: we changed branches when there were no files or directories that were modified or newly created. Let's take a look at some caveats when checking out branches when you have some uncommitted changes in your working directory.

By default, Git precludes the accidental removal or modification of data in your local working directory without your explicit request. Files and directories in your working directory that are not being tracked (i.e., are not in one of Git's object stores) are always left alone; Git won't remove or modify them.

However, if you have local modifications to a file that are different from changes that are present on the new branch you are switching to, Git issues an error message such as the following and refuses to check out the target branch:

```
$ git branch
  bugs/pr-1
  bugs/pr-2
  dev
* main

$ git checkout dev
error: Your local changes to the following files would be overwritten by checkout:
    NewStuff
Please, commit your changes or stash them before you can switch branches.
Aborting
```

In this case, a message warns that something has caused Git to stop the checkout request. But what? You can find out by inspecting the contents of the file *NewStuff*, as it is locally modified in the current working directory, and the target dev branch:

```
# Show what NewStuff looks like in the working directory
$ cat NewStuff
Something
Something else

# Show that the local version of the file has an extra line that
# is not committed in the working directory's current branch (main)
$ git diff NewStuff
diff --git a/NewStuff b/NewStuff
index 0f2416e..5e79566 100644
--- a/NewStuff
+++ b/NewStuff
@@ -1 +1,2 @@
 Something
+Something else

# Show what the file looks like in the dev branch
$ git show dev:NewStuff
Something
A text existing in the dev branch version
```

If Git brashly honored the request to check out the dev branch, your local modifications to *NewStuff* in your working directory would be overwritten by the version from dev. By default, Git detects this potential loss and prevents it from happening.

 If you really don't care about losing changes in your working directory and are willing to throw them away, you can force Git to perform the checkout by using the -f option.

Seeing the error message from the earlier example, you might be prompted to update the file within the *index/staging* directory and then proceed with the branch checkout. However, this isn't quite sufficient because using git add to update the new contents of the file *NewStuff* into the *index/staging* directory only places the contents of that file in the *index/staging* directory; it won't commit it to any branch. Thus Git still can't check out the new branch without losing your change, so it will fail again:

```
# Move file to index/staging directory
$ git add NewStuff

$ git checkout dev
error: Your local changes to the following files would be overwritten by checkout:
    NewStuff
Please, commit your changes or stash them before you can switch branches.
Aborting
```

Indeed, the file would still be overwritten. Clearly, just adding it to the index isn't sufficient.

You could just issue git commit at this point to commit your change into your current branch (main). But suppose you want the change to be made in the new dev branch instead. You seem to be stuck: you can't put your change into the dev branch until you check it out, and Git won't let you check it out because your change is present.

Luckily, there are ways out of this catch-22. One approach uses the *stash* and is described in Chapter 10. Another approach is described in "Merging Changes into a Different Branch" on page 70, where we will merge the changes of the file while at the same time switching to the intended branch.

Git checkout: Working with files versus branches

Although the git checkout command is used to change working branches, it also provides robust options to restore states of files. Consider the following:

```
# change to a dev branch
$ git checkout dev

# restore state for a specific file
```

```
# four commits back from the tip or HEAD commit
$ git checkout dev~4 index.js
```

It can also be used to restore a deleted file in your working directory from the *index/staging* directory:

```
# recover deleted file from index/staging directory
$ rm -rf server.js
$ git checkout server.js
```

When using the `git checkout` command, it can get confusing if you have the same name for a branch and a file. If your goal is to work on a file instead of a branch, you will need to specify -- followed by the filename. Git will understand that it should not interpret subsequent arguments as options:

```
# checkout a file with the same name of a branch
$ git checkout -- file-with-same-branch-name.js
```

New Experimental Commands for Working with Branches

In Git version 2.23.0 (*https://oreil.ly/y3Cxy*), a new command, `git switch`, was introduced to allow you to switch to a specific branch in your repository:

```
$ git switch branch
```

Additionally, the `git restore` command was introduced to allow for restore operations on file states:

```
$ git restore [options] file
```

Both the `git switch` and `git restore` commands are experimental, and their intended behavior may change in the future, as mentioned in the official Git manual pages.

Merging Changes into a Different Branch

Picking up from the previous section, the current state of your working directory conflicted with that of the branch you wanted to switch to. In order to keep your file changes in your working directory and switch to a new branch at the same time, you will need to perform a merge while checking out to your target branch.

You are able to do so by providing the -m option with your `git checkout` command; Git attempts to carry your local change into the new working directory by performing a merge operation between your local modifications and the state of the file in the target branch:

```
$ git checkout -m dev
M       NewStuff
Switched to branch "dev"
```

In this example, Git has modified the file *NewStuff* and checked out the `dev` branch successfully. This merge operation occurs entirely in your working directory; it does not introduce a merge commit on any branch. The reason for this is because, via the `-m` option, Git performed a three-way merge between your current branch, the current state of your working directory, and the target branch you are checking out to. It is not an explicit merge between two branches.

In the event a merge conflict happens while switching branches with the `-m` option, you will need to resolve the conflict manually. Git will modify the affected file and place *conflict resolution markers* within the file. We will learn more about merges and helpful techniques to resolve merge conflicts in Chapter 6:

```
# Conflict resolution markers (<<<,===,>>>) in the NewStuff file as a result
# of merge conflict when merging while switching branches

$ cat NewStuff
Something
<<<<<<< dev:NewStuff
A text existing in the dev branch version
=======
Something else
>>>>>>> local:NewStuff
```

If Git can check out a branch, change to it, and merge your local modifications cleanly without any merge conflicts, then the checkout request succeeds.

Suppose you're on the `main` branch in your development repository and you've made some changes to the *NewStuff* file. Moreover, you realize that the changes you made really should be made on another branch, perhaps because they fix Problem Report 1 and should be committed on the `bugs/pr-1` branch.

Here is the setup. Start on the `main` branch. Make some changes to some files, which are represented here by adding the text `Some bug fix` to the file *NewStuff*:

```
$ git show-branch
! [bugs/pr-1] Fix Problem Report 1
 ! [bugs/pr-2] Added Bob's fixes.
  ! [dev] Started developing NewStuff
   * [main] Added Bob's fixes.
----
  +  [dev] Started developing NewStuff
  +  [dev,] Improve the new development
  +  [dev~2] Start some new development.
 +   [bugs/pr-1] Fix Problem Report 1
+++* [bugs/pr-2] Added Bob's fixes.

$ echo "Some bug fix" >> NewStuff

$ cat NewStuff
Something
Some bug fix
```

At this point, you realize that all this work should be committed on the bugs/pr-1 branch and not the main branch. For reference, here is what the *NewStuff* file looks like in the bugs/pr-1 branch prior to the checkout in the next step:

```
$ git show bug/pr-1:NewStuff
Something
```

To carry your changes into the desired branch, simply attempt to check it out:

```
$ git checkout -m bug/pr-1
M       NewStuff
Switched to branch "bug/pr-1"

$ cat NewStuff
Something
Some bug fix
```

Here, Git was able to correctly merge the changes from your working directories and the target branch and leave them in your new working directory structure. You might want to verify that the merge went according to your expectations by using git diff:

```
$ git diff
diff --git a/NewStuff b/NewStuff
index 0f2416e..b4d8596 100644
--- a/NewStuff
+++ b/NewStuff
@@ -1 +1,2 @@
 Something
+Some bug fix
```

That one-line addition (+Some bug fix) is correct.

Finding Base Branch Information for Merged Branches

A merge operation between branches does not eliminate any of the source or target branches' names. A merge is the complement of a branch. When you merge, the content of one or more branches is joined with an implicit target branch.

Because the original commit from which a branch was started is not explicitly identified, that commit (or its equivalent) can be found algorithmically using the name of the original branch from which the new branch forked:

```
$ git merge-base original-branch new-branch
```

We will learn more about the complex process of merging branches in Chapter 6.

Creating and Checking Out a New Branch

In "Creating Branches" on page 61, we learned how to create branches, and in "Switching (Checking Out) Branches" on page 66, we learned how to switch to a specific branch. Sometimes you may want to create a new branch and switch to it at the same time. Git provides a shortcut for this with the -b *new-branch* option:

```
$ git checkout -b new-branch
```

As an example use case, we will start with the same setup as the previous one, except now we will create a new branch instead of switching to an existing branch. In other words, we are in the main branch, editing files, and we want all of the changes to be committed on an entirely new branch named bugs/pr-3. The sequence is as follows:

```
$ git branch
  bugs/pr-1
  bugs/pr-2
  dev
* main

$ git checkout -b bugs/pr-3
M       NewStuff
Switched to a new branch "bugs/pr-3"

$ git show-branch
! [bugs/pr-1] Fix Problem Report 1
 ! [bugs/pr-2] Added Bob's fixes.
  * [bugs/pr-3] Added Bob's fixes.
   ! [dev] Started developing NewStuff
    ! [main] Added Bob's fixes.
-----
    + [dev] Started developing NewStuff
    + [dev.] Improve the new development
    + [dev~2] Start some new development.
+      [bugs/pr-1] Fix Problem Report 1
++*++ [bugs/pr-2] Added Bob's fixes.
```

To reiterate, the command:

```
$ git checkout -b new-branch start-point
```

is exactly the same as the following two commands in sequence, assuming your working directory is clean:

```
$ git branch new-branch start-point
$ git checkout new-branch
```

When you are using the -b *new-branch* option to create and switch to a new branch, if the name of the new branch conflicts with an existing branch name, Git will not allow you to complete the command:

```
$ git checkout -b shiny-branch-name
fatal: A branch named 'shiny-branch-name' already exists.
```

You may bypass this default behavior with the -B *new-branch* option. This method will switch and reset the branch, causing you to lose any prior work done in the branch with the same name:

```
$ git checkout -B shiny-branch-name
Switched to and reset branch shiny-branch-name
```

```
# Equivalent to the following two commands in sequence
# -f option is used to discard any local changes in your working directory

$ git branch -f branch [start-point]
$ git checkout branch
```

Detached HEAD

By default, every time you check out to a branch, you are typically checked out at the tip or HEAD commit of the named branch. However, Git also allows you to specifically check out to any commit, either by referencing the commit via a tag name or by directly addressing it using the commit SHA (object ID) in the *start-point* option with the git checkout command.

In such cases, when you check out to a specific commit, you will be in a state known as detached HEAD mode. Figure 3-6 illustrates this concept. Take note of the HEAD pointer and the named branch main; they both point to different commits.

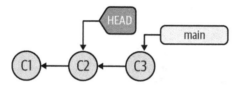

Figure 3-6. Detached HEAD mode

Git puts you in detached HEAD mode when you do the following:

- Check out a commit that is not the tip of a branch, by direct reference or via a named tag.

- Check out a tracking branch. You might do this to explore changes recently brought into your repository from a remote repository.

- Start a git bisect operation, as described in "Using git bisect" on page 177.

- Use the git submodule update command.

Let's explore detached HEAD mode with an example:

```
# Using a cloned repository of Git source code!
$ cd git

$ git checkout v2.9.0-rc2
Note: switching to 'v2.9.0-rc2'.

You are in 'detached HEAD' state. You can look around, make experimental
changes and commit them, and you can discard any commits you make in this
state without impacting any branches by switching back to a branch.

If you want to create a new branch to retain commits you create, you may
```

```
do so (now or later) by using -c with the switch command. Example:

   git switch -c <new-branch-name>

Or undo this operation with:

   git switch -

Turn off this advice by setting config variable advice.detachedHead to false

HEAD is now at 49fa3dc761 Git 2.9-rc2
```

As mentioned in the preceding output, while in detached HEAD mode, you are free to add new commits as experimental changes in your development project. Figure 3-7 illustrates this concept.

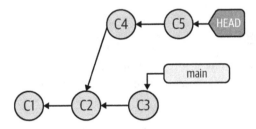

Figure 3-7. New commits while in detached HEAD mode

Commits C4 and C5 in Figure 3-7 are also known as *unreachable commits* in this context: in other words, there is no permanent reference to the commits other than the HEAD while it's in detached HEAD mode. When you switch to another named branch, commits C4 and C5 will eventually be purged by the routine Git garbage collection operation.

If you decide to keep those commits, you must first create a new branch:

```
$ git checkout -b new_branch
```

This will give you a new, proper branch based on the commit where the detached HEAD was. You can then continue with normal development.

 You can also create a named tag pointing to commit C5 to keep those commits and work on commit C5 at a later time. It is easier to do this while you are still in detached HEAD mode. If you switch to another branch, you will need to recover commit C5 via the git reflog command and then add a reference to it.

The output from the git branch command will help you determine whether you are in detached HEAD mode:

```
$ git branch
* (HEAD detached at 49fa3dc761)
  main
```

On the other hand, if you are finished with the detached HEAD and want to simply abandon that state, you can convert to a named branch by simply entering git checkout *branch*:

```
$ git checkout main
Updating files: 100% (3013/3013), done.
Previous HEAD position was 49fa3dc761 Git 2.9-rc2
Switched to branch 'main'
Your branch is up to date with 'origin/main'.

$ git branch
* main
```

Deleting Branches

To delete a branch, you may use the command git branch -d *branch name*. This action will remove the named branch from your local repository:

```
$ git branch -d branch
```

If you plan to also delete remote tracking branches, you will need to provide the -r option together with the command. We will cover remote tracking branches in Chapter 11.

By default, Git prevents you from deleting the branch you are currently working on. Removing your current branch would leave Git unable to determine the state of your working directory. Instead, you must always name a noncurrent branch.

But there is another subtle issue. Git won't allow you to delete a branch that contains commits that are not also present on the current branch, as hinted in the error message in the following example. That is, Git prevents you from accidentally removing development in commits that will be lost if the branch were to be deleted:

```
$ git checkout main
Switched to branch "main"

$ git branch -d bugs/pr-3
error: The branch 'bugs/pr-3' is not fully merged.
If you are sure you want to delete it, run 'git branch -D bugs/pr-3'.
```

Let us examine this with the git show-branch command:

```
$ git show-branch
! [bugs/pr-1] Fix Problem Report 1
 ! [bugs/pr-2] Added Bob's fixes.
  ! [bugs/pr-3] Added a bug fix for pr-3.
   ! [dev] Started developing NewStuff
    * [main] Added Bob's fixes..
-----
   +  [bugs/pr-3] Added a bug fix for pr-3.
```

```
    +   [dev] Started developing NewStuff
    +   [dev₊] Improve the new development
    +   [dev~2] Start some new development.
  +      [bugs/pr-1] Fix Problem Report 1
++++*   [bugs/pr-2] Added Bob's fixes.
```

In this `git show-branch` output, the commit "Added a bug fix for pr-3" is found only on the `bugs/pr-3` branch. If that branch were to be deleted, there would no longer be a way to access that commit.

By stating that the `bugs/pr-3` branch is not *fully merged*, Git is telling you that the line of development represented by the `bugs/pr-3` branch does not contribute to the development of the current branch, `main`.

Again, this is merely a friendly reminder. Git is not mandating that all branches be merged into the `main` branch before they can be deleted. Remember, a branch is simply a name or pointer to a commit that has actual content. Instead, Git is keeping you from accidentally losing content from the branch to be deleted that is not merged into your *current* branch.

If the content from the deleted branch is already present on another branch, checking *that* branch out and then requesting the branch deletion from that context would work. Another approach is to merge the content from the branch you want to delete into your current branch. Then the other intended branch can be safely deleted:

```
$ git merge bugs/pr-3
Updating 7933438..401b78d
Fast forward
 NewStuff |    1 +
 1 files changed, 1 insertions(+), 0 deletions(-)

$ git show-branch
! [bugs/pr-1] Fix Problem Report 1
 ! [bugs/pr-2] Added Bob's fixes.
  ! [bugs/pr-3] Added a bug fix for pr-3.
   ! [dev] Started developing NewStuff
    * [main] Added a bug fix for pr-3.
-----
  + * [bugs/pr-3] Added a bug fix for pr-3.
   +  [dev] Started developing NewStuff
   +  [dev₊] Improve the new development
   +  [dev~2] Start some new development.
  +      [bugs/pr-1] Fix Problem Report 1
++++*   [bugs/pr-2] Added Bob's fixes.

$ git branch -d bugs/pr-3
Deleted branch bugs/pr-3.

$ git show-branch
! [bugs/pr-1] Fix Problem Report 1
 ! [bugs/pr-2] Added Bob's fixes.
  ! [dev] Started developing NewStuff
   * [main] Added a bug fix for pr-3.
----
   * [main] Added a bug fix for pr-3.
  + [dev] Started developing NewStuff
```

```
   +  [dev,] Improve the new development
   +  [dev~2] Start some new development.
   +    [bugs/pr-1] Fix Problem Report 1
 +++* [bugs/pr-2] Added Bob's fixes.
```

Finally, as the error message suggests, you can override Git's safety check by using -D instead of -d. Do this if you are certain you don't want the extra content in that branch.

Git does not maintain any form of historical record of branch *names* being created, moved, manipulated, merged, or deleted. Once a branch name has been removed, it is gone.

The commit history on that branch, however, is a separate question. Git will eventually prune away commits that are no longer referenced and reachable from some named reference, such as a branch name or tag name. If you want to keep those commits, you must either merge them into a different branch, make a branch for them, or point a tag reference to them. Otherwise, without a reference to them, commits and blobs are unreachable and will eventually be collected as garbage by the git gc tool.

 If you accidentally remove a branch or other ref, you can recover it by using the git reflog command. Other commands such as git fsck and configuration options such as gc.reflogExpire and gc.pruneExpire can also help you recover lost commits, files, and branch heads.

Summary

In this chapter, we started by explaining the motivation for using branches in Git. We then learned about some recommended guidelines for working with branches. In "Managing Branches" on page 58, we dove into detailed use cases and scenarios for working with branches in Git on a daily basis for your projects. Specifically, this section dealt with the technicalities of how you will be managing and working with your Git repository's branches. When you approach this chapter as a whole, you will realize that when working with branches, a lot of the heavy lifting is in the way you plan your line of development, from branch naming conventions to an agreed-upon process for systematically introducing changes to your main stable branch, whether those changes are meant to fix a bug or introduce a new set of features for your project. Once you have established this norm, you can leverage the techniques we covered here to effectively work with multiple sets of branches within your repositories.

## CHAPTER 4

Commits

A *commit* is a snapshot capturing the current state of a repository at a moment in time. Commit snapshots are chained together, with each new snapshot pointing to its predecessor. Over time, a sequence of changes is represented as a series of commits.

Git uses a commit as a means to record changes to a repository. At face value, a Git commit is comparable to a check-in or commit found in other version control systems. However, the similarities are only at the surface. Under the hood, the inner mechanics of how Git creates and manages commits are entirely unique.

When you make a commit, Git takes a snapshot of the current state of the index directory and stores it in the object store as discussed briefly in Chapter 2. The snapshot does *not* contain a copy of every file and directory in the index. Instead, Git compares the current state of the index to the previous commit snapshot and derives a list of affected files and directories when you are creating a new commit. Based on this list, Git creates new blob objects for any file that is changed and new tree objects for any directory that has changed, and it reuses any blob or tree object that has not changed.

We will discuss how to prepare the index directory for a commit in Chapter 5. In this chapter, we will focus on what happens when you make a commit. First we will first explore how commits are introduced and understand the importance of atomic changesets. Then we will look at how to identify commits and how to view commit histories.

Git is well suited to frequent commits and provides a rich set of commands for manipulating them. We will show you how several commits, each with small, well-defined changes, can also lead to better organization of changes and easier manipulation of patch sets.

Commits: Recorded Units of Change

A commit is the only method for introducing changes to a repository. This mandate provides auditability and accountability. Under no circumstances should repository data change without a record of the change via a commit! Imagine the chaos if content in the repository changed somehow and there was no record of how it happened, who did it, or why.

Commits are explicitly introduced by developers; this is the most typical scenario. However, there are occasions when Git itself can introduce a commit. For instance, a merge operation creates a new commit in the repository, in addition to any commits made by the developers before the merge. You will learn more about this in Chapter 6.

The frequency with which you create commits is pretty much up to you. Logically, you should introduce a commit at well-defined points in time when your development is at a latent stage, such as when all test suites pass.

You might think it would be time-consuming to compare the entire index to some prior state, yet the whole process is remarkably fast. This is because, as you may recall from Chapter 2, every Git object has an SHA1 hash, and if two objects, even two subtrees, have the same SHA1 hash, the objects in comparison are identical. Thus, Git can avoid swaths of recursive comparisons by pruning subtrees that have the same content.

Nevertheless, this should not mean that you should hesitate to introduce commits regularly.

Atomic Changesets

Every Git commit represents a single atomic changeset (*https://oreil.ly/rlThS*) with respect to the previous state. Regardless of the number of directories, files, lines, or bytes that change with a commit,[1] either all changes apply or none do.

From the perspective of the underlying Git object model, the rationale behind atomicity becomes clearer. A commit snapshot represents the state of the total set of modified files and directories, which also means that it represents a given tree state. Thus, a changeset *between* two snapshots represents a complete transformation from one tree state to another. Again, you can only switch from one state to the other; you cannot make incremental switches. We will discuss how to derive the differences between commits in Chapter 7.

---

[1] Git also records a mode flag indicating the executability of each file. Changes in this flag are also part of a changeset.

As a developer, this is an important principle that you should not undermine. Consider the following workflow of moving a function from one file to another. If you remove the function from the first file with one commit and then add it to the second file with another commit, a small "semantic gap" remains in the history of your repository during which time the function is gone. Two commits occurring in the reverse order is also problematic. In each case, before the first commit and after the second one, your code is semantically consistent, but after the first commit, the code is faulty.

However, with an atomic commit that simultaneously deletes the function from the first file and adds it to the second file, no such semantic gap appears in the history. An understanding of this concept allows you to structure your commits more appropriately.

Git doesn't care *why* files are changing. That is, the content of the changes doesn't matter. You might move a function from one file to another and expect this to be handled as one unitary move. Alternatively, you can commit the removal and then later commit the addition. Git doesn't care. It has nothing to do with the semantics of what is in the files.

Identifying Commits

Every commit in Git can be referenced explicitly or implicitly. Being able to identify individual commits is an essential task for your routine development requirements. For example, to create a branch, you must choose a commit from which to diverge; to compare code variations, you must specify two commits; and to edit the commit history, you must provide a collection of commits.

When you reference a commit explicitly, you are referencing it using its *absolute commit names*, and when you reference a commit implicitly, you are doing so using its *refs, symrefs,* or *relative commit names*.

You've already seen examples of explicit commit references and implicit commit references in code snippets in Chapters 1 through 3. The unique, 40-digit hexadecimal SHA1 commit ID is an explicit reference, whereas HEAD, which always points to the most recent commit in a branch, is an implicit reference; see Table 4-1.

Table 4-1. Difference between explicit and implicit commits

	Explicit	Implicit
Identified via	Absolute commit name	Refs, symrefs, relative commit names
Example	34043c95636aee319d606a7a380697cae4f1bfcc	HEAD, HEAD^2, etc.

At times, when discussing a particular commit with a colleague working on the same data but in a distributed environment, it's best to use a commit name that is guaranteed to be the same in both repositories. On the other hand, if you're working within your own repository and need to refer to the state a few commits back on a branch, a simple relative name works perfectly.

Fortunately, Git provides many different mechanisms for naming a commit, each with advantages and some more useful than others, depending on the context.

Absolute Commit Names

The most rigorous name for a commit is its object ID, the SHA1 hash identifier. The SHA1 hash ID is an *absolute* name, meaning it can only refer to exactly one commit. It doesn't matter where the commit is in the repository's history; the SHA1 hash ID always points to and identifies the same commit.

Each commit ID is *globally* unique, not just for one repository but for any and all repositories. If you compare a reference to a specific commit ID in your repository with another developer's repository and the same commit ID is found, you can be assured that both of you have the same commit and content.

Furthermore, because the data that contributes to a commit ID contains the state of the whole repository tree as well as the prior commit state, you can also be certain that both of you are referencing the same complete line of development leading up to and including the commit.

Because a 40-digit hexadecimal SHA1 number makes for a tedious and error-prone entry, Git allows you to shorten this number to a unique prefix within a repository's object database. Let's take a look at an example from Git's own repository:

```
$ git log -1 --pretty=oneline HEAD
30cc8d0f147546d4dd77bf497f4dec51e7265bd8 ... A regression fix for 2.37

$ git log -1 --pretty=oneline 30c
fatal: ambiguous argument '30c': unknown revision or path not in the working tree.
Use '--' to separate paths from revisions, like this:
'git <command> [<revision>...] -- [<file>...]'

$ git log -1 --pretty=oneline 30cc8d
a5828ae6b52137b913b978e16cd2334482eb4c1f ... A regression fix for 2.37
```

Although a tag name isn't a globally unique name, it is absolute in that it points to a unique commit and doesn't change over time (unless you explicitly change it, of course).

Refs and Symrefs

A *ref* points to an SHA1 hash ID within the Git object store. Technically, a simple ref may *point* to any Git object, but generally it *refers* to a commit object. A *symbolic reference*, or *symref*, is a name that indirectly points to a Git object. Think of it as a shortcut pointing to the actual Git object. It is still just a ref.

Each symbolic ref has a definitive, full name that begins with `refs/`, and each is stored hierarchically within the repository in the *.git/refs/* directory. There are basically three different namespaces represented in `refs/`:

- `refs/heads/`*ref* for your local branches
- `refs/remotes/`*ref* for your remote tracking branches
- `refs/tags/`*ref* for your tags

Local branch names, remote tracking branch names, and tag names are some examples of refs. As an example, a local feature branch named `dev` is really a short form of `refs/heads/dev`. Whereas remote tracking branches are in the `refs/remotes/` namespace, so `origin/main` is a short form of `refs/remotes/origin/main`. Finally, a tag such as `v1.8.17` is short for `refs/tags/v1.8.17`.

When searching or referencing a ref, you may use the fully qualified ref name (`refs/heads/main`) or its abbreviation (`main`). In the event that you are searching for a branch and there is a tag with the same name, Git applies a disambiguation heuristic and uses the first match according to this list from the `git rev-parse` man page:

```
.git/ref
.git/refs/ref
.git/refs/tags/ref
.git/refs/heads/ref
.git/refs/remotes/ref
.git/refs/remotes/ref/HEAD
```

The first matching rule (`.git/`*ref*) is usually used by Git internally. They are `HEAD`, `ORIG_HEAD`, `FETCH_HEAD`, `CHERRY_PICK_HEAD`, and `MERGE_HEAD`.

Technically, the name of the Git directory, *.git*, can be changed. Thus, Git's internal documentation uses the variable `$GIT_DIR` instead of the literal `.git`.

Git internally maintains the following symrefs automatically for particular reasons:

HEAD

> HEAD always refers to the most recent commit on the current branch. When you change branches, Git automatically updates HEAD to refer to the new branch's latest commit.

ORIG_HEAD

> Certain operations, such as merge and reset, record the previous version of HEAD in ORIG_HEAD just prior to adjusting it to a new value. You can use ORIG_HEAD to recover or revert to the previous state or to make a comparison.

FETCH_HEAD

> When remote repositories are used, git fetch records the heads of all branches fetched in the file *.git/FETCH_HEAD*. FETCH_HEAD is a shorthand for the head of the last branch fetched and is valid only immediately after a fetch operation. Using this symref, you can find the HEAD of commits from git fetch even if an anonymous fetch that doesn't specifically name a branch is used. The fetch operation is covered in Chapter 11.

MERGE_HEAD

> When a merge is in progress, the tip of the *other* branch is temporarily recorded in the symref MERGE_HEAD. In other words, MERGE_HEAD is the commit that is being merged into HEAD.

CHERRY_PICK_HEAD

> When cherry-picking is used via the git cherry-pick command, the CHERRY_PICK_HEAD symref will record the commits you have selected for the intended operation. The git cherry-pick command is covered in Chapter 8.

All of these symbolic references are managed by the low-level plumbing command git symbolic-ref.

> Although it is possible to create your own branch with one of these special symbolic names, it isn't a good idea. Also, newer versions of Git have safeguards in place that prevent you from using certain symbolic names (e.g., HEAD).

There is a whole raft of special character variants for ref names. The two most common, the caret (^) and tilde (~), are described in the next section. In another twist on refs, colons can be used to refer to alternate versions of a common file involved in a merge conflict. This procedure is described in Chapter 6.

Relative Commit Names

In addition to Git using absolute commit names, and refs, and symrefs, Git also provides mechanisms for identifying a commit relative to another reference, commonly the tip of a branch. This comes in handy when you are working on your local repository and need to quickly reference changes in past commits.

Again, you've seen some of these names already, such as main and main^`, where main^ always refers to the penultimate commit on the main branch. There are others as well: you can use main^^, main~2, and even a complex name like main~10^2~2^2.

Except for the first or root commit,[2] each commit is derived from at least one earlier commit and possibly many, where direct ancestors are called *parent commits*. For a commit to have multiple parent commits, it must be the result of a merge operation. As a result, there will be a parent commit for each branch contributing to a merge commit.

Within a single generation, the caret is used to select a different parent. Given a commit C, C^1 is the first parent, C^2 is the second parent, and C^n is the nth parent, as shown in Figure 4-1.

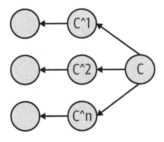

Figure 4-1. Multiple parent names

The tilde is used to go back before an ancestral parent and select a preceding generation. Again, given the commit C, C~1 is the first parent, C~2 is the first grandparent, and C~3 is the first great-grandparent. When there are multiple parents in a generation, the first parent of the first parent is followed. You might also notice

---

2 Yes, you can actually introduce multiple root commits into a single repository. This happens, for example, when two different projects and their entire repositories are brought together and merged into one.

that both C^1 and C~1 refer to the first parent; either name is correct, as shown in Figure 4-2.

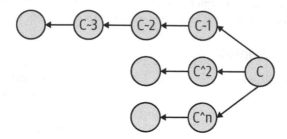

Figure 4-2. Multiple parent names with ancestors

Git supports other abbreviations and combinations as well. The abbreviated forms C^ and C~ are the same as C^1 and C~1, respectively. Also, C^^; is the same as C^1^1, and, because that means "the first parent of the first parent of commit C," it refers to the same commit as C~2.

Keep in mind that, in the presence of a merge operation, an abbreviated expression such as C^ or C^^ may not return a result that you expect, as it would if you were working on a branch with a linear commit history. Figure 4-3 illustrates that C^^ is not the same as C^2.

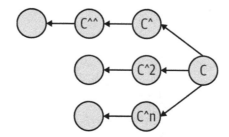

Figure 4-3. C^^ versus C^2

By combining a *ref* and instances of carets and tildes, arbitrary commits may be selected from the ancestral commit graph of *ref*. Remember, though, that these names are relative to the *current* value of *ref*. If a new commit is made on top of *ref*, the commit graph is amended with a new generation, and each "parent" name shifts farther back in the history and graph.

Here's an example from Git's own history when its main branch was at commit a5828ae6b52137b913b978e16cd2334482eb4c1f. Using the command:

```
git show-branch --more=25
```

and limiting the output to the final 25 lines, you can inspect the graph history and examine a complex branch merge structure:

```
$ git reset --hard a5828ae6b52137b913b978e16cd2334482eb4c1f
HEAD is now at a5828ae6b5 Git 2.31

$ git show-branch --more=25
[main] Git 2.31
[main^] Merge branch 'jn/mergetool-hideresolved-is-optional'
[main^^2] doc: describe mergetool configuration in git-mergetool(1)
[main^^2^] mergetool: do not enable hideResolved by default
[main^^2~2] mergetool: add per-tool support and overrides for the hideResolved flag
[main~2] Merge branch 'tb/pack-revindex-on-disk'
[main~2^2] pack-revindex.c: don't close unopened file descriptors
[main~3] Merge tag 'l10n-2.31.0-rnd2' of git://github.com/git-l10n/git-po
[main~3^2] l10n: zh_CN: for git v2.31.0 l10n round 1 and 2
[main~3^2^] Merge branch 'master' of github.com:vnwildman/git
[main~3^2^^2] l10n: vi.po(5104t): for git v2.31.0 l10n round 2
[main~3^2~2] Merge branch 'l10n/zh_TW/210301' of github.com:l10n-tw/git-po
[main~3^2~2^2] l10n: zh_TW.po: v2.31.0 round 2 (15 untranslated)
[main~3^2~3] Merge branch 'po-id' of github.com:bagasme/git-po
[main~3^2~3^2] l10n: Add translation team info
[main~3^2~4] Merge branch 'master' of github.com:Softcatala/git-po
[main~3^2~4^2] l10n: Update Catalan translation
[main~3^2~5] Merge branch 'russian-l10n' of github.com:DJm00n/git-po-ru
[main~3^2~5^2] l10n: ru.po: update Russian translation
[main~3^2~6] Merge branch 'pt-PT' of github.com:git-l10n-pt-PT/git-po
[main~3^2~6^2] l10n: pt_PT: add Portuguese translations part 1
[main~3^2~7] l10n: de.po: Update German translation for Git v2.31.0
[main~4] Git 2.31-rc2
[main~5] Sync with Git 2.30.2 for CVE-2021-21300
[main~5^2] Git 2.30.2
[main~6] Merge branch 'jt/transfer-fsck-across-packs-fix'


$ git rev-parse main~3^2~2^
8278f870221711c2116d3da2a0165ab00368f756
```

Between `main~3` and `main~4`, a merge took place that introduced a couple of other merges as well as a simple commit named `main~3^2~2^2`. That happens to be commit `8278f870221711c2116d3da2a0165ab00368f756`.

The command `git rev-parse` is the final authority on translating any form of commit name—tag, relative, shortened, or absolute—into an actual, absolute commit hash ID within the object database.

Commit History

The primary command to show the history of commits is `git log`. It has more options, parameters, bells, whistles, colorizers, selectors, formatters, and doodads than the fabled `ls`. But don't worry. Just as with `ls`, you don't need to learn all the details right away. Next, we will dive into the nooks and crannies of commit history for a repository.

Viewing Old Commits

When you execute the `git log` command, the output will include every associated commit and its log messages in your commit history, reachable from the specified starting point.

As an example, if you execute the `git log` command without any additional options, it is the same as executing the command `git log HEAD`. The result will be an output of all commits starting with the `HEAD` commit and all reachable commits way back through the commit graph (commit graphs will be discussed in the following section). The results are given in reverse chronological order by default, but keep in mind that, when Git traverses back through your commit history, the reverse order adheres to the commit graph and not the time when the snapshot was taken.

Being explicit on the starting point for the log output using the command `git log` *commit* can be useful for viewing the history of a branch. Let's use the command to view an example output from the Git repository itself:

```
$ git log main -2
commit 30cc8d0f147546d4dd77bf497f4dec51e7265bd8 (HEAD -> main, ...)
Author: Junio C Hamano <gitster@pobox.com>
Date:   Sat Jul 2 17:01:34 2022 -0700

    A regression fix for 2.37

    Signed-off-by: Junio C Hamano <gitster@pobox.com>

commit 0f0bc2124b25476504e7215dc2af92d5748ad327
Merge: e4a4b31577 4788e8b256
Author: Junio C Hamano <gitster@pobox.com>
Date:   Sat Jul 2 21:56:08 2022 -0700

    Merge branch 'js/add-i-delete'

    Rewrite of "git add -i" in C that appeared in Git 2.25 didn't
    correctly record a removed file to the index, which was fixed.

    * js/add-i-delete:
      add --interactive: allow `update` to stage deleted files
```

Log information is an authoritative source of truth. However, rolling back through the entire commit history of a large repository is likely not very practical or meaningful. Typically, a limited range of history is more informative and easier to work on.

One way to constrain history is to specify a commit range, a technique that we will cover later in this chapter. You are able to limit the history range using the form *since..until*. Given a range, `git log` shows all commits following *since* and running through *until*. You can also specify a count as a natural place to start, for example, `git log -3`.

Here's an example:

```
$ git log --pretty=short --abbrev-commit main~9..main~7

commit be7935ed8b
Author: Junio C Hamano <gitster@pobox.com>

    Merged the open-eintr workaround for macOS

commit 58d581c344
Author: Elijah Newren <newren@gmail.com>

    Documentation/RelNotes: improve release note for rename detection work
```

Here, `git log` shows the commits between `main~9` and `main~7`, or the seventh and eighth prior commits on the main branch. You'll learn about ranges in "Commit Ranges" on page 96.

In the example, we introduced two formatting options, `--pretty=short` and `--abbrev-commit`. The former adjusts the amount of information about each commit and has several variations, including `oneline`, `short`, `medium`, and `full`, to name a few. The latter simply requests that the SHA1 hash IDs be abbreviated.

You can also use the *format:string* option to specify how the log information is customized and displayed.

Here's an example:

```
$ git log --pretty=format:"%an was the author of commit %h, %ar with%nthe commit titled: [%s]%n" \
> --abbrev-commit main~9..main~7

Junio C Hamano was the author of commit be7935ed8b, 12 days ago with
the commit titled: [Merged the open-eintr workaround for macOS]

Elijah Newren was the author of commit 58d581c344, 12 days ago with
the commit titled: [Documentation/RelNotes: improve release note for rename detection work]
```

You can provide the option `-n` together with the `git log` command to limit the output to at most *n* commits. This restricts the output according to the specified number. In addition, combining the `-p` option will print the *patch*, or changes introduced by the commit, while limiting the result sets. This helps you get more details regarding a commit by providing more context.

Here's an example:

```
$ git log -1 -p 4fe86488
commit 4fe86488e1a550aa058c081c7e67644dd0f7c98e
Author: Jon Loeliger <jdl@freescale.com>
Date:   Wed Apr 23 16:14:30 2008 -0500

    Add otherwise missing --strict option to unpack-objects summary.

    Signed-off-by: Jon Loeliger <jdl@freescale.com>
    Signed-off-by: Junio C Hamano <gitster@pobox.com>
```

```
diff --git a/Documentation/git-unpack-objects.txt b/Documentation/git-unpack-objects.txt
index 3697896..50947c5 100644
--- a/Documentation/git-unpack-objects.txt
+++ b/Documentation/git-unpack-objects.txt
@@ -8,7 +8,7 @@ git-unpack-objects - Unpack objects from a packed archive

 SYNOPSIS
 --------
-'git-unpack-objects' [-n] [-q] [-r] <pack-file>
+'git-unpack-objects' [-n] [-q] [-r] [--strict] <pack-file>
```

If you would like to know which files changed in a commit along with a tally of how many lines were modified in each file, the `--stat` option will be your go-to option.

Here's an example:

```
$ git log --pretty=short --stat main~9..main~7

commit be7935ed8bff19f481b033d0d242c5d5f239ed50
Author: Junio C Hamano <gitster@pobox.com>

    Merged the open-eintr workaround for macOS

Documentation/RelNotes/2.31.0.txt | 5 +++++
1 file changed, 5 insertions(+)

commit 58d581c3446cb616b216307d6b47539bccd494cf
Author: Elijah Newren <newren@gmail.com>

    Documentation/RelNotes: improve release note for rename detection work

Documentation/RelNotes/2.31.0.txt | 2 +-
1 file changed, 1 insertion(+), 1 deletion(-)
```

Another command to display objects from the Git object store is `git show`. You can also use it to inspect a commit:

```
$ git show HEAD~2
```

The output will show the commit log message and the textual diff for files included in the commits.

Commit Graphs

So far we have been using the `git log` command with options that display results in a linear format. Although it is useful to understand the commit history leading up to a certain point in the timeline of a project, it isn't always clear in this flattened view that two consecutive commits may not belong to a single branch.

The `--graph` option used in combination with the `git log` command prints out a textual representation of the repository's commit history. In this view, you are able to visualize the forks from a commit and the point in which branches merge in the timeline of the repository.

Following is a simplified commit history for the Git source code from its early days:

```
$ git log 89d21f4b649..0a02ce72d9 --oneline --graph
* 0a02ce72d9 Clean up the Makefile a bit.
* 839a7a06f3 Add the simple scripts I used to do a merge with content conflicts.
*   b51ad43140 Merge the new object model thing from Daniel Barkalow
|\
| * b5039db6d2 [PATCH] Switch implementations of merge-base, port to parsing
| * ff5ebe39b0 [PATCH] Port fsck-cache to use parsing functions
| * 5873b67eef [PATCH] Port rev-tree to parsing functions
| * 175785e5ff [PATCH] Implementations of parsing functions
| * 6eb8ae00d4 [PATCH] Header files for object parsing
* | a4b7dbef4e [PATCH] fix bug in read-cache.c which loses files when merging...
* | 1bc992acac [PATCH] Fix confusing behaviour of update-cache --refresh on...
* | 6ad6d3d36c Update README to reflect the hierarchical tree objects...
* | 64982f7510 [PATCH] (resend) show-diff.c off-by-one fix
* | 75118b13bc Pass a "merge-cache" helper program to execute a merge on...
* | 74b2428f55 [PATCH] fork optional branch point normazilation
* | d9f98eebcd Ignore any unmerged entries for "checkout-cache -a".
* | 5e5128ed1c Remove extraneous ',' ';' and '.' characters from...
* | 08ca0b04ba Make the revision tracking track the object types too.
* | d0d7cbe730 Make "commit-tree" check the input objects more carefully.
* | 7d60ad7cc9 Make "parse_commit" return the "struct revision" for the commit.
|/
* 6683463ed6 Do a very simple "merge-base" that finds the most recent...
* 15000d7899 Make "rev-tree.c" use the new-and-improved "mark_reachable()"
* 01796b0e91 Make "revision.h" slightly better to use.
```

 The `--oneline` option is shorthand for `--pretty=oneline` `--abbrev-commit` used together.

The repository's commit history is usually visualized as a graph[3] for the purpose of reference when discussing certain Git commands. It is most often related to operations that might modify the commit history of the repository. We will discuss rewriting commit histories in Chapter 8.

If you recall, in the "Visualizing the Git Object Store" on page 33, we included a figure to help you visualize the layout and relationship between objects stored in the Git object store. That figure is reproduced here as Figure 4-4.

---

3 A *graph* is a collection of nodes and a set of edges between the nodes. Commonly, the directed acyclic graph (DAG) diagram is used when explaining Git commit history.

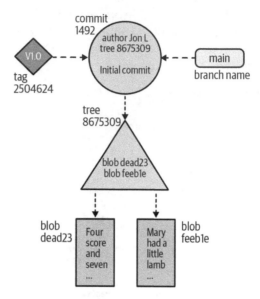

Figure 4-4. Git objects

If we were to map out a repository's commit history using Figure 4-4, even for a small repository with just a handful of commits, merges, and patches, that map would become too unwieldy to render in this kind of detail. Figure 4-5 shows a more complete but still somewhat simplified commit graph in the same format. Imagine how it would appear if all commits and all data structures were rendered.

Figure 4-6 shows the same commit graph as Figure 4-5 but without depicting the tree and blob objects. Branch names are also shown in the commit graphs as supporting reference.

We can further simplify Figure 4-5 with an important observation about commits: each commit introduces a tree object that references one or more blob objects and represents the entire state of the repository when a commit snapshot was made. Therefore, a commit can be pictured as just a name, simplifying the blueprint of the repository's commit history immensely.

Figures 4-5 and 4-6 are examples of a directed acyclic graph (DAG). A DAG has the following important properties:

- The edges within the graph are all directed from one node to another.
- Starting at any node in the graph, there is no path along the directed edges that leads back to the starting node.

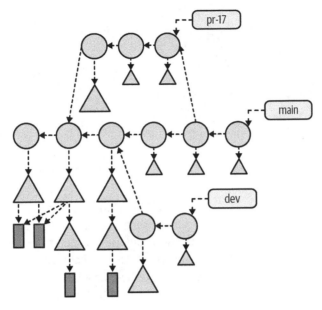

Figure 4-5. Full commit graph

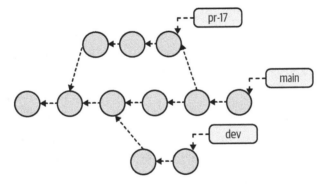

Figure 4-6. Simplified commit graph

Git implements the history of commits within a repository as a DAG. In the commit graph, each node is a single commit, and all edges are directed from one descendant node to another parent node, forming an ancestor relationship. The individual commit nodes are often labeled as shown in Figure 4-7, and they are used to describe the history of the commits and the relationship between them.

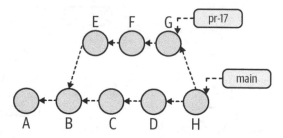

Figure 4-7. Labeled commit graph

An important facet of a DAG is that Git doesn't care about the time or timing (absolute or relative) of commits. The actual timestamp of a commit can be misleading because a computer's clock can be set incorrectly or inconsistently. Within a distributed development environment, the problem is exacerbated. What is certain, though, is that if commit Y points to parent X, then X captures the repository state prior to the repository state of commit Y, regardless of what timestamps might be on the commits.

Building on that notion, Figure 4-7 shows the following:

- Time is roughly left to right.
- A is the root commit because it has no parent, and B occurred after A.
- Both E and C occurred after B, but no claim can be made about the relative timing between C and E; either could have occurred before the other.
- The commits E and C share a common parent, B. Thus, B is the origin of a branch.
- The main branch begins with commits A, B, C, and D.
- Meanwhile, the sequence of commits A, B, E, F, and G forms the branch named pr-17. The branch pr-17 points to commit G, as discussed in Chapter 3.
- Commit H is a merge commit, where the pr-17 branch has been merged into the main branch. The merge operation is discussed in more detail in Chapter 6.
- Because it's a merge, H has more than one commit parent—in this case, D and G.
- After this commit is made, main will be updated to refer to the new commit H, but pr-17 will continue to refer to G.

In time, as you learn and reference many DAG diagrams of commits, you will soon notice a recurring pattern:

- Normal commits have exactly one parent, which is the previous commit in the history. When you make a change, your change is the difference between your new commit and its parent.
- There is usually only one commit with zero parents: the root commit.
- A merge commit has more than one parent commit.
- A commit with more than one *child* is the place where history began to diverge and formed a new branch.

In practice, the fine points of intervening commits are considered unimportant. Also, the implementation detail of a commit pointing back to its parent is often elided, as shown in Figure 4-8.

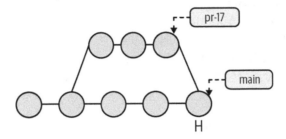

Figure 4-8. Commit graph without arrows

Time is still vaguely left to right, two branches are shown, and there is one identified merge commit (H), but the actual directed edges are simplified because they are implicitly understood.

The commit graphs are a fairly abstract representation of the actual commit history, in contrast to tools that provide concrete representations of commit history graphs. With these tools, though, time is usually represented from bottom to top, from the oldest to the most recent commit. Conceptually, it is the same information. In the next section we will briefly discuss the freely distributed gitk tool.[4] In addition to gitk, a variety of other tools are available as either a paid or free version.

Using gitk to view the commit graph

A commit graph can help you visualize a complicated structure and relationship. The gitk command can draw a picture of a repository DAG representing the repository's commit history.

---

4 The gitk command is not a *git* subcommand; it is its own independent command and installable package.

Let's look at an example of a simple repository with two branches and simple commits to add files:

```
$ mkdir commit-graph-repo
# Operations to add new files, create new branch and merge branch
...
...
$ gitk
```

The gitk program can do a lot of things, but let's just focus on the DAG for now. The graph output looks something like Figure 4-9.

Figure 4-9. Merge viewed with gitk

 There is no permanent record of branch start points, but Git can algorithmically determine them via the git merge-base command.

Commit Ranges

The git log command operates on a series of commits and is one of many commands that allow you to traverse the commit history of your repository. To be precise, when you specify commit Y as a starting point to git log, you are actually requesting Git to show the log for all commits that are reachable from commit Y.

In a Git commit graph, the set of reachable commits is the set of commits that you can reach from a given commit by traversing the directed parent links. Conceptually and in terms of dataflow, the set of reachable commits is the set of ancestor commits that flow into and contribute to a given starting commit.

 In graph theory, a node X is said to be reachable from another node A if you can start at A, travel along the arcs of the graph according to the rules, and arrive at X. The set of reachable nodes for node A is the collection of all nodes reachable from A.

There are several options in Git that allow you to include and exclude commits within a specified range. These options are not limited to the git log command; they are also applicable for other supported Git subcommands. For example, you can exclude a specific commit X and all commits reachable from X with the expression ^X. Typically, a range is used to examine a branch or part of a branch.

A range is denoted with a double-period notion (..), as in *start..end*, where *start* and *end* may be specified as described in "Identifying Commits" on page 81.

A commit range, *start..end*, is defined as the set of commits inclusive of *end* and exclusive of *start*. Usually this is simplified to just the phrase "in *end* but not *start*." Figure 4-11 provides an illustrated explanation.

In "Viewing Old Commits" on page 88, you saw how to use a commit range with git log. The example used the range main~9..main~7 to specify the eighth and seventh prior commits on the main branch. To visualize the range, consider the commit graph in Figure 4-10. Branch M is shown over a portion of its commit history that is linear.

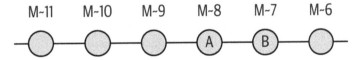

Figure 4-10. Linear commit history

Recall that time flows from left to right, so M~11 is the oldest commit shown, M~6 is the most recent commit shown, and A is the eighth prior commit.

The range M~9..M~7 represents two commits, the eighth and seventh oldest commits, which are labeled A and B. The range does not include M~9 (recall the phrase "in M~7 but not M~9").

Commit Ranges as a Set Operation

When we view commit ranges as a mathematical set operation, it provides added clarity. Commits reachable from any provided commits form a set, and commits reachable from any provided commits with a ^ in front are removed from the set. For example:

```
$ git log ^X Y
```

can be paraphrased as "give me all commits that are reachable from Y and don't give me any commit leading up to and including X."

The double-period notation X..Y is shorthand for ^X Y. Thus, the following may be used interchangeably:

```
$ git log X..Y
$ git log ^X Y
```

Combining the two forms, the commit range X..Y is mathematically equivalent to ^X Y. Reiterating this as a set subtraction: list everything leading up to Y minus everything leading up to and including X.

There are two other range permutations as well. If you leave either the *start* or *end* commit out of the range, HEAD is assumed. Thus:

- ..*end* is equivalent to HEAD..*end*.

- *start*.. is equivalent to *start*..HEAD.

Returning to the commit series from the earlier example, when viewed as a set operation, here's how M~9..M~7 specifies just two commits, A and B:

1. Begin with everything leading up to M~7, as shown in the first line of Figure 4-11.

   a. Find everything leading up to and including M~9, as shown in the second line of the figure.

      i. Subtract M~9 from M~7 to get the commits shown in the third line of the figure.

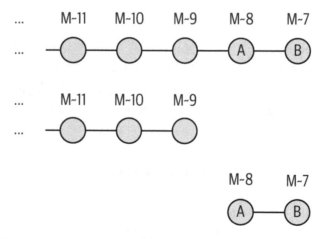

Figure 4-11. Interpreting ranges as set subtraction

When your repository history is a simple linear series of commits, it's fairly easy to understand how a range works. But when branches or merges are involved in the graph, things can become a bit tricky, so it's important to understand the rigorous definition.

Let's look at a few more examples. Keep in mind that these examples are abstract representations only and are designed to be simple and easy to comprehend. The merge operation is used to support the concept, and its technical aspects will be described in detail in Chapter 6.

We start with the case of a main branch with a linear history, as shown in Figure 4-12. The sets B..E, ^B E, and C, D, and E are equivalent.

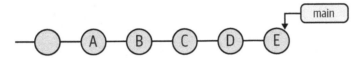

Figure 4-12. Simple linear history

In Figure 4-13, the main branch at commit V was merged into the feature branch at B.

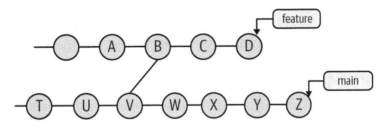

Figure 4-13. main branch merged into feature branch

The range feature..main represents those commits in main but not in feature. Because each commit on the main branch prior to and including V (i.e., the set {..., T, U, V}) contributes to feature, those commits are excluded, leaving W, X, Y, and Z.

The inverse of the previous example is shown in Figure 4-14. Here, feature has been merged into main.

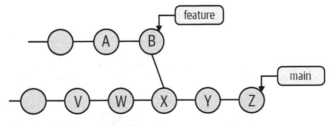

Figure 4-14. feature branch merged into main branch

In this example, the range `feature..main`, again representing those commits in `main` but not in `feature`, is the set of commits on the `main` branch leading up to and including V, W, X, Y, and Z.

However, we have to be a little careful and consider the full history of the `feature` branch. Consider the case where it originally started as a branch of `main` and then merged again, as shown in Figure 4-15.

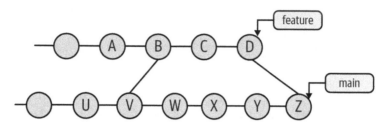

Figure 4-15. A branch and a merge

In this case, `feature..main` contains only the commits W, X, Y, and Z. Remember, the range will exclude *all* commits that are reachable (going back or left over the graph) from `feature` (i.e., the commits D, C, B, A, and earlier), as well as V, U, and earlier from the other parent of B. The result is just W through Z.

Finally, just as *start..end* can be thought of as representing a set subtraction operation, the notation A...B (using three periods) represents the symmetric difference between A and B, or the set of commits that are reachable from either A or B but not from both. Because of the function's symmetry, neither commit can really be considered a start or end. In this sense, A and B are equal.

More formally, the set of revisions in the symmetric difference between A and B, A...B is given by thte following:

```
$ git rev-list A B --not $(git merge-base --all A B)
```

Let's look at the example in Figure 4-16.

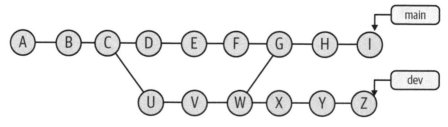

Figure 4-16. Example of symmetric difference

The commits that contribute to `main` are (I, H, . . . , B, A, W, V, U). The commits that contribute to dev are (Z, Y, . . . , U, C, B, A).

The union of those two sets is (A, . . . , I, U, . . . , Z). The merge base between `main` and `dev` is commit W. In more complex cases, there might be multiple merge bases, but here we have only one. The commits that contribute to W are (W, V, U, C, B, and A); those are also the commits that are common to both `main` and `dev`, so they need to be removed to form the symmetric difference: (I, H, Z, Y, X, G, F, E, D).

It may be helpful to think of the symmetric difference between two branches, A and B, as "show everything in branch A or in branch B but only back to the point where the two branches diverged."

We can compute each piece of the symmetric difference definition:

```
A...B = (A OR B) AND NOT (merge-base --all A B)
```

Now that we've described what commit ranges are, how to write them, and how they work, it's important to reveal that Git doesn't actually support a true range operator. It is purely a notational convenience that A..B represents the underlying ^A B form. Git actually allows much more powerful commit set manipulation on its command line. Commands that accept a range are actually accepting an arbitrary sequence of included and excluded commits. For example, you could use:

```
$ git log ^dev ^feature ^bugfix main
```

to select those commits in `main` but not in any of the dev, feature, or bugfix branches.

Once again, all of these examples may be a bit abstract, but the power of range representation really comes to light when you consider that any branch name can be used as part of the range. As described in "Tracking Branches" on page 244, if one of your branches represents the commits from another repository, you can quickly discover the set of commits that are in *your* repository and are not in another repository!

Summary

We started this chapter by introducing commits as a recorded unit of change, further explaining the importance of commits needing to be recorded as an atomic change-set. Next, we gradually built up your proficiency in commits by first introducing you to the various ways in which a commit can be identified. We stressed the importance of learning how to identify commits because this is the building block for many intermediate to advanced Git commands and concepts that will help you confidently tackle any complex requirements that may come your way when dealing with repositories in future projects. We also discussed how you can view a repository's commit history along with methods to effectively constrain a range or set of the history to better understand how a repository came to being in its current state. Understanding commit ranges may be tricky in the beginning, but you will be able to comprehend the overall idea when you start analyzing repository commit history with specific use cases, especially those that require you to traverse the commit history to a specific state of the repository.

## CHAPTER 5

File Management and the Index

When you work in any version control system, you edit in your working directory and commit your changes to your repository for safekeeping. Git also works in this way but inserts an intermediate layer, the index, between the working directory and the repository. The *index*, also known as the *staging directory*, is used to stage, or collect, alterations to any files as a final step before the commit.

The index can be regarded as a cache of the current state of your working directory and plays an important role when you are creating a new commit, when you are querying the status of your repository, and when you are performing a merge operation between two branches. (Merges are covered in Chapter 6.) For the purpose of explaining the fundamentals, we will focus on the importance of the index directory in relation to commits, which are covered in Chapter 4.

In this chapter, we will explain how the index or staging directory in Git is unique compared to other version control systems. We will also explain how to manage the index and your collections of files while describing how to add and remove a file from your repository. We will show you how to rename a file in Git and how to catalog the state of the index, before concluding with how to make Git ignore temporary and other irrelevant files that need not be tracked for version control in your repository.

Importance of the Index

When you manage your code with Git, you edit in your working directory, accumulate changes in your index, and commit whatever has amassed in the index as a single changeset. This concept makes more sense when you think of it from the perspective of writing a newspaper article. You prepare a draft version, your editor reviews and proposes changes, you incorporate those changes, and finally the article is published.

The draft represents your working directory in Git, the editor's changes represent what you will incorporate into your index directory, and the published article is the final commit.

Technically, you can think of Git's index as a set of intended or prospective modifications. You add, remove, move, or repeatedly edit files right up to the culminating commit, which actualizes the accumulated changes in the repository. Thus most of the critical work actually precedes the commit step. Figure 5-1 illustrates this concept.

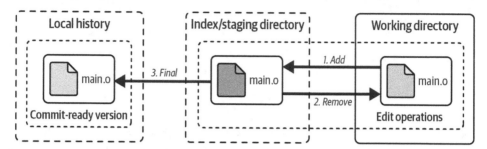

Figure 5-1. Index and file operations concept

In Figure 5-1, the version of main.o in the "Local history" block represents the final version of the file from the index/staging directory after concluding any edit operations on the file.

As explained in "Index" on page 28, the index is one of the most important data structures in Git (see the Git technical documentation (*https://oreil.ly/dBb9O*)). It is a binary file, and it contains a sorted list of file pathnames in its virtual state along with its permissions and a reference to the SHA1 ID of the corresponding blob objects. Essentially, the index contains the virtual tree state, representing a tree object that will be referenced by a future commit. (Blob and tree objects are discussed in Chapter 2.)

The operations to add, remove, or edit files commonly use Git's porcelain (high-level) commands, which hide the details of the index from you and make your job easier. As an example, you can query the state of the index at any time with the command `git status`. This command explicitly calls out what files Git considers staged. It does so by comparing the virtual tree state with your working tree and displays the differences as an output.

You can also peer into the internal state of Git with plumbing (low-level) commands, such as `git ls-files`. The following snippet shows an example output of the index using this command:

```
$ git ls-files -s
100644 e69de29bb2d1d6434b8b29ae775ad8c2e48c5391 0    README.md
100644 6ff87c4664981e4397625791c8ea3bbb5f227e69 0    NewFile.md
```

In other words, Git's index doesn't contain any file content; it simply tracks what you want to commit. When you run `git commit`, Git checks the index rather than your working directory to discover what to commit.

When staging a file into the index, you'll also likely find the `git diff` command to be useful. (Diffs are discussed extensively in Chapter 7.) This command can display two different sets of changes: `git diff` displays the changes that remain in your working directory and are not staged, and `git diff --cached` shows changes that are staged and will therefore contribute to your next commit.

 `git diff --staged` is a synonym for `git diff --cached`. The commands can be used interchangeably.

You can use both variations of `git diff` to guide you through the process of staging changes. Initially, `git diff` is a large set of all modifications, and `--cached` is empty. As you stage, the former set will shrink, and the latter set will grow. If all your working changes are staged and ready for a commit, the `--cached` will be full and `git diff` will show nothing.

File Classifications in Git

Since the index is a transitory state, a dynamic layer between your working directory and Git's object store, it is important to understand how Git keeps track of the state of your files.

Git classifies your files into three groups: tracked, ignored, and untracked:

Tracked
> A tracked file is any file already in the repository or any file that is staged in the index. To add a new file, *somefile*, to this group, run `git add` *somefile*.

Ignored
> An ignored file must be explicitly declared invisible or ignored in the repository even though it may be present within your working directory. A software project tends to have a good number of ignored files. Commonly ignored files include temporary and scratch files, personal notes, compiler output, and most files generated automatically during a build. Git maintains a default list of files to ignore, and you can configure your repository to recognize others. Ignored files are discussed in detail in "The .gitignore File" on page 118.

Untracked

An untracked file is any file not found in either of the previous two categories. Git considers the entire set of files in your working directory and subtracts both the tracked files and the ignored files to yield what is untracked.

Let's explore the different categories of files by creating a brand-new working directory and repository and then working with some files:

```
# Initialize new empty git repository
$ cd /tmp/my_stuff
$ git init --initial-branch=main

$ git status
On branch main

No commits yet

nothing to commit (create/copy files and use "git add" to track)

# Add new file with some content
$ echo "New data" > data

$ git status
On branch main

No commits yet

Untracked files:
(use "git add <file>..." to include in what will be committed)
    data

nothing added to commit but untracked files present (use "git add" to track)
```

In the preceding snippet, we initialized a new Git repository with a default branch name `main` using the `--initial-branch` option with the `git init` command.

In the new, empty repository, there are no files, thus the tracked, ignored, and untracked sets are empty. Once we created *data* and ran `git status`, Git reported a single, untracked file.

Next, we will simulate how to explicitly ignore a file in the Git repository:

```
# Manually create an example junk file
$ touch main.o

$ git status
On branch main

No commits yet

Untracked files:
(use "git add <file>..." to include in what will be committed)
    data
    main.o

nothing added to commit but untracked files present (use "git add" to track)

# Explicitly add main.o as an ignored file via .gitignore file
```

```
$ echo main.o > .gitignore

$ git status
On branch main

No commits yet

Untracked files:
(use "git add <file>..." to include in what will be committed)
    .gitignore
    data

nothing added to commit but untracked files present (use "git add" to track)
```

This example replicates what editors and build environments produce, often leaving temporary or transient files among your source code. Such files shouldn't be tracked as source files in a repository. To have Git ignore a file within a directory, simply add that file's name to the special file *.gitignore*. We will revisit the *.gitignore* file later in this chapter.

Thus, in the code snippet, the *main.o* file is ignored, but `git status` now shows a new, untracked file called *.gitignore*. Although the *.gitignore* file has special meaning to Git, it is managed just like any other normal file within your repository. Until *.gitignore* is added, Git considers it untracked.

The next few sections demonstrate different ways to change the tracked status of a file as well as how to add or remove it from the index.

Using git add

Making a commit is a two-step process: first you stage your changes and then you commit the changes.

The command `git add` stages a file. If a file is untracked, the command `git add` converts that file's status to tracked. When `git add` is used on a directory name, all of the files and subdirectories beneath it are staged recursively.

Let's continue the example from the previous section:

```
$ git status
  On branch main

  No commits yet

  Untracked files:
    (use "git add <file>..." to include in what will be committed)

        .gitignore
        data

# Track both new files.
$ git add data .gitignore

$ git status
```

```
On branch main

No commits yet

Changes to be committed:
  (use "git rm --cached <file>..." to unstage)

      new file: .gitignore
      new file: data
```

The first `git status` shows you that two files are untracked and reminds you that to make a file tracked, you simply need to use `git add`. After `git add`, both *data* and *.gitignore* are staged and tracked and are ready to be added to the repository on the next commit. Figure 5-2 illustrates this concept.

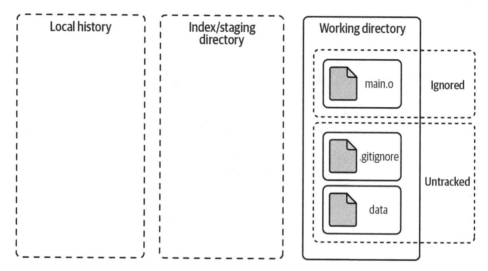

Figure 5-2. Index and file classifications in Git

In terms of Git's object model, the entirety of each file at the moment you issued `git add` was copied into the object store and indexed by its resulting SHA1 name. Staging a file is also called *caching a file*[1] or *putting a file in the index*.

You can use `git ls-files` to peer under the object model hood and find the SHA1 values for those staged files:

```
$ git ls-files --stage
100644 0487f44090ad950f61955271cf0a2d6c6a83ad9a 0       .gitignore
100644 534469f67ae5ce72a7a274faf30dee3c2ea1746d 0       data
```

Figure 5-3 captures this visually.

---

1 You did see the `--cached` in the `git status` output, didn't you?

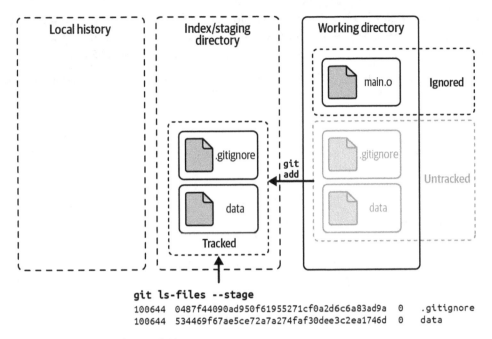

```
git ls-files --stage
100644  0487f44090ad950f61955271cf0a2d6c6a83ad9a  0    .gitignore
100644  534469f67ae5ce72a7a274faf30dee3c2ea1746d  0    data
```

Figure 5-3. Index and staged files

Most of the day-to-day changes within your repository will likely be simple edits. After any edit and before you commit your changes, run `git add` to update the index with the absolute latest and greatest version of your file. If you don't, you'll have two different versions of the file: one captured in the object store and referenced from the index, and the other in your working directory.

To continue the example, let's change the file *data* so it's different from the one in the index and use the arcane `git hash-object` *file* command (which you'll hardly ever invoke directly) to directly compute and print the SHA1 hash for the new version:

```
$ git ls-files --stage
100644 0487f44090ad950f61955271cf0a2d6c6a83ad9a 0      .gitignore
100644 534469f67ae5ce72a7a274faf30dee3c2ea1746d 0      data

# edit "data" to contain...
$ cat data
New data
And some more data now

$ git hash-object data
e476983f39f6e4f453f0fe4a859410f63b58b500
```

After the file is amended, the previous version of the file in the object store and index has SHA1 534469f67ae5ce72a7a274faf30dee3c2ea1746d. However, the updated version of the file has SHA1 e476983f39f6e4f453f0fe4a859410f63b58b500.

Let's update the index using the `git add` command to contain the new version of the file:

```
$ git add data
$ git ls-files --stage
100644 0487f44090ad950f61955271cf0a2d6c6a83ad9a 0        .gitignore
100644 e476983f39f6e4f453f0fe4a859410f63b58b500 0        data
```

Figure 5-4 captures this visually. Note the new SHA1 ID for *data*.

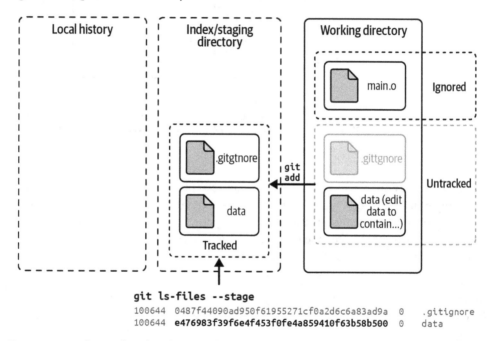

Figure 5-4. Index and updated staged files

The index now has the updated version of the file. Again, "the file *data* has been *staged*," or loosely speaking, "the file *data* is *in the index*." The latter phrase is less accurate because the file is actually in the object store, and the index merely refers to it virtually. The seemingly idle play with SHA1 hashes and the index brings home a key point: think of `git add` not as "add this file" but more as "add this index content."

In any event, the important thing to remember is that the version of a file in your working directory can be out of sync with the version staged in the index. When it comes time to make a commit, Git uses the version in the index.

The --interactive option to either git add or git commit can be a useful way to explore which files you would like to stage for a commit.

Notes on Using git commit

Following are some brief pointers on how the index is affected when you are working with commits.

Using git commit --all

The -a or --all option to git commit causes Git to automatically stage all unstaged, tracked file changes, including removals of tracked files from the working copy before it performs the commit.

Let's see how this works by setting up a few files with different staging characteristics:

```
# Setup test repository
$ mkdir /tmp/commit-all-example
$ cd /tmp/commit-all-example
$ git init --initial-branch=main
Initialized empty Git repository in /tmp/commit-all-example/.git/

$ echo something >> ready
$ echo something else >> notyet
$ git add ready notyet
$ git commit -m "Setup"
[main (root-commit) 63ae368]] Setup
 2 files changed, 2 insertions(+)
 create mode 100644 notyet
 create mode 100644 ready

# Modify file "ready" and "git add" it to the index
# edit ready
$ git add ready

# Modify file "notyet", leaving it unstaged
# edit notyet

# Add a new file in a subdirectory, but don't add it
$ mkdir subdir
$ echo Nope >> subdir/new
```

Next, we use git status to see what a regular commit (without command-line options) would do:

```
$ git status
On branch main
Changes to be committed:
(use "git restore --staged <file>..." to unstage)
    modified:   ready

Changes not staged for commit:
(use "git add <file>..." to update what will be committed)
```

```
    (use "git restore <file>..." to discard changes in working directory)
        modified:   notyet

Untracked files:
  (use "git add <file>..." to include in what will be committed)
        subdir/
```

Here, the index is prepared to commit just the one file named *ready* because it's the only file that's been staged.

However, if you run `git commit --all`, Git recursively traverses the entire repository; stages all known, modified files; and commits them. In this case, when your editor presents the commit message template, it should indicate that the modified and known file *notyet* will, in fact, be committed as well:

```
# Please enter the commit message for your changes. Lines starting
# with '#' will be ignored, and an empty message aborts the commit.
#
# On branch main
# Changes to be committed:
#       modified:   notyet
#       modified:   ready
#
# Untracked files:
#       subdir/
#
```

However, because the directory named *subdir/* is new and no filename or path within it is tracked, not even the `--all` option causes it to be committed. Concluding the commit with an appropriate message will result in the following output:

```
[main a6f75bb] Some --all thing.
 2 files changed, 2 insertions(+)
```

While Git recursively traverses the repository looking for modified and removed files, the completely new *subdir/* directory and all of its files do not become part of the commit; they remain in the working directory.

For convenience, Git allows you to combine the two steps, `git add` and `git commit`, when you change an existing tracked file in the repository:

```
$ git commit -m trackedfile
```

But if you move or remove a file, you don't have that luxury. The two steps must then be separate:

```
$ git rm somefile
$ git commit
```

Writing Commit Log Messages

If you do not directly supply a log message on the command line, Git launches an editor and prompts you to write one. Git selects which editor to launch from your configuration, as described in "Configuration Files" on page 20.

If you are in the editor writing a commit log message and for some reason decide to abort the operation, simply exit the editor without saving; this results in an empty log message, prompting Git to abort the commit:

```
$ git commit ready

# Configured Editor launched
# Exit editor without writing a commit message

Aborting commit due to empty commit message.
```

If it's too late for that because you've already saved, just delete the entire log message and save again. Git will not process an empty (no text) commit.

Using git rm

The command `git rm` is, naturally, the inverse of `git add`. It removes a file from both the repository and the working directory. However, because removing a file tends to be more problematic (if something goes wrong) than adding a file, Git treats the removal of a file with a bit more care.

Git is able to remove a file in two situations: when you need to remove a file from the index only and when you need to remove a file from both the index and the working directory simultaneously. Since Git will not automatically remove a file from the working directory, you can use the regular `rm` command for that purpose.

Removing a file from your directory and the index does not remove the file's existing history from the repository. Any versions of the file that are part of its history already committed in the repository remain in the object store and retain that history.

Continuing the example from "File Classifications in Git" on page 105, let's "accidentally" introduce an additional file that shouldn't be staged and see how to remove it:

```
$ echo "random stuff" > oops

$ git rm oops
fatal: pathspec 'oops' did not match any files

# You can't use "git rm" on files Git is not tracking
# Use "rm oops" to delete the file from the working directory
```

Because `git rm` is also an operation on the index, the command won't work on a file that hasn't been previously added to the repository or index; Git must first be aware of a file in order to track it. So let's accidentally stage the *oops* file:

```
# Accidentally stage "oops" file
$ git add oops

$ git status
On branch main

No commits yet

Changes to be committed:
(use "git rm --cached <file>..." to unstage)
    new file:   .gitignore
    new file:   data
    new file:   oops
```

To convert a file from staged to unstaged, use `git rm --cached`. Let's observe how this affects the index:

```
$ git ls-files --stage
100644 0487f44090ad950f61955271cf0a2d6c6a83ad9a 0       .gitignore
100644 e476983f39f6e4f453f0fe4a859410f63b58b500 0       data
100644 6bece861cc8fd34181e6d43264acfe1503486538 0       oops

$ git rm --cached oops
rm 'oops'

$ git ls-files --stage
100644 0487f44090ad950f61955271cf0a2d6c6a83ad9a 0       .gitignore
100644 e476983f39f6e4f453f0fe4a859410f63b58b500 0       data
```

The `git rm --cached` command removes the file from the index and leaves it in the working directory:

```
$ git status
On branch main

No commits yet

Changes to be committed:
(use "git rm --cached <file>..." to unstage)
    new file:   .gitignore
    new file:   data

Untracked files:
(use "git add <file>..." to include in what will be committed)
    oops
```

In contrast, the `git rm` command removes the file from both the index and the working directory.

Using `git rm --cached` to make a file untracked while leaving a copy in the working directory is dangerous because you may forget that it is no longer being tracked. Using this approach also overrides Git's check that the working file's contents are current. Be cautious about which command you intend to use.

If you want to remove a file once it's been committed, just stage the request through a simple `git rm` *filename*:

```
$ git commit -m "Add some files"
[main (root-commit) 57cbafa] Add some files
2 files changed, 2 insertions(+)
create mode 100644 .gitignore
create mode 100644 data

$ git rm data
rm 'data'

$ git status
On branch main
Changes to be committed:
(use "git restore --staged <file>..." to unstage)
    deleted:    data
```

Before Git removes a file, it checks to make sure the version of the file in the working directory matches the latest version in the current branch (the version in the most recent commit, the HEAD). This verification precludes the accidental loss of any changes (due to your editing) that may have been made to the file.

Use `git rm -f` to *force* the removal of your file. Force is an explicit mandate and removes the file even if you have altered it since your last commit.

And in case you *really* meant to keep a file that you accidentally removed, simply add it back:

```
$ git add data
fatal: pathspec 'data' did not match any files
```

Darn! Git removed the working copy too! But don't worry. Version control systems are good at recovering old versions of files:

```
$ git checkout HEAD -- data
$ cat data
New data
And some more data now

$ git status
On branch main
nothing to commit, working tree clean
```

Using git mv

Suppose you need to move or rename a file. You can use a combination of `git rm` on the old file and `git add` on the new file, or you can use `git mv` directly. Given a repository with a file named *stuff* that you want to rename *newstuff*, the following sequences of commands are equivalent Git operations:

```
$ mv stuff newstuff
$ git rm stuff
$ git add newstuff
```

and

```
$ git mv stuff newstuff
```

In both cases, Git removes the pathname *stuff* from the index; adds a new pathname, *newstuff*; keeps the original content for *stuff* in the object store; and reassociates that content with the pathname *newstuff*.

Picking up from the earlier example, and since *data* is back in the example repository, let's rename it and commit the change:

```
# Check the index before renaming file
$ git ls-files --stage
100644 0487f44090ad950f61955271cf0a2d6c6a83ad9a 0    .gitignore
100644 e476983f39f6e4f453f0fe4a859410f63b58b500 0    data

$ git mv data mydata

$ git status
On branch main
Changes to be committed:
(use "git restore --staged <file>..." to unstage)
      renamed:    data -> mydata

# Check the index with the renamed file
# Note that the SHA1 ID remains the same with the new pathname
$ git ls-files --stage
100644 0487f44090ad950f61955271cf0a2d6c6a83ad9a 0    .gitignore
100644 e476983f39f6e4f453f0fe4a859410f63b58b500 0    mydata

$ git commit -m "Moved data to mydata"
[main 4b7a819] Moved data to mydata
 1 file changed, 0 insertions(+), 0 deletions(-)
 rename data => mydata (100%)
```

If you happen to check the history of the file, you may be a bit disturbed to see that Git has apparently lost the history of the original *data* file and remembers only that it renamed *data* to the current name:

```
$ git log mydata
commit 4b7a81923c636716d2b035574ca569018c723f21 (HEAD -> main)
Author: Prem Kumar Ponuthorai <ppremk@gmail.com>
Date:   Mon Apr 5 23:56:05 2021 +0200

Moved data to mydata
```

Git does still remember the whole history, but the display is limited to the particular filename you specified in the command. The `--follow` option asks Git to trace back through the log and find the full history associated with the content:

```
$ git log --follow mydata
commit 4b7a81923c636716d2b035574ca569018c723f21 (HEAD -> main)
Author: Prem Kumar Ponuthorai  <ppremk@gmail.com>
Date:   Mon Apr 5 23:56:05 2021 +0200

    Moved data to mydata

commit 57cbafaf8f20187395f6806aa7bc579fcbf7acde
Author: Prem Kumar Ponuthorai  <ppremk@gmail.com>
Date:   Mon Apr 5 23:37:48 2021 +0200

    Add some files
```

One of the classic problems with version control systems is that renaming a file can cause the system to lose track of the file's history. Git preserves this information even after a rename.

A Note on Tracking Renames

Let's take a look at SVN, an example of a traditional revision control system, and then compare it with Git to see how the two systems keep track of files renamed in different ways.

SVN does a lot of work tracking when a file is renamed and moved around because it only keeps track of diffs between files. If you move a file, it's essentially the same as deleting all the lines from the old file and adding them to the new one. But it would be inefficient to transfer and store all the contents of the file again whenever you do a simple rename; imagine renaming a whole subdirectory that contains thousands of files.

To alleviate this situation, SVN tracks each rename explicitly. If you want to rename *hello.txt* to *subdir/hello.txt*, you must use `svn mv` instead of `svn rm` and `svn add` on the files. Otherwise, SVN has no way to see that it's a rename and must go through the inefficient delete/add sequence just described.

Next, given this exceptional feature of tracking a rename, the SVN server needs a special protocol to tell its clients, "Please move *hello.txt* into *subdir/hello.txt*." Furthermore, each SVN client must ensure that it performs this operation correctly.

Git, on the other hand, doesn't keep track of a rename. You can move or copy *hello.txt* anywhere you want, but doing so affects only tree objects. (Remember that tree objects store the relationships between content, whereas the content itself is stored in blobs.) A look at the differences between two trees makes it obvious that the same unique blob has moved to a new place. And even if you don't explicitly examine the differences, every part of the system knows it already has that blob, so every part knows it doesn't need another copy of it.

In this situation, as in many other places, Git's simple hash-based storage system simplifies a lot of things that baffle or elude other version control systems.

Problems with Tracking a Rename

Tracking the renaming of a file engenders a perennial debate among developers of version control systems.

A simple rename is fodder enough for dissension. The argument becomes even more heated when the file's name changes and then its content changes. Then the scenarios turn the parley from practical to philosophical: Is that "new" file really a rename, or is it merely similar to the old one? How similar should the new file be before it's considered the same file? If you apply someone's patch that deletes a file and re-creates a similar one elsewhere, how is that managed? What happens if a file is renamed in two different ways on two different branches? Is it less error-prone to automatically detect renames in such a situation, as Git does, or to require the user to explicitly identify renames, as SVN does?

In real-life situations, it seems that Git's system for handling file renames is superior, compared to the same effortful methods in SVN; but, that said, there is no perfect system for handling renames…yet.

The .gitignore File

Earlier in this chapter, you saw how to use the *.gitignore* file to exclude *main.o*, an irrelevant file. As in that example, you can skip any file by adding its name to *.gitignore* in the same directory. Additionally, you can ignore the file everywhere by adding it to the *.gitignore* file in the topmost directory of your repository. But Git also supports a much richer mechanism.

A *.gitignore* file can contain a list of filename patterns that specify what files to ignore.

The pattern format of *.gitignore* is as follows:

- Blank lines are ignored. Lines starting with a pound sign (#) can be used for comments, but # doesn't represent a comment if it follows other text on the line.

- A simple, literal filename matches a file in any directory with that name.

- A directory name is marked by a trailing slash (/). This matches the named directory and any subdirectory but does not match a file or a symbolic link.

- A pattern containing shell globbing characters, such as an asterisk (*), is expanded as a shell glob pattern. Just as in standard shell globbing, the match cannot extend across directories, and so an asterisk can match only a single file or directory name. But an asterisk can still be part of a pattern that includes slashes to specify directory names (e.g., *debug/*.o*).

- An initial exclamation point (!) inverts the sense of the pattern on the rest of the line. Additionally, any file excluded by an earlier pattern but matching an inversion rule is included. An inverted pattern overrides lower precedence rules.

Following is an example based on the preceding explanations:

```
$ cat .gitignore
# Example Pattern Format of a .gitignore file

# Below is not a comment. The "#" is part of an expression as its first character
\#*.tmp

# Literal filename
somefile.log

# Directory exclusion
my_package/

# Glob pattern expression
*.[oa]
*.log
debug/*.o

# Inverting a glob pattern expression (do not ignore the important.log file)
!important.log
```

Table 5-1 lists some example output to match the globbing patterns supported by the *.gitignore* file.

Table 5-1. Globbing pattern example output

Globbing pattern	Matches
*.log	.log important.log file.log dir/anotherfile.log
*.[oa]	file.o file.a
tmp/	tmp/files.log tmp/subdir/files.log parent/tmp/files.log grandparent/tmp/files.log

Globbing pattern	Matches
file.log	file.log dir/file.log
dir/**/file	dir/file dir/subdir/file dir/subdir/subsubdir/file
**/file	dir/file anotherdir/file file
file?.log	file1.log file2.log
!important.log	important.log dir/important.log *(the above files will not be ignored)*

 Two asterisks (**) used adjacently in globbing patterns that include a directory name may match differently, as per the examples in Table 5-1.

Furthermore, Git allows you to have a *.gitignore* file in any directory within your repository. Each file affects its directory and all subdirectories. The *.gitignore* rules also cascade: you can override the rules in a higher directory by including an inverted pattern (using the initial !) in one of the subdirectories.

To resolve a hierarchy with multiple *.gitignore* directories and to allow command-line addenda to the list of ignored files, Git honors the following precedence, from highest to lowest:

- Patterns specified on the command line.
- Patterns read from *.gitignore* in the same directory.
- Patterns in parent directories, proceeding upward. Hence, the current directory's patterns overrule the parents' patterns, and the parents close to the current directory take precedence over higher parents.
- Patterns from the *.git/info/exclude* file.
- Patterns from the file specified by the configuration variable `core.excludesFile`.

Because a *.gitignore* file is treated as a regular file within your repository, it is copied during clone operations and applies to all copies of your repository. In general, you should place entries into your version-controlled *.gitignore* files only if the patterns apply to *all* derived repositories universally.

If the exclusion pattern is somehow specific to your one repository and should not (or might not) be applicable to anyone else's clone of your repository, then the patterns should instead go into the *.git/info/exclude* file because that file is not propagated during clone operations. Its pattern format and treatment are the same as *.gitignore* files.

Here's another scenario. It's typical to exclude *.o* files, which are generated from source by the compiler. To ignore *.o* files, place **.o* in your top-level *.gitignore*. But what if you also had a particular **.o* file that was, say, supplied by someone else and for which you couldn't generate a replacement yourself? You'd likely want to explicitly track that particular file. You might then have a configuration like this:

```
.
└── my_package
    ├── .gitignore
    ├── vendor_files
    │   └── .gitignore

$ cd my_package
$ cat .gitignore
*.o

$ cd my_package/vendor_files
$ cat .gitignore
!driver.o
```

The combination of rules means that Git will ignore all *.o* files within the repository but will track one exception, the file *driver.o* within the *vendor_files* subdirectory.

Summary

By now, you should have the basic skills to manage files. Nonetheless, keeping track of what file is where in the working directory, index, and repository history can be a little overwhelming. To overcome this, it is important for you to take the time and fully understand the importance of index and file classifications in Git so that you can grasp the importance of the index directory in combination with how Git classifies and tracks files in your project repositories. Once you understand this concept, you can take advantage of the technical aspects of how to add, remove, and even exclude files in your repositories to meet your project goals with ease.

## CHAPTER 6

Merges

Because Git is a distributed version control system, it allows developers in dispersed geographical locations to make and record changes independently, and it permits two or more developers to combine their changes at any time, all without a central repository. Technically, this is an operation that combines two or more different lines of development, and it is formally known as a *merge* in Git.

In this chapter, we'll explain how to merge two or more different lines of development via some simple merge examples, and we'll share some techniques for resolving a merge conflict when it occurs. We will also discuss merge strategies in Git and take a peek at what happens in the Git object store when a merge operation is executed.

Merge: A Technical View

In Git, a merge unifies two or more commit histories of branches. Most often, a merge unites just two branches, although Git supports a merge of three or more branches at the same time.

A merge must occur within a single repository—that is, all the branches to be merged must be present in the same repository. How the branches come to be in the repository is not important. (As you will see in Chapter 11, Git provides mechanisms for referring to other repositories and for bringing remote branches into your current working repository.)

When modifications in one branch do not conflict with modifications found in another branch, Git computes a merge result and creates a new commit that represents the new, unified state. But when branches have conflicts, Git does not resolve the dispute. Instead, Git marks such contentious changes as "unmerged" in the index and leaves reconciliation up to you, the developer (to reiterate what we explained in "Git Characteristics" on page 5, Git waits for you to provide instructions on what to do and when to do it). When Git cannot merge branches automatically, it's also up to you to make the final commit once all conflicts are resolved.

Merge Examples

The `git merge` operation is context sensitive. Your current branch is always the target branch, and changes from other branches are merged into the current branch.

In the following example, we will switch to our *main-branch* to set it as our current branch and merge a *modified-branch* into it:

```
$ git checkout main-branch
$ git merge modified-branch
```

An easier way to remember a merge operation in Git is to think about it in a *source* versus *target* perspective—that is, you have some changes in another branch (*source branch*), and you want to merge that branch into your current branch (*target branch*).

Let's work through a pair of example merges, one without conflicts and one with substantial overlaps. To simplify the examples in this chapter, we'll use multiple branches per the techniques presented in Chapter 3.

Preparing for a Merge

As a general rule, your Git life will be much easier if you start each merge with a clean working directory and index. During a normal merge, Git creates new versions of files and places them in your working directory when it is finished. Furthermore, Git uses the index to store temporary and intermediate versions of files during the operation.

If you have modified files in your working directory or if you've modified the index via `git add` or `git rm`, then your repository has a dirty working directory or index. If you start a merge in a dirty state, Git may be unable to combine the changes from all the branches *and* from those in your working directory or index in one pass.

You don't *have* to start with a clean directory. Git still performs the merge, for example, if the files affected by the merge operation and the dirty files in your working directory are not commonly affected by the introduced change. However, starting with a clean directory is easier and is the tactic we prefer.

Merging Two Branches

For the simplest scenario, let's set up a repository with a single file, create two branches, and then merge the pair of branches together again:

```
$ mkdir merge-conflict

# Initialize new repository
$ git init -b main
Initialized empty Git repository in /merge-conflict/.git/

# Create new file
$ cat > file
Line 1 stuff
Line 2 stuff
Line 3 stuff
^D

# Add and commit file
$ git add file
$ git commit -m "Initial 3 line file"
[main (root-commit) 21a352e] Initial 3 line file
 1 file changed, 3 insertions(+)
 create mode 100644 file
```

Let's create another commit on the main branch:

```
$ cat > other_file
Here is stuff on another file!
^D

$ git add other_file
$ git commit -m "Another file"
[main e5d26c6] Another file
 1 file changed, 1 insertion(+)
 create mode 100644 other_file
```

So far, the repository has one branch with two commits, where each commit introduced a new file. Next, let's change to a different branch and modify the first file:

```
$ git checkout -b alternate main^
Switched to a new branch "alternate"

$ git show-branch
* [alternate] Initial 3 line file
 ! [main] Another file
--
 + [main] Another file
*+ [alternate] Initial 3 line file
```

Here, the alternate branch is initially forked from the main^ commit, one commit behind the current head.

We'll make one more trivial change to the file so that you have something to merge, and then we'll commit it. Remember, it's best to commit outstanding changes and start a merge with a clean working directory:

```
$ cat >> file
Line 4 alternate stuff
^D

$ git commit -a -m "Add alternate's line 4"
[alternate 97e7ffe] Add alternate's line 4
 1 file changed, 1 insertion(+)
```

Now there are two branches, and each has a different line of development work. A second file has been added to the main branch, and a modification has been made to the alternate branch. Because the two changes do not affect the same parts of a common file, a merge should proceed smoothly and without incident.

Because the git merge operation is context sensitive, we need to ensure that the main branch is the target branch and the changes in the alternate branch are merged into it. In this case, we need to check out to the main branch before we continue:

```
$ git checkout main
Switched to branch "main"

# Check to ensure no dirty working directory or index
$ git status
On branch main
nothing to commit, working tree clean

# Yep, ready for a merge!

# Git prompts the default merge message in your default editor
# when you hit return, save, and continue
$ git merge alternate
Merge made by the 'ort' strategy.
 file | 1 +
 1 file changed, 1 insertion(+)
```

You can use another commit graph viewing tool, a part of git log, to see what's been done:

```
$ git log --graph --decorate --pretty=oneline --abbrev-commit

*   2dce921 (HEAD -> main) Merge branch 'alternate'
|\
| * 97e7ffe (alternate) Add alternate's line 4
* | e5d26c6 Another file
|/
* 21a352e Initial 3 line file
```

Conceptually, this is the same commit graph described in "Commit Graphs" on page 90, except that this graph is turned sideways, with the most recent commits at the top rather than at the right. The two branches have split at the initial commit, 21a352e; each branch shows one commit (e5d26c6 and 97e7ffe); and the two branches merge again at commit 2dce921.

Using `git log --graph` is an excellent alternative to graphical tools such as `gitk`. The visualization provided by `git log --graph` is well suited to dumb terminals, such as when you SSH into a server.

Technically, Git performs each merge symmetrically to produce one identical, combined commit that is added to your current branch. The other branch is not affected by the merge. Because the merge commit is added only to your current branch, you can say, "I merged the source branch *into* this target branch."

A Merge with a Conflict

The merge operation can typically proceed without prompting the user when Git can successfully resolve any differences between either side of the merge. But because the merge operation can take any number of independent, varying, and potentially conflict-ridden lines of development, this is not always the case. When this happens, the user is prompted to resolve any conflicts that Git could not resolve automatically.

Let's work through a scenario in which a merge leads to a conflict. We'll begin with the results of the merge from the previous section and introduce independent and conflicting changes on the `main` and `alternate` branches. We'll then merge the `alternate` branch into the `main` branch, face the conflict, resolve it, and commit the final result.

On the `main` branch, we will create a new version of a file named *file* that has a few additional lines in it, and then we'll commit the changes:

```
$ git checkout main

$ cat >> file
Line 5 stuff
Line 6 stuff
^D

$ git commit -a -m "Add line 5 and 6"
[main 6c5634c] Add line 5 and 6
 1 file changed, 2 insertions(+)
```

Next, on the `alternate` branch, let's modify the same file differently. Whereas we made new commits to the `main` branch, the `alternate` branch has not progressed yet:

```
$ git checkout alternate
Switched to branch "alternate"

$ git show-branch
* [alternate] Add alternate's line 4
 ! [main] Add line 5 and 6
--
 + [main] Add line 5 and 6
*+ [alternate] Add alternate's line 4
```

```
# In this branch, "file" left off with "Line 4 alternate stuff"

$ cat >> file
Line 5 alternate stuff
Line 6 alternate stuff
^D

$ cat file
Line 1 stuff
Line 2 stuff
Line 3 stuff
Line 4 alternate stuff
Line 5 alternate stuff
Line 6 alternate stuff

$ git diff
diff --git a/file b/file
index a29c52b..802acf8 100644
--- a/file
+++ b/file
@@ -2,3 +2,5 @@ Line 1 stuff
 Line 2 stuff
 Line 3 stuff
 Line 4 alternate stuff
+Line 5 alternate stuff
+Line 6 alternate stuff

$ git commit -a -m "Add alternate line 5 and 6"
[alternate 0ca87a4] Add alternate line 5 and 6
 1 file changed, 2 insertions(+)
```

Let's review the scenario. The current branch history looks like this:

```
$ git show-branch
* [alternate] Add alternate line 5 and 6
 ! [main] Add line 5 and 6
--
*  [alternate] Add alternate line 5 and 6
 + [main] Add line 5 and 6
*+ [alternate^] Add alternate's line 4
```

To continue, we will check out the main branch and try to perform the merge:

```
$ git checkout main
Switched to branch "main"

$ git merge alternate
Auto-merging file
CONFLICT (content): Merge conflict in file
Automatic merge failed; fix conflicts and then commit the result.
```

When a merge conflict like this occurs, you should almost invariably investigate the extent of the conflict using the git diff command. Here, the single file named *file* has a conflict in its content:

```
$ git diff
diff --cc file
index 4d77dd1,802acf8..0000000
--- a/file
+++ b/file
@@@ -2,5 -2,5 +2,10 @@@ Line 1 stuf
  Line 2 stuff
  Line 3 stuff
  Line 4 alternate stuff
++<<<<<<< HEAD:file
 +Line 5 stuff
 +Line 6 stuff
++=======
+ Line 5 alternate stuff
+ Line 6 alternate stuff
++>>>>>>> alternate:file
```

The git diff command shows the differences between the file in your working
directory and the index. In the traditional diff command output style, the changed
content is presented between <<<<<<< and =======, with an alternate between
======= and >>>>>>>. However, additional plus and minus signs are used in the
combined diff format to indicate changes from multiple sources relative to the final
resulting version.

The previous output shows that the conflict covers lines 5 and 6, where different
changes were deliberately made in the two branches. It's then up to you to resolve the
conflict. When resolving a merge conflict, you are free to choose any resolution you
would like for the file. That includes picking lines from only one branch or the other,
or picking a mix from both branches, or even making up something completely new
and different. Although that last option might not be fixing the conflict entirely, it is
still a valid choice.

In this case, we resolve the conflict by choosing a line from each branch as the
makeup of our resolved version. The edited file now has this content:

```
$ cat file
Line 1 stuff
Line 2 stuff
Line 3 stuff
Line 4 alternate stuff
Line 5 stuff
Line 6 alternate stuff
```

If you are happy with the conflict resolution, to mark it as resolved, you should git
add the file to the index, staging it for the next commit:

```
$ git add file
```

After you have resolved conflicts and staged final versions of each file in the index using `git add`, it is finally time to commit the merge using `git commit`. Git places you in your default editor with a template message that looks like this:

```
Merge branch 'alternate'

# Conflicts:
#       file
#
# It looks like you may be committing a merge.
# If this is not correct, please run
#       git update-ref -d MERGE_HEAD
# and try again.


# Please enter the commit message for your changes. Lines starting
# with '#' will be ignored, and an empty message aborts the commit.
#
# On branch main
# All conflicts fixed but you are still merging.
#
# Changes to be committed:
#       modified:   file
#
```

As usual, the lines beginning with the pound sign (#) are comments and are meant solely for your information while you write a message. All comment lines are ultimately elided from the final commit log message. Feel free to alter or augment the commit message as you see fit, perhaps adding a note about how the conflict was resolved.

When you exit the editor, Git should indicate the successful creation of a new merge commit:

```
$ git commit
# Edit merge commit message
[main f1fa82f] Merge branch 'alternate'

$ git show-branch
! [alternate] Add alternate line 5 and 6
 * [main] Merge branch 'alternate'
--
 - [main] Merge branch 'alternate'
+* [alternate] Add alternate line 5 and 6
```

You can see the resulting merge commit (the tip or HEAD commit) using the following:

```
$ git log
```

Working with Merge Conflicts

As demonstrated by the previous example, there are instances when conflicting changes can't be merged automatically.

Let's create another scenario with a merge conflict to explore the tools Git provides to help resolve disparities. Starting with a common *hello* file containing just the word *hello*, let's create two different branches with two different variants of the file:

```
$ git init -b main
Initialized empty Git repository in /tmp/conflict/.git/

$ echo hello > hello
$ git add hello
$ git commit -m "Initial hello file"
[main (root-commit) e8a1845] Initial hello file
 1 file changed, 1 insertion(+)
 create mode 100644 hello

$ git checkout -b alt
Switched to a new branch "alt"
$ echo world >> hello
$ echo 'Yay!' >> hello
$ git commit -a -m "One world"
[alt 84e436c] One world
 1 file changed, 2 insertions(+)

$ git checkout main
$ echo worlds >> hello
$ echo 'Yay!' >> hello
$ git commit -a -m "All worlds"
[main 0d7dfb7] All worlds
 1 file changed, 2 insertions(+)
```

We now have one branch with the file *hello* and the content "world" and another branch with a different version of the file *hello* and the content "worlds"—a deliberate difference.

As in the earlier example, if you check out to the main branch and try to merge the alt branch into it, a conflict arises:

```
$ git merge alt
Auto-merging hello
CONFLICT (content): Merge conflict in hello
Automatic merge failed; fix conflicts and then commit the result.
```

As expected, Git warns you about the conflict found in the *hello* file.

Locating Conflicted Files

But what if Git's helpful directions scrolled off the screen or there were many files with conflicts? Luckily, Git keeps track of problematic files by marking each one in the index as conflicted or unmerged.

You can also use either the git status command or the git ls-files -u command to show the set of files that remain unmerged in your working tree. Naturally, the git status command provides you with some hints about what you should do to resolve a conflict and conclude the merge:

```
$ git status
On branch main
You have unmerged paths.
(fix conflicts and run "git commit")
(use "git merge --abort" to abort the merge)

Unmerged paths:
(use "git add <file>..." to mark resolution)
    both modified:    hello

no changes added to commit (use "git add" and/or "git commit -a")

$ git ls-files -u
100644 ce013625030ba8dba906f756967f9e9ca394464a 1        hello
100644 e63164d9518b1e6caf28f455ac86c8246f78ab70 2        hello
100644 562080a4c6518e1bf67a9f58a32a67bff72d4f00 3        hello
```

We will explain why there are three different versions of *hello* in "How Git Keeps Track of Conflicts" on page 138.

You can use `git diff` to show what's not yet merged, but it will show all of the gory details too! In the next section, we will learn how to inspect a file with conflicts.

Inspecting Conflicts

When a conflict appears, the working directory copy of each conflicted file is enhanced with *three-way diff* or *merge markers* (also commonly referred to as *conflict resolution markers*, when addressing a merge conflict). Continuing from where the example left off, the resulting conflicted file now looks like this:

```
$ cat hello
hello
<<<<<<< HEAD
worlds
=======
world
>>>>>>> alt
Yay!
```

The merge markers delineate the two possible versions of the conflicting chunk of the file. In one version, the chunk says "worlds"; in the other version, it says "world." See Figure 6-1 for a visual representation of the merge marker delineation.

> The three-way merge marker lines (<<<<<<<, =======, and >>>>>>>) are automatically generated, but they're just meant to be read by you, not (necessarily) a program. You should delete them with your text editor once you resolve the conflict. A quick method to ensure that all markers are deleted is to run the `git diff --check` command, which highlights any remaining merge markers.

You could simply choose one phrase or the other, remove the conflict markers, and then run `git add` and `git commit`, but let's explore some of the other features Git offers to help resolve conflicts.

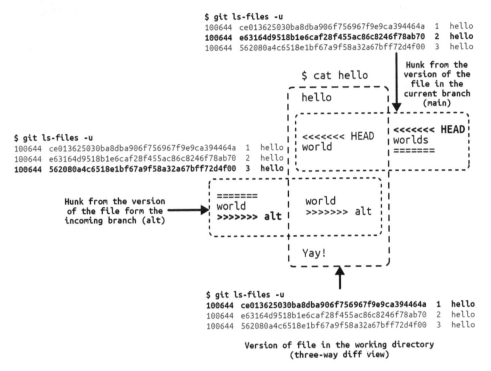

Figure 6-1. Merge marker delineation

git diff with conflicts

Git has a special, merge-specific variant of `git diff` to display the changes made against *both* parents simultaneously. In the example, it looks like this:

```
$ git diff
diff --cc hello
index e63164d,562080a..0000000
--- a/hello
+++ b/hello
@@@ -1,3 -1,3 +1,7 @@@
  hello
++<<<<<<< HEAD
 +worlds
++=======
+ world
++>>>>>>> alt
  Yay!
```

So what does it all mean? It's the simple combination of two diffs: one of the first parent, called HEAD, and one of the second parent, or alt. (Don't be surprised if the second parent is an absolute SHA1 name representing some unnamed commit from some other repository!) To make things easier, Git also gives the second parent the special name MERGE_HEAD.

You can compare both the HEAD and MERGE_HEAD versions against the working directory ("merged") version:

```
$ git diff HEAD
diff --git a/hello b/hello
index e63164d..1f2f61c 100644
--- a/hello
+++ b/hello
@@ -1,3 +1,7 @@
 hello
+<<<<<<< HEAD
 worlds
+=======
+world
+>>>>>>> alt
 Yay!


$ git diff MERGE_HEAD
diff --git a/hello b/hello
index 562080a..1f2f61c 100644
--- a/hello
+++ b/hello
@@ -1,3 +1,7 @@
 hello
+<<<<<<< HEAD
+worlds
+=======
 world
+>>>>>>> alt
 Yay!
```

Note that the line starting with index captures different abbreviated SHA1 IDs.

Alternatively, you can use the git diff --ours command, which is a synonym for git diff HEAD, because it shows the differences between "our" version and the merged version. Similarly, git diff MERGE_HEAD can be written as git diff --theirs.

 You can use git diff --base to see the combined set of changes since the merge base, which would otherwise be rather awkwardly written as follows:

```
$ git diff $(git merge-base HEAD MERGE_HEAD)
```

If you line up the two diffs side by side, all the text except the + columns are the same, so Git prints the main text only once and prints the + columns next to each other. Figure 6-2 illustrates this.

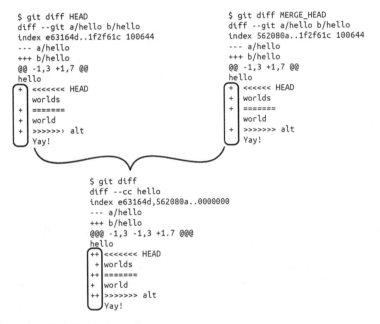

Figure 6-2. Merged diffs side by side

The conflict found by `git diff` has two columns of information prepended to each line of output. A plus sign (+) in a column indicates a line addition, a minus sign (-) indicates a line removal, and a blank indicates a line with no change. The first column shows what's changing versus your version, and the second column shows what's changing versus the other version. The conflict marker lines are new in both versions, so they get a ++. The world and worlds lines are new in only one version or the other, so they have just a single + in the corresponding column.

Suppose you edit the file to pick a third option, like this:

```
$ cat hello
hello
worldly ones
Yay!
```

Then the new `git diff` output is the following:

```
$ git diff
diff --cc hello
index e63164d,562080a..0000000
--- a/hello
+++ b/hello
```

```
@@@ -1,3 -1,3 +1,3 @@@
  hello
- worlds
 -world
++worldly ones
  Yay!
```

If you prefer, you can choose one or the other original version, like this:

```
$ cat hello
hello
world
Yay!
```

The `git diff` output would then be as follows:

```
$ git diff
diff --cc hello
index e63164d,562080a..0000000
--- a/hello
+++ b/hello
```

Wait! Something strange happened there. Where does it show that the world line was added to the base version? Where does it show that the worlds line was removed from the HEAD version? As you have resolved the conflict in favor of the MERGE_HEAD version, Git deliberately omits the diff because it thinks you probably don't care about that section anymore.

Running `git diff` on a conflicted file shows you only the sections that really have a conflict. In a large file with numerous changes scattered throughout, most of those changes don't have a conflict; either one side of the merge changed a particular section or the other side did. When you're trying to resolve a conflict, you rarely care about those sections, so `git diff` trims out uninteresting sections using a simple heuristic: if a section has changes on only one side, that section isn't shown.

This optimization has a slightly confusing side effect: once you resolve something that *used* to be a conflict by simply picking one side or the other, it stops showing up. That's because you modified the section so that it changes only one side or the other (i.e., the side that you didn't choose), so to Git it looks like a section that was never conflicted at all.

This is really more a side effect of the implementation than an intentional feature, but you might consider it useful anyway: `git diff` shows you only those sections of the file that are *still* conflicted, so you can use it to keep track of the conflicts you haven't fixed yet.

git log with conflicts

While you're in the process of resolving a conflict, you can use some special `git log` options to help you figure out exactly where the changes came from and why. Try this:

```
$ git log --merge --left-right -p

commit < 0d7dfb7f23cd5f4d6debedc27f7f85d5c72d5423 (HEAD -> main)
Author: Prem Kumar Ponuthorai  <ppremk@demo.com>
Date:   Thu Sep 2 23:10:35 2021 +0200

    All worlds

diff --git a/hello b/hello
index ce01362..e63164d 100644
--- a/hello
+++ b/hello
@@ -1 +1,3 @@
hello
+worlds
+Yay!

commit > 84e436cd3353739c67fd0fce36e18fc42b31d153 (alt)
Author: Prem Kumar Ponuthorai  <ppremk@demo.com>
Date:   Thu Sep 2 23:09:07 2021 +0200

    One world

diff --git a/hello b/hello
index ce01362..562080a 100644
--- a/hello
+++ b/hello
@@ -1 +1,3 @@
hello
+world
+Yay!
```

This command shows all the commits in both parts of the history that affect the conflicted files in your merge, along with the actual changes each commit introduced. If you wondered when, why, how, and by whom the line `worlds` came to be added to the file, you can see exactly which set of changes introduced it.

The options provided to `git log` are as follows:

- `--merge` shows only commits related to files that produced a conflict.
- `--left-right` displays < if the commit was from the "left" side of the merge ("our" version, the one you started with) or > if the commit was from the "right" side of the merge ("their" version, the one you're merging in).
- `-p` shows the commit message and the patch associated with each commit.

If your repository is more complicated and several files have conflicts, you could also provide the exact filename(s) you're interested in as a command-line option, like this:

```
$ git log --merge --left-right -p hello
```

Our examples here have been kept small for demonstration purposes. Of course, real-life situations are likely to be significantly larger and more complex. One technique to mitigate the pain of large merges with nasty, extended conflicts is to use several small commits with well-defined effects contained to individual concepts.

 Git handles small commits well, so there is no need to wait until the last minute to commit large, widespread changes. Smaller commits and more frequent merge cycles reduce the pain of dealing with complex conflict resolutions.

How Git Keeps Track of Conflicts

Git keeps track of all the information about a conflicted merge by keeping a record of the information in the following areas:

- *.git/MERGE_HEAD* contains the SHA1 of the commit you're merging in. You don't really have to use the SHA1 yourself; Git knows to look in that file whenever you talk about MERGE_HEAD.

- *.git/MERGE_MSG* contains the default merge message used when you `git commit` after resolving the conflicts.

- The Git index contains three copies of each conflicted file: the merge base, "our" version, and "their" version. These three copies are assigned the stage numbers 1, 2, and 3, respectively.

- The conflicted version (merge markers and all) is *not* stored in the index. Instead, it is stored in a file in your working directory. When you run `git diff` without any parameters, the comparison is always between what's in the index and what's in your working directory.

To see how the index entries are stored, you can use the `git ls-files` plumbing command as follows:

```
$ git ls-files -s
100644 ce013625030ba8dba906f756967f9e9ca394464a 1	hello
100644 e63164d9518b1e6caf28f455ac86c8246f78ab70 2	hello
100644 562080a4c6518e1bf67a9f58a32a67bff72d4f00 3	hello
```

The -s option to `git ls-files` shows *all* the files with *all* stages. If you want to see only the conflicted files, use the -u option instead.

In other words, the *hello* file is stored three times, and each has a different hash corresponding to the three different versions. You can look at a specific variant by using `git cat-file`:

```
$ git cat-file -p e63164d951
hello
worlds
Yay!
```

You can also use some special syntax with `git diff` to compare different versions of the file. For example, if you want to see what changed between the merge base and the version you're merging in, you can do this:

```
$ git diff :1:hello :3:hello
diff --git a/:1:hello b/:3:hello
index ce01362..562080a 100644
--- a/:1:hello
+++ b/:3:hello
@@ -1 +1,3 @@
 hello
+world
+Yay!
```

Using the stage numbers to name a version is different from `git diff --theirs`, which shows the differences between their version and the resulting, merged (or still conflicted) version in your working directory. The merged version is not yet in the index, so it doesn't even have a number.

 If you know for certain which version of a file to use to quickly resolve a conflict, the `git checkout` command accepts the `--ours` or `--theirs` option as shorthand for simply checking out (a file from) one side or the other of a conflicted merge. However, these two options can be used only during a conflict resolution.

Continuing with our example, because we fully edited and resolved the working copy version in favor of *their* version, there should be no difference now:

```
$ cat hello
hello
world
Yay!

$ git diff --theirs
* Unmerged path hello
```

All that remains is an *unmerged path reminder* to add it to the index.

Finishing Up a Conflict Resolution

Let's make one last change to the *hello* file before declaring it merged:

```
$ cat hello
hello
everyone
Yay!
```

Now that the file is fully merged and resolved, `git add` reduces the index to just a single copy of the *hello* file again:

```
$ git add hello
$ git ls-files -s
100644 ebc56522386c504db37db907882c9dbd0d05a0f0 0       hello
```

That lone 0 between the SHA1 and the pathname tells you that the stage number for a nonconflicted file is zero.

You must work through all the conflicted files as recorded in the index. You cannot commit as long as there is an unresolved conflict. Therefore, as you fix the conflicts in a file, run `git add` (or `git rm`, `git update-index`, etc.) on the file to clear its conflict status.

 Be careful not to `git add` files with lingering conflict markers (again running the `git diff --check` will yield results of residual merge markers). Although that will clear the conflict in the index and allow you to commit, your file won't be correct.

Finally, you can `git commit` the end result and use `git show` to see the merge commit:

```
$ cat .git/MERGE_MSG
Merge branch 'alt'

# Conflicts:
#       hello

$ git commit
[main d67ecec] Merge branch 'alt'

$ git show
commit d67ecec075281cebb32a9eedd76242b6e9ac76a8 (HEAD -> main)
Merge: 0d7dfb7 84e436c
Author: Prem Kumar Ponuthorai <ppremk@demo.com>
Date:   Sun Sep 5 21:49:53 2021 +0200

    Merge branch 'alt'

diff --cc hello
index e63164d,562080a..ebc5652
--- a/hello
+++ b/hello
@@@ -1,3 -1,3 +1,3 @@@
```

```
hello
- worlds
-world
++everyone
Yay!
```

You should notice two interesting things when you look at a merge commit:

- There is a new, second line in the header that says `Merge:`. Normally, there's no need to show the parent of a commit in `git log` or `git show`, since there is only one parent and it's typically the one that comes right after it in the log. But merge commits typically have two (and sometimes more) parents, and those parents are important to understanding the merge. Hence, `git log` and `git show` always print the SHA1 of each ancestor.

- The diff of a merge commit is not a normal diff. It is always in the combined diff or "conflicted merge" format. A successful merge in Git is simply the combination of other changes that already appeared in the history. Thus, showing the contents of a merge commit shows *only* the parts that are different from one of the merged branches, not the entire set of changes. It also tells you the name of the file in the combined diff format.

Aborting or Restarting a Merge

If you have botched a conflict resolution and want to return to the original conflict state before trying to resolve it again, use the following:

```
$ git checkout -m
```

This will restore the index with the versions of the file that are marked as conflicted (the versions of the file you see when you run `git ls-files -u`).

If you start a merge operation but then decide for some reason that you don't want to complete it, Git provides an easy way to abort the operation. Prior to executing the final `git commit` on the merge commit, use the following:

```
$ git merge --abort
```

This command restores both your working directory and the index to the state immediately prior to the `git merge` command.

If you want to abort or discard the merge after it has finished (i.e., after it has introduced a new merge commit), use the following command:

```
$ git reset --hard ORIG_HEAD
```

Prior to beginning the merge operation, Git saves your original branch `HEAD` in the `ORIG_HEAD` ref for just this purpose.

You should be very careful here, though. If you did not start the merge with a clean working directory and index, you could get into trouble and lose any uncommitted changes you have in your directory.

You can initiate a `git merge` request with a dirty working directory, but if you execute `git reset --hard`, your dirty state prior to the merge is not fully restored. Instead, the reset loses your dirty state in the working directory area. In other words, you requested a --hard reset to the HEAD state! (See "Using git reset" on page 194.)

Merge Strategies

So far, our examples have been easy to handle because there are only two branches. It might seem like Git's extra complexity of directed acyclic graph (DAG)–shaped history and long, hard-to-remember commit IDs isn't really worth it. And maybe it isn't for such a simple case. So let's look at something a little more complicated.

Imagine that instead of just one person working on your repository, there are three. To keep things simple, suppose that each developer—Alice, Bob, and Cal—is able to contribute changes as commits on three separate eponymous branches within a shared repository.

Because the developers are all contributing to separate branches, let's leave it up to one person, Alice, to manage the integration of the various contributions. In the meantime, each developer is allowed to leverage the development of the others by directly incorporating or merging a coworker's branch, as needed.

Eventually, the developers develop a repository with a commit history, as shown in Figure 6-3.

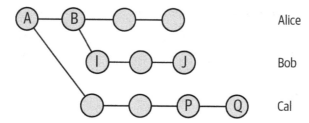

Figure 6-3. Potential merge setup

Imagine that Cal started the project and Alice joined in. Alice worked on it for a while, then Bob joined in. In the meantime, Cal has been working away on his own version.

Eventually, Alice merged in Bob's changes, and Bob kept on working without merging Alice's changes back into his tree. There are now three different branch histories (Figure 6-4).

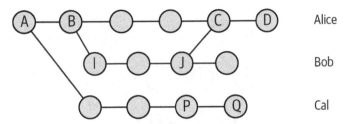

Figure 6-4. After Alice merges in Bob

Let's imagine that Bob wants to get Cal's latest changes. The diagram is looking pretty complicated now, but this part is still relatively easy. Trace up the tree from Bob, through Alice, until you reach the point where she first diverged from Cal. That's A, the merge base between Bob and Cal. To merge from Cal, Bob needs to take the set of changes between the merge base, A, and Cal's latest, Q, and three-way-merge them into his own tree, yielding commit K. The result is the history shown in Figure 6-5.

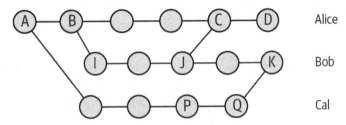

Figure 6-5. After Bob merges in Cal

 You can always find the merge base between two or more branches by using git merge-base. It is possible for there to be more than one equally valid merge base for a set of branches.

So far, so good.

Alice now decides that she, too, wants to get Cal's latest changes, but she doesn't realize Bob has already merged Cal's tree into his. So she just merges Cal's tree into hers. That's another easy operation because it's obvious where she diverged from Cal. The resulting history is shown in Figure 6-6.

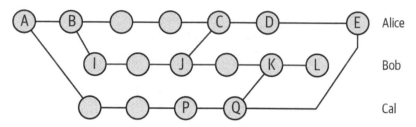

Figure 6-6. After Alice merges in Cal

Next, Alice realizes that Bob has done some more work, L, and wants to merge from him again. What's the merge base (between L and E) this time?

Unfortunately, the answer is ambiguous. If you trace all the way back up the tree, you might think the original revision from Cal is a good choice. But that doesn't really make sense: both Alice and Bob now have Cal's *newest* revision. If you ask for the differences from Cal's original revision to Bob's latest version, it will also include Cal's newer changes, which Alice already has, and which is likely to result in a merge conflict.

What if you use Cal's latest revision as the base? That's better but still not quite right: if you take the diff from Cal's latest to Bob's latest, you get *all* of Bob's changes. But Alice already has *some* of Bob's changes, so you'll probably get a merge conflict there too.

And what if you use the version that Alice last merged from Bob, version J? Creating a diff from there to Bob's latest will include only the newest changes from Bob, which is what you want. But it will also include the changes from Cal, which Alice already has!

What to do?

This kind of situation is called a *criss-cross merge* because changes have been merged back and forth between branches. If changes moved in only one direction (e.g., from Cal to Alice to Bob but never from Bob to Alice or from Alice to Cal), then merging would be simple. Unfortunately, life isn't always that easy.

The Git developers originally wrote a straightforward mechanism to join two branches with a merge commit, but scenarios like the one just described soon led them to realize that a more clever approach was needed. Hence, the developers generalized, parameterized, and introduced alternate, configurable merge strategies to handle different scenarios.

Let's look at the various strategies and see how to apply each one.

Degenerate Merges

There are two common degenerate scenarios that lead to merges, and they are called *already up-to-date* and *fast-forward*. Because neither of these scenarios actually introduces a new merge commit after performing the `git merge`,[1] some might consider them not to be true merge strategies.

Already up-to-date

When all the commits from the other branch (its HEAD) are already present in your target branch, even if it has advanced on its own, the target branch is said to be already up-to-date. As a result, no new commits are added to your branch.

For example, if you perform a merge and immediately follow it with the exact same merge request, then you will be told that your branch is already up-to-date:

```
# Show that alt is already merged into main
$ git show-branch
! [alt] One world
 * [main] Merge branch 'alt'
--
 - [main] Merge branch 'alt'
+* [alt] One world

# Try to merge alt into main again
$ git merge alt
Already up to date.
```

Figures 6-7, 6-8, and 6-9 illustrate what we have just explained.

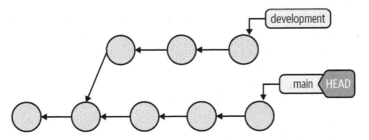

Figure 6-7. Merge between two branches

---

1 Yes, you can force Git to create one anyway by using the `--no-ff` option in the fast-forward case. However, you should fully understand why you want to do so.

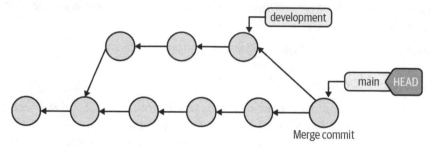

Figure 6-8. Merge commit

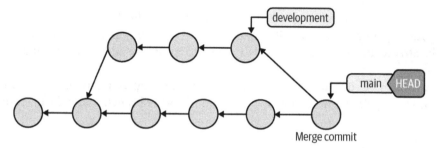

Figure 6-9. Merge commit again (already up-to-date)

Fast-forward

A fast-forward merge happens when your HEAD branch is already fully present and represented in the other branch. This is the inverse of the already up-to-date case.

Because your HEAD is already present in the other branch (likely due to a common ancestor), Git simply tacks onto your HEAD the new commits from the other branch. Git then moves your branch HEAD to point to the final, new commit. Naturally, the index and your working directory are also adjusted accordingly to reflect the new, final commit state.

The fast-forward case is particularly common on tracking branches because they simply fetch and record the remote commits from other repositories. Your local tracking branch HEADs will always be fully present and represented because that is where the branch HEAD was after the *previous* fetch operation. See Chapter 11 for more details.

Figures 6-10 and 6-11 visualize the concept we just discussed.

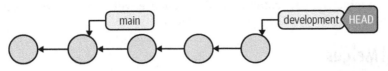

Figure 6-10. Before fast-forward merge

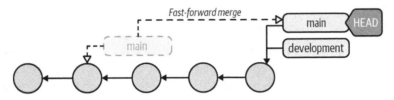

Figure 6-11. After fast-forward merge

It is important for Git to handle these cases without introducing actual commits. Imagine what would happen in the fast-forward case if Git created a commit. Merging branch A into B would first produce Figure 6-12. Then merging B into A would produce Figure 6-13, and merging back again would yield Figure 6-14.

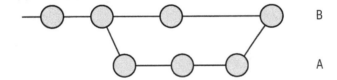

Figure 6-12. First nonconverging merge

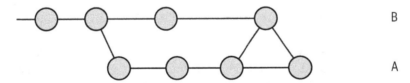

Figure 6-13. Second nonconverging merge

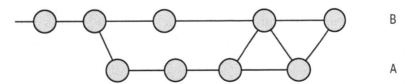

Figure 6-14. Third nonconverging merge

Each new merge is a new commit, so the sequence will never converge on a steady state and reveal that the two branches are identical.

Normal Merges

The following merge strategies produce a final commit, known as the *merge commit*, which is added to your current branch and represents the combined state of the merge:

Resolve
> The resolve strategy operates on only two branches, locating the common ancestor as the merge basis and performing a direct three-way merge by applying the changes from the merge base to the tip of the other branch HEAD onto the current branch.

Recursive
> The recursive strategy is similar to the resolve strategy in that it can join only two branches at once. However, it is designed to handle the scenario where there is more than one merge base between the two branches. In this case, Git forms a temporary merge of all the common merge bases and then uses *that* as the base from which to derive the resulting merge of the two given branches via a normal three-way merge algorithm.
>
> The temporary merge basis is thrown away, and the final merge state is committed on your target branch.

Octopus
> The octopus strategy is specifically designed to merge more than two branches simultaneously. Conceptually, it is fairly simple; internally, it calls the recursive merge strategy multiple times, once for each branch you are merging.
>
> However, this strategy cannot handle a merge that requires any form of conflict resolution that would necessitate user interaction. In such a case, you are forced to do a series of normal merges, resolving the conflicts one step at a time.

Merge-ort
> The merge-ort strategy implements the recursive strategy, but internally it is a complete rewrite from the ground up. It boasts a significant performance improvement and resolves some long-standing issues regarding imprecise merge outcomes.
>
> It does so by caching and reusing internal computational commons when implementing a merge. The merge-ort strategy also allows developers who are working in repositories with partial clones to conclude more merge operations without

having to download the full tree from the upstream repository. We will be discussing partial clones in Chapter 17.

Recursive merges

A simple criss-cross merge example is shown in Figure 6-15.

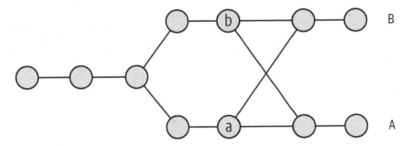

Figure 6-15. Simple criss-cross merge

The nodes a and b are both merge bases for a merge between A and B. Either one could be used as the merge base and yield reasonable results. In this case, the recursive strategy would merge a and b into a temporary merge base, using that as the merge base for A and B.

Because a and b could have the same problem, merging them could require another merge of still older commits. That is why this algorithm is called recursive.

Octopus merges

The main reasons why Git supports merging multiple branches all at once are for generality and design elegance. In Git, a commit can have no parents (the initial commit), one parent (a normal commit), or more than one parent (a merge commit). Once you have more than one parent, there is no particular reason to limit that number to only two, so Git data structures support multiple parents.[2] The octopus merge strategy is a natural consequence of the general design decision to allow a flexible list of commit parents.

Octopus merges look nice in diagrams, so Git users tend to use them as often as possible. You can just imagine the rush of endorphins a developer gets when merging six branches of a program into one. Besides looking pretty, octopus merges don't actually do anything extra. You could just as easily make multiple merge commits, one per branch, and accomplish exactly the same thing.

---

2 That's the "Zero, One, or Infinity Principle" at work.

The largest known octopus merge to date is between 66 parent branches, which resulted in a single merge commit in the Linux kernel code base (*https://oreil.ly/m4Kui*).

Specialty Merges

There are two special merge strategies that you should be aware of because they can sometimes help you solve strange problems. Feel free to skip this section if you don't have a strange problem. The two special strategies are *ours* and *subtree*.

These merge strategies each produce a final commit, added to your current branch, that represents the combined state of the merge:

Ours

> The ours strategy merges in any number of other branches, but it actually discards changes from those branches and uses only the files from the current branch. The result of an ours merge is identical to the current HEAD, but any other named branches are also recorded as commit parents. This is useful if you know you already have all the changes from the other branches but want to combine the two histories anyway. That is, it lets you record that you have somehow performed the merge, perhaps directly by hand, and that future Git operations shouldn't try to merge the histories again. Git can treat this as a real merge no matter how it came to be.

Subtree

> The subtree strategy merges in another branch, but everything in that branch is merged into a particular subtree of the current tree. You don't specify which subtree; Git determines that automatically.

Ours and subtree merges

You can use these two merge strategies together. For example, once upon a time, the `gitweb` program (which is now part of Git) was developed outside the main `git.git` repository. But at revision `0a8f4f`, its entire history was merged into `git.git` under the `gitweb` subtree. If you wanted to do something similar, you could proceed as follows:

1. Copy the current files from the `gitweb.git` project into the *gitweb* subdirectory of your project.

2. Commit them as usual.

3. Pull from the `gitweb.git` project using the ours strategy:

   ```
   $ git pull -s ours gitweb.git main
   ```

You use `ours` here because you know that you already have the latest version of the files and you have already put them exactly where you want them (which is not where the normal *recursive* strategy would have put them).

4. In the future, you can continue to pull the latest changes from the `gitweb.git` project using the `subtree` strategy:

```
$ git pull -s subtree gitweb.git main
```

Because the files already exist in your repository, Git knows automatically which subtree you put them in and performs the updates without any conflicts.

Applying Merge Strategies

So how does Git know or determine which strategy to use? Or, if you don't like Git's choice, how do you specify a different one?

Git tries to keep the algorithms it uses as simple and inexpensive as possible, so it first tries using the already up-to-date and fast-forward strategies to eliminate trivial scenarios, if possible.

If you specify more than one other branch to be merged into your current branch, Git has no choice but to try the octopus strategy because that is the only one capable of joining more than two branches in a single merge.

Failing those special cases, Git must use a default strategy that works reliably in all other scenarios. Originally, resolve was the default merge strategy used by Git.

In criss-cross merge situations such as those described previously, where there is more than one possible merge base, the resolve strategy works like this: pick one of the possible merge bases (either the last merge from Bob's branch or the last merge from Cal's branch) and hope for the best. This is actually not as bad as it sounds. It often turns out that Alice, Bob, and Cal have all been working on different parts of the code. In that case, Git detects that it's remerging some changes that are already in place and just skips duplicate changes, avoiding the conflict. Or, if there are slight changes that do cause a conflict, at least the conflicts should be fairly easy for a developer to handle.

Because resolve is no longer Git's default, if Alice wanted to use it, she would make an explicit request by explicitly specifying which merge strategy to use via the command:

```
$ git merge -s resolve Bob
```

In 2005, Fredrik Kuivinen contributed the recursive merge strategy. It is more general than resolve and has been shown to result in fewer conflicts, without fault, on the Linux kernel. It also handles merges with renames quite well.

In the previous example, where Alice wants to merge all of Bob's work, the recursive strategy would work like this:

1. Start with the most recent revision from Cal that *both* Alice and Bob have. In this case, that's Cal's most recent revision, Q, which has been merged into both Bob's and Alice's branches.

2. Calculate the diff between that revision and the most recent revision that Alice merged from Bob, and patch that in.

3. Calculate the diff between that combined version and Bob's latest version, and patch that in.

This method is called *recursive* because there may be extra iterations, depending on how many levels of criss-crossing and merge bases Git encounters. And it works. Not only does the recursive method make intuitive sense, but it has also been proven to result in fewer conflicts in real-life situations than the simpler resolve strategy. That's why recursive is currently the default strategy for git merge.

Of course, no matter which strategy Alice chooses to use, the final history looks the same (Figure 6-16).

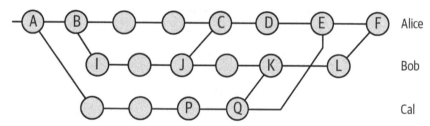

Figure 6-16. Final criss-cross merge history

With recent internal improvements introduced via the new merge-ort strategy, merge-ort is the default strategy in the latest version of Git.

Merge Drivers

Each of the merge strategies described in this chapter uses an underlying merge driver to resolve and merge each individual file. A *merge driver* accepts the names of three temporary files that represent the common ancestor, the target branch version, and the other branch version of a file. The driver modifies the target branch version to have the merged result.

The text merge driver leaves the usual three-way merge markers (<<<<<<<<, ========, and >>>>>>>).

The `binary` merge driver keeps the target branch version of the file and leaves the file marked as a conflict in the index. Effectively, that forces you to handle binary files by hand.

The final built-in merge driver, `union`, simply leaves all the lines from both versions in the merged file.

Through Git's attribute mechanism, Git can tie specific files or file patterns to specific merge drivers. Most text files are handled by the `text` driver and most binary files by the `binary` driver. Yet, for special needs that warrant an application-specific merge operation, you can create and specify your own custom merge driver and tie it to your specific files.

 If you think you need custom merge drivers, you may want to investigate custom diff drivers as well!

How Git Thinks About Merges

At first, Git's automatic merging support seems nothing short of magical, especially compared to the more complicated and error-prone merging steps needed in other version control systems.

Let's take a look at what's going on behind the scenes to make it all possible.

Merges and Git's Object Model

In most version control systems, each commit has only one parent. On such a system, when you merge `some_branch` into `my_branch`, you create a new commit on `my_branch` with the changes from `some_branch`. Conversely, if you merge `my_branch` into `some_branch`, this creates a new commit on `some_branch` containing the changes from `my_branch`. Merging branch A into branch B and merging branch B into branch A are two different operations.

However, the Git designers noticed that each of these two operations results in the same set of files when you're done. The natural way to express either operation is simply to say, "Merge all the changes from `some_branch` and `another_branch` into a single branch."

In Git, the merge yields a new tree object with the merged files, but it also introduces a new commit object on only the target branch. After these commands:

```
$ git checkout my_branch
$ git merge some_branch
```

the object model looks like Figure 6-17.

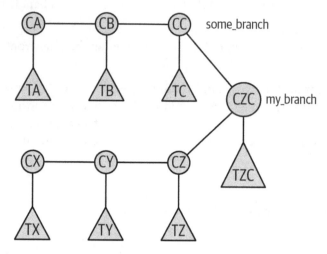

Figure 6-17. Object model after a merge

In Figure 6-17, each Cx is a commit object, and each Tx represents the corresponding tree object. Notice how there is one common merged commit (CZC) that has both CC and CZ as commit parents, but it has only one resulting set of files represented in the TZC tree. The merged tree object symmetrically represents both source branches equally. But because my_branch was the checked-out branch into which the merge happened, only my_branch has been updated to show the new commit on it; some_branch remains where it was.

This is not just a matter of semantics. It reflects Git's underlying philosophy that all branches are created equal.[3]

Squash Merges

Suppose some_branch had contained not just one new commit but 5 or 10 or even hundreds of commits. In most systems, merging some_branch into my_branch would involve producing a single diff, applying it as a single patch onto my_branch, and creating one new element in the history. This is called a *squash commit* because it "squashes" all the individual commits into one big change. As far as the history of my_branch is concerned, the history of some_branch would be lost.

In Git, the two branches are treated as equal, so it's improper to squash one side or the other. Instead, the entire history of commits on both sides is retained. As users,

---

3 And, by extension, so are all complete repository clones.

you can see from Figure 6-17 that you pay for this complexity. If Git had made a squash commit, you wouldn't have to see (or think about) a diagram that diverges and then rejoins again. The history of my_branch could have been just a straight line.

 Git can make squash commits if desired. Just give the --squash option to git merge or git pull. Beware, however! Squashing commits will upset Git's history, and that will complicate future merges because the squashed comments alter the history of commits (see Chapter 9).

The added complexity might appear unfortunate, but it is actually quite worthwhile. For example, this feature means that the git blame and git bisect commands, discussed in Chapter 9, are much more powerful than equivalents in other systems. And as you saw with the recursive merge strategy, Git is able to automate very complicated merges as a result of this added complexity and the resulting detailed history.

 Although the merge operation itself treats both parents as equal, you can choose to treat the first parent as special when you go back through the history later. Some commands (e.g., git log and gitk) support the --first-parent option, which follows only the first parent of every merge. The resulting history looks much the same as if you had used --squash on all your merges.

Why Not Just Merge Each Change One by One?

You might be wondering if it would be possible to have it both ways: a simple, linear history with every individual commit represented. Git could just take all the commits from some_branch and apply them, one by one, onto my_branch. But that wouldn't be the same thing at all.

An important observation about Git's commit histories is that each revision in the history is *real*. (You can read more about treating alternate histories as equal realities in Chapter 12.)

If you apply a *sequence* of someone else's patches on top of your version, you will create a series of entirely new versions with the union of their changes and yours. Presumably, you will test the final version as you always would. But what about all those new, intermediate versions? In reality, those versions never existed: nobody actually produced those commits, so nobody can say for sure whether they ever worked.

Git keeps a detailed history so that you can later revisit what your files were like at a particular moment in the past. If some of your merged commits reflect file versions that never really existed, then you've lost the reason for having a detailed history in the first place!

This is why Git merges don't work that way. If you were to ask, "What was it like five minutes before I did the merge?" the answer would be ambiguous. Instead, you must ask about either `my_branch` or `some_branch` specifically, because both were different five minutes ago, and Git can give the true answer for each one.

Even though you almost always want the standard history merging behavior, Git can also apply a sequence of patches (see Chapter 13). This process is called *rebasing* and is discussed in Chapter 9. The implications of changing commit histories are discussed in "Changing Public History" on page 295.

Summary

In this chapter, we began to discuss merges at a very high level. We kept it lightweight at first by explaining how a merge between two branches takes place, using guided examples of code snippets before introducing merge conflicts. Resolving a merge conflict can be straightforward and does not require deep proficiency in Git. All it requires on your part is a good understanding of how to locate conflicted files and inspect the conflicts in them—specifically, how you read and understand the conflict resolution markers and supplement the use of the `git diff` command (discussed in the next chapter) to further investigate the conflicting files before providing a resolution. These skills are the bare minimum you need to be able to successfully resolve any conflict in your merge operations. In later parts of the chapter, we discussed the inner mechanics of how Git keeps track of conflicts and various merge strategies that Git can apply when combining one or more branches in your repository. That discussion may have felt a little heavy, but we encourage you to revisit it after you've been exposed to a few merging and conflict resolving use cases in your projects.

## CHAPTER 7

Diffs

Before we cover the prowess of Git's `diff` command, it will be beneficial to quickly cover the concept of the Unix and Linux `diff` utilities since the command `git diff` can compare files much akin to its Unix and Linux counterparts. A *diff* is a compact summary of the differences (hence the name "diff") between two items. For example, given two files, the Unix and Linux `diff` commands compare the files line by line and summarize the deviations in a diff, as shown in the following example snippet. More specifically, the deviations list the required changes to convert one file into the other. In the example, `initial` is one version of some prose and `rewrite` is a subsequent revision. The `-u` option produces a unified diff, a standardized format used widely to share modifications:

```
$ cat initial
Now is the time
For all good men
To come to the aid
Of their country.

$ cat rewrite
Today is the time
For all good men
And women
To come to the aid
Of their country.

$ diff -u initial rewrite
--- initial     1867-01-02 11:22:33.000000000 -0500
+++ rewrite     2000-01-02 11:23:45.000000000 -0500
@@ -1,4 +1,5 @@
-Now is the time
+Today is the time
 For all good men
+And women
 To come to the aid
 Of their country.
```

Let's look at the diff in detail. In the header, the original file is denoted by - - - and the new file by + + +. The @@ line provides line number context for both file versions. A line prefixed with a minus sign (-) must be removed from the original file to produce the new file. Conversely, a line with a leading plus sign (+) must be added to the original file to produce the new file. A line that begins with a space is the same in both files and is provided by the -u option as context.

By itself, a diff offers no reason or rationale for a change, nor does it justify the initial or final state. However, a diff offers more than just a digest of how files differ. It provides a formal description of how to transform one file to the other. (You'll find such instructions useful when applying or reverting changes.) In addition, diff can be extended to show differences among multiple files and entire directory hierarchies.

The Unix and Linux diff commands can compute the differences between all pairs of files found in two directory hierarchies. The command diff -r traverses each hierarchy in tandem, twins files by pathname (say, *original/src/main.c* and *new/src/main.c*), and summarizes the differences between each pair. Using diff -r -u produces a set of unified diffs comparing two hierarchies.

Git has its own diff utility and can likewise produce a digest of differences. Moreover, like Unix's diff -r, Git can traverse two tree objects and generate a representation of the variances. But git diff also has its own nuances and powerful features tailored to the particular needs of Git users. Git uses the Myers diff algorithm (*https://oreil.ly/6rq3x*) developed by Eugene W. Myers as its comparison algorithm by default.

In this chapter, we'll cover some of the basics of git diff and some of its special capabilities. You will learn how to use Git to show editorial changes in your working directory as well as arbitrary changes between any two commits within your project history. You will see how Git's diff can help you make well-structured commits during your normal development process, and you will learn how to produce Git patches, which are described in detail in Chapter 13.

 Technically, a tree object represents only one directory level in the repository. It contains information about the directory's immediate files and immediate subdirectories, but it does not catalog the complete contents of all subdirectories. However, because a tree object references the tree objects for each subdirectory, the tree object at the root of the project effectively represents the entire project at a moment in time. Hence, we can paraphrase and say git diff traverses "two" trees.

Forms of the git diff Command

If you pick two different root-level tree objects for comparison, `git diff` yields all the deviations between the two project states. That's powerful. You could use such a diff to convert wholesale from one project state to another. For example, if you and a coworker are developing code for the same project, a root-level diff could effectively sync the repositories at any time.

There are three basic sources for tree or treelike objects to use with `git diff`:

- Any tree object anywhere within the entire commit graph
- Your working directory, also commonly referred to as the *working tree* when discussing Git diffs
- The index or staging directory

Typically, the trees compared in a `git diff` command are named via commits, branch names, or tags, but any commit name discussed in "Identifying Commits" on page 81 suffices. Also, both the file and directory hierarchies of your working directory, as well as the complete hierarchy of files staged in the index, can be treated as trees.

The `git diff` command along with some options can perform fundamental comparisons. Following are some common examples:

`git diff`
> `git diff` shows the difference between your working directory and the index. It exposes what is dirty in your working directory and is thus a candidate to stage for your next commit. This command does not reveal differences between what's in your index and what's permanently stored in the repository (not to mention remote repositories you might be working with, which we will cover in Chapter 11).

`git diff --cached` *commit*
> This command shows the differences between the staged changes in the index and the given *commit*. A common commit for the comparison—and the default if no commit is specified—is HEAD. With HEAD, this command shows you how your next commit will alter the current branch. The command `git diff --staged` is a synonym for `git diff --cached`. This command *does* reveal differences between what's in your index and what's permanently stored in the repository.

git diff *commit*

    This form summarizes the differences between your working directory and the given *commit*. Common variants of this command name HEAD or a particular branch name as the *commit*.

git diff *commit1 commit2*

    If you specify two arbitrary commits, this command displays the differences between the two. The command ignores the index and working directory, and it is the workhorse for arbitrary comparisons between two trees that are already in your repository's Git object store.

The number of parameters on the command line determines what fundamental form is used and what is compared. You can compare any two commits or trees. What's being compared need not have a direct or even an indirect parent–child relationship. If you don't supply a tree object or two, then git diff compares implied sources, such as your index or working directory.

If you need to compare raw content between blob objects in your repository's Git object store, you can do so by executing the command git diff *blob1 blob2*.

Let's examine how these different forms apply to Git's object model. The example in Figure 7-1 shows a project directory with two files. The file *file1* has been modified in the working directory, changing its content from "foo" to "quux." That change has been staged in the index using git add file1, but it is not yet committed.

Versions of the file *file1* from the working directory, the index, and the HEAD have been identified. Even though the version of *file1* that is in the index, db71363, is actually stored as a blob object in the object store, it is indirectly referenced through the virtual tree object that is the index. Similarly, the HEAD version of the file, a23bf, is also indirectly referenced through several steps.

This example nominally demonstrates the changes within *file1*. The solid arrows in the figure point to the tree or virtual tree objects to remind you that the comparison is actually based on complete trees and not just on individual files. For motivated readers, we cover how to reproduce this scenario with code examples in "Simple git diff Example" on page 163.

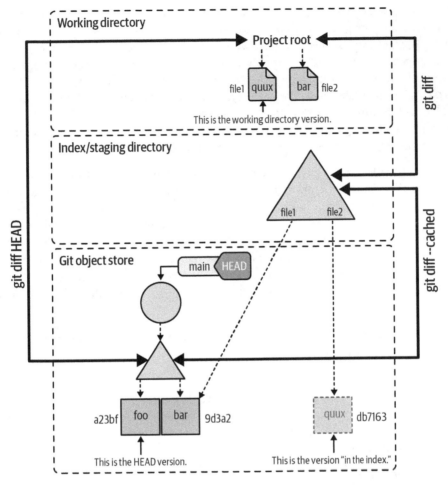

Figure 7-1. Various file versions that can be compared

From Figure 7-1, you can see how using `git diff` without arguments is a good technique for verifying the readiness of your next commit. As long as that command emits output, you have edits or changes in your working directory that are not yet staged. Using a simple `git status` helps you check pending changes on each file. If you are satisfied with your work, use `git add` to stage the file. Once you stage a changed file, the next `git diff` no longer yields diff output for that file. In this way, you can step progressively through each dirty file in your working directory until the differences disappear, meaning that all files and their changes are staged in your index. Don't forget to check for new or deleted files too.

At any time during the staging process, the command `git diff --cached` shows the complementary changes, or those changes that are already staged in the index that will be present in your next commit. When you're finished, `git commit` captures all the changes in your index into a new commit. You are not required to stage all the changes from your working directory for a single commit. In fact, if you find you have conceptually different changes in your working directory that should be made in different commits, you can stage one set at a time, leaving the other edits in your working directory. A commit captures only your staged changes. Repeat the process, staging the next set of files appropriate for a subsequent commit.

The astute reader might have noticed that, although we discussed four fundamental forms of the `git diff` command, only three are highlighted with solid arrows in Figure 7-1. So, what is the fourth? There is only one tree object represented by your working directory, and there is only one tree object represented by the index. In the example, there is one commit in the object store along with its tree. However, the object store is likely to have many commits named by different branches and tags, all of which have trees that can be compared with `git diff`. Thus the fourth form of `git diff` simply compares any two arbitrary commits (trees) already stored within the object store.

In addition to the basic forms of `git diff`, there are myriad options as well. Here are a few of the more useful ones:

`-M`

The `-M` option detects renames and generates a simplified output that records the file rename rather than the complete removal and subsequent addition of the source file. If the rename is not a pure rename but also has some additional content changes, Git calls those out.

`-w` *and* `--ignore-all-space`

Both `-w` and `--ignore-all-space` compare lines without considering changes in whitespace as significant.

`--stat`

The `--stat` option adds statistics about the difference between any two tree states. It reports in a compact syntax how many lines changed, how many were added, and how many were elided.

`--color`

The `--color` option colorizes the output; a unique color represents each of the different types of changes present in the diff.

`--word-diff=[=mode]`

The `--word-diff=[=mode]` option delineates changed words. If you choose the mode to be *color*, the diff output will show changed words using colors for removal and addition. The default mode is *plain*, and it shows words as [-*removed words*-] and {+ *added words* +} in the diff output. Additional modes are described in detail in the `git diff` manual pages.

`--name-only`
> The `--name-only` option is useful for quickly reviewing only names of files that have changed.

`--name-status`
> The `--name-status` option gives a quick summary of the names and the statuses of files that have changed. The status is displayed as `M` for modified, `A` for added, `C` for copied, and `D` for deleted. These and additional statuses are described in detail in the `git diff` manual pages.

`--output=`*file*
> The `--output=`*file* option redirects the output to a specified file instead of to stdout.

Finally, `git diff` may be limited to show diffs for a specific set of files or directories. This is achieved using the *path...* option. A typical use case for three-dot diffs (...) is when you are looking at changes made on a feature branch and you need to compare that branch with the `main` branch, from which it was created, but the `main` branch has already progressed with new changes introduced to it. We will elaborate further on path limiting in "git diff with Path Limiting" on page 171.

> The `-a` option for `git diff` does nothing even remotely like the `-a` option for `git commit`. To get both staged and unstaged changes, use `git diff HEAD`.

Simple git diff Example

Here we construct the scenario presented in Figure 7-1, run through the scenario, and watch the various forms of `git diff` in action. First, let's set up a simple repository with two files in it:

```
$ mkdir /tmp/diff_example
$ cd /tmp/diff_example

$ git init -b main
Initialized empty Git repository in /tmp/diff_example/.git/

$ echo "foo" > file1
$ echo "bar" > file2

$ git add file1 file2

$ git commit -m "Add file1 and file2"
```

```
[main (root-commit) 7915072] Add file1 and file2
 2 files changed, 2 insertions(+)
 create mode 100644 file1
 create mode 100644 file2
```

Next, let's edit *file1* by replacing *foo* with *quux*:

```
$ echo "quux" > file1
```

The *file1* file has been modified in the working directory but has not been staged.
This state is not the situation depicted in Figure 7-1, but you can still make a
comparison. You should expect output if you compare the working directory with the
index version or the existing HEAD version. However, there should be no difference
between the index and the HEAD because nothing has been staged (in other words, the
current HEAD tree is still staged):

```
# diff between working directory versus index
$ git diff
diff --git a/file1 b/file1
index 257cc56..d90bda0 100644
--- a/file1
+++ b/file1
@@ -1 +1 @@
-foo
+quux

# diff between working directory versus HEAD
$ git diff HEAD
diff --git a/file1 b/file1
index 257cc56..d90bda0 100644
--- a/file1
+++ b/file1
@@ -1 +1 @@
-foo
+quux

# diff between the index versus HEAD,
# produces no output since it is still identical
$ git diff --cached
$
```

Applying the maxim just given, `git diff` produced output and so *file1* has some
dirty changes that could be staged. Let's do this now:

```
$ git add file1

$ git status
On branch main
Changes to be committed:
    (use "git restore --staged <file>..." to unstage)
        modified:   file1
```

Here you have exactly duplicated the situation depicted in Figure 7-1. Because *file1*
is now staged, the working directory and the index are synchronized and should not

show any differences. However, there are now differences between the HEAD version and both the working directory and the staged version in the index:

```
# diff between working directory versus index
$ git diff

# diff between working directory versus HEAD
$ git diff HEAD
diff --git a/file1 b/file1
index 257cc56..d90bda0 100644
--- a/file1
+++ b/file1
@@ -1 +1 @@
-foo
+quux

# diff between the index versus HEAD
$ git diff --cached
diff --git a/file1 b/file1
index 257cc56..d90bda0 100644
--- a/file1
+++ b/file1
@@ -1 +1 @@
-foo
+quux
```

If you were to run git commit now, the new commit would capture the staged changes shown by the last command, git diff --cached (which, as mentioned before, has the new synonym git diff --staged).

Now let's add a new scenario because simple diffs are boring. Let's see what would happen if you edited *file1* before making a commit:

```
$ echo "baz" > file1

# diff between working directory versus index
$ git diff
diff --git a/file1 b/file1
index d90bda0..7601807 100644
--- a/file1
+++ b/file1
@@ -1 +1 @@
-quux
+baz

# diff between working directory versus HEAD
$ git diff HEAD
diff --git a/file1 b/file1
index 257cc56..7601807 100644
--- a/file1
+++ b/file1
@@ -1 +1 @@
-foo
+baz

# diff between the index versus HEAD
$ git diff --cached
diff --git a/file1 b/file1
index 257cc56..d90bda0 100644
--- a/file1
```

```
+++ b/file1
@@ -1 +1 @@
-foo
+quux
```

All three diff operations show some form of difference now! But which version will be committed? Remember, `git commit` captures the state present in the index. And what's in the index? It's the content revealed by the `git diff --cached` or `git diff --staged` command, or the version of *file1* that contains the word *quux*! Let's proceed to commit *file1*:

```
$ git commit -m "quux for the win"
[main 27f006d] quux for the win
 1 file changed, 1 insertion(+), 1 deletion(-)
```

Now that the object store has two commits in it, let's try the general form of the `git diff` command:

```
# diff between previous HEAD version versus current HEAD version
$ git diff HEAD^ HEAD
diff --git a/file1 b/file1
index 257cc56..d90bda0 100644
--- a/file1
+++ b/file1
@@ -1 +1 @@
-foo
+quux
```

This diff confirms that the previous commit changed *file1* by replacing *foo* with *quux*.

So is everything synchronized now? No. The working directory copy of *file1* contains *baz*:

```
$ git diff
diff --git a/file1 b/file1
index d90bda0..7601807 100644
--- a/file1
+++ b/file1
@@ -1 +1 @@
-quux
+baz
```

Understanding the git diff Output

While we explored the various forms of `git diff` in action, one thing we did not talk about yet is how to make sense of the output produced by the command. Let's continue from the earlier example to create and edit a new file, *file3*:

```
# add new file3 with five lines
$ echo -e "Line1 \nLine2 \nLine3 \nLine4 \nLine5" >> file3
$ cat file3
Line1
Line2
Line3
Line4
```

```
Line5

# add file3 to the index
$ git add file3
...

# edit file3, remove Line3 and add new Line6 and Line7
...

$ cat file3
Line1
Line2
Line4
Line5
Line6
Line7
```

Figure 7-2 shows the git diff output.

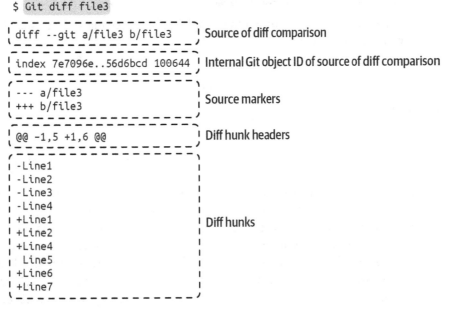

Figure 7-2. git diff output

Following is an explanation of each section of the output:

Source of diff comparison
This block displays the input files the diff is comparing. It is similar to the unified diff format of the Unix diff tool.

Internal Git object ID of source of diff comparison
This block displays the Git object IDs that are being compared. If you run the command git ls-files -s, you will notice that the 7e7096e is the abbreviated

SHA1 ID of *file3*'s content in the index. The `56d6bcd` is the abbreviated SHA1 ID of the version of *file3*'s content in your working directory. If you run the command `git hash-object file3`, the output will produce the full SHA1 ID, which you can verify.

Source markers

This block denotes that the original version of the file is marked with - - - and the modified version of the file is marked with + + +. This will be used to mark the changes that will be displayed in the diff hunk blocks. Keep in mind that diff output displays sections of a file that have changes, so these markers are useful to identify those changes.

Diff hunk headers

Hunk header blocks are enclosed within `@@` characters. They follow this format:

```
@@ oldfile-change-range  newfile-change-range @@
```

The change range follows a format that displays the source marker and start line, followed by lines of changes:

```
[-/+]<start-line>,<lines of change>
```

In our example block, `-1,5 +1,6` is interpreted as:

```
(-)oldfile<starting from line 1>,<5 lines of change>
(+)newfile<starting from line 1>,<6 lines of change>
```

Diff hunks

Comparison diffs for sections of a file with changes are displayed in this block. Since our example file is very small, we have only one diff hunk (the diff hunk includes the hunk header as well). Note that these diff hunks are dynamically generated as needed and are not stored in the repository. Lines of changes that are in the old and new files are displayed with a preceding source marker, and lines without any changes are displayed with a preceding space. In our example, you can see that the old version of *file3* (the version in the index) contains `Line1` to `Line5` (a total of five lines, starting from the first line at the top, `-1,5`), and the new version of *file3* (the version in the working directory) contains `Line1` to `Line7`, excluding `Line3` (a total of six lines, starting from the first line at the top, `+1,6`).

git diff and Commit Ranges

There are two additional forms of `git diff` that warrant some explanation, especially in contrast to `git log`.

The `git diff` command supports a double-dot syntax to represent the difference between two commits. Thus the following two commands are equivalent:

```
$ git diff main bug/pr-1
$ git diff main..bug/pr-1
```

Unfortunately, the double-dot syntax in `git diff` means something quite different from the same syntax in `git log`, which you learned about in Chapter 4. It's worth comparing `git diff` and `git log` in this regard because doing so highlights the relationship of these two commands to changes made in repositories.

Here are some points to keep in mind for the following example:

- `git diff` doesn't care about the history of the files it compares, or anything about branches.
- `git log` is extremely conscious of how one file changed to become another—for example, when two branches diverged and what happened on each branch.

The `log` and `diff` commands perform two fundamentally different operations. Whereas `log` operates on a set of commits, `diff` operates on two different end points.

Imagine the following sequence of events:

1. Someone creates a new branch off the `main` branch to fix bug `pr-1`, calling the new branch `bug/pr-1`.

2. The same developer adds the line "Fix Problem Report 1" to a file in the `bug/pr-1` branch.

3. Meanwhile, another developer fixes bug `pr-3` in the `main` branch, adding the line "Fix Problem Report 3" to the same file in the `main` branch.

In short, one line was added to a file in each branch. If you look at the changes to the branches at a high level, you can see when the `bug/pr-1` branch was launched and when each change was made:

```
$ git show-branch main bug/pr-1
* [main] Added a bug fix for pr-3.
 ! [bug/pr-1] Fix Problem Report 1
--
*   [main] Added a bug fix for pr-3.
 +  [bug/pr-1] Fix Problem Report 1
*+ [main^] Added Bob's fixes.
```

If you type `git log -p main..bug/pr-1`, you will see one commit because the syntax `main..bug/pr-1` represents all those commits in `bug/pr-1` that are not also in `main`. The command traces back to the point where `bug/pr-1` diverged from `main`, but it does not look at anything that happened to `main` since that point:

```
$ git log -p main..bug/pr-1
commit 8f4cf5757a3a83b0b3dbecd26244593c5fc820ea
Author: Jon Loeliger <jdl@example.com>
Date:   Wed May 14 17:53:54 2008 -0500

Fix Problem Report 1

diff --git a/ready b/ready
index f3b6f0e..abbf9c5 100644
--- a/ready
+++ b/ready
@@ -1,3 +1,4 @@
 stup
 znill
 frot-less
+Fix Problem Report 1
```

In contrast, git diff main..bug/pr-1 shows the total set of differences between the two trees represented by the heads of the main and bug/pr-1 branches. History doesn't matter; only the current state of the files does:

```
$ git diff main..bug/pr-1
diff --git a/ready b/ready
index f3b6f0e..abbf9c5 100644
--- a/ready
+++ b/ready
@@ -1,4 +1,4 @@
 stup
 znill
 frot-less
-Fix Problem Report 3
+Fix Problem Report 1
```

To paraphrase the git diff output, you can change the file in the main branch to the version in the bug/pr-1 branch by removing the line "Fix Problem Report 3" and then adding the line "Fix Problem Report 1" to the file.

As you can see, this diff includes commits from both branches. This may not seem crucial with this small example, but consider the example in Figure 7-3 with more expansive lines of development on two branches.

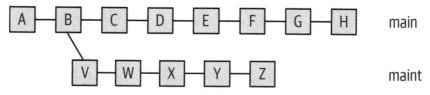

Figure 7-3. git diff larger history

In this case, git log main..maint represents the five individual commits V, W, ..., Z. On the other hand, git diff main..maint represents the differences in the trees at H and Z, an accumulated 11 commits: C, D, ..., H and V, ..., Z.

Similarly, both `git log` and `git diff` accept the form *commit1...commit2* to produce a symmetrical difference. As before, however, `git log` *commit1...commit2* and `git diff` *commit1...commit2* yield different results.

As discussed in "Commit Ranges" on page 96, the command `git log` *commit1... commit2* displays the commits reachable from either commit but not both. Thus `git log main...maint` in the previous example would yield C, D, …, H and V, …, Z.

The symmetric difference in `git diff` shows the differences between a commit that is a common ancestor (or merge base) of *commit1* and *commit2*. Given the same genealogy in Figure 7-3, `git diff main...maint` combines the changes in the commits V, W, …, Z.

git diff with Path Limiting

By default, the command `git diff` operates on the entire directory structure rooted at a given tree object. However, you can leverage the same path-limiting technique employed by `git log` to limit the output of `git diff` to a subset of the repository.

For example, at one point[1] in the development of Git's own repository, `git diff --stat` displayed this:

```
$ git diff --stat main~5 main
 Documentation/git-add.txt            |  2 +-
 Documentation/git-cherry.txt         |  6 +++++
 Documentation/git-commit-tree.txt    |  2 +-
 Documentation/git-format-patch.txt   |  2 +-
 Documentation/git-gc.txt             |  2 +-
 Documentation/git-gui.txt            |  4 +-
 Documentation/git-ls-files.txt       |  2 +-
 Documentation/git-pack-objects.txt   |  2 +-
 Documentation/git-pack-redundant.txt |  2 +-
 Documentation/git-prune-packed.txt   |  2 +-
 Documentation/git-prune.txt          |  2 +-
 Documentation/git-read-tree.txt      |  2 +-
 Documentation/git-remote.txt         |  2 +-
 Documentation/git-repack.txt         |  2 +-
 Documentation/git-rm.txt             |  2 +-
 Documentation/git-status.txt         |  2 +-
 Documentation/git-update-index.txt   |  2 +-
 Documentation/git-var.txt            |  2 +-
 Documentation/gitk.txt               |  2 +-
 builtin-checkout.c                   |  7 ++++-
 builtin-fetch.c                      |  6 ++--
 git-bisect.sh                        | 29 ++++++++++++--------------
 t/t5518-fetch-exit-status.sh         | 37 +++++++++++++++++++++++++++++++++++++
 23 files changed, 83 insertions(+), 40 deletions(-)
```

---

1 d2b3691b61d516a0ad2bf700a2a5d9113ceff0b1

To limit the output to just *documentation* changes, you could instead use `git diff --stat main~5 main Documentation`:

```
$ git diff --stat main~5 main Documentation
 Documentation/git-add.txt             |   2 +-
 Documentation/git-cherry.txt          |   6 +++++
 Documentation/git-commit-tree.txt     |   2 +-
 Documentation/git-format-patch.txt    |   2 +-
 Documentation/git-gc.txt              |   2 +-
 Documentation/git-gui.txt             |   4 ++--
 Documentation/git-ls-files.txt        |   2 +-
 Documentation/git-pack-objects.txt    |   2 +-
 Documentation/git-pack-redundant.txt  |   2 +-
 Documentation/git-prune-packed.txt    |   2 +-
 Documentation/git-prune.txt           |   2 +-
 Documentation/git-read-tree.txt       |   2 +-
 Documentation/git-remote.txt          |   2 +-
 Documentation/git-repack.txt          |   2 +-
 Documentation/git-rm.txt              |   2 +-
 Documentation/git-status.txt          |   2 +-
 Documentation/git-update-index.txt    |   2 +-
 Documentation/git-var.txt             |   2 +-
 Documentation/gitk.txt                |   2 +-
 19 files changed, 25 insertions(+), 19 deletions(-)
```

Of course, you can view the diffs for a single file too:

```
$ git diff main~5 main Documentation/git-add.txt
diff --git a/Documentation/git-add.txt b/Documentation/git-add.txt
index bb4abe2..1afd0c6 100644
--- a/Documentation/git-add.txt
+++ b/Documentation/git-add.txt
@@ -246,7 +246,7 @@ characters that need C-quoting.  `core.quotepath` configuration can be
 used to work this limitation around to some degree, but backslash,
 double-quote and control characters will still have problems.

-See Also
+SEE ALSO
 --------
 linkgit:git-status[1]
 linkgit:git-rm[1]
```

In the following example, also taken from Git's own repository, the `-S"`*string*`"` searches the past 50 commits of the `main` branch for changes containing *string*:

```
$ git diff -S"octopus" main~50
diff --git a/Documentation/RelNotes-1.5.5.3.txt b/Documentation/RelNotes-1.5.5.3.txt
new file mode 100644
index 0000000..f22f98b
--- /dev/null
+++ b/Documentation/RelNotes-1.5.5.3.txt
@@ -0,0 +1,12 @@
+GIT v1.5.5.3 Release Notes
+==========================
+
+Fixes since v1.5.5.2
+--------------------
+
+ * "git send-email --compose" did not notice that non-ascii contents
+   needed some MIME magic.
```

```
+
+ * "git fast-export" did not export octopus merges correctly.
+
+Also comes with various documentation updates.
```

Used with -S, often called the *pickaxe*, Git lists the diffs that contain a change in the number of times the given *string* is used in the diff. Conceptually, you can think of this as "Where is the given *string* either introduced or removed?" You can find an example of the pickaxe used with git log in "Using Pickaxe" on page 184.

How Git Derives diffs

Most version control systems, including CVS and SVN, track a series of revisions and store just the changes between each pair of files. This technique is meant to save storage space and overhead.

Internally, such systems spend a lot of time thinking about things like "the series of changes between A and B." When you update your files from the central repository, for example, SVN remembers that the last time you updated the file you were at revision r1095, but now the repository is at revision r1123. Thus the server must send you the diff between r1095 and r1123. Once your SVN client has these diffs, it can incorporate them into your working copy and produce r1123. (That's how SVN avoids sending you all the contents of all files every time you update.)

To save disk space, SVN also stores its own repository as a series of diffs on the server. When you ask for the diffs between r1095 and r1123, it looks up all the individual diffs for each version between those two versions, merges them together into one large diff, and sends you the result. But Git doesn't work like that.

In Git, as you've seen, each commit contains a *tree*, which is a list of files contained by that commit. Each tree is independent of all other trees. Git users still talk about diffs and patches, of course, because these are still extremely useful. Yet, in Git, a diff and a patch are derived data, not the fundamental data they are in CVS and SVN. If you look in the *.git* directory, you won't find a single diff; if you look in an SVN repository, it consists mostly of diffs.

Just as SVN is able to derive the complete set of differences between r1095 and r1123, Git can retrieve and derive the differences between any two arbitrary states. But SVN must look at each version between r1095 and r1123, whereas Git doesn't care about the intermediate steps.

Each revision has its own tree, but Git doesn't require those to generate the diff; Git can operate directly on snapshots of the complete state at each of the two versions. This simple difference in storage systems is one of the most important reasons why Git is so much faster than other version control systems.

Summary

In this chapter, we explained how the `git diff` command can be a very powerful and useful tool for comparing changes and the state of files within your repositories throughout the development phases of your project. If you are familiar with the Unix and Linux `diff` utilities, then leveraging Git's `diff` command will be much easier. If this is your first encounter, then we urge you to focus on "Simple git diff Example" on page 163 followed by "Understanding the git diff Output" on page 166 so that you are fully acquainted with this tool.

## PART III

Intermediate Skills

In Part III, we prepare you with the intermediate skills that are necessary when working with Git repositories. We begin this part of the book with a discussion about commits and conclude by introducing you to the concept of remote repositories before sharing some good practices for managing your repositories.

The history of your repository consists of commits, and at times, you might need to modify the commit history for valid reasons. Before you can alter commits, you will need to know how to find them. In Chapter 8, we'll teach you how to find specific commits and their metadata. Then, in Chapter 9, we'll share various techniques for altering commits, some of them destructive and others nondestructive to your repository's history. Bear in mind that the skills you learn in this chapter are not limited to operations that are strictly scoped to altering commits; they can also help you in your quest to debug or understand how changes came to be in your repositories. Moving on, in Chapter 10 we'll discuss how you can stash and unstash temporary changes to your work, and we'll discuss the reflog, which keeps a record of supported operations on every ref or commit you introduce.

Finally, in Chapter 11, we will help you understand how best to collaborate and share changes when working with multiple people who need access to your repository. We will also provide some guidance on how to publish your repository and set up a good structure for it for distributed development.

## CHAPTER 8

Finding Commits

Part of a good version control system is the support it provides for "archaeology" and investigating a repository. Git provides several mechanisms to help you locate commits that meet certain criteria within your repository.

In this chapter we'll teach you techniques you can use to find specific commits and their metadata. We'll focus on three methods you can leverage to search through your repository's commit history. The first method is very robust and is helpful in locating a single commit satisfying your search criteria. The second method provides information about commits that introduced changes to a file, and the third method uses a specific search variation with the regular `git log` command.

Besides arming you with search skills in Git when working with commits, this chapter also provides a segue to Chapter 9, where we'll delve into the topic of altering the commits you found.

Using git bisect

The `git bisect` command is a powerful tool for isolating a particular commit based on essentially arbitrary search criteria. It is well suited to those times when you discover that something "wrong" or "bad" is affecting your repository and you know the code had been fine. For example, let's say you are working on the Linux kernel and a test boot fails, but you're positive the boot worked sometime earlier, perhaps the previous week or at a previous release tag. In this case, your repository has transitioned from a known "good" state to a known "bad" state.

But when did that transition occur? Which commit caused it to break? That is precisely the question `git bisect` is designed to help you answer.

The only real search requirement is that, given a checked-out state of your repository, you are able to determine whether it does or does not meet your search requirement. In this case, you have to be able to answer the question, "Does the version of the checked-out kernel build and boot?" You also have to know a good and a bad version of the commit before starting so that the search will be bounded. In short, you should not be providing an incorrect range of commits in your search requirement.

The `git bisect` command internally applies a binary search algorithm when executed; the command systematically chooses a new commit in an ever-decreasing range bounded by good behavior at one end and bad behavior at the other end. Eventually, this narrowing range will pinpoint the one commit that introduced the faulty behavior. Figure 8-1 provides an overarching view of this concept.

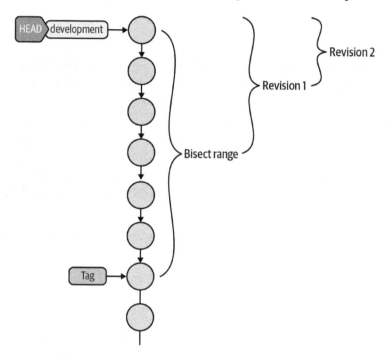

Figure 8-1. Git bisect range revision concept

When in `bisect` mode, there is no need for you to do anything more than provide an initial good and bad commit and then repeatedly answer the question, "Does this version work?"

To start, you first need to identify a good commit and a bad commit. In practice, the bad version is often your current HEAD because that's where you were working when you suddenly noticed something was wrong or were assigned a bug to fix.

Finding an initial good version can be a bit difficult because it's usually buried in your history somewhere. You can probably name or guess some version back in the history of the repository that you know works correctly. This may be a tagged release, like v2.6.25, or some commit 100 revisions ago, like main~100, on your main branch. Ideally, it is close to your bad commit (main~25 is better than main~100) and not buried too far in the past. In any event, you need to know or be able to verify that it is, in fact, a good commit.

It is essential that you start the `git bisect` process from a clean working directory and that your working directory points at the top-level directory of your project. The process necessarily adjusts your working directory to contain various versions of your repository. Starting with a dirty work space is asking for trouble; your working directory could easily be lost. If you have any working changes, you can stash those temporarily. We will discuss stashing in Chapter 10.

Using a clone of the Linux kernel in our example, let's tell Git to begin a search:

```
$ cd linux-2.6
$ git bisect start
```

After initiating a bisection search, Git enters bisect mode, setting up some state information for itself. Git employs a detached HEAD to manage the currently checked-out version of the repository. This detached HEAD is essentially an anonymous branch that can be used to bounce around within the repository and point to different revisions as needed.

 We've decided to leverage an already well-crafted example of `git bisect` using an antiquated version of the Linux kernel. For the curious reader who would like to duplicate this example, HEAD is commit 49fdf6785fd660e18a1eb4588928f47e9fa29a9a here.

Once the search has begun, tell Git which commit is bad. Because this is typically your current version, you can simply default the revision to your current HEAD.

```
# Tell git the HEAD version is broken
$ git bisect bad
```

Similarly, tell Git which version works:

```
$ git bisect good v2.6.27
Bisecting: 3857 revisions left to test after this
[cf2fa66055d718ae13e62451bb546505f63906a2] Merge branch 'for_linus'
    of git://git.kernel.org/pub/scm/linux/kernel/git/mchehab/linux-2.6
```

Identifying a good and bad version delineates a range of commits over which a good-to-bad transition occurs. At each step along the way, Git will tell you how many revisions are in that range. Git also modifies your working directory by checking out a revision that is roughly midway between the good and bad end points. It is now up to you to answer the question, "Is this version good or bad?" Each time you answer this question, Git narrows the search space in half, identifies a new revision, checks it out, and repeats the "good or bad?" question.

Suppose this version is good:

```
$ git bisect good
Bisecting: 1939 revisions left to test after this
[2be508d847392e431759e370d21cea9412848758] Merge git://git.infradead.org/mtd-2.6
```

Notice that 3,857 revisions have been narrowed down to 1,939. Let's do a few more:

```
$ git bisect good
Bisecting: 939 revisions left to test after this
[b80de369aa5c7c8ce7ff7a691e86e1dcc89accc6] 8250: Add more OxSemi devices

$ git bisect bad
Bisecting: 508 revisions left to test after this
[9301975ec251bab1ad7cfcb84a688b26187e4e4a] Merge branch 'genirq-v28-for-linus'
    of git://git.kernel.org/pub/scm/linux/kernel/git/tip/linux-2.6-tip
```

In a perfect bisection run, it takes $\log_2$ of the original number of revision steps to narrow down to just one commit.

Here's what we get after another good and bad answer:

```
$ git bisect good
Bisecting: 220 revisions left to test after this
[7cf5244ce4a0ab3f043f2e9593e07516b0df5715] mfd: check for
    platform_get_irq() return value in sm501

$ git bisect bad
Bisecting: 104 revisions left to test after this
[e4c2ce82ca2710e17cb4df8eb2b249fa2eb5af30] ring_buffer: allocate
    buffer page pointer
```

Throughout the bisection process, Git maintains a log of your answers along with their commit IDs:

```
$ git bisect log
git bisect start
# bad: [49fdf6785fd660e18a1eb4588928f47e9fa29a9a] Merge branch
    'for-linus' of git://git.kernel.dk/linux-2.6-block
git bisect bad 49fdf6785fd660e18a1eb4588928f47e9fa29a9a
# good: [3fa8749e584b55f1180411ab1b51117190bac1e5] Linux 2.6.27
git bisect good 3fa8749e584b55f1180411ab1b51117190bac1e5
# good: [cf2fa66055d718ae13e62451bb546505f63906a2] Merge branch 'for_linus'
    of git://git.kernel.org/pub/scm/linux/kernel/git/mchehab/linux-2.6
git bisect good cf2fa66055d718ae13e62451bb546505f63906a2
# good: [2be508d847392e431759e370d21cea9412848758] Merge
    git://git.infradead.org/mtd-2.6
git bisect good 2be508d847392e431759e370d21cea9412848758
# bad: [b80de369aa5c7c8ce7ff7a691e86e1dcc89accc6] 8250: Add more
    OxSemi devices
git bisect bad b80de369aa5c7c8ce7ff7a691e86e1dcc89accc6
```

```
# good: [9301975ec251bab1ad7cfcb84a688b26187e4e4a] Merge branch
    'genirq-v28-for-linus' of
git://git.kernel.org/pub/scm/linux/kernel/git/tip/linux-2.6-tip
git bisect good 9301975ec251bab1ad7cfcb84a688b26187e4e4a
# bad: [7cf5244ce4a0ab3f043f2e9593e07516b0df5715] mfd: check for
    platform_get_irq() return value in sm501
git bisect bad 7cf5244ce4a0ab3f043f2e9593e07516b0df5715
```

If you get lost during the process, or if you just want to start over for any reason, type **git bisect replay** using the logfile[1] as input. If needed, this is an excellent mechanism to back up one step in the process and explore a different path.

Let's narrow down the defect with five more "bad" answers:

```
$ git bisect bad
Bisecting: 51 revisions left to test after this
[d3ee6d992821f471193a7ee7a00af9ebb4bf5d01] ftrace: make it
    depend on DEBUG_KERNEL

$ git bisect bad
Bisecting: 25 revisions left to test after this
[3f5a54e371ca20b119b73704f6c01b71295c1714] ftrace: dump out
    ftrace buffers to console on panic

$ git bisect bad
Bisecting: 12 revisions left to test after this
[8da3821ba5634497da63d58a69e24a97697c4a2b] ftrace: create
    _mcount_loc section

$ git bisect bad
Bisecting: 6 revisions left to test after this
[fa340d9c050e78fb21a142b617304214ae5e0c2d] tracing: disable
    tracepoints by default

$ git bisect bad
Bisecting: 2 revisions left to test after this
[4a0897526bbc5c6ac0df80b16b8c60339e717ae2] tracing: tracepoints, samples
```

You can use the `git bisect visualize` command to visually inspect the set of commits still within the range of consideration. Git uses the graphical tool `gitk` if the `DISPLAY` environment variable is set. If not, then Git will use `git log` instead. In that case, `--pretty=oneline` might be useful too:

```
$ git bisect visualize --pretty=oneline

fa340d9c050e78fb21a142b617304214ae5e0c2d tracing: disable tracepoints
    by default
b07c3f193a8074aa4afe43cfa8ae38ec4c7ccfa9 ftrace: port to tracepoints
0a16b6075843325dc402edf80c1662838b929aff tracing, sched: LTTng
    instrumentation - scheduler
4a0897526bbc5c6ac0df80b16b8c60339e717ae2 tracing: tracepoints, samples
24b8d831d56aac7907752d22d2aba5d8127db6f6 tracing: tracepoints,
    documentation
97e1c18e8d17bd87e1e383b2e9d9fc740332c8e2 tracing: Kernel Tracepoints
```

---

1 You can generate a logfile by supplying the `git bisect log` command.

The current revision under consideration is roughly in the middle of the range:

```
$ git bisect good
Bisecting: 1 revisions left to test after this
[b07c3f193a8074aa4afe43cfa8ae38ec4c7ccfa9] ftrace: port to tracepoints
```

When you finally test the last revision and Git has isolated the one revision that introduced the problem,[2] it's displayed:

```
$ git bisect good
fa340d9c050e78fb21a142b617304214ae5e0c2d is first bad commit
commit fa340d9c050e78fb21a142b617304214ae5e0c2d
Author: Ingo Molnar <mingo@elte.hu>
Date:   Wed Jul 23 13:38:00 2008 +0200

tracing: disable tracepoints by default

while it's arguably low overhead, we don't enable new features by default.

Signed-off-by: Ingo Molnar <mingo@elte.hu>

:040000 040000 4bf5c05869a67e184670315c181d76605c973931
    fd15e1c4adbd37b819299a9f0d4a6ff589721f6c M  init
```

The method we discussed is a little tedious and can be painful to iterate over a range of revisions to pinpoint the commit that actually borked your repository. Thankfully, Git is able to execute the same operation with a script or command as a shortcut to save us some time when dealing with large revisions to hunt for the culprit commit. Here is how you can achieve the same:

```
# git bisect start <bad-commit-SHA> <good-commit-SHA>
$ git bisect start HEAD v2.6.27

$ git bisect run <command>
...
...
...
fa340d9c050e78fb21a142b617304214ae5e0c2d is first bad commit
commit fa340d9c050e78fb21a142b617304214ae5e0c2d
Author: Ingo Molnar <mingo@elte.hu>
Date:   Wed Jul 23 13:38:00 2008 +0200

tracing: disable tracepoints by default

while it's arguably low overhead, we don't enable new features by default.

Signed-off-by: Ingo Molnar <mingo@elte.hu>

:040000 040000 4bf5c05869a67e184670315c181d76605c973931
    fd15e1c4adbd37b819299a9f0d4a6ff589721f6c M  init
```

---

2 No, this commit did not necessarily introduce a problem. The "good" and "bad" answers were fabricated and landed here.

In the preceding example, *command* can be a script you can execute to tell you whether the currently checked-out version of the code is in a good state or a bad state. Specifically following our example, the script should evaluate if we can boot without failure.

The script needs to exit with code 0 if the current state of the source code is *good* and should exit with a code between 1 and 127, except for 125, if the current state of the code is *bad*.

Finally, when your bisection run is complete and you are finished with the bisection log and the saved state, it is vital that you tell Git that you have finished. As you may recall, the whole bisection process is performed on a detached HEAD:

```
$ git branch
* (no branch, bisect started on main)
  main

$ git bisect reset
Previous HEAD position was <COMMIT-SHA1> ...
Switched to branch "main"

$ git branch
* main
```

Running `git bisect reset` places you back on your original branch.

 You can replace the keywords bad and good with terms that better reflect your search criteria (e.g., if you were performing performance regressions). For this you will need to supply the options `--term-new` and `--term-old` with the `git bisect start` command as follows:

```
git bisect start --term-old fast --term-new slow
git bisect fast
git bisect slow
```

Using git blame

Another tool you can use to help identify a particular commit is `git blame`. This command tells you who last modified each line of a file and which commit made the change:

```
$ git blame -L 35, init/version.c

4865ecf1 (Serge E. Hallyn 2006-10-02 02:18:14 -0700 35)          },
^1da177e (Linus Torvalds  2005-04-16 15:20:36 -0700 36) };
4865ecf1 (Serge E. Hallyn 2006-10-02 02:18:14 -0700 37) EXPORT_SYMBOL_GPL(init_uts_ns);
3eb3c740 (Roman Zippel    2007-01-10 14:45:28 +0100 38)
c71551ad (Linus Torvalds  2007-01-11 18:18:04 -0800 39) /* FIXED STRINGS!
                                                           Don't touch! */
c71551ad (Linus Torvalds  2007-01-11 18:18:04 -0800 40) const char linux_banner[] =
3eb3c740 (Roman Zippel    2007-01-10 14:45:28 +0100 41)       "Linux version "
                                                           UTS_RELEASE "
```

```
3eb3c740 (Roman Zippel    2007-01-10 14:45:28 +0100 42)    (" LINUX_COMPILE_BY "@"
3eb3c740 (Roman Zippel    2007-01-10 14:45:28 +0100 43)    LINUX_COMPILE_HOST ")
3eb3c740 (Roman Zippel    2007-01-10 14:45:28 +0100 44)    (" LINUX_COMPILER ")
3eb3c740 (Roman Zippel    2007-01-10 14:45:28 +0100 45)    " UTS_VERSION "\n";
3eb3c740 (Roman Zippel    2007-01-10 14:45:28 +0100 46)
3eb3c740 (Roman Zippel    2007-01-10 14:45:28 +0100 47) const char linux_proc_banner[] =
3eb3c740 (Roman Zippel    2007-01-10 14:45:28 +0100 48)    "%s version %s"
3eb3c740 (Roman Zippel    2007-01-10 14:45:28 +0100 49)    " (" LINUX_COMPILE_BY
                                                           "@"
3eb3c740 (Roman Zippel    2007-01-10 14:45:28 +0100 50)    LINUX_COMPILE_HOST ")"
3eb3c740 (Roman Zippel    2007-01-10 14:45:28 +0100 51)    " (" LINUX_COMPILER ")
                                                           %s\n";
```

The -L option allows you to specify ranges when used with the git blame command. Here's an example of how to execute the option: git blame -L start-line-no,end-line-no.

Most Git clients today have extensions built in that display the git blame output for each line of a file by default, when open in a text editor window. This helps you to understand who made the last change to the file.

If you are interested in knowing who modified a specific file within a recent time frame, you can limit the range via the *<revisions range>* option of the git blame command as follows:

```
$ git blame --since=1.weeks -- file
```

Using Pickaxe

The -S option to git log is called *pickaxe*. That's brute-force archeology for you.

Whereas git blame tells you about the current state of a file, git log -S*string* searches back through the history of a file's diffs for the given *string*. By searching the actual diffs between revisions, this command can find commits that perform a *change* in both additions and deletions:

```
$ git log -Sinclude --pretty=oneline --abbrev-commit init/version.c
cd354f1... [PATCH] remove many unneeded #includes of sched.h
4865ecf... [PATCH] namespaces: utsname: implement utsname namespaces
63104ee... kbuild: introduce utsrelease.h
1da177e... Linux-2.6.12-rc2
```

In the preceding code, each commit listed on the left (cd354f1, etc.) will either add or delete lines that contain the word *include*. Be careful, though. If a commit both adds and subtracts exactly the same number of instances of lines with your key word, that won't be shown. The commit must have a *change* in the number of additions and deletions in order to count.

Using the option `-G` with the `git log` command will also show commits that match a specified regular expression, regardless of whether the number of additions or removals is balanced or not.

Summary

This chapter was very concise and discussed three specific methods you can use to find the commits that led to certain outcomes in your project. Whether the outcome is a bug, a performance regression, or even a compilation error, a natural next step will be for you to figure out how to fix the situation. The learnings you take from here are often used in combination with skills needed to alter commits, something we will discuss in the next chapter.

## CHAPTER 9

Altering Commits

A commit records the history of your work and keeps your changes sacrosanct. Git provides several tools and commands specifically designed to help you modify and improve the commit history catalogued within your repository.

There are many valid reasons why you might modify or rework a commit or your overall commit sequence. Here are a few examples:

- You can fix a problem before it becomes a legacy issue.
- You can decompose a large, sweeping change into a number of small, thematic commits. Conversely, you can combine individual changes into a larger commit.
- You can incorporate review feedback and suggestions throughout the development lifecycle of your project.
- You can reorder commits into a sequence that doesn't break a build requirement.
- You can order commits into a more logical sequence.
- You can remove debug code that was committed accidentally.
- You can remove sensitive data in code that was committed "accidentally."[1]

As you'll see in Chapter 11, which explains how to share a repository, there are many more reasons to change commits prior to publishing your repository.

For this chapter, we will discuss the philosophy of altering commit histories, its repercussions, and various tooling Git provides for us to be able to alter either a series or a specific commit in our repositories' commit history.

---

[1] If you have not pushed your commit to a remote repository, then that sensitive data is present only in your local repository. You still have the option to alter the commit and purge unreferenced commits from your local repository.

Remember, what gets committed in Git stays in Git (the commit history)! As such, you will need to be cautious of how changes pertaining to sensitive data in code are to be tracked or even version-controlled to avoid trivial alterations to your commits resulting in repository history rewrites.

Philosophy of Altering Commit History

When it comes to manipulating the development history, there are several schools of thought. One philosophy might be termed *realistic history*: every commit is retained and nothing is altered.

One variant of this is known as a *fine-grained* realistic history, where you commit every change as soon as possible, ensuring that each and every step is saved for posterity. Another option is *didactic* realistic history, where you take your time and commit only your best work at convenient and suitable moments.

Given the opportunity to adjust the history—possibly cleaning up a bad intermediate design decision or rearranging commits into a more logical flow—you can create a more "idealistic" history.

In reality, development moves at a fast pace. So, in this chapter, we'll start with our initial commit, and then we'll progressively add commits—including feature additions, typo fixes, and fixes from continuous integration/continuous delivery (CI/CD) (*https://oreil.ly/PThXB*) system outputs, all not necessarily done in a sequenced order. All of this leaves our repo commit history in a messy, uncurated state. What we really want is for our repositories to have a well-structured, curated commit history.

We like to think of this as keeping a journal versus writing a book. In a journal, you record how things happened. The raw details narrate what actually took place from day to day. A book, on the other hand, goes through a few rounds of editing and reviews over time before a final version is published; it's a structured narrative of how things came to be. Keep this analogy in mind as you work your way through the chapter, as it will help you decide which method is right for your projects.

As a developer, you may find value in the full, fine-grained, realistic history because it might provide archaeological details regarding how some good or bad ideas developed. A complete narrative may provide insight into the introduction of a bug or explicate a meticulous bug fix. In fact, an analysis of the history may even yield insight into how a developer or team of developers works and how the development process can be improved.

Many of those details might be lost if a revised history removes intermediate steps. Was a developer able to simply intuit such a good solution? Or did it take several iterations of refinement? What is the root cause of a bug? If the intermediate steps are not captured in the commit history, answers to those types of questions may be lost.

On the other hand, having a clean history showing well-defined steps, each with logical forward progress, can often be a joy to read and a pleasure to work with. There is, moreover, no need to worry about the vagaries of a possibly broken or suboptimal step in the repository history. Also, other developers reading the history may thereby learn a better development technique and style.

So is a detailed realistic history without information loss the best approach? Or is a clean history better? Perhaps an intermediate representation of the development is warranted. Or, with a clever use of Git branches, perhaps you could represent both a fine-grained realistic history and an idealized history in the same repository.

Git gives you the ability to clean up the actual history and turn it into a more idealized or cleaner one before it is published or committed to public record. Whether you choose to do so, to keep a detailed record without alteration, or to pick some middle ground is entirely up to you and your project policies.

Caution About Altering History

As a general guideline, you should feel free to alter and improve your repository commit history as long as no one has obtained a copy of your repository. Or, to be more pedantic, you can alter a specific branch of your repository as long as no one has a copy of that branch. The notion to keep in mind is you shouldn't rewrite, alter, or change any part of a branch that's been made available and might be present in a shared repository.

With the emergence of pull and merge requests on popular Git hosting platforms, you are presented with a variety of options on how specific feature branch histories can be rewritten, even if the feature branch is published. In most situations, the owner or author of this feature branch is a single developer, thus providing the freedom to rewrite commit history for the published feature branch. Of course, if another developer has checked out that specific feature branch, they have done so at their own risk, which may result in issues when reconciling changes.

For example, let's say you've worked on your main branch and made commits A through D available to another developer, as shown in Figure 9-1. Once you make your development history available to another developer, that chronicle is known as a *published history*.

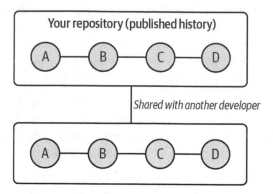

Figure 9-1. Your published history

Let's say you then do further development and produce new commits W through Z as unpublished history on the same branch. This is pictured in Figure 9-2.

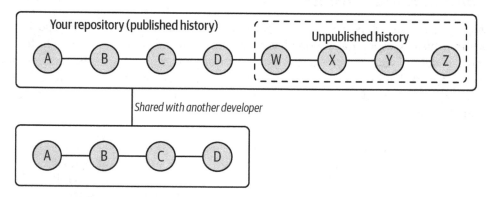

Figure 9-2. Your unpublished history

In this situation, you should be very careful to leave commits earlier than W alone. However, until you republish your main branch, there is no reason you can't modify commits W through Z. This could include reordering, combining, and removing one or more commits or, obviously, adding even more commits as new development.

You might end up with a new and improved commit history, as depicted in Figure 9-3. In this example, commits X and Y have been combined into one new commit; commit W has been slightly altered to yield a new, similar commit, W'; commit Z has been moved earlier in the history; and a new commit, P, has been introduced.

The following sections explore techniques to help you alter and improve your commit history. It is for you to judge whether the new history is better, when the history is good enough, and when the history is ready to be published.

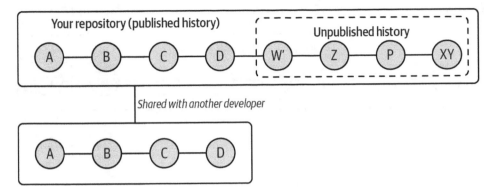

Figure 9-3. *Your new history*

Using git revert

When executed, the git revert *commit* command applies the *inverse* of the given *commit* (where the *commit* represents a snapshot of your repository at a moment in time). Generally, this command is used to introduce a new commit that reverses the effects of a given commit.

The revert doesn't *alter* the existing history within a repository. Instead, it adds a new commit to the history. Thus this command is typically regarded as a safe command to use when altering the commits of a shared repository.

A common application for git revert is to undo the effects of a commit that is buried, perhaps deeply, in the history of a branch. In Figure 9-4, a history of changes has been built up on the main branch. For some reason, perhaps through testing, commit D has been deemed faulty.

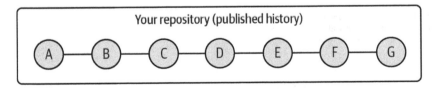

Figure 9-4. *Before simple* git revert

One way to fix the situation is to make edits to undo the effects of D and then commit the reversal directly. You might note in your commit message that the purpose of this commit is to revert the changes that were caused by the earlier commit.

An easier approach is to simply run git revert:

```
$ git revert main~3    # commit D
```

The result looks like Figure 9-5, where commit D' is the inverse of commit D.

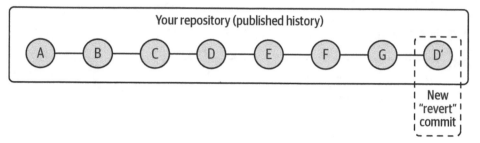

Figure 9-5. After simple `git revert`

Changing the HEAD Commit

One of the easiest ways to alter the most recent commit on your current branch is by using `git commit --amend`. Typically, *amend* implies that the commit has fundamentally the same *content* but some aspect requires adjustment or tidying. The actual commit object that's reintroduced into the object store will, of course, be different.

A frequent use of `git commit --amend` is to fix typos right after a commit. However, this is not the only use. As with any commit, this command can amend any file or files in the repository and can add or delete a file as part of the new commit.

As with a normal `git commit` command, `git commit --amend` prompts you with an editor session in which you may also alter the commit message.

For example, suppose we were working on a speech (yes, we do version-control our speeches) and made the following recent commit:

```
$ git show
commit 0ba161a94e03ab1e2b27c2e65e4cbef476d04f5d
Author: Jon Loeliger <jdl@example.com>
Date:   Thu Jun 26 15:14:03 2008 -0500

Initial speech

diff --git a/speech.txt b/speech.txt
new file mode 100644
index 0000000..310bcf9
--- /dev/null
+++ b/speech.txt
@@ -0,0 +1,5 @@
+Three score and seven years ago
+our fathers brought forth on this continent,
+a new nation, conceived in Liberty,
+and dedicated to the proposition
+that all women are created equal.
```

At this point, the commit is stored in Git's object repository, albeit with small errors in the prose. To make corrections, you could simply edit the file again and make a second commit. That would leave a history like this:

```
$ git show-branch --more=5
[main] Fix timeline typo
[main^] Initial speech
```

However, if you wish to leave a slightly cleaner commit history in your repository, then you can alter this commit directly and replace it. To do this, fix the file in your working directory. Correct the typos, and add or remove files as needed. As with any commit, update the index with your changes using commands such as `git add` or `git rm`. Then issue the `git commit --amend` command:

```
# edit speech.txt as needed.

$ git diff
diff --git a/speech.txt b/speech.txt
index 310bcf9..7328a76 100644
--- a/speech.txt
+++ b/speech.txt
@@ -1,5 +1,5 @@
-Three score and seven years ago
+Four score and seven years ago
 our fathers brought forth on this continent,
 a new nation, conceived in Liberty,
 and dedicated to the proposition
-that all women are created equal.
+that all women and men are created equal.

$ git add speech.txt

$ git commit --amend

# Also edit the "Initial speech" commit message if desired
# In this example we change it a bit...

$ git show-branch --more=5
[main] Initial speech that sounds familiar.

$ git show
commit 47d849c61919f05da1acf983746f205d2cdb0055
Author: Jon Loeliger <jdl@example.com>
Date:   Thu Jun 26 15:14:03 2008 -0500

    Initial speech that sounds familiar.

diff --git a/speech.txt b/speech.txt
new file mode 100644
index 0000000..7328a76
--- /dev/null
+++ b/speech.txt
@@ -0,0 +1,5 @@
+Four score and seven years ago
+our fathers brought forth on this continent,
+a new nation, conceived in Liberty,
+and dedicated to the proposition
+that all women and men are created equal.
```

This command can also edit the meta-information on a commit. For example, by specifying the --author option, you can alter the author of the commit:

```
$ git commit --amend --author "Bob Miller <kbob@example.com>"
# ...just close the editor...

$ git log
commit 0e2a14f933a3aaff9edd848a862e783d986f149f
Author: Bob Miller <kbob@example.com>
Date:   Thu Jun 26 15:14:03 2008 -0500

Initial speech that sounds familiar.
```

 If you've followed closely, you will have noticed that with each git commit --amend, a new commit SHA1 ID was generated (based on the changed content) and reintroduced to the Git object store.

Pictorially, altering the HEAD or top commit using git commit --amend changes the commit graph from that shown in Figure 9-6 to that shown in Figure 9-7.

Figure 9-6. Commit graph before git commit --amend

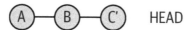

Figure 9-7. Commit graph after git commit --amend

Here, the substance of the C commit is still the same, but it has been altered to obtain C'. The HEAD ref has been changed from the old commit, C, so that it points to the replacement ref, C'.

Using git reset

The git reset command changes your repository and working directory to a known state. Specifically, git reset adjusts the HEAD ref to a given *commit* and, by default, updates the index to match that commit. If desired, git reset can also modify your working directory to mirror the revision of your project represented by the given commit. git reset can be used as part of many other operations. As such, in this section we focus on how the git reset operation can influence and change your repository commit history.

You might construe `git reset` as "destructive" because it can overwrite and destroy changes in your working directory. Indeed, data can be lost. Even if you have a backup of your files, you might not be able to recover your work. However, the whole point of this command is to establish and recover known states for the HEAD, index, and working directory.

When you need to use the `git reset` command, it helps to approach the concept by visualizing a *before* and *after* state of a repository's commit history. To paraphrase: this is the current state or commit history of my repository before I execute a `git reset`; how do I want the commit history or state of the repository to look after executing the reset command? Pictorially, this is best illustrated in Figure 9-8.

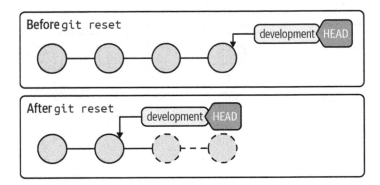

Figure 9-8. Before and after `git reset`

 Another way to understand the concept of using `git reset` is to think of your commit history as a timeline. Your HEAD ref is like a play button that is pointing to a specific moment in the timeline (usually the most recent). When you perform a `git reset`, you are able to *rewind* or *fast-forward* to a moment in the timeline of your repository's commit history.

The `git reset` command has three main options: `--soft`, `--mixed`, and `--hard`. These options influence how either the index or the working directory of your repository will be updated to respect the `git reset` operation.

Let's examine these options. In Figures 9-9 through 9-11, note that the `git reset` command resets the HEAD ref to point to commit B in the commit history of the repository:

`git reset --soft` *commit*

The `--soft` option changes the `HEAD` ref to point to the given *commit*. The contents of your index and working directory are left unchanged. This version of the command has the "least" effect, changing only the state of a symbolic reference so it points to a new commit.

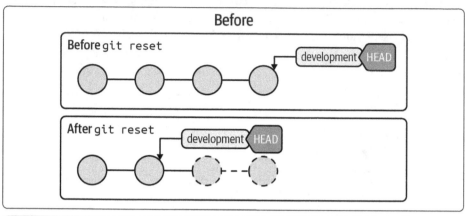

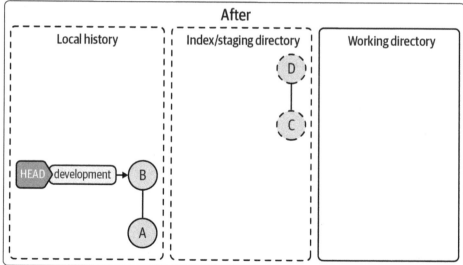

Figure 9-9. Before and after `git reset --soft` *(changes to files that are committed from commits C and D will be reflected in the index or staging directory)*

`git reset --mixed` *commit*

The `--mixed` option changes `HEAD` to point to the given *commit*. Your index contents are also modified to align with the tree structure named by *commit*, but your working directory contents are left unchanged. This version of the command leaves your index as if you had just staged all the changes represented by *commit*, and it tells you what remains modified in your working directory. Note that --mixed is the default mode for git reset.

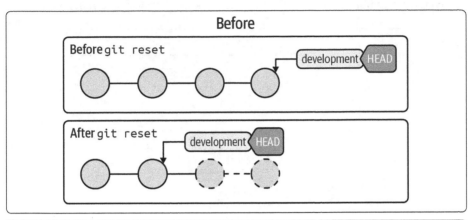

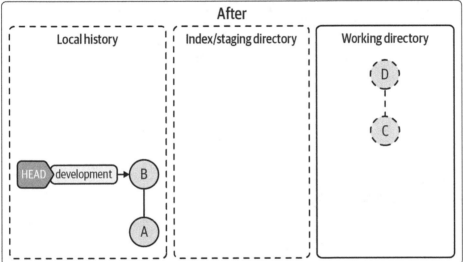

Figure 9-10. Before and after git reset --mixed (changes to files that are committed from commits C and D will be reflected in the working directory)

git reset --hard *commit*

The --hard option changes the HEAD ref to point to the given *commit*. The contents of your index are also modified to agree with the tree structure named by the named *commit*. Furthermore, your working directory contents are changed to reflect the state of the tree represented by the given *commit*.

When changing your working directory, the complete directory structure is altered to correspond to the given *commit*. Modifications are lost, and new files added to the repository but not tracked will stay untouched. Files that are in the given *commit* but no longer exist in your working directory are reinstated.

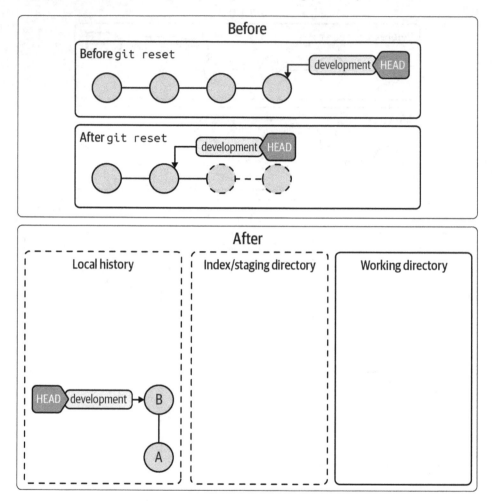

Figure 9-11. Before and after `git reset --hard` *(changes to files that are committed from commits C and D will be lost)*

The effects demonstrated in the previous illustrations are summarized in Table 9-1.

Table 9-1. git reset option effects

Option	HEAD	Index	Working directory
--soft	Yes	Yes	No
--mixed	Yes	No	Yes
--hard	Yes	Yes	Yes

The `git reset` command also saves the original HEAD value in the ref ORIG_HEAD. This is useful, for example, if you wish to use that original HEAD's commit log message as the basis for some follow-up commit. To reuse the commit log message, you will need to supply the --reuse-message=ORIG_HEAD argument.

In terms of the object model, `git reset` moves the current branch HEAD within the commit graph to a specific commit. Just remember, if you specify --hard, your working directory is transformed as well.

Next, let's look at some examples of how `git reset` operates.

We'll start by setting up a branch with several commits on it:

```
$ git init -b main
Initialized empty Git repository in /tmp/reset/.git/

$ echo Do >> main_file

$ git add main_file

$ git commit -m "Do"
[main (root-commit) d8789aa] Do
 1 file changed, 1 insertion(+)
 create mode 100644 main_file

$ echo Fa >> file_1
$ git add file_1
$ git commit -m "Fa"
[main cf6315c] Fa
 1 file changed, 1 insertion(+)
 create mode 100644 file_1

$ ls
file_1    main_file

$ git log --oneline
cf6315c (HEAD -> main) Fa
d8789aa Do
```

Suppose you now add *file_2* and stage the file, then realize that you need to combine this staged change with the previous commit of adding *file_1*, and you want to go back and do it correctly.

Here you can use git reset --soft *commit*:

```
$ echo Mi >> file_2
$ git add file_2

$ git status
On branch main
Changes to be committed:
  (use "git restore --staged <file>..." to unstage)
        new file:   file_2

$ git reset --soft HEAD^

$ git log --oneline
d8789aa (HEAD -> main) Do

# Files in the directory
$ ls
file_1    file_2    main_file

# Git status after reset soft shows that both
# file_2 and file_1 are in the index directory
$ git status
On branch main
Changes to be committed:
  (use "git restore --staged <file>..." to unstage)
        new file:   file_1
        new file:   file_2

# Create new commit with both file_1 and file_2
$ git commit -m "Fa and Mi"
[main 0c8a4ba] Fa and Mi
 2 files changed, 2 insertions(+)
 create mode 100644 file_1
 create mode 100644 file_2

$ git log --oneline
0c8a4ba (HEAD -> main) Fa and Mi
d8789aa Do
```

Recall (from "Identifying Commits" on page 81) that HEAD^ references the commit parent of the current main HEAD, and it represents the state immediately prior to completing the second commit that added *file_1*.

Let's continue:

```
$ echo Re >> file_3
$ echo So >> file_4
```

With the addition of the content from the new files, you may need to alter the sequence of commits to show a logical progression of work.

Here you can use git reset --mixed *commit*:

```
# --mixed is the default reset option,
# thus you don't need to explicitly supply the option
$ git reset HEAD^

$ git log --oneline
d8789aa (HEAD -> main) Do

# Files in the directory
$ ls
file_1    file_2    file_3    file_4    main_file

# Git status after reset mixed shows all files are in the working directory
$ git status
On branch main
Untracked files:
(use "git add <file>..." to include in what will be committed)
        file_1
        file_2
        file_3
        file_4

# Create new commit with all files to reflect
# a logical sequence of commit history
$ git add file_3
$ git commit -m "Re - content from file_3"
[main 61e676f] Re - content from file_3
 1 file changed, 1 insertion(+)
 create mode 100644 file_3

# Continue to add and commit files in the
# correct logical order based on their content
$ git add file_2
$ git commit -m "Mi - content from file_2"
[main 4ecc185] Mi - content from file_2
 1 file changed, 1 insertion(+)
 create mode 100644 file_2

$ git add file_1
$ git commit -m "Fa - content from file_1"
[main 4d72acb] Fa - content from file_1
 1 file changed, 1 insertion(+)
 create mode 100644 file_1

$ git add file_4
$ git commit -m "So - content from file_4"
[main 3ab8f23] So - content from file_4
 1 file changed, 1 insertion(+)
 create mode 100644 file_4


$ git log --oneline
3ab8f23 (HEAD -> main) So - content from file_4
4d72acb Fa - content from file_1
4ecc185 Mi - content from file_2
61e676f Re - content from file_3
d8789aa Do
```

Because the --mixed option resets the index, you must restage any changes you want in the new commit. This gives you the opportunity to re-edit existing files, add other files, or perform other changes before making a new commit.

In some cases, you may want to eliminate the series of new commits entirely because you don't care about its content. To do this, you can use `git reset --hard` *commit*:

```
$ git log --oneline
3ab8f23 (HEAD -> main) So - content from file_4
4d72acb Fa - content from file_1
4ecc185 Mi - content from file_2
61e676f Re - content from file_3
d8789aa Do

$ git reset --hard HEAD~4
HEAD is now at d8789aa Do

$ git log --oneline
d8789aa (HEAD -> main) Do

# Files in the directory
$ ls
main_file

# Git status after reset hard resets the index and working directory
# to reflect the state when main_file was committed
$ git status
On branch main
nothing to commit, working tree clean

# Create new commit with new content and file name
$ echo "Do Re Mi Fa So" >> new_file
$ git add new_file
$ git commit -m "Add new_file"
[main 46623d8] Add new_file
  1 file changed, 1 insertion(+)
  create mode 100644 new_file

$ git log --oneline
46623d8 (HEAD -> main) Add new_file
d8789aa Do
```

The `--hard` option has the effect of pulling the main branch back to a specified state. In our example, it modifies the working directory to mirror the specified (HEAD~4) state, specifically, the state when the *main_file* in your working directory was created.

Although the examples all use HEAD in some form, you can apply `git reset` to any commit in the repository. For example, to eliminate several commits on your current branch, you could use `git reset --hard HEAD~4`, `git reset --hard d8789aa`, or even `git reset --hard ORIG_HEAD`.

But be careful. Just because you can name other commits using a branch name, this is not the same as checking the branch out. Throughout the `git reset` operation, you remain on the same branch. You can alter your working directory to *look like* the head of a different branch, but you are still on your original branch.

Using git cherry-pick

The command `git cherry-pick` *commit* applies the changes introduced by the named *commit* on the current branch. It will introduce a new, distinct commit. Strictly speaking, using `git cherry-pick` doesn't *alter* the existing history within a repository; instead, it adds to the history.

As with other Git operations that introduce changes via the process of applying a diff, you may need to resolve conflicts to fully apply the changes from the given *commit*.

The command `git cherry-pick` is typically used to introduce particular commits from one branch within a repository onto a different branch. A common use is to forward- or back-port commits from a maintenance branch to a development branch.

In Figure 9-12, the `dev` branch has normal development, whereas the `rel_2.3` contains commits for the maintenance of release `2.3`.

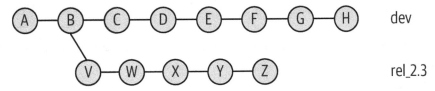

Figure 9-12. Before git `cherry-pick` of one commit

During the course of normal development, a bug is fixed on the development line with commit F. If that bug turns out to also be present in the 2.3 release, the bug fix, F, can be made to the `rel_2.3` branch using `git cherry-pick`:

```
$ git checkout rel_2.3
$ git cherry-pick dev~2    # commit F, above
```

After the `cherry-pick`, the graph resembles Figure 9-13.

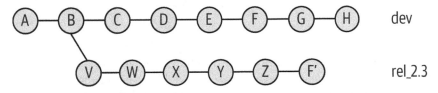

Figure 9-13. After git `cherry-pick` of one commit

In Figure 9-13, commit F' is substantially similar to commit F, but it is a new commit and will have to be adjusted—perhaps with conflict resolutions—to account for its application to commit Z rather than commit E. None of the commits following F are applied after F'; only the named commit is picked and applied.

Another common use for cherry-pick is to rebuild a series of commits by selectively picking a batch from one branch and introducing them onto a new branch.

Suppose you had a series of commits on your development branch, my_dev, as shown in Figure 9-14, and you wanted to introduce them onto the main branch but in a substantially different order.

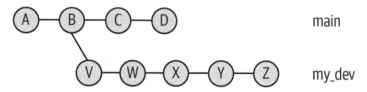

Figure 9-14. Before `git cherry-pick` *shuffle*

To apply them on the main branch in the order Y, W, X, Z, you could use the following commands:

```
$ git checkout main
$ git cherry-pick my_dev~1     # Y
$ git cherry-pick my_dev~3     # W
$ git cherry-pick my_dev~2     # X
$ git cherry-pick my_dev       # Z
```

Afterward, your commit history would look something like Figure 9-15.

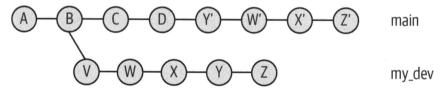

Figure 9-15. After `git cherry-pick` *shuffle*

In situations like this, where the order of commits undergoes fairly volatile changes, it is quite likely that you will have to resolve conflicts. It depends entirely on the relationship between the commits. If they are highly coupled and change overlapping lines, then you will have conflicts that need to be resolved. If they are highly independent, then you will be able to move them around quite readily.

Originally, the `git cherry-pick` command selected and reapplied one commit at a time. However, in later versions of Git, `git cherry-pick` allowed a range of commits to be selected and reapplied in a single command. For example, the following command:

```
# on branch main
$ git cherry-pick X..Z
```

would apply new commits X', Y', and Z' on the main branch. This is particularly handy in porting or moving a large sequence of commits from one line of development to another without necessarily using the entire source branch at one time.

You can also reference a few specific commits when cherry-picking, like this:

```
# on branch rel_2.3
$ git cherry-pick dev~4 dev~2
```

This will apply the fifth D (dev~4) and third F (dev~2) commit from the dev branch to the rel_2.3 branch.

reset, revert, and checkout

The three Git commands `reset`, `revert`, and `checkout` can be somewhat confusing because all appear to perform similar operations. Another reason these three commands can be confusing is that other version control systems have different meanings for the words *reset*, *revert*, and *checkout*.

However, there are some good guidelines and rules for when each command should and should not be used.

If you want to change to a different branch, use `git checkout` or `git switch`. Your current branch and HEAD ref change to match the tip of the given branch.

The `git reset` command does not change your branch. However, if you supply the name of a branch, it will change the state of your current working directory to *look* like the tip of the named branch. In other words, `git reset` is intended to reset the current branch's HEAD reference.

Because `git reset --hard` is designed to recover to a known state, it is also capable of clearing out failed or stale merge efforts, whereas `git checkout` will not. Thus if there were a pending merge commit and you attempted to recover using `git checkout` instead of `git reset --hard`, your next commit would erroneously be a merge commit.

The confusion with `git checkout` is due to its additional ability to extract a file from the object store and put it into your working directory, possibly replacing a version in your working directory in the process. Sometimes the version of that file is one corresponding to the current HEAD version, and sometimes it is an earlier version:

```
# Checkout file.c from index
$ git checkout -- path/to/file.c

# Checkout file.c from rev v2.3
$ git checkout v2.3 -- path/to/file.c
```

Git calls this "checking out a path."

In the former case, obtaining the current version from the object store appears to be a form of a "reset" operation—that is, your local working directory edits of the file are discarded because the file is reset to its current, HEAD version. That is double-plus ungood Git thinking.

In the latter case, an earlier version of the file is pulled out of the object store and placed into your working directory. This has the appearance of being a "revert" operation on the file. That, too, is double-plus ungood Git thinking.

In both cases, it is improper to think of the operation as a Git reset or a revert. In both cases, the file is "checked out" from a particular commit: HEAD and v2.3, respectively.

The `git revert` command works on full commits, not on files.

If another developer has cloned your repository or fetched some of your commits, there are implications for changing the commit history. In this case, you probably should not use commands that alter history within your repository. Instead, use `git revert`; do not use `git reset` or the `git commit --amend` command described in the earlier sections.

Rebasing Commits

The `git rebase` command is used to alter where a sequence of commits is based. This command requires at least the name of the other branch onto which your commits will be relocated. By default, the commits from the current branch that are not already on the other branch are rebased.

A common use for `git rebase` is to keep a series of commits that you are developing up to date with respect to another branch, usually a `main` branch or a tracking branch from another repository.

In Figure 9-16, two branches have been developed. Originally, the topic branch started on the main branch when it was at commit B. In the meantime, it has progressed to commit E.

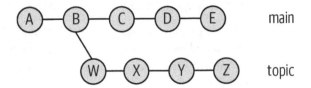

Figure 9-16. Before git rebase

You can keep your commit series up to date with respect to the main branch by writing the commits so that they are based on commit E rather than B. Because the topic branch needs to be the current branch, you can use either:

```
$ git checkout topic
$ git rebase main
```

or

```
$ git rebase main topic
```

After the rebase operation is complete, the new commit graph resembles Figure 9-17.

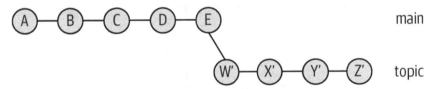

Figure 9-17. After git rebase

Using the git rebase command in situations like the one shown in Figure 9-16 is often called *forward porting*. In this example, the topic branch has been forward-ported to the main branch.

There is no magic to a rebase being a forward or a backward port; both are possible using git rebase. The interpretation is usually left to a more fundamental under-standing of what functionality is considered ahead of or behind another functionality.

In the context of a repository that you have cloned from somewhere else, it is common to forward-port your development branch or branches onto the origin/main tracking branch like this using the git rebase operation. When working with remote repositories, you will see how this operation is requested frequently by a repository maintainer using a phrase such as "Please rebase your patch to the tip-of-main." We discuss remote repositories in Chapter 11.

The `git rebase` command may also be used to completely transplant a line of development from one branch to an entirely different branch using the `--onto` option.

For example, suppose you've developed a new feature on the `feature` branch with the commits P and Q, which were based on the `maint` branch, as shown in Figure 9-18. To transplant the P and Q commits on the `feature` branch from the `maint` to the `main` branch, issue the following command:

```
$ git rebase --onto main maint^ feature
```

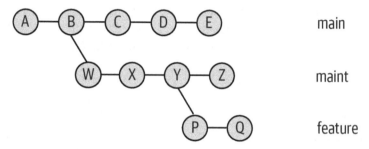

Figure 9-18. Before `git rebase` transplant

The resulting commit graph looks like Figure 9-19.

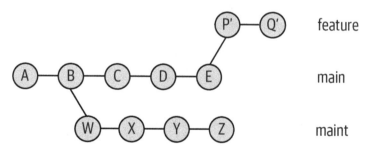

Figure 9-19. After `git rebase` transplant

The rebase operation relocates commits one at a time from each respective original commit location to a new commit base. As a result, each commit that is moved might have conflicts to resolve.

If a conflict is found, the `rebase` operation suspends its processing temporarily so you can resolve the conflict. Any conflict during the rebase process that needs to be resolved should be handled as described in "A Merge with a Conflict" on page 127.

Once all conflicts are resolved and the index has been updated with the results, the rebase operation can be resumed using the `git rebase --continue` command. The command resumes its operation by committing the resolved conflict and proceeding to the next commit in the series being rebased.

If, while inspecting a rebase conflict, you decide that this particular commit really isn't necessary, then you can also instruct the `git rebase` command to simply skip this commit and move to the next one by using `git rebase --skip`. This may not be the correct thing to do, especially if subsequent commits in the series really depend on the changes introduced by this one. The problems are likely to snowball in this case, so it's better to truly resolve the conflict.

Finally, if the `rebase` operation turns out to be the totally wrong thing to do, `git rebase --abort` abandons the operation and restores the repository to the state prior to issuing the original `git rebase`.

Using git rebase -i

Suppose you start writing a haiku (a traditional Japanese poem) and manage to compose two full lines before checking it in:

```
$ git init -b main
Initialized empty Git repository in .git/

$ cat haiku
Talk about colour
No jealous behaviour here

$ git add haiku
$ git commit -m "Start my haiku"
[main (root-commit) 1cc856c] Start my haiku
 1 file changed, 2 insertions(+)
 create mode 100644 haiku
```

Your writing continues, but you decide you really should use the American spelling of *color* instead of the British spelling. So you make a commit to change it:

```
$ git diff
diff --git a/haiku b/haiku
index 088bea0..958aff0 100644
--- a/haiku
+++ b/haiku
@@ -1,2 +1,2 @@
-Talk about colour
+Talk about color
 No jealous behaviour here

$ git commit -a -m "Use color instead of colour"
[main b2c5047] Use color instead of colour
 1 file changed, 1 insertion(+), 1 deletion(-)
```

Finally, you develop the final line and commit it:

```
$ git diff
diff --git a/haiku b/haiku
index 958aff0..cdeddf9 100644
--- a/haiku
+++ b/haiku
@@ -1,2 +1,3 @@
 Talk about color
 No jealous behaviour here
+I favour red wine

$ git commit -a -m "Finish my colour haiku"
[main e0d8d39] Finish my colour haiku
 1 file changed, 1 insertion(+)
```

However, again you (really, it's us) have a spelling quandary and decide to change all British "ou" spellings to the American "o" spelling:

```
$ git diff
diff --git a/haiku b/haiku
index cdeddf9..064c1b5 100644
--- a/haiku
+++ b/haiku
@@ -1,3 +1,3 @@
 Talk about color
-No jealous behaviour here
-I favour red wine
+No jealous behavior here
+I favor red wine

$ git commit -a -m "Use American spellings"
[main 0aff702] Use American spellings
 1 file changed, 2 insertions(+), 2 deletions(-)
```

At this point, you've accumulated a history of commits that looks like this:

```
$ git show-branch --more=4
[main] Use American spellings
[main^] Finish my colour haiku
[main~2] Use color instead of colour
[main~3] Start my haiku
```

After looking at the commit sequence or receiving review feedback, you decide that you prefer to complete the haiku before correcting it and want the following commit history:

```
[main] Use American spellings
[main^] Use color instead of colour
[main~2] Finish my colour haiku
[main~3] Start my haiku
```

But then you also notice that there's no good reason to have two similar commits that correct the spellings of different words. Thus you would also like to squash the main and main^ into just one commit:

```
[main] Use American spellings
[main^] Finish my colour haiku
[main~2] Start my haiku
```

Reordering, editing, removing, squashing multiple commits into one, and splitting one commit into several commits are all easily performed by the git rebase command using the -i or --interactive option. This command allows you to modify the commits that make up a branch and place them back onto the same branch or onto a different branch.

A typical use, and one apropos for this example, modifies the same branch in place. In this case there are three changesets between four commits to be modified; git rebase -i needs to be told the name of the commit beyond that which you actually intend to change:

```
$ git rebase -i main~3
```

You will be placed in an editor on a file that looks like this:

```
pick b2c5047 Use color instead of colour
pick e0d8d39 Finish my colour haiku
pick 0aff702 Use American spellings

# Rebase 1cc856c..0aff702 onto 1cc856c (3 commands)
#
# Commands:
# p, pick <commit> = use commit
# r, reword <commit> = use commit, but edit the commit message
# e, edit <commit> = use commit, but stop for amending
# s, squash <commit> = use commit, but meld into previous commit
# f, fixup [-C | -c] <commit> = like "squash" but keep only the previous
#                     commit's log message, unless -C is used, in which case
#                     keep only this commit's message; -c is same as -C but
#                     opens the editor
# x, exec <command> = run command (the rest of the line) using shell
# b, break = stop here (continue rebase later with 'git rebase --continue')
# d, drop <commit> = remove commit
# l, label <label> = label current HEAD with a name
# t, reset <label> = reset HEAD to a label
# m, merge [-C <commit> | -c <commit>] <label> [# <oneline>]
# .       create a merge commit using the original merge commit's
# .       message (or the oneline, if no original merge commit was
# .       specified); use -c <commit> to reword the commit message
#
# These lines can be re-ordered; they are executed from top to bottom.
#
# If you remove a line here THAT COMMIT WILL BE LOST.
#
# However, if you remove everything, the rebase will be aborted.
```

The first three lines list the commits within the editable commit range you specified on the command line. The commits are initially listed in order from oldest to most recent and have the pick verb on each one. If you were to leave the editor now, each commit would be picked (in order), applied to the target branch, and committed. The lines preceded by a # are helpful reminders that are ignored by the program.

At this point, however, you are free to reorder the commits, squash commits together, change a commit, or delete one entirely. You can also add a commit if you already know the SHA ID. To follow the listed steps, simply reorder the commits in your editor as follows and exit it:

```
pick e0d8d39 Finish my colour haiku
pick b2c5047 Use color instead of colour
pick 0aff702 Use American spellings
```

Recall that the very first commit for the rebase is the "Start my haiku" commit. The next commit will become "Finish my colour haiku," followed by the "Use color..." and "Use American..." commits:

```
$ git rebase -i main~3

# reorder the first two commits and exit your editor

Successfully rebased and updated refs/heads/main.

$ git show-branch --more=4
[main] Use American spellings
[main^] Use color instead of colour
[main~2] Finish my colour haiku
[main~3] Start my haiku
```

Here, the history of commits has been rewritten; the two spelling commits are together, and the two writing commits are together.

Still following the outlined order, your next step is to squash the two spelling commits into just one commit. Again, issue the git rebase -i main~3 command. This time, convert the commit list from:

```
pick e0d8d39 Finish my colour haiku
pick b2c5047 Use color instead of colour
pick 0aff702 Use American spellings
```

to:

```
pick da10180 Finish my colour haiku
pick 3dd2279 Use color instead of colour
squash d83e71c Use American spellings
```

The third commit will be squashed into the immediately preceding commit, and the new commit log message template will be formed from the combination of the commits being squashed together.

In this example, the two commit log messages are joined and offered in an editor:

```
# This is a combination of 2 commits.
# This is the 1st commit message:

Use color instead of colour

# This is the commit message #2:

Use American spellings
```

These messages can be edited down to just the following:

```
Use American spellings
```

Again, all # lines are ignored.

Finally, the results of the rebase sequence can be seen:

```
$ git rebase -i main~3

# squash and rewrite the commit log message

[detached HEAD 0692bda] Use American spellings
 Date: Sun Oct 3 14:36:00 2021 +0200
 1 file changed, 3 insertions(+), 3 deletions(-)
Successfully rebased and updated refs/heads/main.

$ git show-branch --more=4
[main] Use American spellings
[main^] Finish my colour haiku
[main~2] Start my haiku
```

Although the reordering and squash steps demonstrated here occurred in two separate invocations of git rebase -i main~3, the two phases could have been performed in one. It is also perfectly valid to squash multiple sequential commits into one commit in a single step.

rebase Versus merge

In addition to the problem of simply altering history, the rebase operation has further ramifications of which you should be aware.

Rebasing a sequence of commits to the tip of a branch is similar to merging the two branches; in either case, the new head of that branch will have the combined effect of both branches represented.

You might ask yourself, "Should I use merge or rebase on my sequence of commits?" In Chapter 11, this will become an important question—especially when multiple developers, repositories, and branches come into play.

The process of rebasing a sequence of commits causes Git to generate entirely new sequences of commits. They have new SHA1 commit IDs, are based on a new initial state, and represent different diffs even though they involve changes that achieve the same ultimate state.

When faced with a situation like that shown in Figure 9-16, rebasing it into Figure 9-17 doesn't present a problem because no other commit relies on the branch being rebased. However, even within your own repository you might have additional branches based on the one you wish to rebase. Consider the graph shown in Figure 9-20.

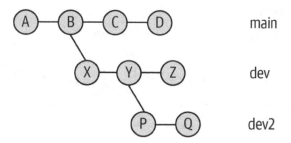

Figure 9-20. Before `git rebase` *multibranch*

You might think that executing the command:

```
# Move onto tip of main the dev branch
$ git rebase main dev
```

would yield the graph in Figure 9-21. But it does not.

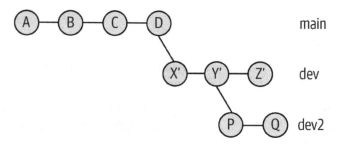

Figure 9-21. Desired `git rebase` *multibranch*

Instead, you get the following output, and you obtain the graph in Figure 9-22. This is because, during a rebase, Git stores all changes made by commits in the current branch to a temporary location internally and then reapplies them to the target branch, one by one, in order:

```
$ git rebase main dev
Successfully rebased and updated refs/heads/dev.
```

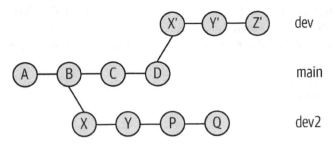

Figure 9-22. Actual git rebase multibranch

The commits X', Y', and Z' are the new versions of the old commits that stem from B. The old X and Y commits both still exist in the graph because they are still reachable from the dev2 branch. However, the original Z commit has been removed because it is no longer reachable. The branch name that *was* pointing to it has been moved to the new version of that commit.

The branch history now looks like it has duplicate commit messages in it too:

```
$ git show-branch
* [dev] Z
 ! [dev2] Q
  ! [main] D
---
*     [dev] Z
*     [dev^] Y
*     [dev~2] X
* +   [main] D
* +   [main^] C
  +   [dev2] Q
  +   [dev2^] P
  +   [dev2~2] Y
  +   [dev2~3] X
*++ [main~2] B
```

But remember, these are different commits that do essentially the same change. If you merge a branch with one of the new commits into another branch that has one of the old commits, Git has no way of knowing that you're applying the same change twice. The result is duplicate entries in git log, most likely a merge conflict, and general confusion. It's a situation that you should find a way to clean up.

If this resulting graph is actually what you want, then you're done. More likely, moving the entire branch (including subbranches) is what you really want. To achieve that graph, you will, in turn, need to rebase the dev2 branch on the new Y' commit on the dev branch:

```
$ git rebase dev^ dev2
Successfully rebased and updated refs/heads/dev2.

$ git show-branch
! [dev] Z
 * [dev2] Q
  ! [main] D
---
 *  [dev2] Q
 *  [dev2^] P
+   [dev] Z
+*  [dev2~2] Y
+*  [dev2~3] X
+*+ [main] D
```

And this is the graph shown in Figure 9-21.

Another situation that can be extremely confusing is rebasing a branch that has a merge on it. For example, suppose you had a branch structure like that shown in Figure 9-23.

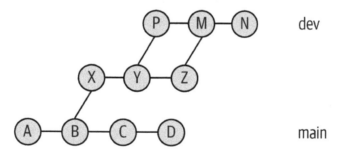

Figure 9-23. Before git rebase merge

If you want to move the entire dev branch structure from commit N down through to commit X off of B and onto D, as shown in Figure 9-24, then you might expect simply to use the command git rebase main dev.

Again, however, that command yields some surprising results:

```
$ git rebase main dev
Successfully rebased and updated refs/heads/dev.
```

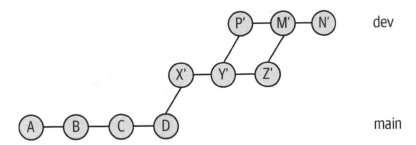

Figure 9-24. Desired `git rebase` merge

It *looks* like it did the right thing. After all, Git says that it applied all the (nonmerge) commit changes. But did it really get things right?

```
$ git show-branch
* [dev] N
 ! [main] D
--
*   [dev] N
*   [dev^] P
*   [dev~2] Z
*   [dev~3] Y
*   [dev~4] X
*+  [main] D
```

All those commits are now in one long string!

What happened here?

Git needs to move the portion of the graph reachable from dev back to the merge base at B, so it found the commits in the range main..dev. To list all those commits, Git performs a topological sort on that portion of the graph to produce a linearized sequence of all the commits in that range. Once that sequence has been determined, Git applies the commits one at a time starting on the target commit, D. Thus we say that "rebase has linearized the original branch history (with merges) onto the main branch," as shown in Figure 9-25.

Again, if that is what you wanted, or if you don't care that the graph shape has been altered, then you are done. But if, in such cases, you want to explicitly preserve the branching and merging structure of the entire branch being rebased, then use the --rebase-merges option. Because this option tries to preserve the merge commits, if there were any resolved merge conflicts, you may need to resolve or reapply the changes manually:

```
$ git rebase --rebase-merges main dev
Successfully rebased and updated refs/heads/dev.
```

We can see that the resulting graph structure maintains the original merge structure using the `git log` command:

```
$ git log --oneline --all
* 061f9fd... N
*   f669404... Merge branch 'dev2' into dev
|\
| * c386cfc... Z
* | 38ab25e... P
|/
* b93ad42... Y
* 65be7f1... X
* e3b9e22... D
* f2b96c4... C
* 8619681... B
* d6fba18... A
```

 In previous versions of Git, the option `--preserve-merges` was used to achieve the same thing. This option is deprecated in favor of the `--rebase-merges`, which works with interactive rebases.

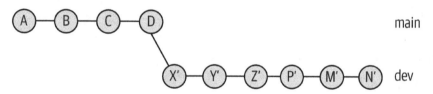

Figure 9-25. `git rebase` merge after linearization

And this looks like the graph in Figure 9-24.

Some of the principles for answering the rebase-versus-merge question apply equally to your own repository as they do to a distributed or multirepository scenario. In Chapter 12, you can read about the additional implications that affect developers using other repositories.

Depending on your development style and your ultimate intent, having the original branch development history linearized when it is rebased may or may not be acceptable. If you have already published or provided the commits on the branch that you wish to rebase, consider the negative ramifications on others.

If the rebase operation isn't the right choice and you still need the branch changes, then merging may be the correct choice.

The following concepts are important to remember:

- Rebase rewrites commits as new commits.

- Old commits that are no longer reachable are gone.
- Any user of one of the old, pre-rebase commits might be stranded.
- If you have a branch that uses a pre-rebase commit, you might need to rebase it in turn.
- If there is a user of a pre-rebase commit in a different repository, they still have a copy of that commit even though it has moved in your repository; the user will now have to fix up their commit history too.

Summary

In general, you should feel empowered to alter a commit or a commit sequence if your effort makes it cleaner and more understandable. This chapter provided you with techniques for implementing the alterations you desire for your projects, and helped you understand the consequences they will have, specifically where repository commit histories are concerned. Of course, as with all software development, there is a trade-off between repeated over-refinement and acceptance of something that is satisfactory. The key here is that you should strive for a clean, well-structured, curated Git commit history that has concise meaning for both you and your collaborators.

## CHAPTER 10

The Stash and the Reflog

Do you ever feel overwhelmed in your daily development cycle when the constant interruptions, demands for bug fixes, and requests from coworkers or managers all pile up and clutter the *real* work you are trying to do? If so, the stash was designed to help you!

In this chapter you will learn how the stash works and how to view the stashed context. Following this, you will learn about the reflog, which records the Git repository's local commits. These features will help you leverage the options Git provides when you need to temporarily stash your current work in order to work on something else.

The Stash

The *stash* is a mechanism for capturing your work in progress, allowing you to save it and return to it at a more convenient time. Sure, you can already do that using Git's existing branch and commit mechanisms, but the stash lets you quickly capture your entire index and working directory with one simple command, leaving your repository clean, uncluttered, and ready for an alternate development direction. Another single command restores the index and the working directory, allowing you to your resume where you left off.

Let's explore how the stash works with some example use cases.

Use Case: Interrupted Workflow

In this scenario, you are happily working in your Git repository and have changed several files and maybe even staged a few in the index. Then you're interrupted. Perhaps a critical bug has been discovered, and you've been asked to fix it immediately. Perhaps your team lead has suddenly prioritized a new feature over everything else and insists that you drop everything to work on it.

Whatever the circumstance, you realize that you must store your work in progress, clean your slate and work tree, and start afresh. This is a perfect opportunity for `git stash`:

```
$ cd the-git-project
# edit a lot, in the middle of something

# High-Priority Workflow Interrupt!
# Must drop everything and do something else now!

$ git stash push
Saved working directory and index state WIP on main: 1En0v80 ...

# edit high-priority change
# add and commit the changes

# continue with stashed work in progress
$ git stash pop
```

And resume where you were!

Since `push` is the default option for the `git stash` command, you can leave out the option when specifying a stash. Git also supplies a default log message when saving a stash, but you can supply your own message to better remind you of what you were working on, for example:

```
$ git stash -m "WIP: Doing real work on my stuff"
```

The acronym *WIP* is a common abbreviation for "work in progress."

Achieving the same effect with other, more basic Git commands requires that you manually create a new branch on which you commit all of your modifications, reestablishing your previous branch to continue your work and then later recovering your saved branch state on top of your new working directory. For the curious, that process roughly follows this sequence:

```
# ... normal development process interrupted ...

# Create new branch on which current state is stored.
$ git checkout -b saved_state

# Store work in progress
$ git add files
$ git commit -m "Saved state"

# Back to previous branch for immediate update.
```

```
$ git checkout main

# edit emergency fix
$ git add fixed-files
$ git commit -m "Fix something."

# Recover saved state on top of working directory.
$ git checkout saved_state
$ git reset --mixed HEAD^

# ... resume working where we left off above ...
```

The preceding process is sensitive to completeness and attention to detail. All of your changes have to be captured when you save your state, and you must remember to move your HEAD back to prevent the restoration process from being disrupted.

The git stash push command will save your current index (when you supply the --staged flag) and working directory state and will clear them out so that they again match the head of your current branch. Although this operation gives the appearance that your modified files and any files updated into the index using, for example, git add or git rm have been lost, they have not. Instead, the contents of your index and working directory are actually stored as independent, regular commits and are accessible through the ref .git/refs/stash. Executing the following command further validates this notion:

```
$ git show-branch stash
[stash] WIP on main: 3889def Some initial files.
```

As you might surmise by the use of pop to restore your state, the two basic stash commands, git stash push and git stash pop, implement a stack of stash states. That allows your interrupted workflow to be interrupted yet again! Each stashed context on the stack can be managed independently of your regular commit process.

The git stash pop command restores the context saved by a previous push operation on top of your current working directory and index (for the stash to pop the previously stored context of an index, you will need to push the staged changes with the option git stash push --staged). And by restore, we mean that the pop operation takes the stash content and *merges* those changes into the current state, rather than just overwriting or replacing files. Nice, huh? Keep in mind that your working directory must match the index for this operation to complete, as stated in the git stash manual pages.

When you use git stash pop, the command may or may not fully succeed in re-creating the full state you originally had at the time it was saved. Because the application of the saved context can be performed on top of a different commit, merging may be required, complete with possible user resolution of any conflicts.

After a successful pop operation, Git will automatically remove your saved state from the stack of saved states. This means that, once applied, the stash state will be "dropped." However, when conflict resolution is needed, Git will not automatically drop the state, just in case you want to try a different approach or want to restore it onto a different commit. Once you clear the merge conflicts and want to proceed, you should use the `git stash drop` command to manually remove the stash from the stash stack. Otherwise, Git will maintain an ever-growing[1] stack of contexts:

```
$ git stash drop
Dropped refs/stash@{0} (7ec158448f301a4fb4f7cb567225ddb1af135bde)
```

In the preceding example, if we had executed `git stash drop` without explicitly referencing the stash entry `stash@{0}`, the most recent stash entry in the stash stack would have been dropped.

If you just want to re-create the context you have saved in a stash state without dropping it from the stack, use `git stash apply`. Thus, a `git stash pop` command is a successful `git stash apply` followed by a `git stash drop`.

> In fact, you can use `git stash apply` to apply the same saved stashed context onto several different commits prior to dropping it from the stack.

However, you should carefully consider whether you want to use `git stash apply` or `git stash pop` to regain the contents of a stash. Will you ever need it again? If not, pop it. Then clean the stashed content and reference out of your object store.

Figure 10-1 illustrates this concept. Here, the repository we are working in already contains a stash stack. The `git stash push` command pushes *file5* and *file6* to the top of the stack (`stash@{0}`). The `git stash apply` command applies the stored stash of *file4* back to the *index* directory but keeps the stash stack entry (`stash@{1}`) intact. The `git stash pop` command restores the stash of *file1*, *file2*, and *file3*, respectively, to the index and working directory and will drop the stash entry from the stack (`stash@{0}`), denoted by the dotted box in the stash stack (`.git/refs/stash`).

---

1 Technically, it's not growing boundlessly. The stash is subject to reflog expiration and garbage collection.

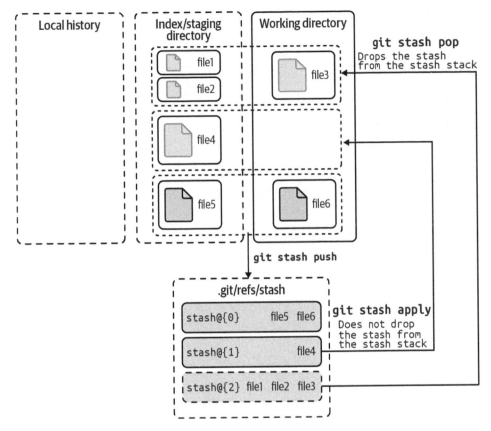

Figure 10-1. Stash concepts

Viewing the stashed context

The `git stash list` command lists the stack of saved contexts from most to least recent. In the following example, we'll work with an existing Git repository containing two files, which we will modify and stash. Then we will add a new file to the repository to show you how to stash new, untracked files you may have in your working directory:

```
$ mkdir my-repo
$ cd my-repo
$ git init -b main
$ cd my-repo
Initialized empty Git repository in /tmp/my-repo/.git/

$ echo "hello" >> file1
$ git add file1
$ git commit -m "Add file 1"
[main (root-commit) 9841192] add file 1
 1 file changed, 1 insertion(+)
 create mode 100644 file1
```

```
$ echo "Git" >> file2
$ git add file2
$ git commit -m "Add file 2"
[main 24d4b0a] add file 2
 1 file changed, 1 insertion(+)
 create mode 100644 file2

$ ls
file1  file2

$ echo "some foo" >> file1

$ git status
On branch main
Changes not staged for commit:
    (use "git add <file>..." to update what will be committed)
    (use "git restore -- <file>..." to discard changes in working directory)

       modified:   file1

no changes added to commit (use "git add" and/or "git commit -a")

$ git stash -m "Tinkered file1"
Saved working directory and index state On main: Tinkered file1

$ git commit --dry-run
On branch main
nothing to commit, working directory clean

$ echo "some bar" >> file2

$ git stash -m "Messed with file2"
Saved working directory and index state On main: Messed with file2

$ git stash list
stash@{0}: On main: Messed with file2
stash@{1}: On main: Tinkered file1

$ echo "new" >> file3

# Stashing will fail for any new untracked file
$ git stash -m "Add new untracked file3"
No local changes to save

# Add the option -u to stash new untracked file to the stash stack
$ git stash -u -m "Add new untracked file3"
Saved working directory and index state On main: Add new untracked file3

$ git stash list
stash@{0}: On main: Add new untracked file3
stash@{1}: On main: Messed with file2
stash@{2}: On main: Tinkered file1
```

Git always numbers the stash entries, with the most recent entry being zero. As entries get older, they increase in numerical order. As such, the different stash entry names are stash@{0} and stash@{1}, as we will explain in "The Reflog" on page 232. The git stash show command shows the index and file changes recorded for a given stash entry, relative to its parent commit:

```
$ git stash show stash@{1}
 file2 |    1 +
```

```
1 file changed, 1 insertion(+)
```

That summary may or may not be the extent of the information you sought. If not, adding -p to the git stash show command so that you can see the diffs might be more useful. Note that, by default, the git stash show command shows the most recent stash entry, stash@{0}.

Because the changes that contribute to making a stash state are relative to a particular commit, showing the state is a state-to-state comparison suitable for git diff, rather than a sequence of commit states suitable for git log. Thus, all the options for git diff may also be supplied to git stash show as well. As we saw previously, --stat is the default, but other options are valid too. Here, -p is used to obtain the patch differences for a given stash state:

```
$ git stash show -p stash@{1}
diff --git a/file2 b/file2
index 5664e30..265404f 100644
--- a/file2
+++ b/file2
@@ -1 +1,2 @@
 git
+some bar
```

Use Case: Updating Local Work in Progress with Upstream Changes

Another classic use case for git stash is when you have local changes that are not entirely complete but you want to pull in the latest changes from the upstream repository to evaluate whether your current changes break the repository with work from the new changes. In the Git manuals, this is referenced as the "pull into a dirty tree" scenario. It goes something like this: you're developing in your local repository and have made several commits. You still have some modified files that haven't been committed yet, but you realize there are upstream changes that you want to make. If you have conflicting modifications, a simple git pull will fail, refusing to overwrite your local changes. One quick way to work around this problem is to use git stash:

```
$ git pull
# ... pull fails due to merge conflicts ...

$ git stash
Saved working directory and index state WIP on main: e4896bd ...

$ git pull
$ git stash pop
Already up to date.
On branch main
...
...
Dropped refs/stash@{0} (39351f8d3bd89116df89a67119831638d6268180)
```

At this point, you may or may not need to resolve conflicts created by the pop.

If you have new, uncommitted (and hence "untracked") files as part of your local development, it is possible that a git pull that would also introduce a file of the same name might fail, thus not wanting to overwrite your version of the new file. In this case, add the --include-untracked option to your git stash so that it *also* stashes your new, untracked files along with the rest of your modifications. That will ensure a completely clean working directory for the pull.

The --all option will gather up the untracked files as well as the explicitly ignored files from the *.gitignore* and *exclude* files.

Finally, for more complex stashing operations where you wish to selectively choose which hunks should be stashed, use the -p or --patch option as described in the manual pages (this is similar to using git add interactively to select the hunk of changes to be stashed).

In a similar scenario, git stash can be used when you want to move modified work out of the way, enabling a clean pull --rebase. This would typically happen just prior to pushing your local commits upstream:

```
# ... edit and commit ...
# ... more editing and working...

$ git commit --dry-run
# On branch main
# Your branch is ahead of 'origin/main' by 2 commits.
#
# Changed but not updated:
#   (use "git add <file>..." to update what will be committed)
#   (use "git restore -- <file>..." to discard changes in working directory)
#
#       modified:   file1.h
#       modified:   file1.c
#
no changes added to commit (use "git add" and/or "git commit -a")
```

At this point, you may decide that the commits you have already made should go upstream, but you also want to leave the modified files here in your working directory. However, Git refuses to pull:

```
$ git pull --rebase
error: cannot pull with rebase: You have unstaged changes.
error: please commit or stash them.
```

This scenario isn't as contrived as it might seem at first. For example, some of us frequently work in a repository where we want to modify a *Makefile*,[2] perhaps to enable debugging, or we need to modify some configuration options for a build. We

---

2 A Makefile is as special file that contains shell commands used by the Make build utility tool in Unix.

don't want to commit those changes, and we don't want to lose them between updates from a remote repository. We just want them to linger in our working directory.

Again, this is where `git stash` helps:

```
$ git stash
Saved working directory and index state WIP on main: 5955d14 Some commit log.

$ git pull --rebase
remote: Counting objects: 63, done.
remote: Compressing objects: 100% (43/43), done.
remote: Total 43 (delta 36), reused 0 (delta 0)
Unpacking objects: 100% (43/43), done.
From ssh://git/var/git/my_repo
   871746b..6687d58  main      -> origin/main
Successfully rebased and updated refs/heads/main.
```

After you pull in upstream commits and rebase your local commits on top of them, your repository is in good shape to send your work upstream. If desired, you can readily push them now:

```
# Push upstream now if desired!
$ git push
```

or after restoring your previous working directory state:

```
$ git stash pop
Auto-merging file1.h
On branch main
Your branch is ahead of 'origin/main' by 2 commits.

Changed but not updated:
    (use "git add <file>..." to update what will be committed)
    (use "git restore -- <file>..." to discard changes in working directory)

        modified:   file1.h
        modified:   file1.c

no changes added to commit (use "git add" and/or "git commit -a")
Dropped refs/stash@{0} (7e2546f5808a95a2e6934fcffb5548651badf00d)

$ git push
```

If you decide to `git push` after popping your stash, remember that only completed, committed work will be pushed. There's no need to worry about pushing your partial, uncommitted work. There is also no need to worry about pushing your stashed content: the stash is purely a local notion.

Figure 10-2 illustration represents a high-level mental model of this concept.

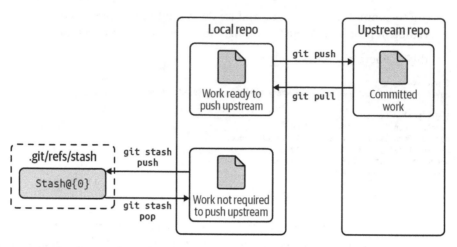

Figure 10-2. Pushing only completed, uncommitted work upstream

Use Case: Converting Stashed Changes Into a Branch

Sometimes, stashing your changes leads to a sequence of development on your branch, and restoring your stashed state on top of those changes may not make sense. In addition, merge conflicts might make popping difficult. Nonetheless, you may still want to recover the work you stashed. In situations like this, Git offers the `git stash branch` command to help you. This command converts the contents of a saved stash into a new branch based on the commit that was current at the time the stash entry was made. Let's see how that works on a repository with a bit of history in it:

```
$ git log --pretty=one --abbrev-commit
d5ef6c9 Some commit.
efe990c Initial commit.
```

Some files are modified and subsequently stashed:

```
$ git stash
Saved working directory and index state WIP on main: d5ef6c9 Some commit.
```

Note that the stash was made against commit d5ef6c9.

Due to other development reasons, more commits are made, and the branch drifts away from the d5ef6c9 state:

```
$ git log --pretty=one --abbrev-commit
2c2af13 Another mod
1d1e905 Drifting file state.
d5ef6c9 Some commit.
efe990c Initial commit.

$ git show-branch -a
[main] Another mod
```

And although the stashed work is available, it doesn't apply cleanly to the current main branch:

```
$ git stash list
stash@{0}: WIP on main: d5ef6c9 Some commit.

$ git stash pop
Auto-merging foo
CONFLICT (content): Merge conflict in foo
Auto-merging bar
CONFLICT (content): Merge conflict in bar
The stash entry is kept in case you need it again.
```

Therefore, we need to reset some state and take a different approach, creating a new branch called mod that contains the stashed changes:

```
$ git reset --hard main
HEAD is now at 2c2af13 Another mod

$ git stash branch mod
Switched to a new branch 'mod'
On branch mod
Changes not staged for commit:
   (use "git add <file>..." to update what will be committed)
   (use "git restore -- <file>..." to discard changes in working directory)

    modified:   bar
    modified:   foo

no changes added to commit (use "git add" and/or "git commit -a")
Dropped refs/stash@{0} (96e53da61f7e5031ef04d68bf60a34bd4f13bd9f)
```

There are several important points to notice here. First, notice that the branch is based on the original commit d5ef6c9, and not on the current HEAD commit 2c2af13:

```
$ git show-branch -a
! [main] Another mod
 * [mod] Some commit.
--
+  [main] Another mod
+  [main^] Drifting file state.
+* [mod] Some commit.
```

Second, because the stash is always reconstituted against the original commit, it will always succeed and hence will be dropped from the stash stack.

Finally, reconstituting the stash state doesn't automatically commit any of your changes onto the new branch. All the stashed file modifications (and index changes, if desired) are still left in your working directory on the newly created and checked-out branch:

```
$ git commit --dry-run
# On branch mod
# Changes not staged for commit:
#   (use "git add <file>..." to update what will be committed)
#   (use "git checkout -- <file>..." to discard changes in working directory)
#
```

```
#     modified:   bar
#     modified:   foo
#
no changes added to commit (use "git add" and/or "git commit -a")
```

At this point, you can commit the changes onto the new branch, presumably as a precursor to further development or merging as you deem necessary:

```
$ git commit -a -m "Stuff from the stash"
[mod 42c104f] Stuff from the stash
 2 files changed, 2 insertions(+), 0 deletions(-)

$ git show-branch
! [main] Another mod
 * [mod] Stuff from the stash
--
 * [mod] Stuff from the stash
+  [main] Another mod
+  [main^] Drifting file state.
+* [mod^] Some commit.
```

Note that this isn't a magic bullet to avoid resolving merge conflicts. If there were merge conflicts when you tried to pop the stash directly onto the main branch earlier, trying to merge the new branch with the main branch will yield the same effects and the same merge conflicts:

```
$ git checkout main
Switched to branch 'main'

$ git merge mod
Auto-merging foo
CONFLICT (content): Merge conflict in foo
Auto-merging bar
CONFLICT (content): Merge conflict in bar
Automatic merge failed; fix conflicts and then commit the result.
```

The ability to create stashes might be appealing, but be careful not to overuse it and create too many stashes. And don't just convert them to named branches to make them linger!

The Reflog

Sometimes Git does something either mysterious or magical and causes one to wonder what just happened. Sometimes you simply want an answer to the question, "Wait, where was I? What just happened?" Other times, you do some operation and realize "Uh-oh, I shouldn't have done that!" But it is too late, and you have already lost the top commit with a week's worth of awesome development.

Not to worry! Git's reflog has you covered in either case! By using the reflog, you can gain the assurance that operations happened as you expected on the branches you intended and that you have the ability to recover lost commits just in case something goes astray.

The *reflog* is a record of changes to the tips of branches within nonbare repositories. Every time an update is made to any ref, including HEAD, the reflog is updated to record how that ref has changed. Think of the reflog as a trail of breadcrumbs showing where you and your refs have been. With that analogy, you can also use the reflog to follow your trail of crumbs and trace back through your branch manipulations.

Some of the basic operations that record reflog updates include:

- Cloning
- Pushing
- Making new commits
- Changing or creating branches
- Rebase operations
- Reset operations

Fundamentally, any Git operation that modifies a ref or changes the tip of a branch is recorded.

By default, the reflog is enabled in nonbare repositories and disabled in bare repositories. Specifically, the reflog is controlled by the Boolean configuration option `core.logAllRefUpdates`. It can be enabled using the command `git configcore.logAllRefUpdates true` and disabled with `false` as desired on a per-repository basis.

 A *bare repository* is a repository that is set up on a server and has no working directory. You can think of it as being similar to a blueprint. When developers on a team make changes to the blueprint, each developer's changes are reflected in a copy of the blueprint, but the blueprint remains unchanged.

So, what does the reflog look like?

```
$ git reflog show
a44d980 HEAD@{0}: reset: moving to main
79e881c HEAD@{1}: commit: last foo change
a44d980 HEAD@{2}: checkout: moving from main to fred
a44d980 HEAD@{3}: rebase -i (finish): returning to refs/heads/main
a44d980 HEAD@{4}: rebase -i (pick): Tinker bar
a777d4f HEAD@{5}: rebase -i (pick): Modify bar
e3c46b8 HEAD@{6}: rebase -i (squash): More foo and bar with additional stuff.
8a04ca4 HEAD@{7}: rebase -i (squash): updating HEAD
1a4be28 HEAD@{8}: checkout: moving from main to 1a4be28
ed6e906 HEAD@{9}: commit: Tinker bar
6195b3d HEAD@{10}: commit: Squash into 'more foo and bar'
488b893 HEAD@{11}: commit: Modify bar
1a4be28 HEAD@{12}: commit: More foo and bar
8a04ca4 HEAD@{13}: commit (initial): Initial foo and bar.
```

Although the reflog records transactions for all refs, `git reflog show` displays the transactions for only one ref at a time. The previous example shows the default ref, HEAD. If you recall that branch names are also refs, you will realize that you can also get the reflog for any branch as well. From the previous example, we can see that there is also a branch named `fred`, so we can display its changes in another command:

```
$ git reflog fred
a44d980 fred@{0}: reset: moving to main
79e881c fred@{1}: commit: last foo change
a44d980 fred@{2}: branch: Created from HEAD
```

Each line records an individual transaction from the history of the ref, starting with the most recent change and going back in time. The leftmost column contains the commit ID at the time the change was made. Entries such as HEAD@{7} from the second column provide convenient names for the commit at each transaction. Thus, HEAD@{0} is the most recent entry, HEAD@{1} records where HEAD was just prior to that, and so on. The oldest entry, HEAD@{13}, is actually the very first commit in this repository. The rest of each line after the colon describes the transaction that occurred. Finally, for each transaction there is a timestamp (not shown) that records when the event took place within your repository.

So what good is all that? Here's the interesting aspect of the reflog: the sequentially numbered HEAD names (e.g., HEAD@{1}) can be used as symbolic names of commits for any Git command that takes a commit, for example:

```
$ git show HEAD@{10}
commit 6195b3dfd30e464ffb9238d89e3d15f2c1dc35b0
Author: Jon Loeliger <jdl@example.com>
Date:   Sat Oct 29 09:57:05 2011 -0500

    Squash into 'more foo and bar'

diff --git a/foo b/foo
index 740fd05..a941931 100644
--- a/foo
+++ b/foo
@@ -1,2 +1 @@
-Foo!
-more foo
+junk
```

That means that as you go about your development process, recording commits, moving to different branches, rebasing, and otherwise manipulating a branch, you can always use the reflog to reference where the branch was. The name HEAD@{1} always references the previous commit for the branch, HEAD@{2} names the HEAD commit just prior to that, and so on. Keep in mind, though, that although the history names individual commits, transactions other than `git commit` are present also. Every time you move the tip of your branch to a different commit, it is logged.

Thus, HEAD@{3} doesn't necessarily mean the third prior git commit operation. More accurately, it means the third prior visited or referenced commit.

Git also supports more English language–like qualifiers for the part of the reference within curly brackets. Maybe you aren't sure exactly how many changes took place since something happened, but you know you want what it looked like yesterday or an hour ago:

```
$ git log 'HEAD@{yesterday}'
commit 1a4be2804f7382b2dd399891eef097eb10ddc1eb
Author: Jon Loeliger <jdl@example.com>
Date:   Sat Oct 29 09:55:52 2011 -0500

More foo and bar

commit 8a04ca4207e1cb74dd3a3e261d6be72e118ace9e
Author: Jon Loeliger <jdl@example.com>
Date:   Sat Oct 29 09:55:07 2011 -0500

Initial foo and bar.
```

Git supports a fairly wide variety of date-based qualifiers for refs. These include words like *yesterday, noon, midnight, afternoon, tea*,[3] names of the days of the week, names of months, A.M. and P.M. indicators, absolute times and dates, and relative phrases like "last monday," "1 hour ago," "10 minutes ago," and combinations of these phrases such as "1 day, 2 hours ago." And, finally, if you omit the actual ref name and just use the @{...} form, the current branch name is assumed. Thus, while on the bugfix branch, using just @{noon} refers to bugfix@{noon}.

 The Git tool responsible for understanding references is git rev-parse. Its manpage is extensive and details more than you would ever care to know about how refs are interpreted.

Although these date-based qualifiers are fairly liberal, they are not perfect. Understand that Git uses a heuristic to interpret them, so exercise some caution when referring to them. Also remember that the notion of time is local and relative to your repository: these time-qualified refs reference the value of a ref in your local repository only. Using the same phrase about time in a different repository will likely yield different results due to different reflogs. Thus, main@{2.days.ago} refers to the state of your local main branch two days ago. If you don't have reflog history to cover that time period, Git should warn you:

---

3 No, really. And yes, that is 5:00 P.M.!

```
$ git log HEAD@{last-monday}
warning: Log for 'HEAD' only goes back to Sat, 29 Oct 2011 09:55:07 -0500.
commit 8a04ca4207e1cb74dd3a3e261d6be72e118ace9e
Author: Jon Loeliger <jdl@example.com>
Date:   Sat Oct 29 09:55:07 2011 -0500

Initial foo and bar.
```

One last warning: don't let the shell trick you. There is a significant difference between these two commands:

```
# Bad!
$ git log dev@{2 days ago}

# Likely correct for your shell
$ git log 'dev@{2 days ago}'
```

The former, without single quotes, provides multiple command-line arguments to your shell, whereas the latter, with quotes, passes the entire ref phrase as one command-line argument. Git needs to see the ref as one word from the shell. To help simplify the word break issue, Git allows several variations:

```
# These should all be equivalent
$ git log 'dev@{2 days ago}'
$ git log dev@{2.days.ago}
$ git log dev@{2-days-ago}
```

One more concern to address: if Git is maintaining a transaction history of every operation performed on every ref in the repository, doesn't the reflog eventually become huge?

Luckily, no. Git automatically runs a garbage collection process occasionally. During this process, some of the older reflog entries are expired and dropped. Normally, a commit that is otherwise not referenced or reachable from some branch or ref will expire after a default of 30 days, and commits that are reachable expire after a default of 90 days. Take a look at Figure 10-3.

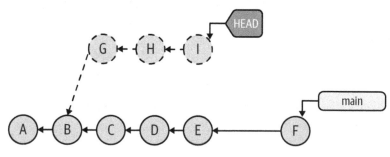

Figure 10-3. Unreachable commits

In Figure 10-3, commits G, H, and I are unreachable commits. Commits A through F are reachable commits. The key here is where the HEAD is pointing to. You can see that for commits G, H, and I, HEAD is in a detached HEAD mode, and those commits are not associated with a branch name. This is a result of directly checking out to commit B, followed by adding new commits from that point on.

If the default garbage collection schedule isn't ideal, the configuration variables gc.reflogExpireUnreachable and gc.reflogExpire can be set to alternate values in your repository. You can use the command git reflog delete to remove individual entries, or use the command git reflog expire to directly cause entries older than a specified time to be immediately removed. The latter command can also be used to forcefully expire the reflog:

```
$ git reflog expire --expire=now --all
$ git gc
```

One last implementation detail: reflogs are stored under the *.git/logs* directory. The file *.git/logs/HEAD* contains the history of HEAD values, whereas the subdirectory *.git/logs/refs/* contains the history of all refs, including the stash. The sub-subdirectory *.git/logs/refs/heads* contains the history for branch heads.

All the information stored in the reflogs, specifically everything under the *.git/logs* directory, is ultimately transitory and expendable. Throwing away the *.git/logs* directory or turning the reflog off harms no Git-internal data structure; it simply means references like main@{4} can't be resolved.

Conversely, having the reflog enabled introduces references to commits that might otherwise be unreachable. If you are trying to clean up and shrink your repository size, removing the reflog may enable the removal of otherwise unreachable (i.e., irrelevant) commits.

Summary

In this chapter we discussed two different tools. The stash tool provides you with a clever mechanism to store any development work in progress so that you can handle interruptions to your workflow and then return to your dev work later. The reflog tool gives you an audit trail of changes that modified a ref or changed the tip of any given branch for a limited period of time in your local development environment. Although these tools focus on commits and changes you are introducing to the repository, you can leverage them whenever you are interrupted from your development workflow to tend to a task that requires your immediate attention.

## CHAPTER 11

Remote Repositories

So far, we've worked almost entirely within one local repository. Now it's time to explore the much-lauded distributed features of Git and learn how to collaborate with other developers via shared repositories.

Working with multiple and remote repositories adds a few new terms to the Git vernacular.

A *clone* is a copy of a repository. A clone contains all the objects from the original repository; as a result, each clone is an independent and autonomous repository and a true, symmetric peer of the original. A clone allows each developer to work locally and independently without centralization, polls, or locks. Ultimately, it's cloning that allows Git to easily scale and permit many geographically distributed contributors.

Essentially, separate repositories are useful under the following conditions:

- When developers work autonomously.
- When a project is expected to diverge significantly along separate development paths. Although the regular branching and merging mechanisms demonstrated in previous chapters can handle any amount of separate development, the resulting complexity may become more trouble than it's worth. Instead, diverged development paths can use separate repositories to be merged again whenever appropriate.

Cloning a repository is just the first step in sharing code. You must also relate one repository to another to establish paths for data exchange. Git establishes these repository connections through what we call *remotes*.

This chapter is divided into five parts, with each part incrementally building on the previous one to explain the concepts of working with remote repositories. In "Part I: Repository Concepts" on page 240, we cover repository concepts and working with a remote repository. In "Part II: Example Using Remote Repositories" on page 251, we provide examples and techniques to share, track, and obtain data across multiple repositories. "Part III: Remote Repository Development Cycle in Pictures" on page 265 reinforces the learning visually by elaborating on the development lifecycle for remote repositories. In "Part IV: Remote Configuration" on page 272, we discuss the many ways you can manage remote configurations for any given repository. And in "Part V: Working with Tracking Branches" on page 275, we tie things up by explaining the importance of working with remote-tracking branches in the best recommended method.

Part I: Repository Concepts

The repository concepts discussed in this part are the building blocks to understanding and working with a Git repository in a shared and distributed environment. The following sections will introduce key principles and important terminology to help you transition to working in a Git repository.

Bare and Development Repositories

A Git repository is either a bare or a development (nonbare) repository.

A *development repository* is used for normal, daily development. It maintains the notion of a current branch and provides a checked-out copy of the current branch in a working directory. All of the repositories mentioned in the book so far have been development repositories.

In contrast, a *bare repository* has no working directory and shouldn't be used for normal development. Also, a bare repository has no notion of a checked-out branch. Think of a bare repository as simply the contents of the *.git* directory. In other words, you shouldn't make commits in a bare repository.

A bare repository might seem to be of little use, but its role is crucial: to serve as an authoritative focal point for collaborative development. Other developers `clone` and `fetch` from the bare repository and `push` updates to it. We'll work through an example later in this chapter that shows how all of this works together.

First, let's examine how the `--bare` flag affects the directory that is initialized when creating a development repository and a bare repository:

```
# Development (nonbare) repo
$ cd /tmp

$ git init -b main fluff
Initialized empty Git repository in /private/tmp/fluff/.git/

$ tree fluff
fluff

0 directories, 0 files

# Bare repo
$ git init --bare -b main fluff-bare
Initialized empty Git repository in /private/tmp/fluff-bare/
fatal: this operation must be run in a work tree

$ tree fluff-bare
fluff
├── HEAD
├── config
├── description
├── hooks
│   ├── applypatch-msg.sample
│   ├── commit-msg.sample
│   ├── fsmonitor-watchman.sample
│   ├── post-update.sample
│   ├── pre-applypatch.sample
│   ├── pre-commit.sample
│   ├── pre-merge-commit.sample
│   ├── pre-push.sample
│   ├── pre-rebase.sample
│   ├── pre-receive.sample
│   ├── prepare-commit-msg.sample
│   ├── push-to-checkout.sample
│   └── update.sample
├── info
│   └── exclude
├── objects
│   ├── info
│   └── pack
└── refs
    ├── heads
    └── tags

8 directories, 17 files
```

If you issue a `git clone` command with the `--bare` option, Git creates a bare repository; otherwise, a development repository is created.

 Notice that we did not say that `git clone --bare` creates a new or empty repository. We said it creates a *bare* repository. And that newly cloned repository will contain a copy of the content from the upstream repository. The command `git init` creates a new and empty repository, and that repository can come in both *development* and *bare* variants. You can compare the earlier created repositories using this diff trick:

```
# execute from the root directory of both the repos
        $ diff -y <(tree fluff/.git/) <(tree fluff-bare)
```

By default, Git enables a reflog (as explained in "The Reflog" on page 232) on development repositories but not on bare repositories. This again anticipates that development will take place in the former and not in the latter. By the same reasoning, no remotes are created in a bare repository.

If you set up a repository into which developers push changes, it should be bare. In effect, this is a special case of the more general best practice that a published repository should be bare.

Repository Clones

The `git clone` command creates a new Git repository based on the original repository that you specify via a filesystem or network address. Git doesn't have to copy all the information from the original to the clone repository. Instead, Git ignores information that is pertinent only to the original repository, such as remote-tracking branches.

> In normal `git clone` use, the local development branches of the original repository, stored within *.git/refs/heads/*, become remote-tracking branches in the new clone under *.git/refs/remotes/*. Remote-tracking branches within *.git/refs/remotes/* in the original repository are not cloned. (The clone doesn't need to know what, if anything, the upstream repository is in turn tracking.)

Tags from the original repository are copied into the clone, as are all objects that are reachable from the copied refs. However, repository-specific information such as hooks (see Chapter 14), configuration files, the reflog, and the stash of the original repository are not reproduced in the clone.

In "Making a local copy of the repository" on page 19, we showed how `git clone` can be used to create a copy of your *my_website* repository:

```
$ git clone my_website new_website
```

Here, *my_website* is considered the original, "remote" repository. The new, resulting clone is *new_website*.

Similarly, `git clone` can be used to clone a copy of a repository from network sites:

```
$ git clone git://git.kernel.org/pub/scm/linux/kernel/git/torvalds/linux.git
```

By default, each new clone maintains a link back to its parent repository via a remote called `origin`. However, the original repository has no knowledge of nor does it maintain a link to any clone. It is purely a one-way relationship.[1]

The name *origin* isn't special in any way. If you don't want to use it, simply specify an alternative name with the `--origin` *name* option during the clone operation.

```
$ git clone git://git.kernel.org/pub/scm/linux/kernel/git/torvalds/linux.git \
> --origin somename
```

Git also configures the default `origin` remote with a default `fetch` refspec (refspecs transfer data to and from a remote repository and are discussed later).

Establishing the `fetch` refspec anticipates that you want to continue updating your local repository by fetching changes from the originating repository. In this case, the remote repository's branches are available in the clone on branch names prefixed with `origin/`, such as `origin/main`, `origin/dev`, or `origin/maint`.

An example refspec looks like the following in your repo configuration file:

```
fetch = +refs/heads/*:refs/remotes/origin/*
```

Remotes

The repository you're currently working in is called the *local* or *current repository*, and the repository with which you exchange files is called the *remote repository*. But the latter term is a bit of a misnomer because the repository may or may not be on a physically remote or even different machine; it could conceivably be just another repository on a local filesystem. In Chapter 12, we discuss how the term *upstream repository* is usually used to identify the remote repository from which your local repository is derived via a clone operation.

Git uses both the remote and the remote-tracking branch to reference and facilitate the connection to another repository. The remote provides a friendly name for the repository and can be used in place of the actual repository URL. A remote also forms part of the name basis for the remote-tracking branches for that repository.

Use the `git remote` command to create, remove, manipulate, and view a remote. All the remotes you introduce are recorded in the *.git/config* file and can be manipulated using `git config`.

Figure 11-1 illustrates this concept.

---

1 Of course, a bidirectional remote relationship can be set up later using the `git remote` command.

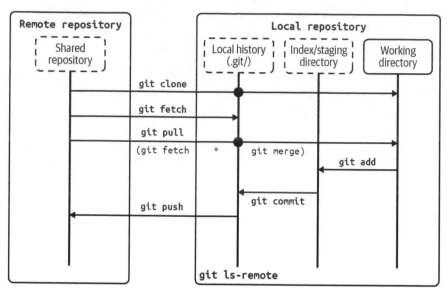

Figure 11-1. Remote git command

Note that for `git clone` and `git pull` operations in Figure 11-1, the update to the local history is represented as a dot.

In addition to `git clone`, other common Git commands that refer to remote repositories include the following:

`git fetch`
Retrieves objects and their related metadata from a remote repository.

`git pull`
Like `git fetch` but also merges changes into a corresponding local branch.

`git push`
Transfers objects and their related metadata to a remote repository.

`git ls-remote`
Shows a list of references along with their associated commit SHA1s, held by a given remote (on an upstream server). This command indirectly answers the question "Is an update available?"

Tracking Branches

Once you clone a repository, you can keep up with changes in the original source repository even as you make local commits and create local branches.

As Git itself has evolved, some terminology around branch names has also evolved and become more standard. To help clarify the purposes of the various branches, different namespaces have been created. Although any branch in your local repository is still considered a local branch, the branches can be further divided into different categories:

- *Remote-tracking branches* are associated with a remote and have the specific purpose of following the changes of each branch in the remote repository.
- A *local-tracking branch* is paired with a remote-tracking branch. It is a type of integration branch that collects both the changes from your local development branch and the changes from the remote-tracking branch.
- Any local, nontracking branch is usually generically called a *topic* or *development branch*.
- Finally, to complete the namespaces, a *remote branch* is a branch located in a nonlocal, remote repository. It is likely an upstream source for a remote-tracking branch.

During a clone operation, Git creates a remote-tracking branch in the clone for each topic branch in the upstream repository. The set of remote-tracking branches is introduced in a new, separate namespace within the local repository that is specific to the remote being cloned. The local repository uses its remote-tracking branches to follow or track changes made in the remote repository:

```
# Clone Repository and create a new local branch
$ cd git-repo

$ git branch -a
  main               <-- # local-tracking branch
* mylocal-branch     <-- # local, nontracking branch (topic or development)
  remotes/origin/main <-- # remote-tracking branches
```

In the preceding code snippet, a "remote branch" was not listed. This scenario could occur when a new branch was created on the remote repository after you performed a clone operation at that moment in time.

 You may recall from "Refs and Symrefs" on page 83 that a local topic branch that you call dev is really named refs/heads/ dev. Similarly, remote-tracking branches are retained in the refs/ remotes/ namespace. Thus the remote-tracking branch origin/ main is actually refs/remotes/origin/main.

Because remote-tracking branches are lumped into their own namespace, there is a clear separation between branches made in a repository by you (topic branches) and those branches that are actually based on another, remote repository (remote-tracking branches). In the early Git days, separate namespaces were just a best practice designed to help prevent you from making accidental conflicts. Today, separate namespaces are considered to be much more than a best practice. They are an integral part of how you are expected to use your branches to interact with your upstream repositories.

All the operations that you can perform on a regular topic branch can also be performed on a tracking branch. However, there are some restrictions and guidelines to observe.

Because remote-tracking branches are used exclusively to follow the changes from another repository, you should effectively treat them as read only. You shouldn't merge or make commits onto a remote-tracking branch. Doing so would cause your remote-tracking branch to become out of sync with the remote repository. Worse, each future update from the remote repository would likely require merging, making your clone increasingly difficult to manage. Proper management of tracking branches is covered in more detail later in this chapter.

Referencing Other Repositories

To coordinate your repository with another repository, you define a remote, which here means a named entity stored in the config file of a repository. It consists of two different parts. The first part states the name of the other repository in the form of a URL. The second part, called a *refspec*, specifies how a ref (which usually represents a branch) should be mapped from the namespace of one repository into the namespace of the other repository.

Let's look at each of these components in turn.

Referring to Remote Repositories

Git supports several types of Uniform Resource Locators (URLs) that can be used to name remote repositories. These URLs specify both an access protocol and the location or address of the data.

Technically, Git's URLs are neither true URLs nor Uniform Resource Identifiers (URIs) because none entirely conform to RFC 1738 or RFC 2396, respectively. However, because of their versatile utility in naming the location of Git repositories, Git's variants are usually referred to as *Git URLs*. Furthermore, the *.git/config* file uses the name url as well.

As you have seen, the simplest form of Git URL refers to a repository on a local filesystem, be it a true physical filesystem or a virtual filesystem mounted locally via the Network File System (NFS). There are two permutations:

```
/path/to/repo.git
file:///path/to/repo
```

Although these two formats are essentially identical, there is a subtle but important distinction between the two. The former uses hard links within the filesystem to directly share exactly the same objects between the current and remote repositories; the latter copies the objects instead of sharing them directly. To avoid issues associated with shared repositories, the `file://` form is recommended.

The other forms of the Git URL referring to repositories on remote systems follow.

When you have a truly remote repository whose data must be retrieved across a network, the most efficient form of data transfer is often called the *Git native protocol*, which refers to the custom protocol used internally by Git to transfer data. Examples of a native protocol URL include the following:

```
git://example.com/path/to/repo.git
git://example.com/~user/path/to/repo.git
```

These forms are used by `git-daemon` to publish repositories for anonymous read. You can both clone and fetch using these URL forms.

For secure, authenticated connections, the Git native protocol can be tunneled over a Secure Shell (SSH) connection using the following URL templates:

```
ssh://[user@]example.com[:port]/path/to/repo.git
ssh://[user@]example.com/path/to/repo.git
ssh://[user@]example.com/~user2/path/to/repo.git
ssh://[user@]example.com/~/path/to/repo.git
```

The third form allows for the possibility of two different usernames. The first is the user under whom the session is authenticated, and the second is the user whose home directory is accessed.

Git also supports a URL form with scp-like syntax. It's identical to the SSH forms, but there is no way to specify a port parameter:

```
[user@]example.com:/path/to/repo.git
[user@]example.com:~user/path/to/repo.git
[user@]example.com:path/to/repo.git
```

Although the HTTP and HTTPS URL variants have been fully supported since the early days of Git, they have undergone some important changes since version 1.6.6:

```
http://example.com/path/to/repo.git
https://example.com/path/to/repo.git
```

Prior to Git version 1.6.6, neither the HTTP nor the HTTPS protocol was as efficient as the Git native protocol. In version 1.6.6, the HTTP protocol was improved dramatically and has become essentially as efficient as the Git native protocol. Git literature refers to this implementation as "smart" in contrast to the prior, so-called "dumb" implementation.

With the HTTP efficiency benefit realized now, the utility of the `http://` and `https://` URL forms will likely become more important and popular. Notably, most corporate firewalls allow HTTP port 80 and HTTPS port 443 to remain open, while the default Git port 9418 is typically blocked. Furthermore, these URL forms are being favored by popular Git hosting sites like GitHub.

Finally, the Rsync protocol can be specified:

```
rsync://example.com/path/to/repo.git
```

The use of Rsync is discouraged because it is inferior to the other options. If absolutely necessary, it should be used only for an initial clone, at which point the remote repository reference should be changed to one of the other mechanisms. Continuing to use the Rsync protocol for later updates may lead to the loss of locally created data.

These protocols, as mentioned earlier, are a way to reference the remote repositories, but in actual essence they also dictate the method in which data from the remote repositories is to be transferred. Each transfer protocol has its own advantages and disadvantages. Generally the concerns are around security (encryption and the need for authenticated access of the repository data which is being transferred), simplicity of configuring the protocols within your network servers, and developer experience in working with remote repositories.

You may be wondering which protocol is better when cloning a repository: SSH or HTTPS.

Both protocols are secure. But when you need to access a remote repository from multiple machines, with the SSH protocol you will have to generate the SSH key for each machine and configure it on the server before you are able to clone. With the HTTPS protocol, you can skip this step since you can be authenticated via a prompt when you perform a clone operation.")))

The refspec

In "Refs and Symrefs" on page 83, we explained how the ref, or reference, names a particular commit within the history of the repository. Usually a ref is the name of a branch. A refspec maps branch names in the remote repository to branch names within your local repository.

Because a refspec must simultaneously name branches from the local repository and the remote repository, complete branch names are common in a refspec and are often required. In a refspec, you typically see the names of development branches with the `refs/heads/` prefix and the names of remote-tracking branches with the `refs/remotes/` prefix. (For brevity, we've omitted the `.git/` when referencing the ref paths.)

Refspecs are added to your repository's *.git/config* when you clone a repository and when you add or update remotes to your repository (we cover how to add remotes later in this chapter). The following snippet is an example:

```
$ cd git-repo
$ cat .git/config
...
...
[remote "origin"]
        url = https://github.com/ppremk/git.git

        # The Refspec
        fetch = +refs/heads/*:refs/remotes/origin/*
...
...
```

The syntax of a refspec is as follows:

```
[+]source:destination
```

It consists primarily of a source ref, a colon (:), and a destination ref. It can be prefixed with a plus sign (+) to indicate that the normal fast-forward safety check will not be performed during the transfer. It can also be prefixed with an asterisk (*) to allow a limited form of wildcard matching on branch names.

In some uses, the *source* ref is optional; in others, the colon and *destination* ref are optional.

Refspecs are used by both the `git fetch` and `git push` commands. The trick to using a refspec is to understand the data flow it specifies. The refspec itself is always *source*:*destination*, but the roles of *source* and *destination* depend on the Git operation being performed. This relationship is summarized in Table 11-1.

Table 11-1. Refspec data flow

Operation	Source	Destination
push	Local ref being pushed	Remote ref being updated
fetch	Remote ref being fetched	Local ref being updated

A typical `git fetch` command uses a refspec such as this:

```
+refs/heads/*:refs/remotes/remote/*
```

This refspec might be paraphrased as follows:

All the source branches from a remote repository in namespace refs/heads/ are 1) mapped into your local repository using a name constructed from the *remote* name and 2) placed under the refs/remotes/*remote* namespace.

Because of the asterisks, this refspec applies to multiple branches as found in the remote's refs/heads/ namespace. It is *exactly* this specification that causes the remote's topic branches to be mapped into your repository's namespace as remote-tracking branches and separates them into subnames based on the remote name.

Although not mandatory, it is a convention and a common best practice to place the branches for a given *remote* under refs/remotes/*remote*/* (e.g., refs/remotes/origin/*).

Use git show-ref to list the references within your current repository. Use git ls-remote *repository* to list the references in a remote repository.

Because git pull's first step is fetch, the fetch refspecs apply equally to git pull.

You should not make commits or merges onto a remote-tracking branch identified on the righthand side of a pull or fetch refspec. Those refs will be used as remote-tracking branches.

During a git push operation, you typically want to provide and publish the changes you made on your local topic branches. To allow others to find your changes in the remote repository after you upload them, your changes must appear in that repository as topic branches. Thus, during a typical git push command, the source branches from your repository are sent to the remote repository using a refspec such as this:

```
+refs/heads/*:refs/heads/*
```

This refspec can be paraphrased as follows:

From the local repository, take each branch name found under the source namespace refs/heads/ and place it in a similarly named, matching branch under the destination namespace refs/heads/ in the remote repository.

The first refs/heads/ refers to your local repository (because you're executing a push), and the second one refers to the remote repository. The asterisks ensure that all branches are replicated.

Multiple refspecs can be given on the `git fetch` and `git push` command lines. Within a remote definition, multiple fetch refspecs, multiple push refspecs, or a combination of both may be specified.

What if you don't specify a refspec at all on a `git push` command? How does Git know what to do or where to send data?

First, without an explicit remote given to the command, Git assumes you want to use `origin`. Without a refspec, `git push` will send your commits to the remote for all branches that are common between your repository and the upstream repository. Any local branch that is not already present in the upstream repository will not be sent upstream; branches must already exist and match names. Thus new branches must be explicitly pushed by name. Later they can be defaulted with a simple `git push`. As such, the default refspec makes the following two commands equivalent:

```
$ git push origin branch
$ git push origin branch:refs/heads/branch
```

For examples, see "Adding and Deleting Remote Branches" on page 280.

Part II: Example Using Remote Repositories

Now you have the basis for some sophisticated sharing via Git. Without a loss of generality and to make examples easy to run on your own system, this section shows multiple repositories on one physical machine. In real life, they'd probably be located on different hosts across the internet. Other forms of remote URL specification may be used because the same mechanisms apply to repositories on physically disparate machines as well.

Let's explore a common use case for Git. For the sake of illustration, let's set up a repository that all developers consider authoritative, although technically it's no different from other repositories. In other words, authority lies in how everyone agrees to treat the repository, not in some technical or security measure.

This agreed-on authoritative copy is often placed in a special directory known as a *depot*. There are often good reasons for setting up a depot. For instance, your organization could reliably and professionally back up the filesystems of some large server. You want to encourage your coworkers to check everything into the main copy within the depot in order to avoid catastrophic losses. The depot will be the remote origin for all developers.

The following sections show how to place an initial repository in the depot, clone development repositories out of the depot, do development work within them, and then sync them with the depot.

To illustrate parallel development on this repository, a second developer will clone it, work with their repository, and then push their changes back into the depot for all to use.

Creating an Authoritative Repository

You can place your authoritative depot anywhere on your filesystem; for this example, let's use */tmp/Depot*. No actual development work should be done directly in the */tmp/Depot* directory or in any of its repositories. Instead, individual work should be performed in a local clone.

In practice, this authoritative upstream repository would likely already be hosted on some server, perhaps `git.kernel.org`, GitHub, or one of your private machines.

These steps, however, outline what is necessary to transform a repository into another bare clone repository capable of being the authoritative upstream source repository.

The first step is to populate */tmp/Depot* with an initial repository. Assuming you want to work on website content that is already established as a Git repository in *~/ my_website*, make a copy of the *~/my_website* repository and place it in */tmp/Depot/ my_website.git*:

```
# Assume that ~/my_website is already a Git repository
$ cd /tmp/Depot/
$ git clone --bare ~/my_website my_website.git
Cloning into bare repository 'my_website.git'...
done.
```

This `clone` command copies the Git remote repository from *~/my_website* into the current working directory, */tmp/Depot*. The last argument gives the repository a new name, *my_website.git*. By convention, bare repositories are named with a *.git* suffix. This is not a requirement, but it is considered a best practice.

The original development repository has a full set of project files checked out at the top level, and the object store and all of the configuration files are located in the *.git* subdirectory:

```
$ cd ~/my_website/
$ ls -aF
./    fuzzy.txt  index.html  techinfo.txt
../   .git/      poem.html

# Note: The output in your terminal may vary
$ ls -aF .git
./          HEAD          hooks/        logs/
../         config        index         objects/
COMMIT_EDITMSG  description   info/         refs/
```

Because a bare repository has no working directory, its files have a simpler layout:

```
$ cd /tmp/Depot/

$ ls -aF my_website.git
./         HEAD          description     info/        packed-refs
../        config        hooks/          objects/     refs/
```

To view the configuration in the new, bare repository, we can do the following:

```
# In /tmp/Depot/my_website.git

$ cat config
[core]
        repositoryformatversion = 0
        filemode = true
        bare = true
        ignorecase = true
        precomposeunicode = true
[remote "origin"]
        url = ~/users/my_website
```

Because we used the `--bare` option during this clone operation, Git sets the `bare` option to `true`. However, due to the clone operation, a remote named `origin` is already present in the config file. Since we want this copy of the bare repository to be an authoritative source, for this purpose we will remove the `origin` remote by supplying the following command:

```
$ git remote remove origin
$ cat config
[core]
        repositoryformatversion = 0
        filemode = true
        bare = true
        ignorecase = true
        precomposeunicode = true
```

You can now treat this bare */tmp/Depot/my_website.git* repository as the authoritative version.

Make Your Own Origin Remote

Right now, you have two repositories that are virtually identical, except the initial repository has a working directory and the bare clone repository does not.

Moreover, because the *~/my_website* repository in your *home* directory was created using `git init` and *not* via a `clone`, it lacks an `origin`. In fact, it has no remote configured at all:

```
$ cd ~/my_website
$ cat .git/config
[core]
        repositoryformatversion = 0
        filemode = true
        bare = false
        logallrefupdates = true
```

It is easy enough to add one, though. And it's needed if the goal is to perform more development in your initial repository and then push that development to the newly established, authoritative repository in the depot. In a sense, you must manually convert your initial repository into a derived clone.

A developer who clones from the depot will have an `origin` remote created automatically. In fact, if you were to turn around now and clone off the depot, you would see it set up for you automatically too.

The command for manipulating remotes is `git remote`. This operation introduces a few new settings in the *.git/config* file:

```
$ cd ~/my_website
$ git remote add origin /tmp/Depot/my_website

$ cat .git/config
[core]
        repositoryformatversion = 0
        filemode = true
        bare = false
        logallrefupdates = true
[remote "origin"]
        url = /tmp/Depot/my_website
        fetch = +refs/heads/*:refs/remotes/origin/*
```

Here, `git remote` added to our configuration a new `remote` section called `origin`. The name `origin` isn't magical or special. You could have used any other name, but the remote that points back to the original repository is named `origin` by convention.

The remote establishes a link from your current repository to the remote repository found, in this case, at */tmp/Depot/my_website.git* as recorded in the `url` value. As a convenience, the *.git* suffix is not required; both */tmp/Depot/my_html* and */tmp/Depot/my_website.git* will work.

Now, within this repository, the name `origin` can be used as a shorthand reference for the remote repository found in the depot. Note that a default fetch refspec that follows branch name mapping conventions has also been added.

The relationship between a repository that contains a remote reference (the referrer) and that remote repository (the referee) is asymmetric. A remote always points in one direction from referrer to referee. The referee has no idea that some other repository points to it. Another way to say this is that a clone knows where its upstream repository is, but the upstream repository doesn't know where its clones are.

Let's complete the process of setting up the `origin` remote by establishing new remote-tracking branches in the original repository to represent the branches from the remote repository. First, you can see that there is only one branch, as expected, called `main`:

```
# List all branches

$ git branch -a
* main
```

Now, use `git remote update`:

```
$ git remote update
Fetching origin
From /tmp/Depot/my_website
 * [new branch]      main      -> origin/main

$ git branch -a
* main
  remotes/origin/main
```

Git introduced into the repository a new branch called `remotes/origin/main`. It is a remote-tracking branch within the `origin` remote. Nobody does development in this branch. Instead, its purpose is to hold and track the commits made in the remote `origin` repository's `main` branch. You could consider it your local repository's proxy for commits made in the remote; eventually you can use it to bring those commits into your repository.

The phrase `Fetching origin`, produced by the `git remote update` command, means that the *local* repository's notion of the `origin` has been updated based on information brought in from the remote repository.

 The generic `git remote update` command caused every remote within this repository to be updated by checking for and then fetching any new commits from each repository named in a remote.

Rather than generically updating all remotes, you can restrict the operation to fetch updates from a single remote by supplying the desired remote name on the `git remote update` command:

```
$ git remote update remote_name
```

Also, using the `-f` option when the remote is initially added causes an immediate `fetch` from that remote repository:

```
$ git remote add -f origin repository
```

Now you're done linking your repository to the remote repository in your depot.

Developing in Your Repository

Let's do some development work in the repository and add another poem, *fuzzy.txt*:

```
$ cd ~/my_website

$ git show-branch -a
* [main] add new file
 ! [origin/main] add new file
--
*+ [main] add new file

$ cat fuzzy.txt
Fuzzy Wuzzy was a bear
Fuzzy Wuzzy had no hair
Fuzzy Wuzzy wasn't very fuzzy,
Was he?

$ git add fuzzy.txt
$ git commit -m "Add a new poem"
[main 2daf640] Add new poem
 1 files changed, 4 insertions(+)
 create mode 100644 fuzzy.txt

$ git show-branch -a
* [main] Add new poem
 ! [origin/main] add new file
--
*  [main] Add new poem
*+ [origin/main] add new file
```

At this point, your repository has one more commit than the repository in */tmp/Depot*. Perhaps more interesting is that your repository has two branches, one (main) with the new commit on it and the other (origin/main) that is tracking the remote repository.

Pushing Your Changes

Any change that you commit is completely local to your repository; it is not yet present in the remote repository. A convenient way to get your commits from your main branch into the origin remote repository is to use the git push command. Depending on your version of Git, the main parameter on this command was assumed:

```
$ git push origin main
Enumerating objects: 4, done.
Counting objects: 100% (4/4), done.
Delta compression using up to 8 threads
Compressing objects: 100% (3/3), done.
Writing objects: 100% (3/3), 343 bytes | 343.00 KiB/s, done.
Total 3 (delta 0), reused 0 (delta 0), pack-reused 0
To /tmp/Depot/my_website
   7e876fd..2daf640  main -> main
```

All that output means that Git has taken your main branch changes, bundled them up, and sent them to the remote repository named origin. Git has also performed one more step here: it has taken those same changes and added them to the origin/main branch in your repository as well. Git doesn't actually round-trip the changes. After all, the commits are already in your repository. Git is smart enough to instead simply fast-forward the remote-tracking branch.

Now both local branches, main and origin/main, reflect the same commit within your repository:

```
$ git show-branch -a
* [main] Add a new poem
 ! [origin/main] Add a new poem
 --
*+ [main] Add a new poem
```

You can also probe the remote repository and verify that it, too, has been updated. If your remote repository is on a local filesystem, as it is here, then you can easily check by going to the depot directory:

```
$ cd /tmp/Depot/my_website.git
$ git show-branch
[main] Add a new poem
```

When the remote repository is on a physically different machine, a plumbing command can be used to determine the branch information of the remote repository:

```
$ cd ~/my_website

$ git ls-remote
From /tmp/Depot/my_website
2daf64034a769ee02f8cedd9fcb2e43b04fe7c17    HEAD
2daf64034a769ee02f8cedd9fcb2e43b04fe7c17    refs/heads/main
```

 In our example, the From path outputs the local *Depot* directory. Generally, this will be a URL of the remote Git repository if it was on a different server where the repository is hosted.

You can then show that those commit IDs match your current, local branches using something like git rev-parse HEAD or git show *commit-id*:

```
$ git rev-parse HEAD
2daf64034a769ee02f8cedd9fcb2e43b04fe7c17
```

Adding a New Developer

Once you have established an authoritative repository, it's easy to add a new developer to a project simply by letting them clone the repository and begin working.

Let's introduce Lisa to the project by giving them their own cloned repository in which to work:

```
$ cd /tmp/lisa
$ git clone /tmp/Depot/my_website.git
Cloning into 'my_website'...
done.

$ ls
my_website
$ cd my_website

$ ls
fuzzy.txt  index.html  poem.html  techinfo.txt

$ git branch
* main

$ git log -1
commit 6f168803f6f1b987dffd5fff77531dcadf7f4b68
Author: Jon Loeliger <jdl@example.com>
Date:   Sat Nov 6 18:57:37 2021 +0100

    Add a new poem
```

Immediately, you can see from `ls` that the clone has a working directory populated with all the files under version control. That is, Lisa's clone is a development repository, and not a bare repository. Good. Lisa will be doing some development too.

From the `git log` output, you can see that the most recent commit is available in Lisa's repository. Additionally, because Lisa's repository was cloned from a parent repository, it has a default remote called `origin`. Lisa can find out more information about the `origin` remote within their repository:

```
$ git remote show origin
* remote origin
Fetch URL: /tmp/Depot/my_website.git
Push  URL: /tmp/Depot/my_website.git
HEAD branch: main
Remote branch:
  main tracked
Local branch configured for 'git pull':
  main merges with remote main
Local ref configured for 'git push':
  main pushes to main (up to date)
```

The complete contents of the configuration file after a default clone show how it contains the `origin` remote:

```
$ cat .git/config
[core]
            repositoryformatversion = 0
            filemode = true
            bare = false
            logallrefupdates = true
            ignorecase = true
            precomposeunicode = true
[remote "origin"]
        url = /tmp/Depot/my_website.git
        fetch = +refs/heads/*:refs/remotes/origin/*
[branch "main"]
        remote = origin
        merge = refs/heads/main
```

In addition to having the `origin` remote in their repository, Lisa has a few branches. They can list all branches in their repository by using `git branch -a`:

```
$ git branch -a
* main
  remotes/origin/HEAD -> origin/main
  remotes/origin/main
```

The `main` branch is Lisa's main development branch. It is the normal, local topic branch. It is also a local-tracking branch associated with the correspondingly named `main` remote-tracking branch. The `origin/main` branch is a remote-tracking branch to follow the commits from the `main` branch of the `origin` repository. The `origin/HEAD` ref indicates which branch the remote considers the active branch, through a symbolic name. Finally, the asterisk next to the `main` branch name indicates that it is the current, checked-out branch in this repository.

We can confirm this by running the `git branch` command with option `-vv` to provide verbose output that shows the relationship of the local and linked remote-tracking branch as explained:

```
$ git branch -vv
* main 2daf640 [origin/main] Add a new poem
```

Let's have Lisa make a commit that alters the new poem and then push that to the main depot repository. Lisa thinks the last line of the poem should be "Wuzzy?", makes this change, and commits it:

```
$ git diff

diff --git a/fuzzy.txt b/fuzzy.txt
index 0d601fa..608ab5b 100644
--- a/fuzzy.txt
+++ b/fuzzy.txt
@@ -1,4 +1,4 @@
 Fuzzy Wuzzy was a bear
 Fuzzy Wuzzy had no hair
 Fuzzy Wuzzy wasn't very fuzzy,
-Was he?
+Wuzzy?
```

```
$ git commit fuzzy.txt
[main c426244] Make the name pun complete!
 1 file changed, 1 insertion(+), 1 deletion(-)
```

Lisa completes their development cycle by pushing their changes to the depot, using git push as before:

```
$ git push
Enumerating objects: 5, done.
Counting objects: 100% (5/5), done.
Delta compression using up to 8 threads
Compressing objects: 100% (3/3), done.
Writing objects: 100% (3/3), 330 bytes | 330.00 KiB/s, done.
Total 3 (delta 1), reused 0 (delta 0), pack-reused 0
To /tmp/Depot/my_website.git
   2daf640..a5f8133  main -> main
```

Getting Repository Updates

Let's suppose that Lisa goes on vacation, and, in the meantime, you make further changes and push them to the depot repository. Let's assume you did this after getting Lisa's latest changes.

Your commit looks like this:

```
$ cd ~/my_website
$ git diff
diff --git a/index.html b/index.html
index 40b00ff..063ac92 100644
--- a/index.html
+++ b/index.html
@@ -1,5 +1,7 @@
 <html>
 <body>
 My web site is awesome!
+<br/>
+Read a <a href="fuzzy.txt">new</a> poem!
 </body>
 <html>

$ git commit -m "Add a new poem link." index.html
[main 89cfd9f] Add a new poem link.
 1 file changed, 2 insertions(+)
```

Using the default push refspec, push your commit upstream (the depot):

```
$ git push
Enumerating objects: 5, done.
Counting objects: 100% (5/5), done.
Delta compression using up to 8 threads
Compressing objects: 100% (3/3), done.
Writing objects: 100% (3/3), 333 bytes | 333.00 KiB/s, done.
Total 3 (delta 1), reused 0 (delta 0), pack-reused 0
To /tmp/Depot/my_website.git
   e023cd1..c4e45f7  main -> main
```

Now, when Lisa returns they'll want to refresh their clone of the repository. The primary command for doing this is git pull:

```
$ git pull
remote: Enumerating objects: 5, done.
remote: Counting objects: 100% (3/3), done.
remote: Compressing objects: 100% (3/3), done.
remote: Total 3 (delta 1), reused 0 (delta 0), pack-reused 0
Unpacking objects: 100% (3/3), 943 bytes | 235.00 KiB/s, done.
From /tmp/Depot/my_website
   a5f8133..c4e45f7  main       -> origin/main
Updating a5f8133..c4e45f7
Fast-forward
 index.html |   2 ++
 1 file changed, 2 insertions(+)
```

The fully specified git pull command allows both the repository and multiple refspecs to be specified: git pull *options repository refspecs*.

If the repository is not specified on the command line, either as a Git URL or indirectly through a remote name, then the default remote origin is used. If you don't specify a refspec on the command line, the fetch refspec of the remote is used. If you specify a repository (directly or using a remote) but no refspec, Git fetches the HEAD ref of the remote.

The git pull operation is fundamentally two steps, each implemented by a separate Git command. Namely, git pull implies git fetch followed by either git merge or git rebase. By default, the second step is merge because this is almost always the desired behavior.

Because pull also performs the second merge or rebase step, git push and git pull are not considered opposites. Instead, git push and git fetch are considered opposites. Both push and fetch are responsible for transferring data between repositories but in opposite directions.

Sometimes you may want to execute the git fetch and git merge as two separate operations. For example, you may want to fetch updates into your repository to inspect them but not necessarily merge immediately. In this case, you can simply perform the fetch, and then perform other operations on the remote-tracking branch such as git log, git diff, or even gitk. Later, when you are ready, you can perform the merge at your convenience.

Even if you never separate the fetch and merge, you can do complex operations that require you to know what's happening at each step. So let's look at each one in detail.

The fetch step

In the first `fetch` step, Git locates the remote repository. Since the command line didn't specify a direct repository URL or a direct remote name, it assumes the default remote name, `origin`. The information for that remote is in the configuration file:

```
[remote "origin"]
        url = /tmp/Depot/my_website.git
        fetch = +refs/heads/*:refs/remotes/origin/*
```

Git now knows to use the URL */tmp/Depot/my_website* as the source repository. Furthermore, because the command line didn't specify a refspec, Git will use all of the `fetch` = lines from the `remote` entry. Thus every `refs/heads/*` branch from the remote will be fetched.

Next, Git performs a negotiation protocol with the source repository to determine what new commits are in the remote repository and are absent from your repository, based on the desire to fetch all of the `refs/heads/*` refs as given in the `fetch` refspec.

The pull output prefixed by `remote:` reflects the negotiation, compression, and transfer protocol, and it lets you know that new commits are coming into your repository:

```
remote: Counting objects: 5, done.
remote: Compressing objects: 100% (3/3), done.
remote: Total 3 (delta 1), reused 0 (delta 0)
```

Git places the new commits in your repository on an appropriate remote-tracking branch and then tells you what mapping it uses to determine where the new commits belong:

```
From /tmp/Depot/my_website
   a5f8133..c4e45f7  main      -> origin/main
```

Those lines indicate that Git looked at the remote repository */tmp/Depot/my_website*, took *its* `main` branch, brought its contents back to your repository, and placed them on *your* `origin/main` branch. This process is the heart of branch *tracking*. The corresponding commit IDs are also listed, just in case you want to inspect the changes directly. With that, the `fetch` step is finished.

A more recent version of Git (2.29) introduced support for negative refspecs. This means you are able to explicitly call out refspecs you chose to exclude, which takes effect during a `push` or `fetch` operation. To exclude a refspec, you will need to prefix it with `^`; however, this will apply only to the source side of the refspec (+[*source*]:[*destination*]).

Here is an example:

```
# Fetching with a negative refspec

$ git fetch newdev refs/heads/*:refs/remotes/newdev/* ^refs/heads/skip-me
...
...
```

The preceding code will locally fetch all branches in the repository into `remotes/origin` but will exclude fetching the branch with the matching name `skip-me`.

An alternative to this is to edit the config file directly to include the negative refspec:

```
[remote "newdev"]
        url = /tmp/Depot/my_website.git
        fetch = +refs/heads/dev:refs/remotes/origin/dev
        fetch = +refs/heads/stable:refs/remotes/origin/stable
        fetch = ^refs/heads/skip-me
```

 You don't have to fetch all of the topic branches from the remote repository using the `refs/heads/*` wildcard form. If you want only a particular branch or two, list them explicitly:

```
[remote "newdev"]
        url = /tmp/Depot/my_website.git
        fetch = +refs/heads/dev:refs/remotes/origin/dev
        fetch = +refs/heads/stable:refs/remotes/origin/stable
```

The merge or rebase step

In the second step of the `pull` operation, Git performs a `merge` (the default) or a `rebase` operation. In this example, Git merges the contents of the remote-tracking branch, `origin/main`, into your local-tracking branch, `main`, using a special type of merge called a *fast-forward*.

But how did Git know to merge those particular branches? The answer comes from the configuration file:

```
[branch "main"]
        remote = origin
        merge = refs/heads/main
```

Paraphrased, this gives Git two key pieces of information:

> When `main` is the current, checked-out branch, use `origin` as the default remote from which to fetch updates during a `fetch` (or `pull`). Further, during the `merge` step of `git pull`, use `refs/heads/main` from the remote as the default branch to merge into this, the `main` branch.

For readers paying close attention to detail, the first part of that paraphrase is the actual mechanism by which Git determines that `origin` should be the remote used during this parameterless `git pull` command.

The value of the `merge` field in the `branch` section of the configuration file (`refs/heads/main`) is treated like the remote part of a refspec, and it must match one of the *source* refs just fetched during the `git pull` command. It's a little convoluted, but think of this as a hint conveyed from the `fetch` step to the `merge` step of a `pull` command.

Because the merge configuration value applies only during git pull, if you perform a manual application of git merge at this point, you must name the merge source branch on the command line. The branch is likely a remote-tracking branch name, such as this:

```
# Or, fully specified: refs/remotes/origin/main

$ git merge origin/main
Updating a5f8133..c4e45f7
Fast forward
 index.html |    2 ++
 1 files changed, 2 insertions(+), 0 deletions(-)
```

There are slight semantic differences between the merging behavior of branches when multiple refspecs are given on the command line and when they are found in a remote entry. The former causes an octopus merge, wherein all branches are merged simultaneously in an *n*-way operation, whereas the latter does not. Read the git pull manual page carefully!

If you choose to rebase rather than merge, Git will instead forward port the changes on your local-tracking branch to the newly fetched HEAD of the corresponding remote-tracking branch. The operation is the same as that shown in Figure 9-16 and Figure 9-17 in Chapter 9.

The command git pull --rebase will cause Git to rebase (rather than merge) your local-tracking branch onto the remote-tracking branch during only this pull. To make rebase the normal operation for a branch, set the branch.*branch_name*.rebase configuration variable to true:

```
[branch "mydev"]
    remote = origin
    merge = refs/heads/main
    rebase = true
```

And with that, the merge (or rebase) step is also done.

Should you merge or rebase?

So, should you merge or rebase your changes during a pull operation? The short answer is "Do either as you wish." But why would you choose to do one over the other? Here are some issues to consider.

By using merge, you will potentially incur an additional merge commit at each pull to record the updated changes simultaneously present in each branch. In a sense, it is a true reflection of the two paths of development that took place independently and were then, well, merged together. Conflicts will have to be resolved during the merge. Each sequence of commits on each branch will be based on exactly the commit on which it was originally written. When pushed upstream, any merge commits will continue to be present. Some consider these superfluous merges and would rather not see them cluttering up the history. Others consider these merges a more accurate portrayal of the development history and want to see them retained.

As a rebase fundamentally changes the notion of when and where a sequence of commits was developed, some aspects of the development history will be lost. Specifically, the original commit on which your development was originally based will be changed to be the newly pulled HEAD of the remote-tracking branch. That will make the development appear to happen later (in commit sequence) than it actually did. If that's OK with you, it's OK with us. It'll just be different and simpler than if the history was merged. Naturally, you will still have to resolve conflicts during the rebase operation as needed. As the changes that are being rebased are still strictly local within your repository and haven't been published yet, there's really no reason to fear the "don't change history" mantra with this rebase.

With both merge and rebase, you should consider that the new, final content is different from what was present on either development branch independently. As such, it might warrant some form of validation in its new form: perhaps a compilation and test cycle prior to being pushed to an upstream repository.

We tend to like to see simpler, linear histories. During most of our personal development, we are usually not too concerned by a slight reordering of our changes with respect to those of our coworkers that came in on a remote-tracking branch fetch, so we are fond of using the rebase option.

If you really want to set up one consistent approach, consider setting the config option branch.autosetupmerge or branch.autosetuprebase to true, false, or always as desired. There are also a few other options to handle behavior between purely local branches and not just between a local and a remote branch.

Part III: Remote Repository Development Cycle in Pictures

Integrating your local development with changes from an upstream repository is at the very core of the distributed development cycle in Git. Let's take a moment to visualize what happens to both your local repository and an upstream origin repository during clone and pull operations. A few pictures should also clarify the often confusing uses of the same name in different contexts.

Let's start with the simple repository shown in Figure 11-2 as the basis for discussion.

As with all of our commit graphs, the sequence of commits flows from left to right, and the main label points to the HEAD of the branch. The two most recent commits are labeled A and B. Let's follow these two commits, introduce a few more, and watch what occurs.

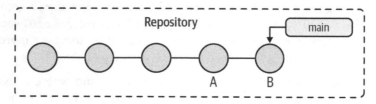

Figure 11-2. Simple repository with commits

Cloning a Repository

A git clone command results in two separate repositories, as shown in Figure 11-3.

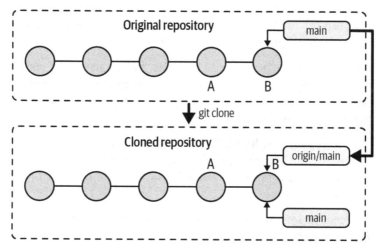

Figure 11-3. Cloned repository

Figure 11-3 illustrates some important results of the clone operation:

- All the commits from the original repository are copied to your clone; you could now easily retrieve earlier stages of the project from your own repository.

- The branch named main from the original repository is introduced into your clone on a new remote-tracking branch named origin/main.

- Within the new clone repository, the new origin/main branch is initialized to point to the main HEAD commit, which is B in the figure.

- A new local-tracking branch called main is created in your clone.

- The new main branch is initialized to point to origin/HEAD, the original repository's active branch HEAD. That happens to be origin/main, so it also points to the exact same commit, B.

After cloning, Git selects the new `main` branch as the current branch and checks it out for you. Thus, unless you change branches, any changes you make after a `clone` will affect your `main` branch.

In all of these figures, development branches in both the original repository and the derived clone repository are distinguished by a dark shaded background, and remote-tracking branches by a lighter shaded background. It is important to understand that both the local-tracking development branches and remote-tracking branches are private and local to their respective repositories. In terms of Git's implementation, however, the dark shaded branch labels belong to the `refs/heads/` namespace, whereas the lighter ones belong to `refs/remotes/`.

Alternate Histories

Once you have cloned and obtained your development repository, two distinct paths of development may result. First, you may do development in your repository and make new commits on your `main` branch, as shown in Figure 11-4. In this figure, your development extends the `main` branch with two new commits, X and Y, which are based on B.

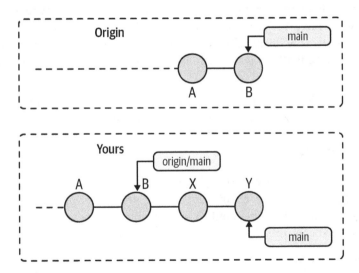

Figure 11-4. Commits in your repository

In the meantime, any other developer who has access to the original repository might have done further development and pushed their changes into that repository. Those changes are represented in Figure 11-5 by the addition of commits C and D.

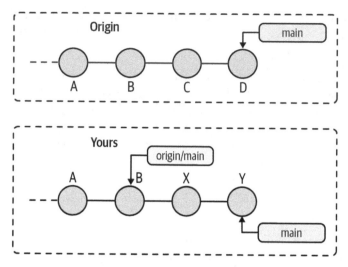

Figure 11-5. Commits in original repository

In this situation, we say that the histories of the repositories have *diverged* or *forked* at commit B. In much the same way that local branching within one repository causes alternate histories to diverge at a commit, a repository and its clone can diverge into alternate histories as a result of separate actions by possibly different people. It is important to realize that this is perfectly fine and that neither history is more correct than the other.

In fact, the whole point of the merge operation is that these different histories may be brought back together and resolved again. Let's see how Git implements that!

Non-Fast-Forward Pushes

If you are developing in a repository model in which you have the ability to git push your changes into the origin repository, then you might attempt to push your changes at any time. This could create problems if some other developer has previously pushed commits.

This hazard is particularly common when you are using a shared repository develop-ment model in which all developers can push their own commits and updates into a common repository at any time.

Let's look again at Figure 11-4, in which you have made new commits, X and Y, based on B.

If you wanted to push your X and Y commits upstream at this point, you could do so easily. Git would transfer your commits to the origin repository and add them to the history at B. Git would then perform a fast-forward merge operation on the main branch, putting in your edits and updating the ref to point to Y. A fast-forward is essentially a simple linear history advancement operation; it was introduced in "Degenerate Merges" on page 145.

On the other hand, suppose another developer had already pushed some commits to the origin repository, and the result looked more like Figure 11-5 when you attempted to push *your* history up to the origin repository. In effect, you are attempting to cause your history to be sent to the shared repository when there is already a different history there. The origin history does not simply fast-forward from B. This situation is called the *non-fast-forward push problem*.

When you attempt your push, Git rejects it and tells you about the conflict with a message like this:

```
$ git push
To /tmp/Depot/my_website
 ! [rejected]        main -> main (non-fast forward)
error: failed to push some refs to '/tmp/Depot/my_website'
```

So what are you really trying to do? Do you want to overwrite the other developer's work, or do you want to incorporate both sets of histories?

If you want to overwrite all other changes, you can! Simply use the -f option on your git push. We just hope you won't need *that* alternate history!

More often, you are not trying to wipe out the existing origin history but just want your own changes to be added. In this case, you must perform a merge of the two histories in your repository before pushing.

Fetching the Alternate History

For Git to perform a merge between two alternate histories, both must be present within one repository on two different branches. Branches that are purely local development branches are a special (degenerate) case of their already being in the same repository.

However, if the alternate histories are in different repositories because of cloning, then the remote branch must be brought into your repository via a fetch operation. You can carry out the operation through a direct git fetch command or as part of a git pull command; it doesn't matter which. In either case, the fetch brings the remote's commits—here, C and D—into your repository. The results are shown in Figure 11-6.

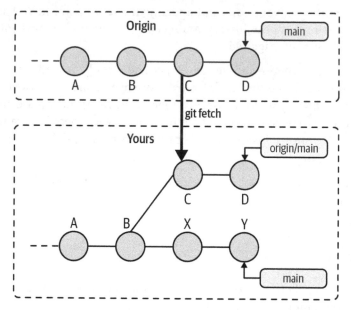

Figure 11-6. Fetching the alternate history

In no way does the introduction of the alternate history with commits C and D change the history represented by X and Y; the two alternate histories both now exist simultaneously in your repository and form a more complex graph. Your history is represented by your main branch, and the remote history is represented by the origin/main remote-tracking branch.

Merging Histories

Now that both histories are present in one repository, all that is needed to unify them is a merge of the origin/main branch into the main branch.

The merge operation can be initiated either with a direct git merge origin/main command or as the second step in a git pull request. In both cases, the techniques for the merge operation are exactly the same as those described in Chapter 6.

Figure 11-7 shows the commit graph in your repository after the merge has successfully assimilated the two histories from commits D and Y into a new merge commit, M. The ref for origin/main remains pointing at D because it hasn't changed, but main is updated to the merge commit, M, to indicate that the merge was into the main branch; this is where the new commit was made.

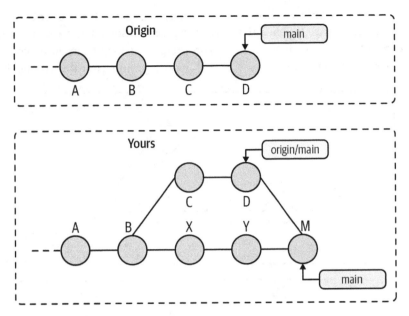

Figure 11-7. Merging histories

Merge Conflicts

Occasionally there will be merge conflicts between the alternate histories. Regardless of the outcome of the merge, the fetch still occurred. All the commits from the remote repository are still present in your repository on the tracking branch.

You can choose to resolve the merge normally, as described in Chapter 6, or you can choose to abort the merge and reset your `main` branch to its prior `ORIG_HEAD` state using the command `git reset --hard ORIG_HEAD`. Doing so in this example would move `main` to the *prior* `HEAD` value, Y, and change your working directory to match. It would also leave `origin/main` at commit D.

 You can brush up on the meaning of `ORIG_HEAD` by reviewing "Refs and Symrefs" on page 83; also see its use in "Aborting or Restarting a Merge" on page 141.

Pushing a Merged History

If you've performed all the steps shown, your repository has been updated to contain the latest changes from both the `origin` repository and your repository. But the converse is not true: the `origin` repository still doesn't have your changes.

If your objective is only to incorporate the latest updates from origin into your repository, then you are finished when your merge is resolved. On the other hand, a simple git push can return the unified and merged history from your main branch back to the origin repository. Figure 11-8 shows the results after the git push.

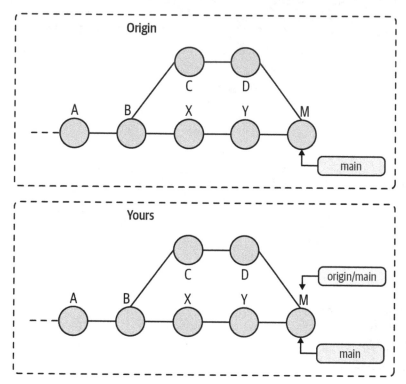

Figure 11-8. Merged histories after push

Finally, observe that the origin repository has been updated with your development even if it has undergone other changes that had to be merged first. Both your repository and the origin repository have been fully updated and are again synchronized.

Part IV: Remote Configuration

Keeping track of all the information about a remote repository reference by hand can become tedious and difficult: you have to remember the full URL for the repository, you must type and retype remote references and refspecs on the command line each time you want to fetch updates, you have to reconstruct the branch mappings, and so on. Repeating the information is also likely to be quite error-prone.

You might also wonder how Git remembers the URL for the remote from the initial clone for use in subsequent fetch or push operations using `origin`.

Git provides three mechanisms for setting up and maintaining information about remotes: using the `git remote` command, using the `git config` command, and editing the *.git/config* file directly. All three mechanisms ultimately result in configuration information being recorded in the *.git/config* file.

Using git remote

The `git remote` command is a more specialized interface, specific to remotes, that manipulates the configuration file data and remote refs. It has several subcommands with fairly intuitive names. Typing `git remote --help` displays a message with subcommand names:

```
$ git remote --help
NAME
        git-remote - Manage set of tracked repositories

SYNOPSIS
        git remote [-v | --verbose]
        git remote add [-t <branch>] [-m <main>] [-f] [--[no-]tags]
          [--mirror=(fetch|push)] <name> <url>
        git remote rename <old> <new>
        git remote remove <name>
        git remote set-head <name> (-a | --auto | -d | --delete | <branch>)
        git remote set-branches [--add] <name> <branch>...
        git remote get-url [--push] [--all] <name>
        git remote set-url [--push] <name> <newurl> [<oldurl>]
        git remote set-url --add [--push] <name> <newurl>
        git remote set-url --delete [--push] <name> <url>
        git remote [-v | --verbose] show [-n] <name>...
        git remote prune [-n | --dry-run] <name>...
        git remote [-v | --verbose] update [-p | --prune] [(<group> | <remote>)...]
```

We shared the `git remote add` and `update` commands in "Make Your Own Origin Remote" on page 253 and the `git remote show` command in "Adding a New Developer" on page 258. We used `git remote add origin` to add a new remote named `origin` to the newly created parent repository in the depot, and we ran the `git remote show origin` command to extract all the information about the `origin` remote. Finally, we used the `git remote update` command to fetch all the updates available in the remote repository into our local repository.

The command `git remote rm` removes the given remote and all of its associated remote-tracking branches from our local repository. To remove just one remote-tracking branch from your local repository, you can use a command like this:

```
$ git branch -r -d origin/dev
```

But you shouldn't really do that unless the corresponding remote branch really has been removed from the upstream repository. Otherwise, your next fetch from the upstream repository is likely to re-create the branch again.

The remote repository may have branches deleted from it by the actions of other developers, even though your copies of those branches may linger in your repository. The `git remote prune` command may be used to remove the names of those stale (with respect to the actual remote repository) remote-tracking branches from your local repository.

To keep even more in sync with an upstream remote, use the command `git remote update --prune` *remote* to first get updates from the remote and then prune stale tracking branches, all in one step.

To rename a remote and all of its refs, use `git remote rename` *old new*:

```
$ git remote rename jon jdl
```

After this command, a ref like `jon/bugfixes` will be renamed `jdl/bugfixes`.

In addition to manipulating the remote name and its refs, you can also update or change the URL of the remote:

```
$ git remote set-url origin git://repos.example.com/stuff.git
```

Using git config

The `git config` command can be used to manipulate the entries in your configuration file directly. This includes several config variables for remotes.

For example, to add a new remote named `publish` with a push refspec for all the branches you would like to publish, you might do something like this:

```
$ git config remote.publish.url 'ssh://git.example.org/pub/repo.git'
$ git config remote.publish.push '+refs/heads/*:refs/heads/*'
```

Each of the preceding commands adds a line to the *.git/config* file. If no publish remote section exists yet, then the first command you issue that refers to that remote creates a section in the file for it. As a result, your *.git/config* contains, in part, the following remote definition:

```
[remote "publish"]
        url = ssh://git.example.org/pub/repo.git
        push = +refs/heads/*:refs/heads/*
```

Use the -l (lowercase *L*) option à la `git config -l` to list the contents of the configuration file with complete variable names:

```
# From a clone of git.git sources

$ git config -l
core.repositoryformatversion=0
core.filemode=true
core.bare=false
core.logallrefupdates=true
remote.origin.url=git://git.kernel.org/pub/scm/git/git.git
remote.origin.fetch=+refs/heads/*:refs/remotes/origin/*
branch.main.remote=origin
branch.main.merge=refs/heads/main
```

Using Manual Editing

Rather than wrestling with either the `git remote` or `git config` command, directly editing the file with your favorite text editor may be easier or faster in some situations. There is nothing wrong with doing so, but it can be error- prone and is usually done only by developers who are very familiar with Git's behavior and the configuration file. Yet having seen the parts of the file that influence various Git behaviors and the changes resulting from commands, you should know enough at this point to understand and manipulate the configuration file.

Multiple Remote Repositories

Operations such as `git remote add` *remote repository-URL* can be executed multiple times to add several new remotes to your repository. With multiple remotes, you can subsequently fetch commits from multiple sources and combine them in your repository. This feature also allows you to establish several push destinations that might receive part or all of your repository.

In Chapter 12, we'll show you how to use multiple repositories in different scenarios during your development.

Part V: Working with Tracking Branches

Because the creation and manipulation of tracking branches is such a vital part of the Git development methodology, it is important to understand how and why Git creates the different tracking branches and how Git expects you to use them in development.

Creating Tracking Branches

In the same way that your `main` branch can be thought of as extending the development brought in on the `origin/main` branch, you can create a new branch based on any remote-tracking branch and use it to extend that line of development.

We've already seen that remote-tracking branches are introduced during a clone operation or when remotes are added to a repository. Git makes it very easy to create a local- and remote-tracking branch pair using a consistent ref name for them. A simple checkout request using the name of a remote-tracking branch causes a new local-tracking branch to be created and associated with the remote-tracking branch. However, Git does this only if your branch name matches just one remote branch name from all of the repository remotes. And by the phrase "branch name matches," Git means the full branch name after the name of the remote in a refspec.

Let's use Git's source repository for some examples. By pulling from both GitHub and git.kernel.org, we'll create a repository that has a collection of branch names from two remotes, most of which are duplicates:

```
# Grab Git source code repository
$ git clone https://github.com/git/git.git
Cloning into 'git'...
...

$ cd git

# add a second remote for the same repo from a different server
$ git remote add korg git://git.kernel.org/pub/scm/git/git.git

$ git remote update
Fetching origin
remote: Enumerating objects: 931, done.
remote: Counting objects: 100% (759/759), done.
remote: Compressing objects: 100% (130/130), done.
remote: Total 931 (delta 650), reused 726 (delta 629), pack-reused 172
Receiving objects: 100% (931/931), 918.29 KiB | 6.47 MiB/s, done.
Resolving deltas: 100% (676/676), completed with 142 local objects.
From https://github.com/git/git
   ...
   ...
Fetching korg
From git://git.kernel.org/pub/scm/git/git
 * [new branch]      main       -> korg/main
 * [new branch]      maint      -> korg/maint
 * [new branch]      master     -> korg/master
 * [new branch]      next       -> korg/next
 * [new branch]      seen       -> korg/seen
 * [new branch]      todo       -> korg/todo
```

For this next section of the code example, we will assume that there is a hypothetical branch that exists only in the `korg` remote. We will explore how you can work with this specific branch from the newly added `korg` remote. If you are following along, this section will not work since the branch will not exist for you:

```
# Find a uniquely named branch and check it out.
$ git branch -a | grep split-blob
  remotes/origin/jc/split-blob

$ git branch
* main

$ git checkout jc/split-blob
branch 'jc/split-blob' set up to track 'jc/split-blob'
Switched to a new branch 'jc/split-blob'

$ git branch
* jc/split-blob
  main
```

Notice that we had to use the full branch name `jc/split-blob` and not simply `split-blob`.

In cases when the branch name is ambiguous, you can directly establish and set up the branch yourself:

```
$ git branch -a | egrep 'maint$'
  remotes/korg/maint
  remotes/origin/maint

$ git checkout maint
hint: If you meant to check out a remote tracking branch on, e.g. 'origin',
...
...
...
fatal: 'maint' matched multiple (2) remote tracking branches

# Just select one of the maint branches.
$ git checkout --track korg/maint
branch 'maint' set up to track 'korg/maint'.
Switched to a new branch 'maint'
```

It is likely that the two branches represent the same commit as found in two different repositories, and you can simply choose one on which to base your local-tracking branch.

If for some reason you wish to use a different name for your local-tracking branch, use the following:

```
$ git branch --track mynext korg/next
branch 'mynext' set up to track 'korg/next'.
```

Under the hood, Git automatically adds a `branch` entry to the *.git/config* to indicate that the remote-tracking branch should be merged into your new local-tracking branch. The collected changes from the previous series of commands yield the following config file:

```
$ cat .git/config
[core]
    repositoryformatversion = 0
    filemode = true
    bare = false
    logallrefupdates = true
    ignorecase = true
    precomposeunicode = true
[remote "origin"]
    url = https://github.com/git/git.git
    fetch = +refs/heads/*:refs/remotes/origin/*
[branch "main"]
    remote = origin
    merge = refs/heads/main
[remote "korg"]
    url = git://git.kernel.org/pub/scm/git/git.git
    fetch = +refs/heads/*:refs/remotes/korg/*
[branch "jc/split-blob"]
    remote = origin
    merge = refs/heads/jc/split-blob
[branch "maint"]
    remote = korg
    merge = refs/heads/maint
[branch "mynext"]
    remote = korg
    merge = refs/heads/next
```

As usual, you can also use `git config` or a text editor to manipulate the `branch` entries in the configuration file.

 When you get lost in the tracking branch mire, use the command `git remote show` *remote* to help sort out all the remotes and branches.

At this point, it should be pretty clear that the default clone behavior introduces the local-tracking branch `main` for the remote-tracking branch `origin/main` as a simplifying convenience just as if you had explicitly checked out the `main` branch yourself.

To reinforce the idea that making commits directly on a remote-tracking branch isn't good form, checking out a remote-tracking branch using early versions of Git (prior to about 1.6.6 or so) caused a detached `HEAD`. As mentioned in "Detached HEAD" on page 74, a detached `HEAD` is essentially an anonymous branch name. Making commits on the detached `HEAD` is possible, but you shouldn't then update your remote-tracking branch `HEAD` with any local commits lest you suffer grief later when fetching new updates from that remote. (If you find you need to keep any such commits on a detached HEAD, use `git checkout -b my_branch` to create a new, local branch on which to further develop your changes.) Collectively, it isn't really a good, intuitive approach.

If you already have a topic branch that you decide should be associated with an upstream repository's remote-tracking branch, you can establish the relationship using the `--set-upstream-to` option. Typically, this is done after adding a new remote, like this:

```
# From in the existing repository root directory run the following
$ git remote add upstreamrepo git://git.example.org/upstreamrepo.git

# Existing branch with a different remote: origin/dev.
# Leave it alone, but associate it with upstreamrepo/dev.
$ git branch --set-upstream-to upstreamrepo/dev
branch dev set up to track 'upstreamrepo/dev'.
```

Ahead and Behind

With the establishment of a local- and remote-tracking branch pair, relative comparisons between the two branches can be made. In addition to the normal `diff`, `log`, and other content-based comparisons, Git offers a quick summary of the number of commits on each of the branches and states which branch it judges to be "ahead of" or "behind" the other branch.

If your local development introduces new commits on a local-tracking branch, it is considered to be ahead of the corresponding remote-tracking branch. Conversely, if you fetch new commits onto remote-tracking branches and they are not present on your local-tracking branch, Git considers your local-tracking branch to be behind the corresponding remote-tracking branch.

The `git status` command usually reports this status:

```
$ git fetch
remote: Enumerating objects: 5, done.
remote: Counting objects: 100% (5/5), done.
remote: Compressing objects: 100% (3/3), done.
remote: Total 3 (delta 2), reused 0 (delta 0), pack-reused 0
Unpacking objects: 100% (3/3), 660 bytes | 220.00 KiB/s, done.
From https://github.com/ppremk/somerepo
   78625f3..cf1abb0  main        -> origin/main


$ git status
On branch main
Your branch is behind 'origin/main' by 1 commit, and can be fast-forwarded.
  (use "git pull" to update your local branch)

nothing to commit, working tree clean
```

To see which commits you have in `main` that are not in `origin/main`, use a command like this:

```
$ git log main..origin/main
commit cf1abb04818c5ee5304c3cdece481442596e34da (origin/main, origin/HEAD)
Author: Prem Kumar Ponuthorai <ppremk@gmail.com>
Date:   Thu Jul 14 20:40:17 2022 +0200

    Update README.md
```

The following code shows how it is possible to be both ahead and behind simultaneously!

```
# Make one local commit on top of previous example
$ git commit -m "Something" README.md
[main 7d28dc3] Something
 1 file changed, 2 insertions(+), 1 deletion(-)

$ git status
On branch main
Your branch and 'origin/main' have diverged,
and have 1 and 1 different commits each, respectively.
  (use "git pull" to merge the remote branch into yours)

nothing to commit, working tree clean
```

In this case, you probably want to use the symmetric difference to see the changes:

```
$ git log origin/main...main
commit 7d28dc31ca6be516a648e434fcfc04a4b14dc1b0 (HEAD -> main)
Author: Prem Kumar Ponuthorai <ppremk@gmail.com>
Date:   Thu Jul 14 20:50:01 2022 +0200

    Something
```

Adding and Deleting Remote Branches

Any new development work you do on branches in your local clone is not visible in the parent repository until you make a direct request to propagate it there. Similarly, a branch deletion in your repository remains a local change and is not removed from the parent repository until you request that it be removed from the remote as well.

In Chapter 3, you learned how to add new branches to and delete existing branches from your repository using the `git branch` command. But `git branch` operates only on a local repository.

To perform similar branch add and delete operations on a remote repository, you need to specify different forms of refspecs in a `git push` command. Recall that the syntax of a refspec is as follows:

```
[+]source:destination
```

Pushes that use a refspec with just a *source* ref (i.e., with no *destination* ref) create a new branch in the remote repository:

```
$ cd ~/my_website

$ git checkout -b foo
Switched to a new branch "foo"

$ git push origin foo
Total 0 (delta 0), reused 0 (delta 0), pack-reused 0
To /tmp/Depot/my_website
 * [new branch]      foo -> foo
```

A push that names only a source is just shorthand for using the same name for both the source and destination ref names. A push that names both a source and a destination ref that are different can be used to create a new destination named *branch* or extend an existing destination remote branch with the content from the local source branch. That is, `git push origin mystuff:dev` will push the local branch `mystuff` to the upstream repository and either create or extend a branch named dev. Thus, due to a series of default behaviors, the following commands have the same effect:

```
$ git push upstream new_dev
$ git push upstream new_dev:new_dev
$ git push upstream new_dev:refs/heads/new_dev
```

Naturally, `upstream` would be a reference to an appropriate upstream repository, which would typically be `origin`.

Pushes that use a refspec with just a *destination* ref (i.e., no *source* ref) cause the *destination* ref to be deleted from the remote repository. To denote the ref as the *destination*, the colon separator must be specified:

```
$ git push origin :foo
To /tmp/Depot/my_website
 - [deleted]         foo
```

If that :*branch* form causes you heartache, you can use a syntactically equivalent form:

```
$ git push origin --delete foo
```

So, what about renaming a remote branch? Unfortunately, there is not a simple solution for this. The short answer is to create a new upstream branch with the new name and then delete the old branch. That's easy enough to do using the `git push` commands, as shown previously:

```
# Create new name at exiting old commit
$ git branch new origin/old
$ git push origin new

# Remove the old name
$ git push origin :old
```

But that's the easy and obvious part. Now, what are the distributed implications? Do you know who has a clone of the upstream repository that was just modified out from underneath them? If you do, they could all just fetch and remote prune to get their repositories updated. But if you don't, then all those other clones will suddenly have dangling tracking branches. And there's no real way to get them renamed in a distributed way.

The bottom line here is that this is just a variant of the "Be careful how you rewrite history" theme.

Bare Repositories and git push

As a consequence of the peer-to-peer semantics of Git repositories, all repositories are of equal stature. You can push to and fetch from development and bare repositories equally, because there is no fundamental implementation distinction between them. This symmetric design is critically important to Git, but it also leads to some unexpected behavior if you try to treat bare and development repositories as exact equals.

Recall that the git push command does not check out files in the receiving repository. It simply transfers objects from the source repository to the receiving repository and then updates the corresponding refs on the receiving end.

In a bare repository, this behavior is all that can be expected because there is no working directory that might be updated by checked-out files. That's good. However, in a development repository that is the recipient of a push operation, it can later cause confusion to anyone using the development repository.

The push operation can update the repository state, including the HEAD commit. That is, even though the developer at the remote end has done nothing, the branch refs and HEAD might change, becoming out of sync with the checked-out files and index.

A developer who is actively working in a repository into which an asynchronous push happens will not see the push. But a subsequent commit by that developer will occur on an unexpected HEAD, creating an odd history. A forced push will lose pushed commits from the other developer. The developer at that repository also may find themselves unable to reconcile their history with either an upstream repository or a downstream clone because they are no longer simple fast-forwards as they should be. And they won't know why: the repository has silently changed out from underneath them.

As a result, you are encouraged to push only into a bare repository. This is not a hard-and-fast rule, but it's a good guide for the average developer and is considered a best practice. There are a few instances and use cases where you might want to push into a development repository, but you should fully understand the implications of doing so. When you *do* want to push into a development repository, you may want to follow one of two basic approaches.

In the first scenario, you really do want to have a working directory with a branch checked out in the receiving repository. You may know, for example, that no other developer will ever be doing active development there, and therefore there is no one who might be blindsided by silent changes being pushed into their repository.

In this case, you may want to enable a hook in the receiving repository to perform a checkout of some branch, perhaps the one just pushed, into the working directory as well. To verify that the receiving repository is in a sane state prior to having an automatic checkout, the hook should ensure that the nonbare repository's working directory contains no edits or modified files and that its index has no files in the staged but uncommitted state when the push happens. When these conditions are not met, you run the risk of losing those edits or changes as the checkout overwrites them.

There is another scenario where pushing into a nonbare repository can work reasonably well. By agreement, each developer who pushes changes must push to a non-checked-out branch that is considered simply a receiving branch. A developer never pushes to a branch that is expected to be checked out. It is up to some developer in particular to manage what branch is checked out and when. Perhaps that person is responsible for handling the receiving branches and merging them into a main branch before it is checked out.

Summary

By now it is apparent that a remote is a reference, or handle, to another repository through a filesystem or network path. As we discussed in this chapter, you use a remote as a shorthand name for an otherwise lengthy and complicated Git URL. You can define any number of remotes in a repository, thus creating terraced networks of repository sharing.

Once a remote is established, Git can transfer data from one repository to another using either a push or a pull model. For example, it's a common practice to occasionally transfer commit data from an original repository to its clone in order to keep the clone in sync. You can also create a remote to transfer data from the clone repository to its original or configure the two to exchange information bidirectionally.

We also discussed that, to keep track of data from other repositories, Git uses remote-tracking branches. Each remote-tracking branch in your repository is a branch that serves as a proxy for a specific branch in a remote repository. You can set up a local-tracking branch that forms the basis for integrating your local changes with the remote changes from a corresponding remote-tracking branch.

Finally, we shared techniques for making your repository available to others. Git generally refers to this as "publishing a repository" and provides several techniques for doing so. The parts in this chapter were designed to iteratively build the skill and conceptual understanding you need to effectively leverage working with remote repositories across all your projects.

## CHAPTER 12

Repository Management

This chapter describes how to publish Git repositories and presents approaches for managing and publishing repositories for cooperative development. It is very discussion oriented and draws together possible schools of thoughts one could adopt when managing Git repositories.

We start by explaining how you can set up and configure your own Git server and expose access for published repositories via available protocols. Next, we discuss possible ways you can structure your repository for either central or distributed access according to your development needs. Following this, we then share some rules of thumb for you to consider in your development journey with Git repositories. Building on this, we cover the importance of understanding the possible roles of developers, mainly the presence of role duality in a developer–maintainer relationship. We also discuss techniques you can leverage when you need to work with multiple distributed repositories, and we conclude the chapter by sharing some context around the concept of forking a repository.

A Word About Servers

The word *server* is used liberally and loosely to mean a variety of different things. Neither Git nor this book is an exception, so let's clarify what a server may or may not be, what it might or might not do, and how Git might use one.

Technically, Git doesn't need a server. In contrast to other version control systems, where a centralized server is often required, there is no need to hang on to the mindset that one is *required* to host Git repositories.

Having a server in the context of a Git repository often requires little more than establishing a convenient, fixed, or known location from which repositories are obtained or updates are exchanged. The Git server might also provide some form of authentication or access control.

Git is happy to exchange files directly with a peer repository on the same machine without the need for some server to broker the deal, or with different machines via a variety of protocols, neiither of which enforces the need for a superior server to exist.

Publishing Repositories

Whether you are setting up an open source development environment in which many people across the internet might develop a project, or you are establishing a project for internal development within a private group, the mechanics of collaboration are essentially the same. The main difference between the two scenarios is the location of the repository and who has access to it.

The term *commit rights* is sort of a misnomer in Git. Git doesn't try to manage access rights; instead, it leaves it to other tools, such as SSH, which are better suited to the task. You can always commit in any repository to which you have (Unix) access via SSH and cding to that repository, or to which you have direct rwx-mode access.

The concept might better be paraphrased as "Can I update the published repository?" In that expression, you can see the issue is really the question "Can I push changes to the published repository?"

In "Referring to Remote Repositories" on page 246, we cautioned you about using the remote repository URL form */path/to/repo.git* because it might exhibit problems characteristic of repositories that use shared files. However, if you were setting up a common depot containing several similar repositories, you would want to use a shared, underlying object store. In this case, you expect the repositories to be monotonically increasing in size without objects and refs being removed from them. This situation can benefit from large-scale sharing of the object store by many repositories, thus saving tremendous volumes of disk space. To achieve this space savings, consider using the `--reference` `repository` option, the `--local` option, or the `--shared` option during the initial bare repository clone setup step for your published repositories.

For any situation in which you publish a repository, we strongly advise that you publish a bare one.

Repositories with Controlled Access

It might be sufficient for your project to publish a bare repository in a known location on a filesystem in your organization that everyone can access.

Naturally, access in this context means that all developers can see the filesystem on their machines and have traditional Unix (or Unix-like system) ownership and read/write permissions. In these scenarios, using a filename URL such as */path/to/Depot/project.git* or *file://path/to/Depot/project.git* might suffice. Although the performance might be less than ideal, an NFS-mounted[1] filesystem can provide such sharing support.

Slightly more complex access is called for if multiple development machines are used. Within a corporation, for example, the IT department might provide a central server for the repository depot and keep it backed up. Each developer might then have a desktop machine for development. If direct filesystem access such as NFS is not available, you could use repositories named with SSH URLs, but this still requires each developer to have an account on the central server.

In the following example, the same repository published in */tmp/Depot/my_website.git* earlier in this chapter is accessed by a developer who has SSH access to the hosting machine:

```
desktop$ cd /tmp
desktop$ git clone ssh://example.com/tmp/Depot/my_website.git
Initialize my_website/.git
Initialized empty Git repository in /tmp/my_website/.git/
jdl@example.com's password:
remote: Counting objects: 27, done.
Receiving objects: 100% (27/27), done.objects:    3% (1/27)
Resolving deltas: 100% (7/7), done.
remote: Compressing objects: 100% (23/23), done.
remote: Total 27 (delremote: ta 7), reused 0 (delta 0)
```

When that clone is made, it records the source repository using the following URL: *ssh://example.com/tmp/Depot/my_website.git*.

Similarly, other commands such as `git fetch` and `git push` can now be used across the network:

```
desktop$ git push
jdl@example.com's password:
Counting objects: 5, done.
Compressing objects: 100% (3/3), done.
Writing objects: 100% (3/3), 385 bytes, done.
Total 3 (delta 1), reused 0 (delta 0)
To ssh://example.com/tmp/Depot/my_website.git
   55c15c8..451e41c  main -> main
```

---

1 NFS stands for "Network File System."

In both of these examples, the password requested is the normal Unix login password for the remote hosting machine.

 If you need to provide network access with authenticated developers but are not willing to provide login access to the hosting server, check out the Gitolite project. It is an access control layer on top of Git. Start here:

```
$ git clone https://github.com/sitaramc/gitolite.git
```

If you do not need the overhead of setting up your own servers, there are many alternative Git hosting solutions available, with different pricing tiers from free to pro and enterprise.

Again, depending on the desired scope of access, such SSH access to machines may be within a group or corporate setting or may be available across the internet.

Repositories with Anonymous Read Access

If you want to share code, you'll probably want to set up a hosting server to publish repositories and allow others to clone them. Anonymous, read-only access is often all that developers need to clone or fetch from these repositories. A common and easy solution is to export them using git-daemon and also perhaps an HTTP daemon.

Again, the actual realm across which you can publish your repository is as limited or as broad as access to your HTTP pages or your git-daemon. That is, if you host these commands on a public-facing machine, anyone can clone and fetch from your repositories. If you put them behind a corporate firewall, only those people inside the corporation will have access (in the absence of security breaches).

Publishing repositories using git-daemon

Setting up git-daemon (*https://oreil.ly/YxLNI*) allows you to export your repositories using the Git-native protocol.

You must mark repositories as "OK to be exported" in some way. Typically, this is done by creating the file *git-daemon-export-ok* in the top-level directory of the bare repository. This mechanism gives you fine-grained control over which repositories the daemon can export.

Instead of marking each repository individually, you can run git-daemon with the --export-all option to publish all identifiable (by having both an *objects* and a *refs* subdirectory) repositories found in its list of *directories*. There are many git-daemon options that limit and configure which repositories will be exported.

One common way to set up `git-daemon` on a server is to enable it as an `inetd` service. This involves ensuring that your *etc/services* has an entry for Git. The default port is 9418, though you may use any port you like. A typical entry might be as follows:

```
git     9418/tcp     # Git version control system
```

Once you add that line to *etc/services*, you must set up an entry in your *etc/inetd.conf* to specify how `git-daemon` should be invoked.

A typical entry might look like this:

```
# Place on one long line in /etc/inetd.conf

git stream tcp nowait nobody /usr/bin/git-daemon
        git-daemon --inetd --verbose --export-all
        --base-path=/pub/git
```

Using `xinetd` instead of `inetd`, place a similar configuration in the file *etc/xinetd.d/ git-daemon*:

```
# description: The git server offers access to git repositories
service git
{
    disable         = no
    type            = UNLISTED
    port            = 9418
    socket_type     = stream
    wait            = no
    user            = nobody
    server          = /usr/bin/git-daemon
    server_args     = --inetd --export-all --base-path=/pub/git
    log_on_failure  += USERID
}
```

You can make it look as if repositories are located on separate hosts, even though they're just in separate directories on a single host, through a trick supported by `git-daemon`. The following example entry allows a server to provide multiple, virtually hosted Git daemons:

```
# Place on one long line in /etc/inetd.conf

git stream tcp nowait nobody /usr/bin/git-daemon
        git-daemon --inetd --verbose --export-all
        --interpolated-path=/pub/%H%D
```

In the preceding command, `git-daemon` will fill in the %H with a fully qualified hostname and the %D with the repository's directory path. Because %H can be a logical hostname, different sets of repositories can be offered by one physical server.

Typically, an additional level of directory structure, such as *software* or *scm*, is used to organize the advertised repositories. If you combine `--interpolated-path=/pub/%H%D` with a *software* repository directory path, the bare repositories to be published will be physically present on the server, in directories such as these:

```
/pub/git.example.com/software/
/pub/www.example.org/software/
```

You would then advertise the availability of your repositories at URLs such as these:

```
git://git.example.com/software/repository.git
git://www.example.org/software/repository.git
```

Here, the %H is replaced by the host git.example.com or www.example.org, and the %D is replaced by the full repository name, such as /software/repository.git.

The important point of this example is that it shows how a single git-daemon can be used to maintain and publish multiple, separate collections of Git repositories that are physically hosted on one server but are presented as logically separate hosts. The repositories available from one host might be different from those offered by a different host.

Publishing repositories using an HTTP daemon

Sometimes an easier way to publish repositories with anonymous read access is to simply make them available through an HTTP daemon. If you also set up gitweb, visitors can load a URL into their web browsers, see an index listing of your repository, and negotiate using familiar clicks and the browser Back button. Visitors do not need to run Git in order to download files.

You will need to make one configuration adjustment to your bare Git repository before it can be properly served by an HTTP daemon—enable the hooks/post-update option as follows:

```
$ cd /path/to/bare/repo.git
$ mv hooks/post-update.sample hooks/post-update
```

Verify that the *post-update* script is executable, or use chmod 755 on it just to be sure. Finally, copy that bare Git repository into a directory served by your HTTP daemon. You can now advertise that your project is available using a URL such as:

```
http://www.example.org/software/repository.git
```

 If you see an error message such as:

```
...not found: did you run git update-server-info
     on the server?
```

or

```
Perhaps git-update-server-info needs to be run there?
```

then chances are good that you aren't running the hooks/post-update command properly on the server.

Publishing repositories using Smart HTTP

Publishing a repository via the newer, so-called Smart HTTP mechanism is pretty simple in principle, but you may want to consult the full online documentation for the process as found in the manual page of the `git-http-backend` command. What follows here is a simplified extraction of some of that material, which should get you started:

- First, this setup is really geared for use with Apache. Thus the examples that follow show how to modify Apache configuration files. On an Ubuntu system, these are found in */etc/apache2*.

- Second, some mapping, from your advertised repository names to the repository layout on the disk as made available to Apache, needs to be defined. As with the `git-http-backend` documentation, the mapping here makes `http://$host name/git/foo/bar.git` correspond to */var/www/git/foo/bar.git* under Apache's file view.

- Third, three Apache modules are required and must be enabled: `mod_cgi`, `mod_alias`, and `mod_env`.

Define some variables and a script alias that points to the `git-http-backend` command, like this:

```
SetEnv GIT_PROJECT_ROOT /var/www/git
SetEnv GIT_HTTP_EXPORT_ALL
ScriptAlias /git/ /usr/libexec/git-core/git-http-backend/
```

The location of your `git-http-backend` may be different. For example, Ubuntu places it in */usr/lib/git-core/git-http-backend*.

Now you have a choice: you can allow anonymous read access but require authenticated write access to your repository, or you can require authentication for read and write.

For anonymous read access, set up a `LocationMatch` directive:

```
<LocationMatch "^/git/.*/git-receive-pack$">
    AuthType Basic
    AuthName "Git Access"
    Require group committers
    ...
</LocationMatch>
```

For authenticated read access, set up a `Location` directive for the repository or a parent directory of the repository:

```
<Location /git/private>
    AuthType Basic
    AuthName "Private Git Access"
    Require group committers
    ...
</Location>
```

Further recipes exist within the manual page to set up coordinated gitweb access, and show how to serve multiple repository namespaces as well as configure accelerated access to static pages.

Publishing repositories via Git and HTTP daemons

Although using a web server and browser is certainly convenient, think carefully about how much traffic you plan to handle on your server. Development projects can become large, and HTTP is less efficient than the native Git protocol.

You can provide both HTTP and Git daemon access, but it might take some adjusting and coordination between your Git daemon and your HTTP daemon. Specifically, it may require a mapping with the --interpolated-path option to git-daemon and an Alias option to Apache to provide seamless integration of the two views of the same data. Further details on the --interpolated-path option are available in the git daemon manual page, whereas details about the Apache Alias option can be found in the Apache documentation or its configuration file, */etc/apache2/mods-available/alias.conf*.

Repositories with Anonymous Write Access

Technically, you may use the Git native protocol URL forms to allow anonymous write access into repositories served by git-daemon. Doing so requires that you enable the receivepack option in the published repositories config file:

```
[daemon]
        receivepack = true
```

You might do this on a private LAN where every developer is trusted, but it is not considered a best practice. Instead, you should consider tunneling your Git push needs over an SSH connection.

Repository Publishing Advice

Before you go wildly setting up server machines and hosting services just to host Git repositories, consider what your needs really are and why you want to offer Git repositories. Perhaps your needs are already satisfied by existing companies, websites, or services.

For private code, or even for public code, where you place a premium on the value of service, you might consider using a commercial Git hosting service. If you are offering an open source repository and have minimal service needs or expectations, there are a multitude of Git hosting services available. Some offer upgrades to supported services as well. Platforms such as GitHub, GitLab, and Bitbucket are some popular examples available in the mainstream.

The more complicated situations arise when you have private code that you want to keep in-house, and therefore you must set up and maintain your own main depot for repository hosting. Oh, and don't forget your own backups! Even then, there are enterprise-ready versions of Git hosting platforms that provide all of that functionality, available as subscription- or license-based models.

If you need to set up your own servers, the usual approach is to use the Git-over-SSH protocol and require all users of the repository to have SSH access to the hosting server. On the server itself, a semigeneric user account and group (e.g., `git` or `gituser`) are usually created. All repositories are group-owned by this user and typically live in some file space (e.g., */git*, */opt/git*, or */var/git*) set aside for this purpose. Here's the key: that directory must be owned by your `gituser` group, be writable by that group, and have the sticky group bit set.

Now, when you want to create a new, hosted repository called `newrepo.git` on your server, just `ssh` into the server and do this:

```
$ ssh git.my-host.example.com

$ cd /git
$ mkdir newrepo.git
$ cd newrepo.git
$ git init --shared --bare
```

Those last four commands can be simplified as follows:

```
$ git --git-dir /git/newrepo.git init --shared
```

At this point, the bare repository structure exists, but it remains empty. The important aspect of this repository, though, is that it is now receptive to a push of initial content from any user authorized to connect with the server:

```
# from some client
$ cd /path/to/existing/initial/repo.git
$ git push git+ssh://git.my-host.example.com/git/newrepo.git main
```

The whole process of executing that `git init` on the server in such a way that subsequent pushes will work is at the heart of the Git web hosting services.

Repository Structure

Although Git is a distributed system, you are still able to realize a central working model, where one version of the repository can be the source of truth for everyone who works on the repository. The following section elaborates on this concept.

Shared Repository Structure

Some version control systems use a centralized server to maintain a repository. In this model, every developer is a client of the server, which maintains the authoritative version of the repository. Given the server's jurisdiction, almost every versioning operation must contact the server to obtain or update repository information. Thus, for two developers to share data, all information must pass through the centralized server; no direct sharing of data between developers is possible.

With Git, in contrast, a shared, authoritative, and centralized repository is merely a convention. Each developer still has a clone of the depot's repository, so there's no need for every request or query to go to a centralized server. For instance, simple log history queries can be made privately and offline by each developer.

One of the reasons that some operations can be performed locally is that a checkout retrieves not just the particular version you ask for, the way most centralized version control systems operate, but the entire history. Hence, you can reconstruct any version of a file from the local repository.

Furthermore, nothing prevents a developer from either establishing an alternate repository and making it available on a peer-to-peer basis with other developers or sharing content in the form of patches and branches.

In summary, Git's notion of a shared, centralized repository model is purely one of social convention and agreement.

Distributed Repository Structure

Large projects often have a highly distributed development model consisting of a single central yet logically segmented repository. Although the repository still exists as one physical unit, logical portions are relegated to different people or teams that work largely or wholly independently.

 When it's said that Git supports a distributed repository model, this doesn't mean that a single repository is broken up into separate pieces and spread around many hosts. Instead, the distributed repository is just a consequence of Git's distributed development model. Each developer has their own repository that is complete and self-contained. Each developer and their respective repository might be spread out and distributed around the network.

How the repository is partitioned or allocated to different maintainers is largely immaterial to Git. The repositories might have a deeply nested directory structure or they might be more broadly structured. For example, different development teams might be responsible for certain portions of a codebase along submodule, library, or functional lines. Each team might raise a champion to be the maintainer, or steward, of its portion of the codebase and agree as a team to route all changes through this appointed maintainer.

The structure may even evolve over time as different people or groups become involved in the project. Furthermore, a team could likely form intermediate repositories that contain combinations of other repositories, with or without further development. There may be specific stable or release repositories, for instance, each with an attendant development team and a maintainer.

It may be a good idea to allow the large-scale repository iteration and dataflow to grow naturally and according to peer review and suggestion rather than impose a possibly artificial layout in advance. Git is flexible, so if development in one layout or flow doesn't seem to work, it is quite easy to change it to a better one.

How the repositories of a large project are organized, or how they coalesce and combine, is again largely immaterial to the workings of Git; Git supports any number of organizational models. Remember that the repository structure is not absolute. Moreover, the connection between any two repositories is not prescribed. Git repositories are peers.

So how is a repository structure maintained over time if no technical measures enforce the structure? In effect, the structure is a web of trust for the acceptance of changes. Repository organization and dataflow between repositories is guided by social or political agreements. Out-of-the-box features from many Git hosting platforms allow for such agreements to be enforced according to your development needs; this is another reason to consider taking advantage of such platforms.

The question is "Will the maintainer of a target repository allow your changes to be accepted?" Conversely, do you have enough trust in the source repository's data to fetch it into your own repository?

Living with Distributed Development

The following sections will describe common best practices, guidelines, and rules of thumb when you are working with one or more shared Git repositories.

Changing Public History

Once you have published a repository from which others might make a clone, you should consider it static and refrain from rewriting the history of any branch. Although this is not an absolute guideline, avoiding rewinds and alterations of published history simplifies the life of anyone who cloned your repository.

Let's say you publish a repository that has a branch with commits A, B, C, and D. Anyone who cloned your repository gets those commits. Suppose Alice clones your repository and heads off to do some development based on your branch.

In the meantime, you decide, for whatever reason, to fix something in commit C. Commits A and B remain the same, but starting with commit C, the branch's notion of commit history changes. You could slightly alter C or make some totally new commit, X. In either case, republishing the repository leaves commits A and B as they were, but will now offer, say, X and then Y instead of C and D.

Alice's work is now greatly affected. Alice cannot send you patches, make a pull request, or push her changes to your repository because her development is based on commit D.

Furthermore, because patches are based on commit D, they won't apply. Suppose Alice issues a pull request and you attempt to pull her changes; you may be able to fetch them into your repository (depending on your tracking branches for Alice's remote repository), but the merges will almost certainly have conflicts. The failure of this push is due to a non-fast-forward push problem.

In short, the basis for Alice's development has been altered. You have pulled the commit rug out from underneath her development feet.

The situation is not irrecoverable, though. Git can help Alice, especially if she uses the `git rebase --onto` command to relocate her changes onto your new branch after fetching the new branch into her repository. The `--onto <newbase>` option allows you to set a starting point, where you can create the new commit.

Also, there are times when it is appropriate to have a branch with a dynamic history. For example, within the Git repository itself there is a so-called proposed updates branch, pu, which is specifically labeled and advertised as being rewound, rebased, or rewritten frequently. You, as a cloner, are welcome to use that branch as the basis for your development, but you must remain conscious of the branch's purpose and take special effort to use it effectively.

So why would anyone publish a branch with a dynamic commit history? One common reason is specifically to alert other developers about possible and fast-changing directions some other branch might take. You can also create such a branch for the sole purpose of making available, even temporarily, a published changeset that other developers can use.

Separate Commit and Publish Steps

One of the clear advantages of a distributed version control system is the separation of commit and publish. A commit just saves a state in your private repository; publishing through patches or push/pull makes the change public, which effectively freezes the repository history. Other version control systems, such as CVS or SVN, have no such conceptual separation. To make a commit, you must publish it simultaneously.

By making commit and publish separate steps, a developer is much more likely to make precise, mindful, small, and logical steps with patches. Indeed, any number of small changes can be made without affecting any other repository or developer. The commit operation is offline in the sense that it requires no network access to record positive, forward steps within your own repository.

Git also provides mechanisms for refining and improving commits (as discussed in Chapter 9), transforming them into nice, clean sequences prior to making them public. Once you are ready, the commits can be made public in a separate operation.

No One True History

Development projects within a distributed environment have a few quirks that might not be obvious at first. And although these quirks might initially be confusing and their treatment often differs from other nondistributed version control systems, Git handles them in a clear and logical manner.

As development takes place in parallel among different developers of a project, each has created what they believe to be the correct history of commits. As a result, there is my repository and my commit history, your repository and your commit history, and possibly several others being developed, simultaneously or otherwise.

Each developer has a unique notion of history, and each history is correct. There is no one true history. You cannot point to one and say, "This is the *real* history."

Presumably, the different development histories have formed for a reason, and ultimately the various repositories and different commit histories will be merged into one common repository. After all, the intent is likely to be advancement toward a common goal.

When various branches from the different repositories are merged, all of the variations are present. The merged result states, effectively, "The merged history is better than any one independently."

Git expresses this history ambivalence toward branch variations when it traverses the commit directed acyclic graph (DAG). So if Git, when trying to linearize the commit sequence, reaches a merge commit, it must select one branch or the other first. What criterion would it use to favor or select one branch over another? The spelling of the author's last name? Perhaps the timestamp of a commit? That might be useful.

Even if you decide to use timestamps and agree to use Coordinated Universal Time (UTC) and extremely precise values, it doesn't help. Even that recipe turns out to be completely unreliable! (The clocks on a developer's computer can be wrong either intentionally or accidentally.)

Fundamentally, Git doesn't care what came first. The only real, reliable relationship that can be established between commits is the direct parent relationship recorded in the commit objects. At best, the timestamps offer a secondary clue, usually accompanied by various heuristics to allow for errors such as unset clocks.

In short, neither time nor space operates in well-defined ways, so Git must allow for the effects of quantum physics.

Git as Peer-to-Peer Backup

The process of uploading files to the internet and letting individuals make a copy was how the source code for the Linux kernel was "backed up" for years. And it worked!

In some ways, Git is just an extension of the same concept. Nowadays, when you download the source code to the Linux kernel using Git, you're downloading not just the latest version but the entire history leading up to that version.

This concept has been leveraged by projects that allow system administrators to manage their /etc configuration directories with Git, and even allow users to manage and back up their home directories. Remember, just because you use Git doesn't mean you are required to share your repositories; it does, however, make it easy to version-control your repositories right onto your Network Attached Storage (NAS) box for a backup copy.

Knowing Your Place

When participating in a distributed development project, it is important to know how you, your repository, and your development efforts fit into the larger picture. Besides the obvious potential for development efforts in different directions and the requirement for basic coordination, the mechanics of how you use Git and its features can greatly affect how smoothly your efforts align with other developers working on the project.

These issues can be especially problematic in a large-scale distributed development effort, as is often found in open source projects. By identifying your role in the overall effort and understanding who the consumers and producers of changes are, many of the issues can be easily managed.

Upstream and Downstream Flows

There isn't a strict relationship between two repositories that have been cloned one from the other. However, it's common to refer to the parent repository as being *upstream* from the new, cloned repository. Reflexively, the new, cloned repository is often described as being *downstream* from the original parent repository.

Furthermore, the upstream relationship extends "up" from the parent repository to any repository from which it might have been cloned. It also extends "down" past your repository to any that might be cloned from yours.

However, it is important to recognize that this notion of upstream and downstream is *not* directly related to the clone operation. Git supports a fully arbitrary network between repositories. New remote connections can be added, and your original clone remote can be removed to create arbitrary new relationships between repositories.

If there is any established hierarchy, it is purely one of convention. Bob agrees to send their changes to you; in turn, you agree to send your changes on to someone further upstream; and so forth.

The important aspect of the repository relationship is how data is exchanged between them. That is, any repository to which you send changes is usually considered upstream of you. Similarly, any repository that relies on yours for its basis is usually considered downstream of yours.

It's purely subjective but conventional. Git itself doesn't care and doesn't track the stream notion in any way. Upstream and downstream simply help us visualize where patches are going.

Of course, it's possible for repositories to be true peers. If two developers exchange patches or push and fetch from each other's repositories, then neither is really upstream or downstream from the other.

The Maintainer and Developer Roles

Two common roles are the maintainer and the developer. The maintainer serves primarily as an integrator or moderator, and the developer primarily generates changes. The maintainer gathers and coordinates the changes from multiple developers and ensures that all are acceptable with respect to some standard. In turn, the maintainer makes the whole set of updates available again. That is, the maintainer is also the publisher.

The maintainer's goal should be to collect, moderate, accept, or reject changes and then ultimately publish branches that project developers can use. To ensure a smooth development model, maintainers should not alter a branch once it has been published. In turn, a maintainer expects to receive changes from developers that are relevant and that apply to published branches.

A developer's goal, beyond improving the project, is to get their changes accepted by the maintainer. After all, changes kept in a private repository do no one else any good. The changes need to be accepted by the maintainer and made available for others to use and exploit. Developers need to base their work on the published branches in the repositories that the maintainer offers.

In the context of a derived clone repository, the maintainer is usually considered to be upstream from developers.

Because Git is fully symmetric, there is nothing to prevent a developer from considering themselves to be a maintainer for other developers further downstream. But they must now understand that they are in the middle of both an upstream and a downstream dataflow and must adhere to the maintainer and developer contract (see the next section) in this dual role.

Because this dual or mixed-mode role is possible, upstream and downstream is not strictly correlated to being a producer or consumer. You can produce changes with the intent of them going either upstream or downstream.

Maintainer–Developer Interaction

The relationship between a maintainer and a developer is often loose and ill-defined, but there is an implied contract between them. The maintainer publishes branches for the developer to use as their basis. Once the branches are published, though, the maintainer has an unspoken obligation not to change the published branches because this would disturb the basis upon which development takes place.

In the opposite direction, the developer, by using the published branches as their basis, ensures that when their changes are sent to the maintainer for integration, they apply cleanly without problems, issues, or conflicts and per contribution guidelines established by the maintainers.

It may seem as if this makes for an exclusive, lockstep process. Once published, the maintainer can't do anything until the developer sends in changes. And then, after the maintainer applies updates from one developer, the branch will necessarily have changed and thus will have violated the "won't change the branch" contract for some other developers. If this were true, then truly distributed, parallel, and independent work could never really take place.

Thankfully, it is not that grim at all! Instead, Git is able to look back through the commit history on the affected branches, determine the merge basis that was used as the starting point for a developer's changes, and apply them even though other changes from other developers may have been incorporated by the maintainer in the meantime.

With multiple developers making independent changes and with all of them being brought together and merged into a common repository, conflicts are still possible. It is up to both the maintainer and developer to identify and resolve such problems. The maintainer can either resolve these conflicts directly or reject changes from a developer if they would create conflicts. These days, most modern Git hosting platforms have features that allow both the maintainer and developer to systematically track and resolve such changes when presented with them.

Role Duality

There are two basic mechanisms for transferring commits between an upstream and a downstream repository.

The first uses `git push` or `git pull` to directly transfer commits, whereas the second uses `git format-patch` and `git am` to send and receive representations of commits, respectively. The method you use is primarily dictated by agreement within your development team and, to some extent, direct access rights, as discussed in Chapter 11.

Using `git format-patch` and `git am` to apply patches achieves the exact same blob and tree object *content* as if the changes had been delivered via a `git push` or incorporated with a `git pull`. However, the actual commit object will be different because the metadata information for the commit will be different between a push or pull and a corresponding application of a patch.

In other words, using push or pull to propagate a change from one repository to another copies that commit exactly, whereas patching copies only the file and directory data exactly. Furthermore, push and pull can propagate merge commits between repositories. Merge commits cannot be sent as patches.

Because it compares and operates on the tree and blob objects, Git is able to understand that two different commits for the same underlying change in two different repositories, or even on different branches within the same repository, really represent the same change. Thus it is no problem for two different developers to apply the same patch sent via email to two different repositories. As long as the resulting content is the same, Git treats the repositories as having the same content.

Let's see how these roles and dataflows combine to form a duality between upstream and downstream producers and consumers:

Upstream consumer

An upstream consumer is a developer upstream from you, who accepts your changes either as patch sets or as pull requests. Your patches should be rebased to the consumer's current branch HEAD. Your pull requests should either be directly mergeable or already merged by you in your repository. Merging prior to the pull ensures that conflicts are resolved correctly by you, relieving the upstream consumer of that burden. This upstream consumer role could be a maintainer who turns around and publishes what they have just consumed.

Downstream consumer

A downstream consumer is a developer downstream from you, who relies on your repository as the basis for work. A downstream consumer wants solid, published topic branches. You shouldn't rebase, modify, or rewrite the history of any published branch.

Upstream producer/publisher

An upstream publisher is a person upstream from you, who publishes repositories that are the basis for your work. This is likely to be a maintainer with the tacit expectation that they will accept your changes. The upstream publisher's role is to collect changes and publish branches. Again, those published branches should not have their histories altered, given that they are the basis for further downstream development. A maintainer in this role expects developer patches to apply and expects pull requests to merge cleanly.

Downstream producer/publisher

A downstream producer is a developer downstream from you, who has published changes either as a patch set or as a pull request. The goal of a downstream producer is to have changes accepted into your repository. A downstream producer consumes topic branches from you and wants those branches to remain stable, with no history rewrites or rebases. Downstream producers should regularly fetch updates from upstream and should also regularly merge or rebase development topic branches to ensure they apply to the local upstream branch HEADs. A downstream producer can rebase their own local topic branches at any time because it doesn't matter to an upstream consumer that it took several iterations for this developer to make a good patch set that has a clean, uncomplicated history.

Figure 12-1 captures this role duality. Note that the relationship between the actors is represented as a bidirectional flow for each persona.

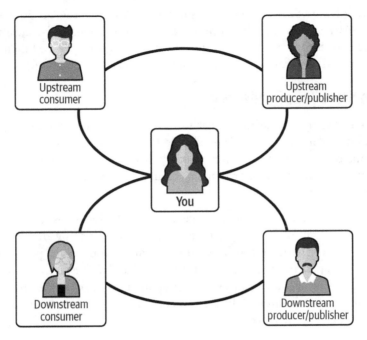

Figure 12-1. Role duality visualized

Working with Multiple Repositories

In this section, we discuss techniques you can leverage when you need to work with multiple distributed repositories.

Your Own Workspace

As the developer of content for a project using Git, you should create your own private copy, or clone, of a repository to do your development. This development repository should serve as your own work area where you can make changes without fear of colliding with, interrupting, or otherwise interfering with another developer.

Furthermore, because each Git repository contains a complete copy of the entire project, as well as the entire history of the project, you can feel free to treat your repository as if it is completely and solely yours. In effect, it actually is!

One benefit of this paradigm is that it allows each developer complete control within their working directory area to make changes to any part, or even to the whole system, without worrying about interaction with other development efforts. If you need to change a part, you have the part and can change it in your repository without affecting other developers. Likewise, if you later realize that your work is not useful or relevant, you can throw it away without affecting anyone else or any other repository.

As with any software development, this is not an endorsement to conduct wild experimentation. Always consider the ramifications of your changes, because ultimately, you may need to merge your changes into the main repository. It will then be time to pay the piper, and any arbitrary changes may come back to haunt you.

Where to Start Your Repository

Faced with a wealth of repositories that ultimately contribute to one project, it may seem difficult to determine where you should begin your development. Should your contributions be based on the main repository directly, or perhaps on the repository where other people are focused on some particular feature? Or maybe a stable branch of a release repository somewhere?

Without a clear sense of how Git can access, use, and alter repositories, you may be caught in some form of the "can't get started for fear of picking the wrong starting point" dilemma. Or perhaps you have already started your development in a clone based on some repository you picked but now realize that it isn't the right one. Sure, it's related to the project and may even be a good starting point, but maybe there is some missing feature found in a different repository. It may even be hard to tell until well into your development cycle.

Another frequent starting point dilemma comes from a need for project features that are being actively developed in two different repositories. Neither of them is, by itself, the correct clone basis for your work.

You could just forge ahead with the expectation that your work and the work in the various repositories will all be unified and merged into one main repository. You are certainly welcome to do so, of course. But remember that part of the gain from a distributed development environment is the ability to do concurrent development. Take advantage of the fact that the other published repositories with early versions of their work are available.

Another pitfall comes if you start with a repository that is at the cutting edge of development and find that it is too unstable to support your work, or that it is abandoned in the middle of your work.

Fortunately, Git supports a model in which you can essentially pick any arbitrary repository from a project as your starting point, even if it is not the perfect one, and then convert, mutate, or augment that repository until it does contain all the right features.

If you later wanted to separate your changes back out to different respective upstream repositories, you may have to make judicious and meticulous use of separate topic branches and merges to keep it all in check.

On the one hand, you can fetch branches from multiple remote repositories and combine them into your own, yielding the right mix of features that are available elsewhere in existing repositories. On the other hand, you can reset the starting point in your repository back to a known stable point earlier in the history of the project's development.

Converting to a Different Upstream Repository

The first and simplest kind of repository mixing and matching is to switch the basis (usually called the *clone origin*) repository, the one you regard as your origin and with which you synchronize regularly.

For example, suppose you need to work on feature F, and you decide to clone your repository from the mainline, M, as shown in Figure 12-2.

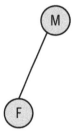

Figure 12-2. Simple clone to develop feature F

You work for a while before learning that there is a better starting point closer to what you would really like, but it is in repository P. One reason you might want to make this sort of change is to gain functionality or feature support that is already in repository P.

Another reason stems from longer-term planning. Eventually, the time will come when you need to contribute the development that you have done in repository F back to some upstream repository. Will the maintainer of repository M accept your changes directly? Perhaps not. If you are confident that the maintainer of repository P will accept them, then you should arrange for your patches to be readily applicable to that repository instead.

Presumably, P was once cloned from M, or vice versa, as shown in Figure 12-3. Ultimately, P and M are based on the same repository for the same project at some point in the past.

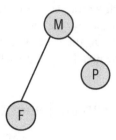

Figure 12-3. Two clones of one repository

The question often asked is whether repository F, originally based on M, can now be converted so that it is based on repository P, as shown in Figure 12-4. This is easy to do using Git because it supports a peer-to-peer relationship between repositories and provides the ability to readily rebase branches.

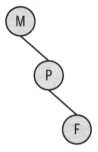

Figure 12-4. Feature F restructured for repository P

In a sense, Git knows how to make up the difference from one repository to the next. Part of the peer-to-peer protocol to fetch branches from another repository is an exchange of information stating what changes each repository has or is missing. As a result, Git is able to fetch just the missing or new changes and bring them into your repository.

Git is also able to review the history of the branches and determine where the common ancestors from the different branches are, even if they are brought in from different repositories. If they have a common commit ancestor, then Git can find it and construct a large, unified view of the commit history with all the repository changes represented.

Using Multiple Upstream Repositories

As another example, suppose that the general repository structure looks like Figure 12-5. Here, some mainline repository, M, will ultimately collect all the development for two different features from repositories F1 and F2.

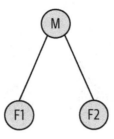

Figure 12-5. Two feature repositories

However, you need to develop some super feature, S, that involves using aspects of features found in only F1 and F2. You could wait until F1 is merged into M and then wait for F2 to also be merged into M. That way, you will then have a repository with the correct, total basis for your work. But unless the project strictly enforces some project lifecycle that requires merges at known intervals, there is no telling how long this process might take.

You might start your repository, S, based off of the features found in F1 or, alternatively, off of F2 (see Figure 12-6).

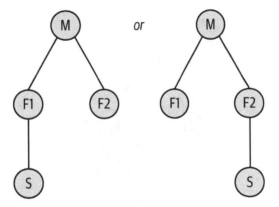

Figure 12-6. Possible starting repositories for S

However, with Git it is possible to instead construct a repository, S, that has both F1 and F2 in it; this is shown in Figure 12-7.

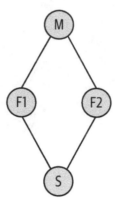

Figure 12-7. Combined starting repository for S

In Figure 12-7, it is unclear whether repository S is composed of the entirety of F1 and F2 or just some part of each. In fact, Git supports both scenarios. Suppose repository F2 has branches F2A and F2B with features A and B, respectively, as shown in Figure 12-8. If your development needs feature A but not B, then you can selectively fetch just that F2A branch into your repository S along with whatever part of F1 is also needed.

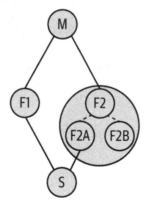

Figure 12-8. Two feature branches in F2

Forking Projects

Anytime you clone a repository, the action can be viewed as *forking* the project. Forking is functionally equivalent to branching in some other version control systems, but Git has a separate concept called branching, so don't call it that. Unlike a branch, a Git fork doesn't exactly have a name. Instead, you simply refer to it by the filesystem directory (or remote server, or URL) into which you cloned.

The term *fork* comes from the idea that when you create a fork, you create two simultaneous paths that the development will follow. It's like a fork in the road of development. As you might imagine, the term *branch* is based on a similar analogy involving trees. There's no inherent difference between the "branching" and "forking" metaphors—the terms simply capture two intents. Conceptually, the difference is that branching usually occurs within a single repository, whereas forking usually occurs at the whole repository level.

Although you *can* fork a project readily with Git, doing so may be more of a social or political choice than a technical one. For public or open source projects, having access to a copy or clone of the entire repository, complete with its history, is both an enabler of and a deterrent to forking.

To fork or not?

Historically, forking a project was often motivated by perceptions of a power grab, a reluctance to cooperate, or the abandonment of a project. A difficult person at the hub of a centralized project can effectively grind things to a halt. A schism may develop between those who are "in charge" of a project and those who are not. Often, the only perceived solution is to effectively fork a new project. In such a scenario, it may be difficult to obtain a copy of the history of the project and start over.

Forking is the traditional term for what happens when one developer of an open source project becomes unhappy with the main development effort, takes a copy of the source code, and starts maintaining their own version.

Forking, in this sense, has traditionally been considered a negative thing; it means the unhappy developer couldn't find a way to get what they wanted from the main project. So they go off and try to do it better themselves, but now there are *two* projects that are almost the same. Obviously, neither one is good enough for everybody, or one of them would be abandoned. So most open source projects make heroic efforts to *avoid* forking.

Forking may or may not be bad. On the one hand, perhaps an alternate view and new leadership is exactly what is needed to revitalize a project. On the other hand, it may simply contribute to strife and confusion on a development effort.

Reconciling forks

In contrast, Git tries to remove the stigma of forking. The real problem with forking a project is not the creation of an alternate development path. Every time a developer downloads or clones a copy of a project and starts hacking on it, they have created an alternative development path, if only temporarily.

In his work on the Linux kernel, Linus Torvalds eventually realized that forking is a problem only if the forks don't eventually merge back together. Thus he designed Git to look at forking totally differently: Git *encourages* forking. But Git also makes it easy for anyone to merge two forks whenever they want.

Technically, reconciling a forked project with Git is facilitated by its support for large-scale fetching and importing of one repository into another and for extremely easy branch merging.

Although many social issues may remain, fully distributed repositories seem to reduce tensions by lessening the perceived importance of the person at the center of a project. Because an ambitious developer can easily inherit a project and its complete history, they may feel it is enough to know that, if needed, the person at the center could be replaced and development could still continue!

Today, where open source is becoming a way of life for developers, forking is adopted to implement a structured and well-implemented method on popular Git hosting platforms such as GitHub, for the community to consume and actively contribute back to popular projects. In this light, forking enables the core maintainers to work cleanly and establish secure access to their projects, all while keeping a stable production codebase for their repositories.

Forking projects at GitHub

Many people in the software community dislike the term *forking*. But this is because it usually results in infinitely diverging copies of the software. Our focus should not be on the dislike for the concept of forks but rather on the quantity of divergence before bringing the two lines of code back together again.

Forking at GitHub typically has a far more positive connotation. Much of the site is built around the premise of short-lived forks. Any drive-by developer can make a copy (fork) of a public repository, make code changes they think are appropriate, and then offer them back to the core project owner. Repository maintainers are able to view all forked copies of their repository in a centralized view.

The forks offered back to the core project are called *pull requests*. Pull requests afford visibility to forks and facilitate smart management of these diverging branches. A conversation can be attached to a pull request, thus providing context as to why a request was accepted or returned to the sender for additional polish.

Well-maintained projects have the attribute of a frequently maintained pull request queue. Project contributors should process through the pull request queue, either accepting, commenting on, or rejecting all pull requests. This signals a level of care about and active maintenance of the codebase and the greater community surrounding the project.

Although GitHub has been intentionally designed to facilitate good use of forks, the negative form of forking—hostile wrangling of the codebase in an isolationist direction—is still possible on GitHub. However, there is a notably low volume of this misbehavior. Misbehavior can be attributed in large part to the visibility of forks and their potential divergence from the primary codebase in the network commit graph.

Summary

In this chapter, each solution discussed has its place. Deciding which solution is right for you and your project will depend on your own requirements and philosophy. However, no matter which approach you adopt, Git implements a distributed development model. For example, even if your team centralizes the repository, each developer has a complete, private copy of that repository and can work independently. The work is distributed, yet it is coordinated through a central, shared repository. The repository model and the development model are independent of each other's orthogonal characteristics. In reality, you will probably already be working with repositories on a Git hosting platform. As such, sections in this chapter discussing repository structure, repository publishing advice, living with distributed development, and knowing your place will prove beneficial and give you enough knowledge to lead you in using the right solution for your project and team.

## PART IV

Advanced Skills

In the following chapters, we discuss topics that help you understand alternative methods in which you are able to propagate changes between repositories that are shared and developed among distributed collaborators. We discuss a simple yet effective mechanism to share those changes via patches, which you can send via email.

We also start exposing you to the possibility of extending the standard execution flow for a handful of Git operations. This is something you can benefit from in the event you need to implement a custom execution workflow beyond the standard Git operations in your daily routine. Although popular Git hosting platforms now support modern development workflow features, knowing this technique adds an extra trick up your sleeve when you need a workflow feature that is not readily available out of the box.

Chapter 15 is going to help you when you need to modularize your projects and manage them in separate Git repositories. We discuss two commonly used methods to achieve this with some examples demonstrating technical implementation to reference dependent Git repositories. In Chapter 16 we push the skills you learned in the intermediate section a little further. We share some elegant techniques to help you craft or group related hunks of changes as an atomic commit, teach you how to find lost commits and demonstrate the usage of the `git rev-list` command. The showcase of this chapter is the `git-filter-repo` tool. It is the Swiss Army knife you need for all your repository commit and history fixing and manipulation. We firmly advise you to spend a good amount of time in this section.

## CHAPTER 13

Patches

Git allows development work to be transferred directly and immediately from one repository to another using both a push model and a pull model. It does so via the various supported protocols we discussed in "Referring to Remote Repositories" on page 246.

As a quick recap, recall that Git implements its own transfer protocol to exchange data between repositories. To save time and space, Git's transfer protocol performs a small handshake, determines what commits in the source repository are missing from the target, and finally transfers a binary, compressed form of the commits. The receiving repository incorporates the new commits into its local history, augments its commit graph, and updates its branches and tags as needed.

HTTP can also be used to exchange development between repositories. Although HTTP is not nearly as efficient as Git's native protocol, it is just as capable of moving commits to and fro. Both protocols ensure that a transferred commit remains identical in both the source and destination repositories.

In modern Git hosting platforms, the operation to systematically incorporate changes from multiple working copies of repositories into a centralized source of truth is almost the same as it is with HTTP. New workflows and features are introduced above the underlying base layers of the push-and-pull model. In fact, you may already know of these as *pull requests* or *merge requests*, depending on your Git hosting platform of choice. We will cover pull requests in detail in Chapter 18.

However, these features and protocols aren't the only mechanisms for exchanging commits and keeping distributed repositories synchronized. In fact, there are times when using these protocols is infeasible. Drawing on tried-and-true methods from an earlier Unix development era, Git also supports a "patch and apply" operation, where the data exchange typically occurs via email.

Git implements three specific commands to facilitate the exchange of a patch:

- `git format-patch` generates a patch in email form.
- `git send-email` sends a Git patch through a Simple Mail Transfer Protocol (SMTP) feed.
- `git am` applies a patch found in an email message.

The typical use case is fairly simple. You and one or more developers start with a clone of a common repository and begin collaborative development. You do some work, make a few commits to your copy of the repository, and eventually decide it's time to convey your changes to your partners. You choose the commits you would like to share and choose with whom to share the work. Because the patches are sent via email, each intended recipient can elect to apply none, some, or all of the patches.

In this chapter, we start by explaining when you might want to use patches and then provides some examples on how to generate, send, and (if you're a recipient) apply a patch. Since patching is basically combining changes from one repository to another, we also discuss the concept of how patching differs from merging.

Why Use Patches?

Although the Git protocol is much more efficient than HTTP, there are at least two compelling reasons to undertake the extra effort required by patches: one is technical and the other is sociological:

- In some situations, neither the Git native protocol nor HTTP can be used to exchange data between repositories in either a push or a pull direction or both.

  For example, a corporate firewall may forbid opening a connection to an external server using Git's protocol or port. Additionally, SSH may not be an option. Moreover, even if HTTP is permitted, which is common, you could download repositories and fetch updates, but you may not be able to push changes back out. In situations like this, email is the perfect medium for communicating patches.

- One of the great advantages of a peer-to-peer development model such as Git is collaboration. Patches, especially those sent to a public mailing list, are a means of openly distributing proposed changes for peer review.

  Prior to permanently applying the patches to a repository, other developers can discuss, critique, rework, test, and either approve or veto posted patches. Because the patches represent precise changes, acceptable patches can be directly applied to a repository.

Even if your development environment allows you the convenience of a direct push or pull exchange, you may still want to employ a "patch, email, review, and apply" paradigm to gain the benefits of peer review.

You might even consider a project development policy whereby each developer's changes must be peer reviewed as patches on a mailing list prior to directly merging them via `git pull` or `git push`. This would give you all the benefits of peer review with the ease of pulling changes directly!

And there are still other reasons to use patches.

In much the same way that you might cherry-pick a commit from one of your own branches and apply it to another branch, using patches allows you to selectively choose commits from another developer's repository without having to fully fetch and merge everything from that repository.

Of course, you could ask the other developer to place the desired commits on a separate branch and then fetch and merge that branch alone, or you could fetch their whole repository and then cherry-pick the desired commits out of the tracking branches. But you might have some reason for *not* wanting to fetch the repository.

If you want an occasional or explicit commit—say, an individual bug fix or a particular feature—then applying the attendant patch may be the most direct way to get that specific improvement.

Git's very own source code is in fact maintained using this patching model. It is constantly updated via the Git mailing list, where maintainers and contributors are active. If you are interested in participating in the mailing list without subscribing to it, you may post a question or comment to the mailing list at *git@vger.kernal.org*.

Although you may find the source code for Git on GitHub, it is just a mirror copy hosted on the platform.

Generating Patches

The `git format-patch` command generates a patch in the form of an email message. It creates one piece of email for each commit you specify. You can specify the commits using any technique discussed in "Identifying Commits" on page 81.

Common use cases include the following:

- A specified number of commits, such as `-2`
- A commit range, such as `main~4..main~2`
- A single commit, often the name of a branch, such as `origin/main`

Although the Git diff machinery is at the heart of the `git format-patch` command, it differs from `git diff` in two key ways:

- Whereas `git diff` generates one patch with the combined differences of all the selected commits, `git format-patch` generates one email message for each selected commit.

- `git diff` doesn't generate email headers. In addition to the actual diff content, `git format-patch` generates an email message complete with headers that list the commit author, the commit date, and the commit log message associated with the change.

> `git format-patch` and `git log` should seem very similar. As an interesting experiment, compare the output of the following two commands: `git format-patch -1` and `git log -p -1 --pretty=email`.

Let's start with a fairly simple example. Suppose you have a repository with just one file in it, named *file*. Furthermore, the content of that file is a series of single capitalized letters, A through D. Each letter was introduced into the file one line at a time and was committed using a log message corresponding to that letter:

```
$ mkdir patch-demo ; cd patch-demo
$ git init -b main
$ echo A > file
$ git add file
$ git commit -m "Add A"
 [main (root-commit) 11200ff] Add A
  1 file changed, 1 insertion(+)
  create mode 100644 file
$ echo B >> file ; git commit -m "Add B" file
 [main ace6f32] Add B
  1 file changed, 1 insertion(+)
$ echo C >> file ; git commit -m "Add C" file
 [main b621372] Add C
  1 file changed, 1 insertion(+)
$ echo D >> file ; git commit -m "Add D" file
 [main d578a1c] Add D
  1 file changed, 1 insertion(+)
```

Thus, the commit history now has four commits:

```
$ git show-branch --more=4 main
[main] Add D
[main^] Add C
[main~2] Add B
[main~3] Add A
```

The easiest way to generate patches for the most recent *n* commits is to use a `-n` option, like this:

```
$ git format-patch -1
0001-Add-D.patch

$ git format-patch -2
0001-Add-C.patch
0002-Add-D.patch

$ git format-patch -3
0001-Add-B.patch
0002-Add-C.patch
0003-Add-D.patch
```

By default, Git generates each patch in its own file with a sequentially numbered name derived from the commit log message. The command outputs the filenames as it executes.

You can also specify which commits to format as patches by using a commit range. Suppose you expect other developers to have repositories based on commit B of your repository, and suppose you want to patch their repositories with all the changes you made between B and D.

Based on the previous output of `git show-branch`, you can see that B has the version name `main~2` and that D has the version name `main`. So you would specify these names as a commit range in the `git format-patch` command.

Although you're including three commits in the range (B, C, and D), you end up with two email messages representing two commits: the first contains the diffs between B and C, and the second contains the diffs between C and D. See Figure 13-1.

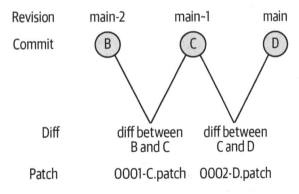

Figure 13-1. *git format-patch with a commit range*

Here is the output of the command:

```
$ git format-patch main~2..main
0001-Add-C.patch
0002-Add-D.patch
```

Each file is a single email, conveniently numbered in the order that it should be subsequently applied. Here is the first patch:

```
$ cat 0001-Add-C.patch
From b621372d83c034eb8b962574d5ad01449b93f6b7 Mon Sep 17 00:00:00 2001
From: Prem Kumar Ponuthorai <ppremk@gmail.com>
Date: Wed, 5 Jan 2022 12:48:32 +0100
Subject: [PATCH 1/2] Add C

---
 file | 1 +
 1 file changed, 1 insertion(+)

diff --git a/file b/file
index 35d242b..b1e6722 100644
--- a/file
+++ b/file
@@ -1,2 +1,3 @@
 A
 B
+C
--
2.37.0
```

And here is the second:

```
$ cat 0002-Add-D.patch
From d578a1c3031e995f5234d1a25f36e470842484eb Mon Sep 17 00:00:00 2001
From: Prem Kumar Ponuthorai <ppremk@gmail.com>
Date: Wed, 5 Jan 2022 12:48:46 +0100
Subject: [PATCH] Add D

---
 file | 1 +
 1 file changed, 1 insertion(+)

diff --git a/file b/file
index b1e6722..8422d40 100644
--- a/file
+++ b/file
@@ -1,3 +1,4 @@
 A
 B
 C
+D
--
2.37.0
```

Let's continue the example and make it more complex by adding another branch, named `alt`, based on commit B.

While the main developer added individual commits with the lines C and D to the `main` branch, the `alt` developer added the commits (and lines) X, Y, and Z to their branch:

```
# Create branch alt at commit B
  (retrieve commit B SHA by running git log --oneline command, your SHA ID may differ from ours)
$ git checkout -b alt ace6f32
Switched to a new branch 'alt'
```

```
$ echo X >> file ; git commit -m "Add X" file
[alt 43250ac] Add X
  1 file changed, 1 insertion(+)
$ echo Y >> file ; git commit -m "Add Y" file
[alt fd1ca23] Add Y
  1 file changed, 1 insertion(+)
$ echo Z >> file ; git commit -m "Add Z" file
[alt cc9993c] Add Z
  1 file changed, 1 insertion(+)
```

The commit graph looks like Figure 13-2.

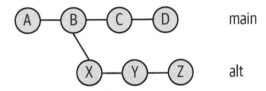

Figure 13-2. Patch graph with alt branch

You can draw an ASCII graph with all your refs using the option
`--all`, like this:

```
$ git log --graph --pretty=oneline --abbrev-commit --all
* cc9993c (HEAD -> alt) Add Z
* fd1ca23 Add Y
* 43250ac Add X
| * d578a1c (main) Add D
| * b621372 Add C
|/
* ace6f32 Add B
* 11200ff Add A
```

Suppose further that the main developer merged the alt branch at commit Z into
main at commit D to form merge commit E. Finally, they made one more change that
added F to the main branch:

```
$ git checkout main
$ git merge alt

# Resolve the conflicts however you'd like
# We used the sequence: A, B, C, D, X, Y, Z

$ git add file
$ git commit -m "Add all lines"
[main 5727615] Add all lines

$ echo F >> file ; git commit -m "Add F" file
[main 9ab717f] Add F
  1 file changed, 1 insertion(+)
```

The commit graph now looks like Figure 13-3.

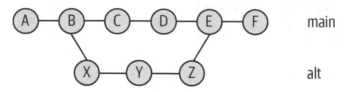

Figure 13-3. History of two branches

A display of the commit branch history looks like this:

```
$ git show-branch --more=10
! [alt] Add Z
 * [main] Add F
--
 * [main] Add F
+* [alt] Add Z
+* [alt^] Add Y
+* [alt~2] Add X
 * [main~2] Add D
 * [main~3] Add C
+* [main~4] Add B
+* [main~5] Add A
```

Patching can be surprisingly flexible when you have a complicated revision tree. Let's take a look.

You must be careful when specifying a commit range, especially when it covers a merge. In the current example, you might expect that the range D..F would cover the two commits for E and F, and it does. But commit E contains all the content merged into it from *all* its merged branches:

```
# Format patches D..F
$ git format-patch main~2..main
0001-Add-X.patch
0002-Add-Y.patch
0003-Add-Z.patch
0004-Add-F.patch
```

Remember, a commit range is defined as including all commits leading up to the range *end point* but excluding all commits leading up to and including the range *starting point* state. In the case of D..F, this means that all the commits contributing to F (every commit in the example graph) are included, but all the commits leading up to and including D (A, B, C, and D) are eliminated. The merge commit itself won't generate a patch.

Detailed Range Resolution Explained

To figure out a range, follow these steps. Start at the end point commit and include it. Work backward along every parent commit that contributes to it and include those. Recursively include the parent of every commit that you have included so far. When

---

you are done including all the commits that contribute to the end point, go back and start with the start point. Remove the start point. Work back over every parent commit that contributes to the start point and remove those too. Recursively remove every parent commit that you have removed so far.

Referring to Figure 13-3, with the case of our D..F range, start with F and include it. Back up to the parent commit, E, and include it. Then look at E and include its parents, D and Z. Now recursively include the parents of D, giving C and then B and A. Down the Z line, recursively include Y and X and then B again, and finally A again. (Technically, B and A aren't included *again*; the recursion can stop when it sees an already-included node.) Effectively, all commits are now included. Now go back and start with the start point, D, and remove it. Remove its parent, C, and recursively its parent, B, and its parent, A.

You should be left with the set F E Z Y X. But E is a merge; so remove it, leaving F Z Y X, which is exactly the reverse of the generated set.

Issue `git rev-list --no-merges -v` *since..until* to verify the set of commits for which patches will be generated before you actually create your patches.

You can also reference a single commit as a variation of the `git format-patch` commit range. However, Git's interpretation of such a command is slightly nonintuitive.

Git normally interprets a single commit argument as "all commits that lead up to and contribute to the given commit." In contrast, `git format-patch` treats a single commit parameter as if you had specified the range `commit..HEAD`. It uses your commit as the starting point and takes HEAD as the end point. Thus, the generated patch series is implicitly in the context of the currently checked-out branch.

In our ongoing example, when the `main` branch is checked out and a patch is made specifying commit A, all seven patches are produced:

```
$ git branch
  alt
* main

# From commit A
$ git format-patch main~5
0001-Add-B.patch
0002-Add-C.patch
0003-Add-D.patch
0004-Add-X.patch
0005-Add-Y.patch
0006-Add-Z.patch
0007-Add-F.patch
```

But when the `alt` branch is checked out and the command specifies the same A commit, only those patches contributing to the tip of the `alt` branch are used:

```
$ git checkout alt
Switched to branch "alt"

$ git branch
* alt
  main

$ git format-patch main~5
0001-Add-B.patch
0002-Add-X.patch
0003-Add-Y.patch
0004-Add-Z.patch
```

Even though commit A is specified, you don't actually get a patch for it. The root commit is somewhat special in that there isn't a previously committed state against which a diff can be computed. Instead, a patch for it is effectively a pure addition of all the initial content.

If you really want to generate patches for every commit up to a named *end-commit*, including the initial root commit, then use the `--root` option, like this:

```
$ git format-patch --root <end-commit-SHA>
```

The initial commit generates a patch as if each file in it was added based on */dev/null* (this convention denotes an added or removed file):

```
$ git format-patch --root main~5
$ cat 0001-Add-A.patch
From 11200ff80b78bd777d8832b112eaddcdd8b899db Mon Sep 17 00:00:00 2001
From: Prem Kumar Ponuthorai
<ppremk@gmail.com>
Date: Wed, 5 Jan 2022 12:47:17 +0100
Subject: [PATCH] add file A

---
file | 1 +
1 file changed, 1 insertion(+)
create mode 100644 file

diff --git a/file b/file
new file mode 100644
index 0000000..f70f10e
--- /dev/null
+++ b/file
@@ -0,0 +1 @@
+A
--
2.37.0
```

Treating a single commit as if you had specified *commit*`..HEAD` may seem unusual, but this approach has a valuable use in one particular situation. When you specify a *commit* on a branch that's different from the branch you currently have checked out, the command emits patches that are in your current branch but *not* in the named branch. In other words, it generates a set of patches that can bring the other branch in sync with your current branch.

To illustrate this feature, assume you've checked out the main branch:

```
$ git branch
  alt
* main
```

Now you specify the alt branch as the *commit* parameter:

```
$ git format-patch alt
0001-Add-C.patch
0002-Add-D.patch
0003-Add-F.patch
```

The patches for commits C, D, and F are exactly the same set of patches in the main branch but not in the alt branch.

The power of this command, coupled with a single commit parameter, becomes apparent when the named commit is the HEAD ref of a tracking branch from someone else's repository.

For example, if you clone Alice's repository and your main development is based on Alice's main, then you would have a tracking branch named something like alice/main.

After you have made some commits on your main branch, the command git format-patch alice/main generates the set of patches that you must send them to ensure that their repository has at least all of your main content. They may have *more* changes from other sources in their repository already, but that is not important here. You have isolated the set from your repository (the main branch) that is known not to be in theirs.

Thus, git format-patch is specifically designed to create patches for commits that are in your repository in a development branch but are not already present in the upstream repository.

Patches and Topological Sorts

Patches generated by git format-patch are emitted in topological order. For a given commit, the patches for all parent commits are generated and emitted before the patch for this commit is emitted. This ensures that a correct ordering of patches is always created, but a correct ordering is not necessarily unique: there may be multiple correct orders for a given commit graph.

Let's see what this means by looking at some of the possible generation orders for patches that could ensure a correct repository if the recipient applies them in order. Example 13-1 shows a few of the possible topological sort orders for the commits of our example graph.

Example 13-1. Some topological sort orders

```
A B C D X Y Z E F

A B X Y Z C D E F

A B C X Y Z D E F

A B X C Y Z D E F

A B X C Y D Z E F
```

Remember, even though patch creation is driven by a topological sort of the selected nodes in the commit graph, only some of those nodes will actually produce patches.

The first ordering in Example 13-1 is the ordering that Git picked for `git format-patch main~5`. Because A is the first commit in the range and no `--root` option was used, there isn't a patch for it. Commit E represents a merge, so no patch is generated for it, either. Thus, the patches are generated in the order B C D X Y Z F.

Whatever patch sequence Git chooses, it is important to realize that Git has produced a *linearization* of all the selected commits, no matter how complicated or branched the original graph was.

Mailing Patches

Once you have generated a patch or a series of patches, the next logical step is to send them to another developer or to a development list for review, with the ultimate goal of it being picked up by a developer or upstream maintainer and applied to another repository.

The formatted patches are generally intended to be sent via email by directly importing them into your Mail User Agent (MUA), or by using Git's `git send-email` command. You are not obliged to use `git send-email`; it is merely a convenience. As you will see in the next section, there are also other tools that use the patch file directly.

If you want to send a generated patch file to another developer, there are several ways to do it: you can run `git send-email`, you can point your mailer directly to the patches, or you can include the patches in an email.

Using `git send-email` is straightforward. In this example, the patch *0001-Add-A.patch* is sent to a mail list called `devlist@example.org`:

```
$ git send-email --to devlist@example.org 0001-Add-A.patch
0001-Add-A.patch
(mbox) Adding cc: Prem Kumar Ponuthorai <ppremk@gmail.com> from line 'From: Prem Kumar Ponuthorai
<ppremk@gmail.com>'

From: Prem Kumar Ponuthorai <ppremk@gmail.com>
To: devlist@example.org
Cc: Prem Kumar Ponuthorai <ppremk@gmail.com>
Subject: [PATCH] Add A
Date: Wed,  5 Jan 2022 15:13:38 +0100
Message-Id: <20220105141338.79674-1-ppremk@gmail.com>
X-Mailer: git-send-email 2.33.0
MIME-Version: 1.0
Content-Transfer-Encoding: 8bit

    The Cc list above has been expanded by additional
    addresses found in the patch commit message. By default
    send-email prompts before sending whenever this occurs.
    This behavior is controlled by the sendemail.confirm
    configuration setting.

    For additional information, run 'git send-email --help'.
    To retain the current behavior, but squelch this message,
    run 'git config --global sendemail.confirm auto'.

Send this email? ([y]es|[n]o|[e]dit|[q]uit|[a]ll): y

OK. Log says:
Sendmail: /usr/sbin/sendmail -i devlist@example.org ppremk@gmail.com
From: Prem Kumar Ponuthorai <ppremk@gmail.com>
To: devlist@example.org
Cc: Prem Kumar Ponuthorai <ppremk@gmail.com>
Subject: [PATCH] add file A
Date: Wed,  5 Jan 2022 15:13:38 +0100
Message-Id: <20220105141338.79674-1-ppremk@gmail.com>
X-Mailer: git-send-email 2.33.0
MIME-Version: 1.0
Content-Transfer-Encoding: 8bit

Result: OK
```

There are many options for either utilizing or working around a myriad of SMTP issues or features. What's critical is ensuring that you know your SMTP server and port. Likely, it is the traditional `sendmail` program or a valid outbound SMTP host, such as `smtp.my-isp.com`.

Don't set up SMTP open relay servers just to send your Git email. Doing so will contribute to spam mail problems.

The `git send-email` command has many configuration options, which are documented in its manual page.

You may find it convenient to record your special SMTP information in your global configuration file by setting, for example, the value `sendemail.smtpserver` and `sendemail.smtpserverport` using commands similar to these:

```
$ git config --global sendemail.smtpserver smtp.my-isp.com
$ git config --global sendemail.smtpserverport 465
```

Depending on your MUA, you may be able to directly import an entire file or directory of patches into a mail folder. If so, this can greatly simplify sending a large or complicated patch series.

Here is an example in which a traditional `mbox`-style mail folder is created using `format-patch` and is then directly imported into `mutt`, where the message can be addressed and sent (`mbox` is the format for mail message storage on Unix systems, and `mutt` is a text-based mail client for Unix systems):

```
$ git format-patch --stdout main~2..main > mbox

$ mutt -f mbox

q:Quit  d:Del  u:Undel  s:Save  m:Mail  r:Reply  g:Group  ?:Help
   1 N    Dec 29 Jon Loeliger    (  15) [PATCH] X
   2 N    Dec 29 Jon Loeliger    (  16) [PATCH] Y
   3 N    Dec 29 Jon Loeliger    (  16) [PATCH] Z
   4 N    Dec 29 Jon Loeliger    (  15) [PATCH] F
```

The latter two mechanisms, using `send-email` and directly importing a mail folder, are the preferred techniques for sending email because both are reliable and not prone to messing with the carefully formatted patch contents. You are less likely, for example, to hear a developer complain about a wrapped line if you use one of these techniques.

On the other hand, you may find that you need to directly include a generated patch file in a newly composed email in popular MUAs such as Gmail, Thunderbird, and Microsoft Outlook, to name a few. In these cases, the risk of disturbing the patch is much greater. Care should be taken to turn off any form of HTML formatting and to send plain ASCII text that has not been allowed to flow or word-wrap in any way.

Depending on your recipient's ability to handle mail or contingent on your development list policies, you may or may not want to use an attachment for the patch. In general, inlining attachment of patches is the simpler, more correct approach. It also facilitates an easier patch review. However, if the patch is inlined, then some of the headers generated by `git format-patch` might need to be trimmed, leaving just the `From:` and `Subject:` headers in the email body.

If you find yourself frequently including your patches as text files in newly composed emails and are annoyed at having to delete the superfluous headers, you might want to try the following command: `git format-patch --pretty=format:%s%n%n%b` *commit*. You might also configure that as a Git global alias, as described in "Configuration Files" on page 20.

Regardless of how the patch mail is sent, it should look essentially identical to the original patch file when received, albeit with more and different mail headers.

The similarity of the patch file format before and after transport through the mail system is not an accident. The key to this operating successfully is to use plain text and to prevent any MUAs from altering the patch format through such operations as line wrapping. If you can preclude such interdictions, a patch will remain usable irrespective of how many Mail Transfer Agents (MTAs) carry the data.

Use `git send-email` if your MUA is prone to wrap lines on outbound mail.

There are a host of options and configuration settings to control the generation of email headers for patches. Your project probably has some conventions that you should follow. For example, if you are consistently adding headers to the patch email as generated, then you might investigate the configuration option `format.headers`.

If you have a series of patches, you might want to funnel them all to a common directory with the `-o` *directory* option to `git format-patch`. Afterward, you can use `git send-email` *directory* to send them all at once. In this case, use either `git format-patch --cover-letter` or `git send-email --compose` to write a guiding, introductory cover letter for the entire series.

There are also options to accommodate various social aspects of most development lists. For example, use `--cc` to add alternate recipients, to add or omit each `Signed-off-by:` address as a `Cc:` recipient, or to select how a patch series should be threaded on a list.

You can read more about these options in the `git send-email` manual pages.

Applying Patches

Git has two basic commands that apply patches. The higher-level porcelain command, `git am`, is partially implemented in terms of the plumbing command `git apply`.

The command `git apply` is the workhorse of the patch application procedure. It accepts `git diff-` or `diff`-style outputs and applies them to the files in your current working directory. Though different in some key respects, it performs essentially the same role as Larry Wall's `patch` command (the patch program for Unix systems).

Because a diff contains only line-by-line edits and no other information (such as author, date, or log messages), it cannot perform a commit and log the change in your repository. Thus, when `git apply` is finished, the files in your working directory are left modified. (In special cases, it can use or modify the index as well.)

In contrast, the patches formatted by `git format-patch`, either before or after they have been mailed, contain the extra information necessary to make and record a proper commit in your repository. Although `git am` is configured to accept patches generated by `git format-patch`, it is also able to handle other patches if they follow some basic formatting guidelines.[1] Note that `git am` creates commits on the current branch.

Let's complete the patching process example we've been working on using the same repository from "Generating Patches" on page 317 (patch, email, review, and apply). We will use the following use case in which one developer has constructed a complete patch set, *0001-Add-B.patch* through *0007-Add-F.patch*, and has sent it or otherwise made it available to another developer. The other developer has an early version of the repository and wants to now apply the patch set.

First we'll look at a naïve approach that exhibits common problems that are ultimately impossible to resolve. Then we'll examine a second approach that proves successful.

Here are the patches from the original repository:

```
$ git format-patch -o /tmp/patches main~5
/tmp/patches/0001-Add-B.patch
/tmp/patches/0002-Add-C.patch
/tmp/patches/0003-Add-D.patch
/tmp/patches/0004-Add-X.patch
/tmp/patches/0005-Add-Y.patch
/tmp/patches/0006-Add-Z.patch
/tmp/patches/0007-Add-F.patch
```

---

1 By the time you adhere to the guidelines detailed in the manual page for `git am` (a "From:", a "Subject:", a "Date:", and a patch content delineation), you might as well call it an email message anyway.

These patches could have been received by the second developer via email and stored on disk, or they may have been placed directly in a shared filesystem.

Let's construct an initial repository as the target for this series of patches. (How this initial repository is constructed is not really important—it may well have been cloned from the initial repository.) The key to long-term success is a moment in time when both repositories are known to have the exact same file content.

Let's reproduce that moment by cloning the earlier repository and resetting it to contain the same file, *file*, with the initial contents, A. This ensures we have exactly the same repository content as was present at the very beginning of the original repository:

```
$ cd /tmp
$ git clone ~/patch-demo am
Cloning into 'am'...
done.
$ cd am

# Get initial commit SHA via git log --oneline command
# then reset to that SHA
$ git reset --hard 11200ff

# Disconnect from upstream, to
  demonstrate patching (not necessary but why not?)
$ git remote remove origin
$ git log --oneline
11200ff (HEAD -> main) Add A
```

A direct application of `git am` shows some problems:

```
$ git am /tmp/patches/*
Applying: Add B
Applying: Add C
Applying: Add D
Applying: Add X
error: patch failed: file:1
error: file: patch does not apply
Patch failed at 0004 Add X
hint: Use 'git am --show-current-patch=diff' to see the failed patch
When you have resolved this problem, run "git am --continue".
If you prefer to skip this patch, run "git am --skip" instead.
To restore the original branch and stop patching, run "git am --abort".
```

This is a tough failure mode, and it might leave you in a bit of a quandary about how to proceed. A good approach in this situation is to look around a bit:

```
$ git show-branch --more=10
[main] Add D
[main^] Add C
[main~2] Add B
[main~3] Add A
```

That's pretty much as expected. No file was left dirty in your working directory, and Git successfully applied patches up to and including D.

Often, looking at the patch itself and the files that are affected by the patch helps clear up the problem. Let's use the hint provided by Git:

```
$ git am --show-current-patch=diff
---
 file | 1 +
 1 file changed, 1 insertion(+)

diff --git a/file b/file
index 35d242b..7f9826a 100644
--- a/file
+++ b/file
@@ -1,2 +1,3 @@
 A
 B
+X
--
2.37.0

$ cat file
A
B
C
D
```

 When the `git am` command is executed, the directory *.git/rebase-apply* is created. It contains various contextual information for the entire series of patches and the individual parts (author, log message, etc.) of each patch.

This is a difficult spot. The file has four lines in it, but the patch applies to a version of that same file with just two lines. As the `git am` command output indicated, this patch doesn't actually apply:

```
error: patch failed: file:1
error: file: patch does not apply
Patch failed at 0004 Add X.
```

You may know that the ultimate goal is to create a file in which all the letters are in order, but Git is not able to figure that out automatically. There just isn't enough context to determine the right conflict resolution yet.

As with other actual file conflicts, `git am` offers a few suggestions:

```
When you have resolved this problem run "git am --continue".
If you would prefer to skip this patch, run "git am --skip" instead.
To restore the original branch and stop patching run "git am --abort".
```

Unfortunately, there isn't even a file content conflict that can be resolved and resumed in this case.

You might think you could just skip the X patch, as suggested:

```
$ git am --skip
Applying: Add Y
error: patch failed: file:1
error: file: patch does not apply
Patch failed at 0005 Add Y
hint: Use 'git am --show-current-patch=diff' to see the failed patch
When you have resolved this problem, run "git am --continue".
If you prefer to skip this patch, run "git am --skip" instead.
To restore the original branch and stop patching, run "git am --abort".
```

But as with this Y patch, all subsequent patches fail now too. It's clear that the patch series isn't going to apply cleanly with this approach.

You can try to recover from here, but that will be tough to do without knowing the original branching characteristics that led to the patch series being presented to `git am`. Recall that the X commit was applied to a new branch that originated at commit B. That means the X patch would apply correctly if it were applied again to that commit state. You can verify this: reset the repository back to just the A commit, clean out the *rebase-apply* directory, apply the B commit using `git am /tmp/patches/0001-B.patch`, and see that the X commit will apply too!

```
# Reset back to commit A
$ git reset --hard main~3
HEAD is now at 11200ff Add A

# remove .git/rebase-apply directory
$ rm -rf .git/rebase-apply/

$ git am /tmp/patches/0001-Add-B.patch
Applying: Add B

$ git am /tmp/patches/0004-Add-X.patch
Applying: Add X
```

 Cleaning up a failed, botched, or hopeless `git am` and restoring the original branch can be simplified to just `git am --abort`.

The success of applying *0004-Add-X.patch* to commit B provides a hint about how to proceed. However, you can't really apply patches X, Y, and Z because then the later patches C, D, and F would not apply. And you don't really want to bother re-creating the exact original branch structure, even temporarily. Even if you were willing to re-create it, how would you know what the original branch structure was?

Knowing the basis file to which a diff can be applied is a difficult problem for which Git provides an easy technical solution. If you look closely at a patch or diff file generated by Git, you will see new, extra information that isn't part of a traditional Unix diff summary. The extra information that Git provides for the patch file *0004-Add-X.patch* is shown in Example 13-2.

Example 13-2. New patch context in 0004-Add-X.patch

```
diff --git a/file b/file
index 35d242b..7f9826a 100644
--- a/file
+++ b/file
```

Just after the diff --git a/file b/file line, Git adds the new line index 35d242b..7f9826a 100644. This information is designed to answer with certainty the following question: "What is the original state to which this patch applies?"

The first number on the index line, 35d242b, is the SHA1 hash of the blob within the Git object store to which this portion of the patch applies. That is, 35d242b is the file as it exists with just the two lines:

```
$ git show 35d242b
A
B
```

And that is exactly the version of *file* to which this portion of the X patch applies. If that version of the file is in the repository, then Git can apply the patch to it.

This mechanism—having a current version of a file; having an alternate version; and locating the original, base version of a file to which the patch applies—is called a *three-way merge*. Git is able to reconstruct this scenario using the -3 or --3way option to git am.

Let's clean up the failed effort; reset back to the first commit state, A; and try to reapply the patch series:

```
# Get rid of temporary "git am" context, if needed.
$ rm -rf .git/rebase-apply/

# Use "git log" to locate commit A, it was SHA1 573956b
# Reset back to commit A. The SHA1 will be different for you.
$ git reset --hard 11200ff
HEAD is now at 11200ff Add A

$ git show-branch --more=10
[main] Add A
```

Now, using the -3 option, apply the patch series:

```
$ git am -3 /tmp/patches/*
Applying: Add B
Applying: Add C
```

```
Applying: Add D
Applying: Add X
Using index info to reconstruct a base tree...
M       file
Falling back to patching base and 3-way merge...
Auto-merging file
CONFLICT (content): Merge conflict in file
error: Failed to merge in the changes.
Patch failed at 0004 Add X
hint: Use 'git am --show-current-patch=diff' to see the failed patch
When you have resolved this problem, run "git am --continue".
If you prefer to skip this patch, run "git am --skip" instead.
To restore the original branch and stop patching, run "git am --abort".
```

That's much better!

Just as before, the simple attempt to patch the file failed, but instead of quitting, Git has changed to the three-way merge. This time, Git recognizes it is able to perform the merge, but a conflict remains because overlapping lines were changed in two different ways.

Because Git is not able to correctly resolve this conflict, the `git am -3` command is temporarily suspended. It is now up to you to resolve the conflict before resuming the command.

Again, the strategy of looking around can help determine what to do next and how to proceed:

```
$ git status
On branch main
You are in the middle of an am session.
  (fix conflicts and then run "git am --continue")
  (use "git am --skip" to skip this patch)
  (use "git am --abort" to restore the original branch)

Unmerged paths:
  (use "git restore --staged <file>..." to unstage)
  (use "git add <file>..." to mark resolution)
    both modified:   file

no changes added to commit (use "git add" and/or "git commit -a")
```

As indicated previously, the file *file* still needs to have a merge conflict resolved.

The contents of *file* show the traditional conflict merge markers, which must be resolved via an editor:

```
$ cat file
A
B
<<<<<<< HEAD
C
D
=======
X
>>>>>>> Add X
```

```
# Fix conflicts in "file"
$ vi file

$ cat file
A
B
C
D
X
```

After resolving the conflict and cleaning up, resume the `git am -3` command:

```
$ git am -3 --continue
Applying: Add X
You still have unmerged paths in your index.
You should 'git add' each file with resolved conflicts to mark them as such.
You might run `git rm` on a file to accept "deleted by them" for it.
When you have resolved this problem, run "git am --continue".
If you prefer to skip this patch, run "git am --skip" instead.
To restore the original branch and stop patching, run "git am --abort".
```

Did you forget to use `git add`? We sure did!

```
$ git add file
$ git am -3 --continue
Applying: Add X
Applying: Add Y
Using index info to reconstruct a base tree...
M    file
Falling back to patching base and 3-way merge...
Auto-merging file
Applying: Add Z
Using index info to reconstruct a base tree...
M    file
Falling back to patching base and 3-way merge...
Auto-merging file
Applying: Add F
```

Finally, success!

```
$ cat file
A
B
C
D
X
Y
Z
F

$ git show-branch --more=10
[main] F
[main^] Z
[main~2] Y
[main~3] X
[main~4] D
[main~5] C
[main~6] B
[main~7] A
```

Applying these patches didn't construct a replica of the branch structure from the original repository. All patches were applied in a linear sequence, and this is reflected in the main branch commit history. You can verify this by running the `git log --graph --oneline` command:

```
$ git log --graph --oneline
* 37e3f43 (HEAD -> main) Add F
* 3a2d1df Add Z
* 3484b10 Add Y
* f18328e Add X
* 68cf338 Add D
* a9e1a1b Add C
* 06d2fad Add B
* 11200ff Add A
```

Another interesting thing to keep in mind is that the patch `Author` and `AuthorDate` will follow per the original commit and patch, whereas the data for the committer reflects the actions of applying the patch and committing it to this branch and repository:

```
# The patch demo was applied the following day
  after the inital example was set up
$ git log --pretty=fuller -1 a9e1a1b
commit a9e1a1bad95082f597b781bb4b22694eaacd9698
Author:     Prem Kumar Ponuthorai <ppremk@gmail.com>
AuthorDate: Wed Jan 5 12:48:32 2022 +0100
Commit:     Prem Kumar Ponuthorai <ppremk@gmail.com>
CommitDate: Thu Jan 6 16:30:03 2022 +0100

    Add C
```

Bad Patches

The obligation to create robust, identical content in multiple distributed repositories around the world is an onerous task. It is no wonder that a perfectly good patch can be trashed by any number of mail-related failures. Ultimately, the onus is on Git to ensure that the complete patch email, review, and apply cycle can faithfully reconstruct identical content through an unreliable transport mechanism.

Patch failures stem from many areas, many mismatched tools, and many different philosophies. But perhaps the most common failure is simply not maintaining the exact line-handling characteristics of the original content. This usually manifests itself as line wrappings due to text being reflowed by either the sender or receiver MUA or by any of the intermediate MTAs. Luckily, the patch format has internal consistency checks that prevent this type of failure from corrupting a repository.

This should not be a challenge when you work with modern Git hosting platforms, which provide rich feature sets enabling systematic and seamless integration of merge changes across distributed development repositories and between development teams into a centralized, single source of truth, the upstream repository, for a given project.

Patching Versus Merging

Git can handle situations in which patches have been applied and the changes have been pulled in the same repository. Even though the commit in the receiving repository ultimately differs from the commit in the original repository from which the patch was made, Git can use its ability to compare and match content to sort matters out.

Later, for example, subsequent diffs will show no content changes. The log message and author information will also be the same as they were conveyed in the patch mail, but information such as the date and SHA1 will be different.

Directly fetching and merging a branch with a complex history will yield a different history in the receiving repository than the history that results from a patching sequence. Remember, one of the effects of creating a patch sequence on a complex branch is to topologically sort the graph into a linearized history. Hence, applying it to another repository yields a linearized history that wasn't in the original. Another point worth noting is that, when creating patches, *merge commits* are not generated as part of the patching operation.

Depending on your development style and your ultimate intent, having the original development history linearized within the receiving repository may or may not be a problem for you and your project. At the very least, you have lost the complete branch history that led to the patch sequence. At best, you simply don't care how you arrived at the patch sequence.

Summary

We began this chapter by discussing the rationale for using patches. Patching can be very impactful when you want to share changes with collaborators who may not have direct access to popular Git hosting platforms but share a common codebase of a shared version of your project repository. Using the techniques we shared for generating and applying patches, you will be able to start sharing commits between repositories using the patch method. When resorting to patching instead of merging commits, we strongly advise you to understand how this will affect your team overall, because this decision could influence how repository histories are recorded.

## CHAPTER 14

Hooks

Git hooks allow you to tweak standard Git operations. You can use a Git hook to run one or more arbitrary scripts whenever a particular event, such as a commit or a patch, occurs in your repository. Typically, an event is broken down into several prescribed steps, and you can tie a custom script to each step. When the Git event occurs, the appropriate script is called at the outset of each step.

Hooks belong to and affect a specific repository and are not copied during a clone operation. In other words, hooks you set up in your private repository are not propagated to and do not alter the behavior of the new clone. If, for some reason, your development process mandates hooks in each developer's personal development repository, arrange to copy the directory *.git/hooks* through some other (non-clone) method.

Do not confuse this with initializing a new repository. When the `git init` command is specified, Git copies available hooks to the new repository; these can include the default sample hooks Git provides or some custom hooks you specify in a configurable path defined via the *template directory* mechanism.

In this chapter, we start by discussing the available types of Git hooks and how to install them, then guide you through the process of creating a simple Git hook. We also explain how and when Git hooks can be used to alter standard Git operations.

Types of Hooks

A hook runs either in the context of your current, local repository or in the context of the remote repository. For example, fetching data into your repository from a remote repository and making a local commit can cause local hooks to run; pushing changes to a remote repository may cause hooks in the remote repository to run. Such hooks are also known as *client-side* and *server-side* hooks (with *client* referring to the local repository and *server* referring to the remote repository). Typically, server-side or remote hooks refer to the hooks enabled in the centralized or upstream copy of the repository.

Most Git hooks fall into one of two categories:

- A *"pre" hook* runs before an action completes and can be used to approve, reject, or adjust a change before it's applied.

- A *"post" hook* runs after an action completes and can be used to trigger notifications (such as email) or launch additional processing, such as running a build or closing a bug.

As a general rule, if a *pre*-action hook exits with a nonzero status (the convention to indicate failure), the Git action is aborted. In contrast, the exit status of a *post*-action hook is generally ignored because the hook can no longer affect the outcome or completion of the action.

A Note on Using Hooks

In general, Git developers advocate using hooks with caution. A hook, they say, should be a method of last resort, to be used only when you can't accomplish the same result in some other way. For example, if you want to specify a particular option each time you make a commit, check out a file, or create a branch, a hook is unnecessary. You can accomplish these tasks with a Git alias (see "Configuration Files" on page 20) or with shell scripts to augment `git commit`, `git checkout`, and `git branch`, respectively.[1]

At first blush, a hook may seem to be an appealing and straightforward solution. However, its use has several implications:

- A hook changes the behavior of Git. If a hook performs an unusual operation, other developers familiar with Git may run into surprises when using your repository.

- A hook can slow down operations that are otherwise fast. For example, developers are often enticed to hook Git to run unit tests before anyone makes a commit, but this makes committing slow. In Git, a commit is supposed to be a fast operation, thus encouraging frequent commits to prevent the loss of data. Making a commit run slowly makes Git less enjoyable.

---

1 As it happens, running a hook at commit time is such a common requirement that a precommit hook exists for that, even though it isn't strictly necessary.

- A hook script that is buggy can interfere with your work and productivity. The only way to work around a hook is to disable it. In contrast, if you use an alias or shell script instead of a hook, then you can always fall back on the normal Git command wherever that makes sense.

- A repository's collection of hooks is not automatically replicated. Hence, if you install a commit hook in your repository, it won't reliably affect another developer's commits. This is partly for security reasons—a malicious script could easily be smuggled into an otherwise innocuous-looking repository—and partly because Git simply has no mechanism to replicate anything other than blobs, trees, and commits.

Junio's Overview of Hooks

Junio Hamano wrote the following about Git hooks on the Git mailing list. Their ideas can be paraphrased as follows.

There are five valid reasons to hook a Git command/operation:

1. To countermand the decision made by the underlying command. The `update` hook and the `pre-commit` hook are two hooks used for this purpose.

2. To manipulate data generated after a command starts to run. Modifying the commit log message in the `commit-msg` hook is an example.

3. To operate on the remote end of a connection that you access only via the Git protocol. A `post-update` hook that runs `git update-server-info` does this very task.

4. To acquire a lock for mutual exclusion. This is rarely a requirement, but sufficient hooks are available to achieve it.

5. To run one of several possible operations, depending on the outcome of the command. The `post-checkout` hook is a notable example.

Each of these five requirements requires at least one hook. You cannot realize a similar result from outside the Git command.

On the other hand, if you always want some action to occur before or after running a Git operation locally, you don't need a hook. For instance, if your postprocessing depends on the effects of a command (item 5 in the list), but the results of the command are plainly observable, then you don't need a hook.

With those "warnings" behind us, we can state that hooks exist for very good reasons and that their use can be incredibly advantageous.

Installing Hooks

Each hook is a script, and the collection of hooks for a particular repository can be found in the *.git/hooks* directory. As already mentioned, Git doesn't replicate hooks between repositories; if you `git clone` or `git fetch` from another repository, you won't inherit that repository's hooks. You have to copy the hook scripts by hand.

Each hook script is named after the event with which it is associated. For example, the hook that runs immediately before a `git commit` operation is named *.git/hooks/pre-commit*.

A hook script must follow the normal rules for Unix scripts: it must be executable (`chmod a+x .git/hooks/pre-commit`) and must start with a line indicating the language in which the script is written (e.g., `!/bin/bash` or `!/usr/bin/perl`).

If a particular hook script exists and has the correct name and file permissions, Git uses it automatically.

Example Hooks

Depending on your exact version of Git, you may find some hooks in your repository at the time it's created. Hooks are copied automatically from your Git template directory when you create a new repository. On Debian and Ubuntu, for example, the hooks are copied from */usr/share/git-core/templates/hooks*. Most Git versions include some example hooks that you can use, and these are preinstalled for you in the *templates* directory.

Let's examine these preinstalled hooks by initializing a new repository:

```
$ mkdir hooks-sample && cd hooks-sample
$ git init -b main
$ tree .git
.git
├── HEAD
├── config
├── description
├── hooks
│   ├── applypatch-msg.sample
│   ├── commit-msg.sample
│   ├── fsmonitor-watchman.sample
│   ├── post-update.sample
│   ├── pre-applypatch.sample
│   ├── pre-commit.sample
│   ├── pre-merge-commit.sample
│   ├── pre-push.sample
│   ├── pre-rebase.sample
│   ├── pre-receive.sample
│   ├── prepare-commit-msg.sample
│   ├── push-to-checkout.sample
│   └── update.sample
├── info
│   └── exclude
```

```
├── objects
│   ├── info
│   └── pack
└── refs
    ├── heads
    └── tags

8 directories, 17 files
```

Here's what you need to know about the example hooks:

- The template hooks probably don't do exactly what you want. You can read them, edit them, and learn from them, but you rarely want to use them as is.
- Even though the hooks are created by default, all the hooks are initially disabled. Depending on your version of Git and your operating system, the hooks are disabled either by removing the execute bit or by appending *.sample* to the hook filename. The latest versions of Git have executable hooks named with a *.sample* suffix.
- To enable an example hook, you must remove the *.sample* suffix from its filename (`mv .git/hooks/pre-commit.sample .git/hooks/pre-commit`).

Originally, each example hook was simply copied into the *.git/hooks/* directory from the *template* directory with its execute permission removed. You could then enable the hook by setting its execute bit.

That worked fine on systems like Unix and Linux, but it didn't work well on Windows. In Windows, file permissions work differently, and, unfortunately, files are executable by default. This meant the example hooks were executable by default, causing great confusion among new Git users because all the hooks ran when none should have.

Because of this problem with Windows, newer versions of Git suffix each hook filename with *.sample* so that it won't run even if it's executable. To enable the example hooks you need, you'll have to rename the appropriate scripts yourself.

If you aren't interested in the example hooks, it is perfectly safe to remove them from your repository using `rm .git/hooks/*`. You can always get them back by copying them from their home in the *templates* directory.

In addition to the template examples, there are more example hooks in Git's *contrib* directory, a portion of the Git source code. The supplemental files may also be installed along with Git on your system. On Debian and Ubuntu, for example, the contributed hooks are installed in */usr/share/doc/git-core/contrib/hooks*. On Fedora, they are in */usr/share/git-core/contrib/$$hooks*.

Creating Your First Hook

To explore how a hook works, let's create a new repository and install a simple hook. First we'll create the repository and populate it with a few files:

```
$ mkdir hooktest && cd hooktest
$ git init -b main
Initialized empty Git repository in /somepath/.git/

$ touch a b c

$ git add a b c

$ git commit -m 'Added a, b, c'
[main (root-commit) 10f32fe] Added a, b, c
 3 files changed, 0 insertions(+), 0 deletions(-)
 create mode 100644 a
 create mode 100644 b
 create mode 100644 c
```

Next, let's create a pre-commit hook to prevent checking in changes that contain the word *broken*. We will create a new hook with the following name (for this example, we will assume that there is no preinstalled sample hook file of the same name):

```
# Create the hook
$ touch .git/hooks/pre-commit
```

Using your favorite text editor, put the following code block in the newly created file called *.git/hooks/pre-commit*:

```
#!/bin/bash
echo "Hello, I'm a pre-commit script!" >&2
if git diff --cached | grep '^\+' | grep -q 'broken'; then
        echo "ERROR: Can't commit the word 'broken'" >&2
        exit 1  # reject
fi
exit 0  # accept
```

The script generates a list of all the differences about to be checked in, extracts the lines to be *added* (i.e., those lines that begin with a + character), and scans those lines for the word *broken*.

There are many ways to test for the word *broken*, but most of the obvious ones result in subtle problems. We're not talking about how to "test" for the word *broken* but rather about how to find the text to be scanned for the word *broken*.

For example, you might have tried the following test:

```
if git ls-files | xargs grep -q 'broken'; then
```

or, in other words, searched for the word *broken* in all files in the repository. But this approach has two problems. If someone else had already committed a file containing the word *broken*, then this script would prevent all future commits (until you fix it), even if those commits are totally unrelated. Moreover, the Unix grep command has no way of knowing which files will actually be committed; if you add *broken* to file b, make an unrelated change to a, and then run `git commit a`, there's nothing wrong with your commit because you're not trying to commit b. However, a script with this test would reject it anyway.

 If you write a `pre-commit` script that restricts what you're allowed to check in, it's almost certain that you'll need to bypass it some-day. You can bypass the `pre-commit` hook either by using the `--no-verify` option to `git commit` or by temporarily disabling your hook.

Now that we've created the `pre-commit` hook, let's make sure it's executable:

```
# Set execute bit
$ chmod a+x .git/hooks/pre-commit
```

And now we can test that it works as expected:

```
$ echo "perfectly fine" >a

$ echo "broken" >b

# Try to commit all files, even a 'broken' one.
$ git commit -m "test commit -a" -a
Hello, I'm a pre-commit script!
ERROR: Can't commit the word 'broken'

# Selectively committing un-broken files works.
$ git commit -m "test only file a" a
Hello, I'm a pre-commit script!
[main 5468656] test only file a
 1 file changed, 1 insertion(+)

# And committing 'broken' files won't work.
$ git commit -m "test only file b" b
Hello, I'm a pre-commit script!
ERROR: Can't commit the word 'broken'
```

Observe that even when a commit works, the `pre-commit` script still emits `"Hello"`. This would be annoying in a real script, so you should use such messages only while debugging the script. Notice also that, when the commit is rejected, `git commit` doesn't print an error message; the only message is the one produced by the script. To avoid confusing the user, always print an error message from a "pre" script if it's going to return a nonzero ("reject") exit code.

Given those basics, let's talk about the different hooks you can create.

Available Hooks

To discover what hooks are available in your version of Git, run `git help hooks`. Also refer to the Git documentation to find all the command-line parameters as well as the input and output of each hook.

Commit-Related Hooks

When you run `git commit`, Git executes a process like that shown in Figure 14-1.

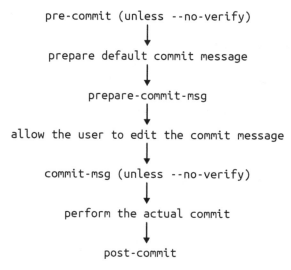

Figure 14-1. Commit hook processing

 None of the commit hooks run for anything other than `git commit`. For example, `git rebase`, `git merge`, and `git am` don't run your commit hooks by default. (Those commands may run other hooks, though.) However, `git commit --amend` *does* run your commit hooks.

Each hook has its own purpose, as follows:

- The `pre-commit` hook gives you the chance to immediately abort a commit if something is wrong with the content being committed. The `pre-commit` hook runs before the user is allowed to edit the commit message, so the user won't enter a commit message only to discover the changes are rejected. You can also use this hook to automatically modify the content of the commit.

- `prepare-commit-msg` lets you modify Git's default message before it is shown to the user. For example, you can use this to change the default commit message template.

- The `commit-msg` hook can validate or modify the commit message after the user edits it. For example, you can leverage this hook to check for spelling mistakes or reject messages with lines that exceed a certain maximum length.

- `post-commit` runs after the commit operation has finished. At this point, you can update a log file, send email, or trigger an autobuilder, for instance. Some people use this hook to automatically mark bugs as fixed if, say, the bug number is mentioned in the commit message. In real life, however, the `post-commit` hook is rarely useful, because the repository that you `git commit` in is rarely the one that you share with other people. (The `update` hook is likely more suitable.)

Patch-Related Hooks

When you run `git am`, Git executes a process as follows (see Figure 14-2):

- `applypatch-msg` examines the commit message attached to the patch and determines whether or not it's acceptable. For example, you can choose to reject a patch if it has no `Signed-off-by:` header. You can also modify the commit message at this point if desired.

- The `pre-applypatch` hook is somewhat misnamed, because this script actually runs *after* the patch is applied but before committing the result. This makes it exactly analogous to the `pre-commit` script when doing `git commit`, even though its name implies otherwise. In fact, many people choose to create a `pre-applypatch` script that runs `pre-commit`.

- `post-applypatch` is analogous to the `post-commit` script.

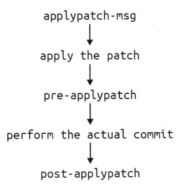

Figure 14-2. Patch hook processing

Despite what you might expect from the names of the hooks shown in Figure 14-2, `git apply` does not run the `applypatch` hooks, only `git am` does. This is because `git apply` doesn't actually commit anything, so there's no reason to run any hooks.

Push-Related Hooks

When you run `git push`, the *receiving end* of Git executes a process like the one shown in Figure 14-3.

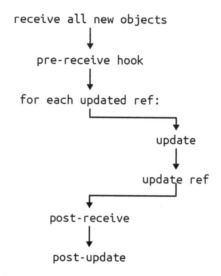

Figure 14-3. Receive hook processing

 All push-related hooks run on the receiver, not the sender. Thus, the hook scripts that run are in the *.git/hooks* directory of the receiving repository, not the sending one. Output produced by remote hooks is still shown to the user doing the `git push`.

As you can see in the diagram, the very first step of `git push` is to transfer all the missing objects (blobs, trees, and commits) from your local repository to the remote one. There is no need for a hook during this process because all Git objects are identified by their unique SHA1 hash; your hook cannot modify an object because it would change the hash. Furthermore, there's no reason to reject an object, because `git gc` cleans up anyway if the object turns out to be unneeded.

Instead of manipulating the objects themselves, push-related hooks are called when it's time to update the refs (branches and tags):

- `pre-receive` receives a list of all the refs that are to be updated, including their new and old object pointers. The only thing the prereceive hook can do is accept or reject all the changes at once, which is of limited use. You might consider it a feature, though, because it enforces transactional integrity across branches. Yet, it's not clear why you'd need such a thing; if you don't like that behavior, use the `update` hook instead.

- The `update` hook is called exactly once for each ref being updated. The update hook can choose to accept or reject updates to individual branches, without affecting whether other branches are updated or not. Also, for each update you can trigger an action such as closing a bug or sending an email acknowledgment. It's usually better to handle such notifications here than in a `post-commit` hook, because a commit is not really considered "final" until it's been pushed to a shared repository.

- Like the prereceive hook, `post-receive` receives a list of all the refs that have just been updated. Anything that `post-receive` can do could also be done by the `update` hook, but sometimes `post-receive` is more convenient. For example, if you want to send an update notification email message, `post-receive` can send just a single notification about all updates instead of a separate email for each update. The `post-receive` hook supersedes the `post-update` hook since it will receive the old and new values for all changed refs.

- The `post-update` hook is meant for notifications only and does not change the outcome of a `git push` operation.

Other Local Repository Hooks

Finally, there are a few miscellaneous hooks, and by the time you read this there may be even more. (Again, you can find the list of available hooks quickly with the command `git help hooks`.)

- The `pre-rebase` hook (*https://oreil.ly/44zID*) runs when you attempt to rebase a branch. This is useful because it can stop you from accidentally running `git rebase` on a branch that shouldn't be rebased because it's already been published.

- `post-checkout` runs after you check out a branch or an individual file. For example, you can use this to automatically create empty directories (Git doesn't know how to track empty directories) or to set file permissions or Access Control Lists (ACLs) on checked-out files (Git doesn't track ACLs). You might think of using this to modify files after checking them out—for example, to do RCS-style variable substitution—but it's not such a good idea because Git will think the files have been locally modified.

- `post-merge` runs after you perform a merge operation. This is rarely used. If your `pre-commit` hook does some sort of change to the repository, you might need to use a `post-merge` script to do something similar.

- `pre-auto-gc` helps `git gc --auto` decide whether or not it's time to clean up. You can make `git gc --auto` skip its `git gc` task by returning nonzero from this script. This will rarely be needed, however.

To Hook or Not

By extending the standard Git operations, Git hooks open up the possibilities for us to extend our development workflows. For reasons cautioned in section "A Note on Using Hooks" on page 340, we reiterate that you should consider using hooks only as a last resort. If and when you resort to using hooks, you need to ensure a good mechanism to ensure that the hooks are updated and consistent for all developers who will be depending on them (recall that hooks are not propagated during a clone). This at times requires efforts that outweigh the benefits of developing and maintaining hooks for the purposes of easing or enforcing consistency in your workflows.

Modern Git hosting platforms provide you with features and functionalities that you could leverage to achieve the same without the added complexity or extraneous efforts in maintaining custom hooks you will be writing. Git hosting platforms such as GitHub or GitLab provide you with built-in features that enable you to extend the core functionalities of their platform, which promotes a robust collaborative development for your team. This could be anything from satisfying set standards of code review, successfully compiling of automated test suite runs, and even code linting, for that matter. With well-defined requirements, you should be able to practically judge whether or not a Git hook is necessary or whether you should use features of Git hosting platforms to get the result you need (assuming you are hosting your repositories in any of the modern Git hosting platforms).

Summary

This chapter elaborated on a concise overview of Git hooks. We started by discussing the various types of hooks before learning how to install and create your own Git hook with a simple use case. Later we explored the available hooks, ranging from hooks that deal with commits and patches to hooks that get triggered before regular Git operations. As attractive as using hooks may seem, it does come with added overheads, and you will need to decide for yourself whether it's worth the trade-off or not.

## CHAPTER 15

Submodules

It's common to have a lot of applications that rely on one utility library or set of libraries. In such situations, you want each of your applications to be developed, shared, branched, and merged in its own Git repository, either because that's the logical unit of separation or perhaps because of code ownership issues.

But dividing your applications in this way creates a problem. Each application relies on a particular version of the shared library, and you need to keep track of exactly which version. If someone upgrades the library by accident to a version that hasn't been tested, they might end up breaking your application. Furthermore, the utility library isn't developed all by itself; usually people are tweaking it to add new features that they need in their own applications. Eventually, they want to share those new features with everybody else writing other applications; that's what a utility library is for.

Several strategies are commonly used in an attempt to address this issue, including conducting partial checkouts, importing dependent code directly into the project, or even copying the dependent project as a subfolder in the project. But these are not elegant solutions; in fact, some people view them as "hacks."

Git addresses this issue with submodules. A *submodule* is simply a project that is part of your Git repository but also exists independently in its own source control repository. Git's mechanism for indicating a direct reference to another Git repository is through a gitlink. In this chapter, we start by explaining how to use gitlinks, and then we provide several techniques for working with submodules. We round out the chapter with a discussion of the `subtree` command as an alternative to submodules.

Gitlinks

A *gitlink* is a link from a tree object to a commit object. Recall from Chapter 2 that each commit object points to a tree object and that each tree object points to a set of blobs and trees, which correspond (respectively) to files and subdirectories. A commit's tree object uniquely identifies the exact set of files, filenames, and permissions attached to that commit. Also recall from "Commit Graphs" on page 90 that the commits themselves are connected to each other in a directed acyclic graph (DAG). Each commit object points to zero or more parent commits, and together they describe the history of your project.

What we haven't discussed yet is how tree objects can point to commit objects through gitlinks. Let's do that now.

We'll start by creating a `superproject` repository to import the Git source code into:

```
$ cd /tmp
$ mkdir myapp
$ cd myapp

# Start the new superproject
$ git init -b main
Initialized empty Git repository in /tmp/myapp/.git/

$ echo hello >hello.txt

$ git add hello.txt

$ git commit -m 'first commit'
[main (root-commit) 2f8e120] first commit
 1 file changed, 1 insertion(+)
 create mode 100644 hello.txt
```

Next, we will import the `git` project directly:

```
$ ls
hello.txt

# clone in a repository as a submodule
$ git submodule add https://github.com/git/git.git  git
Cloning into 'git'...
remote: Enumerating objects: 329719, done.
remote: Counting objects: 100% (338/338), done.
remote: Compressing objects: 100% (156/156), done.
remote: Total 329719 (delta 214), reused 271 (delta 182), pack-reused 329381
Receiving objects: 100% (329719/329719), 194.04 MiB | 27.39 MiB/s, done.
Resolving deltas: 100% (246495/246495), done.
Updating files: 100% (4167/4167), done.


$ ls
git  hello.txt

$ git add git

$ git commit -m 'import git'
[main 62079a5] import git
```

```
2 files changed, 4 insertions(+)
create mode 100644 .gitmodules
create mode 160000 git
```

 Normally, `git add git` and `git add git/` (with the POSIX-compliant trailing slash indicating that *git* must be a directory) would be equivalent. But that's not true if you want to create a gitlink! In the sequence we just showed, adding a slash to make the command `git add git/` won't create a gitlink at all; it will just add all the files in the *git* directory, which is probably not what you want.

Observe the resulting tree of the superproject:

```
$ git ls-tree HEAD
100644 blob fc7f9429d5ca844b0a71bd9cc9062318eaea08bd .gitmodules
160000 commit 4e2a4d1dd44367d7783f33b169698f2930ff13c0     git
100644 blob ce013625030ba8dba906f756967f9e9ca394464a hello.txt
```

The *git* subdirectory is of type `commit` and has mode `160000`. That makes it a gitlink.

Git usually treats gitlinks as simple pointer values or references to other repositories. Most Git operations, such as `clone`, do not dereference the gitlinks and then act on the subproject's repository.

For example, if you push your project into another repository, it won't push in the subproject's commit, tree, and blob objects. If you clone your superproject's repository, the directories in your subproject's repository will be empty.

For example, in the following code, the *git* subproject directory remains empty after the `clone` command:

```
$ cd /tmp

$ git clone myapp app2
Cloning into 'app2'...
done.

$ cd app2

$ ls
git/  hello.txt

$ ls git

$ du git
0       git
```

An important feature of gitlinks is that they link to objects that are *allowed to be missing* from your repository. After all, they're supposed to be part of some other repository.

Because gitlinks can link to missing objects, this implementation allows for partial checkouts. You don't have to check out every subproject; you can check out just the ones you need.

Submodules

Submodules are a powerful piece of the Git toolchain, but sometimes they are perceived as being complex. Submodules are, at the highest level, a facility for the composition of Git repositories (Figure 15-1).

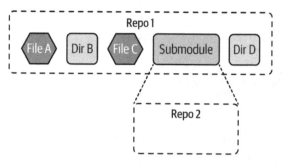

Figure 15-1. Nested repos

Submodules offer great precision, pointing not only to the network address of the nested repository but also to the commit hash of the nested repository (Figure 15-2).

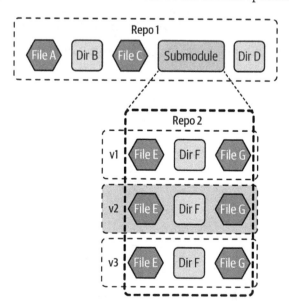

Figure 15-2. Nested repos pointing to precise revision

Because each commit ref has, within a repo, a unique identifier to a specific point in the graph and all parent states that led up to that point, pointing to the ref of another repo records that precise state in the commit history of the parent project.

Why Submodules?

The most common driving factor behind the use of submodules is modularization. Submodules provide a componentization of a source codebase in the absence of such a modularization at the binary level (DLL, JAR, SO). Solutions such as Maven Multimodule Projects (*https://oreil.ly/yLgCm*) and Gradle Multiproject Builds (*https://oreil.ly/woFw3*) are well-known Java solutions for componentized binary or semibinary dependency management that don't require the entire source base to be checked out to a monolithic folder. Likewise, the .NET space has assemblies (*https://oreil.ly/irYSR*) that allow for binary consumption of subcomponents and plug-ins. Driving the use of submodules in the Objective-C ecosystem is the contrasting sparseness of options for modularity and the inclusion of compiled binaries.

Git submodules leave the existing directory structure of a subcomponent intact, provided the separation of components falls along directory fault lines, while enabling precise labeling and version control of each component that contributes to an aggregate project.

Working with Submodules

The `git submodule` command is actually just a 755-line Unix shell script called *git-submodule.sh* (*https://oreil.ly/A1uH4*). Its job is simple: to follow gitlinks and check out the corresponding repositories for you.

The `git submodule` command needs to know one important bit of information before it can do anything: where can it find the repository for your submodule? It retrieves that information from a file called *.gitmodules*, which looks like this:

```
# git is the name of the submodule repository
[submodule "git"]
        path = git
        url = https://github.com/git/git.git
```

Let's initialize a new repository with a file, followed by some Git operations working with a submodule repository:

```
# Create in a temporary directory
$ mkdir superproject && cd superproject
$ git init -b main
Initialized empty Git repository in /tmp/superproject/.git/

$ echo "hello from super project" > sp-readme.md
$ git add sp-readme.md
$ git commit -m "Initial commit"
[main (root-commit) 3689ee7] Initial commit
 1 file changed, 1 insertion(+)
 create mode 100644 sp-readme.md
```

```
$ git status
On branch main
nothing to commit, working tree clean
```

In the subsections that follow, we highlight some Git operations for working with a submodule repository.

Adding a submodule

When adding a submodule to an existing repository via the `git submodule add` command, Git creates the *.gitmodules* file along with a subdirectory containing all the files for the submodule you added. These files are automatically staged in your index directory:

```
# To follow along, create a new repository in your GitHub personal account
# from this template repo https://github.com/ppremk/example-submodule-template
# Click on the green "Use this template" button to create a copy of the repo

# Add an existing submodule from the clone URL of your repo on GitHub

$ git submodule add https://github.com/ppremk/example-submodule.git
Cloning into '/tmp/superproject/example-submodule'...
remote: Enumerating objects: 4, done.
remote: Counting objects: 100% (4/4), done.
remote: Compressing objects: 100% (4/4), done.
remote: Total 4 (delta 0), reused 0 (delta 0), pack-reused 0
Receiving objects: 100% (4/4), done.


$ ls
example-submodule sp-readme.md

$ git status
On branch main
Changes to be committed:
  (use "git restore --staged <file>..." to unstage)
        new file:    .gitmodules
        new file:    example-submodule

# Proceed to commit the submodule

$ git commit -m "Add submodule"
[main ecc6142] Add submodule
 2 files changed, 4 insertions(+)
 create mode 100644 .gitmodules
 create mode 160000 example-submodule
```

 The newly added submodule's project git history will remain as a standalone history and will not be part of the superproject's history. Also, take note of the file mode `160000` for the *example-submodule* directory, which makes it a gitlink.

Cloning a repository

When you clone a repository that already has a submodule, there are a few caveats you need to keep in mind. Take a look at the following example, which attempts to clone a repository with submodules:

```
# Create a bare repository version of the earlier repo
# This will allow for pushing changes from a clone copy of the repository
$ cd ..
$ git clone --bare /tmp/superproject /tmp/superproject-upstream
Cloning into bare repository '/tmp/superproject-upstream'...
done.

# Clone the new upstream repository with the example submodule
$ git clone /tmp/superproject-upstream superproject-clone-1
Cloning into 'superproject-clone -1'...
done.

# Create another new clone for later demo
$ git clone /tmp/superproject-upstream superproject-clone-2
Cloning into 'superproject-clone -2'...
Done.

$ cd superproject-clone-1
$ ls
example-submodule sp-readme.md

$ cd example-submodule && ls
$
```

The subdirectory for the submodules will be empty because the submodules are not initialized during the superproject's clone operation. In order to initialize the submodule, you can do the following:

```
$ cd ..
$ git submodule update --init
Submodule 'example-submodule' (https://github.com/ppremk/example-submodule.git) registered for path
  'example-submodule'
Cloning into '/tmp/superproject-clone/example-submodule'...
Submodule path 'example-submodule': checked out '3b294591ab02a849bdc29f545658cd74f6832bcb'

$ cd example-submodule && ls
LICENSE        README.md
```

If the submodules of your superproject contain even more submodules, you can add the --recursive option to the command to initialize all of them together:

```
$ git submodule update --init --recursive
```

However, a better way to initialize the submodule directory and files when cloning a superproject is to use the --recurse-submodules option with the clone URL, like this:

```
$ git clone --recurse-submodules /tmp/superproject-upstream superproject-clone
```

submodule add versus submodule init

The `git submodule add` command will add an entry to the *.gitmodules* file and populate a new Git repository with a clone of the added repository, whereas the `git submodule init` command will copy the settings from the *.gitmodules* file into your *.git/config* file:

```
$ pwd
/tmp/app2

$ git submodule init
Submodule 'git' (https://github.com/git/git.git) registered for path 'git'

$ cat .git/config
[core]
        repositoryformatversion = 0
        filemode = true
        bare = false
        logallrefupdates = true
[remote "origin"]
        url = /tmp/myapp
        fetch = +refs/heads/*:refs/remotes/origin/*
[branch "main"]
        remote = origin
        merge = refs/heads/main
[submodule "git"]
        active = true
        url = https://github.com/git/git.git
```

The `git submodule init` command adds only the last two lines.

The `git submodule init` step allows you to reconfigure your local submodules to point at a different repository from the one in the official *.gitmodules* file.

Consider the following scenario.

If you make a clone of someone's project that uses submodules, you might want to keep your own copy of the submodules and point your local clone at that. In this case, you wouldn't want to change the module's official location in *.gitmodules*, but you would want `git submodule` to look at your preferred location. So `git submodule init` copies any missing submodule information from *.gitmodules* into *.git/config*, where you can safely edit it. Just find the [submodule] section referring to the submodule you're changing, and edit the URL.

Finally, run `git submodule update` to update the files from your copy of the submodule, or, if needed, to force a complete new clone of the initial subproject repository by deleting the existing files:

```
# Force a complete new clone by removing what's there
# if required when pointing to your own clone version of submodule
$ pwd
/tmp/app2

$ rm -rf git
```

```
$ git submodule update
Cloning into '/tmp/app2/git'...
Submodule path 'git': checked out '4e2a4d1dd44367d7783f33b169698f2930ff13c0'
```

Changing submodules from within a superproject

While working on the main superproject, you may need to make simultaneous changes to the dependent submodule files. You make changes in submodules the same way you would make changes in any Git repository.

There is one important thing you need to bear in mind, though! When cloning a superproject with `--recurse-submodules` or fetching updates using the `git submodule update` command, the files in the submodule directory are updated and will be in a *detached HEAD state*.

This means any changes you need to introduce will need to be done on a local tracking branch for the submodule files.

By way of example, take a look at the following:

```
$ pwd
/tmp/superproject-clone-1

$ cd example-submodule
$ git status
HEAD detached at 3b29459
nothing to commit, working tree clean

$ git branch -a
* (HEAD detached at 3b29459)
  main
  remotes/origin/HEAD -> origin/main
  remotes/origin/main
```

 For the purpose of learning and not adding complexity to an already complex subject, we will be directly updating the main branch in this example. In reality, you will need to adhere to the development workflow of your project, in which case a new feature branch will need to be introduced prior to merging new changes into the main stable branch of the submodule!

Next, we'll introduce changes directly to the submodule by checking out to the `main` local tracking branch:

```
$ pwd
/tmp/superproject-clone-1/example-submodule

$ git checkout main
Switched to branch 'main'
Your branch is up to date with 'origin/main'.
```

```
$ echo "Add new submodule file" > new-submodule-file.md
$ git add new-submodule-file.md
$ git commit -m "Add new submodule file"
[main 03c93dc] Add new submodule file
 1 file changed, 1 insertion(+)
 create mode 100644 new-submodule-file.md

$ git status
On branch main
Your branch is ahead of 'origin/main' by 1 commit.
  (use "git push" to publish your local commits)

nothing to commit, working tree clean
```

Now we'll continue to push the changes to the submodule's remote upstream URL:

```
$ git push
Enumerating objects: 4, done.
Counting objects: 100% (4/4), done.
Delta compression using up to 8 threads
Compressing objects: 100% (2/2), done.
Writing objects: 100% (3/3), 355 bytes | 355.00 KiB/s, done.
Total 3 (delta 0), reused 0 (delta 0), pack-reused 0
To https://github.com/ppremk/example-submodule.git
   3b29459..03c93dc  main -> main
```

If you prefer to push changes committed in the submodule project from the superproject directory, you can do so by supplying the command `git push --recurse-submodules=on-demand`.

In the preceding example, we pushed the changes of the submodule directly to the remote upstream URL from within the subdirectory. While this cleanly updated the submodule's remote URL, it left the superproject in an outdated state; the superproject is still pointing to the old commit SHA when the submodule was initially added:

```
$ cd ..
$ git status
On branch main
Your branch is up to date with 'origin/main'.

Changes not staged for commit:
  (use "git add <file>..." to update what will be committed)
  (use "git restore <file>..." to discard changes in working directory)
        modified:   example-submodule (new commits)

no changes added to commit (use "git add" and/or "git commit -a")
```

Running `git status` in the superproject's directory gives a brief update stating there are new commits in the submodule directory. If you would like to get a detailed status of what has changed, you can set `status.submoduleSummary` to `true` in the Git configuration:

```
$ git config --local status.submoduleSummary true
$ git status
On branch main
Your branch is up to date with 'origin/main'.

Changes not staged for commit:
  (use "git add <file>..." to update what will be committed)
  (use "git restore <file>..." to discard changes in working directory)
        modified:   example-submodule (new commits)

Submodules changed but not updated:

* example-submodule 3b29459...03c93dc (1):
  > Add new submodule file

no changes added to commit (use "git add" and/or "git commit -a")

$ git add example-submodule
$ git commit -m "Add new submodule changes"
[main e044d76] Add new submodule changes
 1 file changed, 1 insertion(+), 1 deletion(-)


$ git push
Enumerating objects: 3, done.
Counting objects: 100% (3/3), done.
Delta compression using up to 8 threads
Compressing objects: 100% (2/2), done.
Writing objects: 100% (2/2), 330 bytes | 330.00 KiB/s, done.
Total 2 (delta 0), reused 0 (delta 0), pack-reused 0
To /tmp/superproject-upstream
   ecc6142..e044d76  main -> main
```

 Ensuring that the superproject records the latest commit SHA of the submodule is an important step. Failing to do so will leave your superproject referencing an outdated commit of the referenced submodule when a new clone or submodule update operation is done for the superproject.

Pulling submodule updates

There are two methods for updating the submodule project for your superproject. One method is through a standard Git *fetch* operation followed by a *merge* operation. You will need to do this from the subdirectory of your submodule (just as you would with any standard Git repository). This enables you to selectively choose which branch of your submodule you want to update.

The other method is to use the git submodule update --remote command. By default, this operation will update the latest changes from the main branch of the submodule in your local submodule:

```
$ pwd
/tmp/superproject

$ git submodule update --remote
remote: Enumerating objects: 4, done.
remote: Counting objects: 100% (4/4), done.
remote: Compressing objects: 100% (2/2), done.
remote: Total 3 (delta 0), reused 3 (delta 0), pack-reused 0
Unpacking objects: 100% (3/3), 335 bytes | 111.00 KiB/s, done.
From https://github.com/ppremk/example-submodule
   3b29459..03c93dc  main        -> origin/main
Submodule path 'example-submodule': checked out '03c93dc48b60829baed35f8f78959a41b89dd832'


$ cd example-submodule && ls
LICENSE                README.md              new-submodule-file.md
```

 When working with submodules, a recommended workflow for collaborative development is to point your reference to a production-ready or stable version of the submodule. Commonly, the maintainers of the submodule can include a named *stable* branch to achieve this. To configure your submodule to track a specific branch, you can set the configuration as follows:

```
git config -f .gitmodules submodule.example-submodule.branch
  <stable-branch-name>
```

The -f .gitmodules option will ensure that the *.gitmodules* file is updated for consistency for every collaborator to track the specific branch.

Pulling updates of a superproject that uses a submodule

When getting updates for the superproject via the git pull command, Git fetches the referenced submodule repository changes, but it does not update them.

To complete the update for the superproject, you will need to run the git submodule update command:

```
# Let us now switch the second cloned repository for this example
$ pwd
/tmp/superproject-clone-2

$ git pull
remote: Enumerating objects: 3, done.
remote: Counting objects: 100% (3/3), done.
remote: Compressing objects: 100% (2/2), done.
remote: Total 2 (delta 0), reused 0 (delta 0), pack-reused 0
Unpacking objects: 100% (2/2), 310 bytes | 310.00 KiB/s, done.
From /tmp/superproject-upstream
   ecc6142..e044d76  main        -> origin/main
```

```
Updating ecc6142..e044d76
Fast-forward
 example-submodule | 2 +-
 1 file changed, 1 insertion(+), 1 deletion(-)

$ cd example-submodule && ls
$

$ cd ..
$ git submodule update --init --recursive
Submodule 'example-submodule' (https://github.com/ppremk/example-submodule.git) registered for...
Cloning into '/tmp/superproject-clone-2/example-submodule'...
Submodule path 'example-submodule': checked out '03c93dc48b60829baed35f8f78959a41b89dd832'

$ cd example-submodule && ls
LICENSE                README.md                new-submodule-file.md
```

When you are updating the superproject, keep in mind that some new submodules may have been added to the project, or the submodule's remote upstream URL might have changed for valid reasons. To be cautious, we recommend that you run the `git submodule update --init` command to ensure that every new submodule is initialized when pulling in changes for the superproject.

> To combine the `git pull` and `git submodule update --init` steps, use the command `git pull --recurse-submodules`.

When there are changes to a submodule's remote upstream URL, running the `git submodule sync` command followed by the `git submodule update --init` command will ensure that your superproject gets the latest updated changes:

```
# First update your local git config file with the new upstream URL for the submodule
$ git submodule sync --recursive
$ git submodule update --init --recursive
```

Switching branches when working with superprojects that have submodules

Working with multiple branches in your superprojects that reference submodules can get confusing. This is because the submodule's working tree is not updated to match the commit captured in the superproject when switching branches.

We recommend that you use the `git checkout` or `git switch` command with the `--recurse-submodules` option every time you work with a superproject that contains submodules. The `--recurse-submodules` option will ensure that the correct state of the submodules is in sync with the branch you are checked out to at any given time:

```
$ git checkout --recurse-submodules <branch-name>
```

The preceding command's output is the same as the following:

```
$ git checkout <branch-name>
$ git submodule update --recursive
```

Submodules and Credential Reuse

A traditional `git clone user@hostname:pathtorepo` is acceptable for a standalone Git repository. However, this is a less desirable address for a `git submodule add URL` command because the username will be saved in the submodule metadata at the superproject repository level. This username will be preserved and unintentionally used by all other repository cloning developers.

In a business where access control to repositories is decided on a per-user basis, it would be undesirable to store a specific username as part of the *.gitmodules* recorded address for a submodule. It would be nice if the superproject's username used during cloning was passed along to the submodule's cloning operation.

The Git submodule commands are known to take the credentials given during the superproject cloning operation and pass them down (Figure 15-3) to any actions invoked by `--recurse-submodules`. This leaves the *.gitmodules* address free of any usernames and usable by any developer authorized to clone the project.

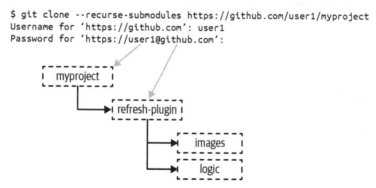

Figure 15-3. Reuse of credentials in submodules

Git Subtrees

Git subtrees are commonly considered alternatives to Git submodules. With subtrees, you are able to add the subproject as a subdirectory of your project with the option of including the entire history of the subproject or squashing the commits as a single commit. Unlike submodules, subtrees do not require the *.gitmodules* file and gitlinks as extra configurations. `git subtree` is installed automatically when you install Git for most modern package managers. If you need to install this extension manually, the steps are explained in the Git repository's contribution documentation (*https://oreil.ly/4viZZ*).

 Subtrees are not to be confused with the *subtree merge strategy*! Git also allows you to extract the history for a given subdirectory from your project via the `git submodule split` command.

In the following example, we'll once again initialize a new repository with a file. Then, in the subsections that follow, we'll provide some Git operations for working with Git subtrees:

```
# Create in a temporary directory
$ mkdir superproject && cd superproject
$ git init -b main
Initialized empty Git repository in /tmp/superproject/.git/

$ echo "hello from super project" > sp-readme.md
$ git add sp-readme.md
$ git commit -m "Initial commit"
[main (root-commit) a5b6866] Initial commit
 1 file changed, 1 insertion(+)
 create mode 100644 sp-readme.md

$ git status
On branch main
nothing to commit, working tree clean
```

Adding a Subproject

When you add a subproject using the subtree method, the `git subtree add` command will also add a new subdirectory in your superproject with all of the subproject's relevant files. However, with the `subtree` command, you will be combining the subproject's Git history with your superproject's Git history:

```
# To follow along, create a new repository in your GitHub personal account
# from this template repo https://github.com/ppremk/example-subtree-template
# Click on the green "Use this template" button to create a copy of the repo


# Create some dummy commits on your copy of the example-subtree repo
# directly from the GitHub WebUI

$ ls
sp-readme.md

$ git log --oneline --graph
* a5b6866 (HEAD -> main) Initial commit

# Add an existing subtree from the clone URL of your repo on GitHub
# Specify which branch of the subproject you want to reference via
# the subtree add command
# Ensure that you have the git subtree extension installed (just in case)
```

```
$ git subtree add --prefix=example-subtree https://github.com/ppremk/example-subtree.git main
git fetch https://github.com/ppremk/example-subtree.git main
remote: Enumerating objects: 15, done.
remote: Counting objects: 100% (15/15), done.
remote: Compressing objects: 100% (13/13), done.
remote: Total 15 (delta 5), reused 4 (delta 0), pack-reused 0
Unpacking objects: 100% (15/15), 2.87 KiB | 367.00 KiB/s, done.
From https://github.com/ppremk/example-subtree
 * branch             main        -> FETCH_HEAD
Added dir 'example-subtree'


$ ls
example-subtree sp-readme.md

# Note the commit history of the subproject has been combined
# with the superproject's git history

$ git log --oneline --graph
*    78d0604 (HEAD -> main) Add 'example-subtree/' from commit '08d39b...'
|\
| * 08d39b1 Final update to README.md
| * 87c0990 One more update to README.md
| * 473e4f9 Update README.md
| * e5d123a Initial commit
* a5b6866 Initial commit
```

In the preceding example, the `subtree` command has essentially grafted the working tree of the subproject into the existing tree of the superproject. If the history of the subproject is irrelevant and you can do without it, you can specify the `--squash` option to keep a clean combined history:

```
$ git reset --hard a5b6866
HEAD is now at a5b6866 Initial commit

$ git log --oneline --graph
* a5b6866 (HEAD -> main) Initial commit

# Squash the commit history of the subproject

$ git subtree add --prefix=example-subtree \
> https://github.com/ppremk/example-subtree.git main --squash
git fetch https://github.com/ppremk/example-subtree.git main
From https://github.com/ppremk/example-subtree
 * branch             main        -> FETCH_HEAD
Added dir 'example-subtree'


$ ls
example-subtree sp-README.md

$ git log --oneline --graph
*    525f638 (HEAD -> main) Merge commit '5d3ce7...' as 'example-subtree'
|\
| * 5d3ce7a Squashed 'example-subtree/' content from commit 08d39b1
* a5b6866 Initial commit
```

Shortening the subtree URL helps when executing the related commands:

```
$ git remote add subremote-origin
  https://github.com/ppremk/example-subtree.git
```

Pulling Subproject Updates

Where there is a new update to the subproject, you can pull the latest changes into your referenced subproject from the superproject as follows:

```
$ cd example-subtree && ls
LICENSE              README.md           another-new-file.md new-file.md

# Add a new file directly on the GitHub WebUI for your example-subtree repo

$ cd ..

$ git subtree pull --prefix=example-subtree subremote-origin main --squash
remote: Enumerating objects: 18, done.
remote: Counting objects: 100% (18/18), done.
remote: Compressing objects: 100% (15/15), done.
remote: Total 18 (delta 6), reused 4 (delta 0), pack-reused 0
Unpacking objects: 100% (18/18), 3.50 KiB | 511.00 KiB/s, done.
From https://github.com/ppremk/example-subtree
 * branch          main        -> FETCH_HEAD
 * [new branch]    main        -> subremote-origin/main
Merge made by the 'ort' strategy.
 example-subtree/sparkling-file.md | 1 +
 1 file changed, 1 insertion(+)
 create mode 100644 example-subtree/sparkling-file.md


# Note squashed updates of subprojects are added as a merge commit in the superproject
$ git log --oneline --graph
*   c468ae8 (HEAD -> main) Merge commit '8bc211...'
|\
| * 8bc211a Squashed 'example-subtree/' changes from 08d39b1..ff9255a
* | 525f638 Merge commit '5d3ce7a...' as 'example-subtree'
|\|
| * 5d3ce7a Squashed 'example-subtree/' content from commit 08d39b1
* a5b6866 Initial commit


$ cd example-subtree && ls
LICENSE     README.md       another-new-file.md new-file.md     parkling-file.md
```

Changing the Subproject from Within the Superproject

When making changes to the subproject, bear in mind that the commits that record the changes to the subproject will be part of the superproject's commit history (on the branch on which it is currently active). This makes it much more direct in comparison to submodules when you need to contribute some changes to the upstream URL of the subproject via the subtree method.

You can push changes to a subproject like so:

```
# Makes changes in the subproject directory
$ cd example-subtree

$ touch just-file.md

$ git add just-file.md
$ git commit -m "Add just file from superproject"
[main 0408fed] Add just file from superproject
 1 file changed, 0 insertions(+), 0 deletions(-)
 create mode 100644 example-subtree/just-file.md


$ git log --oneline --graph
* 0408fed (HEAD -> main) Add just file from superproject
*   c468ae8 (HEAD -> main) Merge commit '8bc211...'
|\
| * 8bc211a Squashed 'example-subtree/' changes from 08d39b1..ff9255a
* | 525f638 Merge commit '5d3ce7a...' as 'example-subtree'
|\|
| * 5d3ce7a Squashed 'example-subtree/' content from commit 08d39b1
* a5b6866 Initial commit


# The command will need to be run from the superproject's directory
$ cd ..

$ git subtree push --prefix=example-subtree subremote-origin main
git push using:  subremote-origin main
Enumerating objects: 3, done.
Counting objects: 100% (3/3), done.
Delta compression using up to 8 threads
Compressing objects: 100% (2/2), done.
Writing objects: 100% (2/2), 251 bytes | 251.00 KiB/s, done.
Total 2 (delta 1), reused 0 (delta 0), pack-reused 0
remote: Resolving deltas: 100% (1/1), completed with 1 local object.
To https://github.com/ppremk/example-subtree.git
   ff9255a..3b0c49a  3b0c49a978fe67f811943b778aaa5b3f867a0cf1 -> main
```

Other Git operations, such as cloning a repository, pulling updates of the superproject, and switching branches when working with superprojects that have subprojects added with `git subtree`, require no special Git commands. You can make changes as required using the standard Git commands.

Git Submodule and Subtree Visual Comparison

In the earlier sections, we provided technical examples of how Git submodules and Git subtrees can be included in your projects. Figures 15-4 and 15-5 are rough representations of the conceptual differences between these two tools.

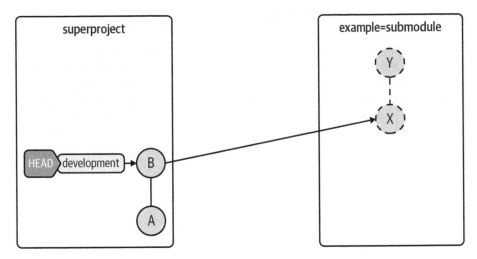

Figure 15-4. Submodules commit history concept

In Figure 15-4, the commit history (HEAD) for the superproject records an explicit reference to the commit SHA of the example-submodule's repository commit history. The commit history for both repos remains separate.

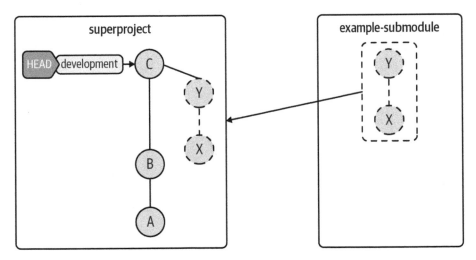

Figure 15-5. Subtree commit history concept

In Figure 15-5, the commit history (HEAD) for the superproject records a new commit SHA in its own repo, combining the example-subtree's repository commit history. The commit history from the example-subtree's repo is ported over as part of the superproject's commit history.

Summary

In this chapter, we demonstrated at a high level the concept of using gitlinks, submodules, and subtrees to combine repositories or projects. The submodule examples were simplified to help teach you the principles that are important when it comes to regular Git operations. As you saw, the use of submodules can be very complex when compared to subtrees. Our advice is to consider carefully whether the complexity is worth it. If your project allows it, there are alternatives, such as dependency management tools, that can help you achieve the same goal without the overhead of maintaining submodules or subtrees. The git-scm manual (*https://oreil.ly/vwnzl*) is another great resource on this topic for extra reference should you need it.

## CHAPTER 16

Advanced Manipulations

In this chapter, we discuss some advanced commands for manipulating Git repositories. These commands range from manipulating files to searching for commits and even support for analyzing and changing a repository to specific requirements. As you already know, manipulating Git repositories does have its consequences, specifically when executing operations that change the repository's Git commit history. As always, proceed with caution when executing such commands.

Interactive Hunk Staging

It's a bit of an ominous moniker; however, interactive hunk staging is an incredibly powerful tool that's used to simplify and organize your development into concise and easily understood commits. If anyone has ever asked you to split your patch up or make single-concept patches, chances are good that this section is for you!

Unless you are a super coder and you both think and develop in concise patches, your day-to-day development process probably resembles that of other developers (including us): a little scattered, perhaps overextended, and likely containing several intertwining ideas. One coding thought leads to another, and pretty soon you've fixed the original bug, stumbled onto another one (but fixed it!), and then added an easy, new feature while you were there. Oh, and you fixed those two typos as well.

And, if you, like us, appreciate having someone review your changes to important code before you ask for it to be accepted upstream, chances are good that having all of those different, unrelated changes will not make for a logical presentation of a single patch. Indeed, some open source projects insist that submitted patches contain separate self-contained fixes. That is, a patch shouldn't serve multiple purposes in one shot. Instead, each idea should stand alone and should be presentable as a well-defined, simple patch that is just large enough to do the job and nothing more.

If more than one idea needs to be upstreamed, more than one patch, perhaps in a sequence, will be needed. Common wisdom suggests that these sorts of patches and patch sequences lead to very solid reviews, quick turnaround, and easy acceptance into mainline upstream development.

So how do these perfect patch sequences come about? Although we strive for a development style that facilitates simple patches, we're not always successful. Nevertheless, Git provides some tools to help formulate good patches. One of those tools enables us to interactively select and commit pieces, or "hunks," of a patch, leaving the rest to be committed in a later patch. Ultimately, you will want to create a new sequence of smaller commits that still sum up to your original work.

What Git won't do for you is decide which conceptual pieces of a patch belong together and which do not. You have to be able to discern the meaning and grouping of hunks that make logical sense together. Sometimes those hunks are all in one file, but other times they are in multiple files. Collectively, all the conceptually related hunks must be selected and staged together as part of one commit.

Furthermore, you must ensure that your selection of hunks still meets any external requirements. For example, if you are writing source code that must be compiled, you will likely want to ensure that the codebase continues to be compilable after each commit. Thus, you must ensure that your patch breakup, when reassembled in smaller parts, still compiles at each commit within the new sequence. Git can't do that for you; that's the part where you have to think.

Staging hunks interactively is easy—just add the -p option to the git add command!

```
$ git add -p file.c
```

Interactive hunk staging looks pretty easy, and it is. But we should probably still have a mental model in mind of what Git is doing with our patches. Remember way back in Chapter 5, we explained how Git maintains the index as a staging area that accumulates your changes prior to committing them. That's still happening. But instead of gathering the changes an entire file at a time, Git is picking apart the changes you have made in your working copy of a file and allowing you to select which individual part or parts to stage in the index, waiting to be committed.

Let's suppose we're developing a program to print out a histogram of whitespace-separated words found in a file. The very first version of this program is the "Hello, World!" program that proves things are starting out on the right compilation track. Here's *main.c*:

```
#include <stdio.h>

int main(int argc, char **argv)
{
    /*
     * Print a histogram of words found in a file.
```

```
     * "Words" are any whitespace-separated  characters.
     * Words are listed in no particular order.
     * FIXME: Implementation needed still!
     */
    printf("Histogram of words\n");
}
```

Add a *Makefile* and *.gitignore*, and put it all in a new repository:

```
$ mkdir /tmp/histogram
# cd /tmp/histogram
$ git init -b main
Initialized empty Git repository in /tmp/histogram/.git/
$ git add main.c Makefile .gitignore

$ git commit -m "Initial histogram program."
[main (root-commit) 42300e7] Initial histogram program.
 3 files changed, 18 insertions(+), 0 deletions(-)
 create mode 100644 .gitignore
 create mode 100644 Makefile
 create mode 100644 main.c
```

Let's do some miscellaneous development until *main.c* looks like this:

```
#include <stdio.h>
#include <stdlib.h>

struct htentry {
    char *item;
    int count;
    struct htentry *next;
};

struct htentry ht_table[256];

void ht_init(void)
{
    /* FIXME: details */
}

int main(int argc, char **argv)
{
    FILE *f;

    f = fopen(argv[1], "r");
    if (f == 0)
        exit(-1);

    /*
     * Print a histogram of words found in a file.
     * "Words" are any whitespace separated characters.
     * Words are listed in no particular order.
     * FIXME: Implementation needed still!
     */
    printf("Histogram of words\n");

    ht_init();
}
```

Notice that this development effort has introduced two conceptually different changes: the hash table structure and storage and the beginnings of the file-reading operation. In a perfect world, these two concepts would be introduced into the program with two separate patches. It will take us a couple of steps to get there, but Git will help us split these changes properly.

Git, along with most of the free world, considers a hunk to be any series of lines from a diff command that are delineated by a line that looks something like this:

```
@@ -1,7 +1,27 @@
```

or this:

```
@@ -9,4 +29,6 @@ int main(int argc, char **argv)
```

In this case, git diff shows two hunks:

```
$ git diff
diff --git a/main.c b/main.c
index 9243ccf..b07f5dd 100644
--- a/main.c
+++ b/main.c
@@ -1,7 +1,27 @@
 #include <stdio.h>
+#include <stdlib.h>
+
+struct htentry {
+        char *item;
+        int count;
+        struct htentry *next;
+};
+
+struct htentry ht_table[256];
+
+void ht_init(void)
+{
+        /* FIXME: details */
+}

 int main(int argc, char **argv)
 {
+        FILE *f;
+
+        f = fopen(argv[1], "r");
+        if (f == 0)
+                exit(-1);
+
     /*
      * Print a histogram of words found in a file.
      * "Words" are any whitespace separated characters.
@@ -9,4 +29,6 @@ int main(int argc, char **argv)
      * FIXME: Implementation needed still!
      */
     printf("Histogram of words\n");
+
+        ht_init();
 }
```

The first hunk starts with the line @@ -1,7 +1,27 @@ and finishes at the start of the second hunk: @@ -9,4 +29,6 @@ int main(int argc, char **argv).

When interactively staging hunks with git add -p, Git offers a choice for each hunk in turn: do you want to stage it?

But let's look at our patch a bit more closely and consider the need to break up the pieces so that conceptually related parts are all gathered up and staged at the same time. That means we'd like to stage all the hash table parts together in one patch and then stage all the file operations in a second patch. Unfortunately, it looks like the first hunk has *both* hash table and file operation pieces in one hunk! That means, for the purposes of the first commit (i.e., the hash table pieces), we want to both stage it and not stage it. Or more precisely, we want to stage *part* of the hunk. If Git asks us only about the first and second hunks, we are in trouble.

But, not to worry! Hunk staging will allow us to *split* a hunk. Anywhere a contiguous sequence of added and deleted lines identified by a plus sign or minus sign in the first column is broken up by original-context text, a split operation may be performed.

Let's see how this works by starting with a git add -p main.c command:

```
$ git add -p
diff --git a/main.c b/main.c
index 4809266..c60b800 100644
--- a/main.c
+++ b/main.c
@@ -1,7 +1,27 @@
 #include <stdio.h>
+#include <stdlib.h>
+
+struct htentry {
+    char *item;
+    int count;
+    struct htentry *next;
+};
+
+struct htentry ht_table[256];
+
+void ht_init(void)
+{
+    /* FIXME: details */
+}

 int main(int argc, char **argv)
 {
+    FILE *f;
+
+    f = fopen(argv[1], "r");
+    if (f == 0)
+        exit(-1);
+
    /*
     * Print a histogram of words found in a file.
     * "Words" are any whitespace separated characters.
Stage this hunk [y,n,q,a,d,/,j,J,g,s,e,?]?
```

After reviewing this hunk and seeing the changes related to the hash table and file operation, you realize you need to both stage and not stage this hunk. So you enter s to split the hunk into two subhunks:

```
Stage this hunk [y,n,q,a,d,/,j,J,g,s,e,?]? s
Split into 2 hunks.
@@ -1,4 +1,18 @@
 #include <stdio.h>
+#include <stdlib.h>
+
+struct htentry {
+    char *item;
+    int count;
+    struct htentry *next;
+};
+
+struct htentry ht_table[256];
+
+void ht_init(void)
+{
+    /* FIXME: details */
+}

 int main(int argc, char **argv)
 {
Stage this hunk [y,n,q,a,d,/,j,J,g,e,?]?
```

Next, you enter y to indicate that you want the first subhunk staged:

```
Stage this hunk [y,n,q,a,d,/,j,J,g,s,e,?]? y
```

This results in the following code, which asks if you want the second subhunk staged:

```
@@ -2,6 +16,12 @@

 int main(int argc, char **argv)
 {
+    FILE *f;
+
+    f = fopen(argv[1], "r");
+    if (f == 0)
+        exit(-1);
+
    /*
     * Print a histogram of words found in a file.
     * "Words" are any whitespace separated characters.
Stage this hunk [y,n,q,a,d,/,K,j,J,g,e,?]?
```

You don't want the second subhunk to be staged, so you enter n:

```
Stage this hunk [y,n,q,a,d,/,j,J,g,s,e,?]? n
```

Finally, Git offers to stage the second hunk. You want it staged, so you enter y:

```
@@ -9,4 +29,6 @@ int main(int argc, char **argv)
     * FIXME: Implementation needed still!
     */
    printf("Histogram of words\n");
+
+    ht_init();
 }
Stage this hunk [y,n,q,a,d,/,j,J,g,s,e,?]? y
```

Let's review. Originally, there were two hunks. But you wanted only part of the first hunk and all of the second hunk staged. So when Git offered you the first hunk, you had to split it into two subhunks. You then staged the first subhunk but not the second subhunk. Then you staged the entire original second hunk.

Verifying that the staged pieces look correct is easy:

```
$ git diff --staged
diff --git a/main.c b/main.c
index 4809266..8a95bb0 100644
--- a/main.c
+++ b/main.c
@@ -1,4 +1,18 @@
 #include <stdio.h>
+#include <stdlib.h>
+
+struct htentry {
+       char *item;
+       int count;
+       struct htentry *next;
+};
+
+struct htentry ht_table[256];
+
+void ht_init(void)
+{
+       /* FIXME: details */
+}

 int main(int argc, char **argv)
 {
@@ -9,4 +23,6 @@ int main(int argc, char **argv)
     * FIXME: Implementation needed still!
     */
    printf("Histogram of words\n");
+
+       ht_init();
 }
```

That looks good, so you can go ahead and commit it. Don't worry that there are lingering differences remaining in the file *main.c*. That's by design because it is the *next* patch! Oh, and don't use the filename with this next `git commit` command because that would use the entire file and not the just the staged parts:

```
$ git commit -m "Introduce a Hash Table."
[main 66a212c] Introduce a Hash Table.
 1 files changed, 16 insertions(+), 0 deletions(-)

$ git diff
diff --git a/main.c b/main.c
index 8a95bb0..c60b800 100644
--- a/main.c
+++ b/main.c
@@ -16,6 +16,12 @@ void ht_init(void)

 int main(int argc, char **argv)
 {
+        FILE *f;
+
+        f = fopen(argv[1], "r");
+        if (f == 0)
+                exit(-1);
+
     /*
      * Print a histogram of words found in a file.
      * "Words" are any whitespace separated characters.
```

And with that, just add and commit the remaining change because it is the total material for the file operations patch:

```
$ git add main.c
$ git commit -m "Open the word source file."
[main e649d27] Open the word source file.
 1 files changed, 6 insertions(+), 0 deletions(-)
```

A glance at the commit history shows two new commits:

```
$ git log --graph --oneline
* e649d27 Open the word source file.
* 66a212c Introduce a Hash Table.
* 3ba81f7 Initial histogram program.
```

And that is a happy patch sequence!

As usual, there are a few caveats and extenuating circumstances for us to point out. For instance, what about that sneaky line:

```
#include <stdlib.h>
```

Doesn't it really belong with the file operation patch and not the hash table patch? Yep. You got us. It does.

That's a bit trickier to handle. But let's do it anyway. We'll have to use the e option. First, reset to the first commit and leave all those changes in your working tree so that you can do it all over again:

```
$ git reset 3ba81f7
Unstaged changes after reset:
M    main.c
```

Do the git add -p again, and split the first patch just like before. But this time, instead of answering y to the first subhunk staging request, answer e and request to edit the patch:

```
$ git add -p
diff --git a/main.c b/main.c
index 4809266..c60b800 100644
--- a/main.c
+++ b/main.c
@@ -1,7 +1,27 @@
 #include <stdio.h>
+#include <stdlib.h>
+
+struct htentry {
+    char *item;
+    int count;
+    struct htentry *next;
+};
+
+struct htentry ht_table[256];
+
+void ht_init(void)
+{
+    /* FIXME: details */
+}
 
 int main(int argc, char **argv)
 {
+    FILE *f;
+
+    f = fopen(argv[1], "r");
+    if (f == 0)
+        exit(-1);
+
     /*
      * Print a histogram of words found in a file.
      * "Words" are any whitespace separated characters.
Stage this hunk [y,n,q,a,d,/,j,J,g,s,e,?]? s
Split into 2 hunks.
@@ -1,4 +1,18 @@
 #include <stdio.h>
+#include <stdlib.h>
+
+struct htentry {
+    char *item;
+    int count;
+    struct htentry *next;
+};
+
+struct htentry ht_table[256];
+
+void ht_init(void)
```

```
+{
+    /* FIXME: details */
+}

 int main(int argc, char **argv)
 {
Stage this hunk [y,n,q,a,d,/,j,J,g,e,?]? e
```

You'll be placed in your favorite editor[1] and allowed to manually edit the patch. Read the comment at the bottom of the editor buffer. Carefully delete the line #include <stdlib.h>. Don't disturb the context lines or the line counts. Git, and most any patch program, will lose its mind if you mess with the context lines.

In this case, because the #include line was removed, it will be swept up in the remainder of the patches that get formed. This effectively introduces it at the correct time in the patch with the other file operation changes.

It is kind of tricky here, but Git now assumes that when you exit your editor, the patch that is left in your editor should be applied and its effects staged. So it offers you the *following* hunk and lets you choose its disposition. Be careful.

Because Git has moved on to the file operation changes, don't stage those changes yet, but do pick up the last hash table change:

```
@@ -2,6 +16,12 @@

 int main(int argc, char **argv)
 {
+    FILE *f;
+
+    f = fopen(argv[1], "r");
+    if (f == 0)
+        exit(-1);
+
    /*
     * Print a histogram of words found in a file.
     * "Words" are any whitespace separated characters.
Stage this hunk [y,n,q,a,d,/,K,j,J,g,e,?]? n
@@ -9,4 +29,6 @@ int main(int argc, char **argv)
     * FIXME: Implementation needed still!
     */
    printf("Histogram of words\n");
+
+    ht_init();
 }
Stage this hunk [y,n,q,a,d,/,K,g,e,?]? y
```

The separation can be verified, noting that the #include <stdlib.h> line has been correctly associated with the file operations now:

```
$ git diff
diff --git a/main.c b/main.c
index 3e77315..c60b800 100644
```

---

1 emacs, right?

```
--- a/main.c
+++ b/main.c
@@ -1,4 +1,5 @@
 #include <stdio.h>
+#include <stdlib.h>

 struct htentry {
     char *item;
@@ -15,6 +16,12 @@ void ht_init(void)

 int main(int argc, char **argv)
 {
+        FILE *f;
+
+        f = fopen(argv[1], "r");
+        if (f == 0)
+                exit(-1);
+
     /*
      * Print a histogram of words found in a file.
      * "Words" are any whitespace separated characters.
```

As before, wrap up with a `git commit` for the hash table patch, then stage and commit the remaining file operation pieces.

We've only touched on the essential responses to the "Stage this hunk?" question. In fact, even more options than those listed in its prompt (i.e., `[y,n,q,a,d,/,K,g,e,?]`) are available. For example, there are also options to delay the fate of a hunk and then revisit it when prompted again later.

Furthermore, although this example had only two hunks in one file, the staging operation generalizes too many hunks, possibly split, in many files. Pulling together changes across multiple files can be a simple process of applying `git add -p` to each file that has a hunk needing to be staged.

However, there is another, outer level to the whole interactive hunk staging process that can be invoked using the `git add -i` command. It can be a bit cryptic, but its purpose is to allow you to select which paths (i.e., files) to stage in the index. As a suboption, you may then select the `patch` option for your chosen paths. This enters the previously described per-file staging mechanism.

Loving git rev-list

One day, Jon received this piece of email:

> Jon,
>
> I'm trying to figure out how to do a date-based checkout from a Git repository into an empty working directory. Unfortunately, winding my way through the Git manual pages makes me feel like I'm playing "Adventure."
>
> Eric

Indeed. Let's see if we can navigate some of those twisty passages.

Date-Based Checkout

It might seem that a command like `git checkout main@{Jan 1, 2011}` should work. However, that command is really using the `reflog` (see "The Stash" on page 221) to resolve the date-based reference for the `main` ref. There are lots of ways this innocent-looking construct might fail: your repository may not have the reflog enabled, you may not have manipulated the `main` ref during that time period, or the reflog may have already-expired refs from that time period. Even more subtly, that construct may not give you your expected answer. It requests the reflog to resolve where your `main` was at the given time that you manipulated the branch, and not according to the branch's commit timeline. They may be related, especially if you developed and committed that history in this repository, but they don't have to be.

Ultimately, this approach can be a misleading dead end. Using the reflog *might* get you what you want. But it can also fail, and it isn't a reliable method.

Instead, use the `git rev-list` command. It is the general-purpose workhorse whose job is to combine a multitude of options, sort through a complex commit history of many branches, intuit potentially vague user specifications, limit search spaces, and ultimately locate selected commits from within the repository history. It then emits one or more SHA1 IDs for use by other tools. Think of `git rev-list` and its myriad options as a commit database frontend query tool for your repository.

In this case, the goal is fairly simple: find the one commit in a repository that existed immediately before a given date on a given branch, and then check it out.

Let's use the actual Git source repository because it has a fairly extensive and explorable history. First, we'll use `rev-list` to find that SHA1. The `-n 1` option limits the output from the command to just one commit ID.

Let's try to locate just the last `main` commit of 2011 from the Git source repository:

```
$ https://github.com/git/git.git
Cloning into 'git'...
remote: Counting objects: 126850, done.
remote: Compressing objects: 100% (41033/41033), done.
remote: Total 126850 (delta 93115), reused 117003 (delta 84141)
Receiving objects: 100% (126850/126850), 27.56 MiB | 1.03 MiB/s, done.
Resolving deltas: 100% (93115/93115), done.

$ cd git
$ git rev-list -n 1 --before="Jan 1, 2012 00:00:00" main
0eddcbf1612ed044de586777b233caf8016c6e70
```

Having identified the commit, you may use it, tag it, reference it, or even check it out. But as the checkout note reminds you, you are on a detached `HEAD`:

```
$ git checkout 0eddcb
Note: switching to '0eddcb'.

You are in 'detached HEAD' state. You can look around, make experimental
changes and commit them, and you can discard any commits you make in this
state without impacting any branches by switching back to a branch.

If you want to create a new branch to retain commits you create, you may
do so (now or later) by using -c with the switch command. Example:

    git switch -c <new-branch-name>

Or undo this operation with:

    git switch -

Turn off this advice by setting config variable advice.detachedHead to false

HEAD is now at 0eddcbf161 Add MYMETA.json to perl/.gitignore
```

But is that really the right commit?

```
$ git log -1 --pretty=fuller
commit 0eddcbf1612ed044de586777b233caf8016c6e70
Author:     Jack Nagel <jacknagel@gmail.com>
AuthorDate: Wed Dec 28 22:42:05 2011 -0600
Commit:     Junio C Hamano <gitster@pobox.com>
CommitDate: Thu Dec 29 13:08:47 2011 -0800

Add MYMETA.json to perl/.gitignore
...
```

The `rev-list` date selection uses the `CommitDate` field, not the `AuthorDate` field. So it looks like the last commit of 2011 in the Git repository happened on December 29, 2011.

Date-based checkout cautions

A few words of caution are in order, though. Git's date handling is implemented using a function called `approxidate()`, meaning not that dates are inherently approximate but rather that Git's interpretation of what you meant is approximated, usually due to insufficient details or precision:

```
$ git rev-list -n 1 --before="Jan 1, 2012 00:00:00" main
0eddcbf1612ed044de586777b233caf8016c6e70

$ git rev-list -n 1 --before="Jan 1, 2012" main
5c951ef47bf2e34dbde58bda88d430937657d2aa
```

We typed those two commands at 11:05 A.M. local time. For lack of a specified *time* in the second command, Git assumed we meant "at this time on Jan 1, 2012." Subsequently, 11 more hours of leeway were available in which to match commits:

```
$ git log -1 --pretty=fuller 5c951ef
commit 5c951ef47bf2e34dbde58bda88d430937657d2aa
Author:     Clemens Buchacher <drizzd@aon.at>
AuthorDate: Sat Dec 31 12:50:56 2011 +0100
```

```
Commit:     Junio C Hamano <gitster@pobox.com>
CommitDate: Sun Jan 1 01:18:53 2012 -0800

Documentation: read-tree --prefix works with existing subtrees
...
```

This commit happened an hour and 18 minutes into the new year—well within the 11 hours past midnight that we accidentally specified in our second command.

Git's Date Parsing

So does Git's date parsing behavior even make sense? Probably.

Git is trying to intuit the intended meaning behind vaguely specified time requests. For example, how should `yesterday` be interpreted? As the previous 24-hour period? As the absolute time period from midnight to midnight of the previous calendar date? As some vague notion of yesterday's business hours? Git happens to use the first interpretation: the 24 hours prior to the current time. Generalizing now, any date used as a starting or ending point in Git uses the current time, and if a date is specified without a time, the current time is used as the demarcation, which is where the notion of "the current time" comes in. If you wanted to be more precise about just exactly *when* yesterday, you could have said something like `noon yesterday` or `5pm yesterday`.

One more caution about date-based checkout: although you may get a valid answer to your query for a specific commit, that same question at some later date may yield a different answer. For example, consider a repository with several lines of development happening on different branches. As previously, when you request the commit `--before` *date* on a given branch, you get an answer for the branch as it exists just then. At some later point in time, however, new commits from other branches might be merged into your branch, altering the notion of which commit might satisfy your search conditions. In the previous January 1, 2012, example, someone might merge in a commit from another branch that is closer to midnight on December 31, 2011, than to December 29, 2011, at 13:08:47.

Retrieve an Old Version of a File

Sometimes in the course of software archeology, you simply want to retrieve an old version of a file from the repository history. It seems like overkill to use the techniques of a date-based checkout as described in "Date-Based Checkout" on page 382 because that causes a complete change in your working directory state for every directory and file just to get one file. In fact, it is even likely that you want to keep your current working directory state but replace the current version of just one file by reverting it to an earlier version.

The first step is to identify a commit that contains the desired version of the file. The direct approach is to use an explicit branch, tag, or ref already known to have the correct version. In the absence of that information, some searching has to be done. And when searching the commit history, you should think about using some `rev-list` techniques to identify commits that have the desired file. As previously seen, dates can be used to select interesting commits. Git also allows the search to be restricted to a particular file or set of files. Git calls this approach *path limiting*. It provides the ultimate guide to possible previous commits that might contain different versions of a file, or as Git calls them, *paths*.

Again, let's explore Git's source repository itself to see what previous versions of, say, *date.c* are available:

```
$ https://github.com/git/git.git
Cloning into 'git'...
remote: Counting objects: 126850, done.
remote: Compressing objects: 100% (41033/41033), done.
remote: Total 126850 (delta 93115), reused 117003 (delta 84141)
Receiving objects: 100% (126850/126850), 27.56 MiB | 1.03 MiB/s, done.
Resolving deltas: 100% (93115/93115), done.

# In our example we have replaced the default branch name to main
# using the git branch -M command
$ git rev-list main -- date.c
974c919d36d944e9005def346fb363d8a83399f7
f1e9c548ce45005521892af0299696204ece286b
...
89967023da94c0d874713284869e1924797d30bb
ecee9d9e793c7573cf3730fb9746527a0a7e94e7
```

Uh, yeah, something like 120-odd lines of SHA1 commit IDs. Fun! But what does it all mean? And how do you use it?

Because we didn't specify the `-n 1` option, all matching commit IDs have been generated and printed. The default is to emit them in reverse chronological order. So this means commit `ee646e` contains the most recent version of the file *date.c*, and `ecee9d9` contains the oldest version. In fact, looking at commit `ecee9d9` shows the file being introduced into the repository for the first time:

```
$ git show --stat ecee9d9 --pretty=short
commit ecee9d9e793c7573cf3730fb9746527a0a7e94e7
Author: Edgar Toernig <froese@gmx.de>

    [PATCH] Do date parsing by hand...

 Makefile      |   4 +-
 cache.h       |   3 +
 commit-tree.c |  27 +--------
 date.c        | 184 ++++++++++++++++++++++++++++++++++++++++++++++++++++++
 4 files changed, 191 insertions(+), 27 deletions(-)
```

Where you go from here to find your desired commit is kind of sketchy. You could do `git log` operations on randomly selected SHA1 values from that `rev-list` list output. Or you could binary-search the timestamps on commits from that list. Earlier, we used the -n 1 option to select the most recent commit. It's really hard to say what trick might work in your selection process to identify the precise commit that contains the version of a file that is interesting to you.

But once you *have* identified one of those commits, how do you use it? What does that version of *date.c* look like? What if we wanted to retrieve it in place?

There are three slightly different approaches you can use to get that version of a file. The first form directly checks out the named version and overwrites the existing version in your working directory:

```
$ git checkout ecee9d9 date.c
Updated 1 path from 0cd8a2506a
```

In two other very similar commands, Git accepts the form *commit:path* to name the desired file (i.e., path) as it existed at the time the commit happened, and writes the specified version of the file to be written to stdout. What you do with that output is up to you, though. You could pipe the output to other commands, or create files:

```
$ git show ecee9d9:date.c > date.c-oldest
```

or:

```
$ git cat-file -p 89967023:date.c > date.c-first-change
```

The difference between these two forms is a bit esoteric. The former filters the output file through any applicable text conversion filters, whereas the latter is a more basic plumbing command and does not do any filtering. Differences might show up between these two commands when manipulating binaries, when textconv filters are set up, or possibly during some newline-handling transformations. If you want the raw data, use the cat -p form. If you want the transformed version as it would be when checked out or added to the repository, use the show form.

Recovering a Lost Commit

Occasionally, an ill-timed git reset command or an accidental branch deletion leaves you wishing you hadn't lost the development it represented and that you could recover it somehow. The usual approach to recovering such work is to inspect your reflog as shown in Chapter 10. Sometimes the reflog isn't available, perhaps because it has been turned off (e.g., core.logAllRefUpdates = false), because you are manipulating a bare repository directly, or because the reflog has simply expired. For whatever reason, sometimes the reflog cannot help you recover a lost commit.

The git fsck Command

Although not foolproof, Git provides the command `git fsck` to help locate lost data. The word *fsck* is an old abbreviation for "file system check." Although this command does not check your filesystem, it does have many characteristics and algorithms that are quite similar to a traditional filesystem check and results in some of the same output data as well.

Understanding how `git fsck` works is predicated on a good understanding of Git's data structures as described in Chapter 2. Normally, every object in the Git repository, whether it is a blob, tree, commit, or tag, is connected to another object and anchored to a branch name, tag name, or some other symbolic ref, such as a reflog name.

However, various commands and manipulations can leave objects in the object store that are not linked into the complete data structure somehow. These objects are called *unreachable* or *dangling*. They are unreachable because a traversal of the full data structure that starts from every named ref and follows every tag, commit, commit parent, and tree object reference will never encounter the lost object. In a sense, it is out there dangling on its own.

But traversing the ref-based commit graph isn't the only way to walk every object in the database! You can simply list the objects in your object store using `ls`:

```
$ cd path/to/some/repo
$ ls -R .git/objects/
.git/objects/:
25  3b  73  82  info  pack

.git/objects/25:
7cc5642cb1a054f08cc83f2d943e56fd3ebe99

.git/objects/3b:
d1f0e29744a1f32b08d5650e62e2e62afb177c

.git/objects/73:
8d05ac5663972e2dcf4b473e04b3d1f19ba674

.git/objects/82:
b5fee28277349b6d46beff5fdf6a7152347ba0

.git/objects/info:

.git/objects/pack:
```

In this simple example, the set of objects in the repository has been listed without doing a traversal of the refs and commits.

By carefully comparing the total set of objects with those reachable via a traversal of the ref-based commit graph, you can determine all of the unreferenced objects. From the previous example, the second object listed turns out to be an unreferenced blob (i.e., file):

```
$ git fsck
Checking object directories: 100% (256/256), done.
dangling blob 3bd1f0e29744a1f32b08d5650e62e2e62afb177c
```

Let's follow an example to see how a lost commit can occur and how `git fsck` can recover it. First, construct a simple, new repository with a single simple file in it:

```
$ mkdir /tmp/lost
$ cd /tmp/lost
$ git init -b main
Initialized empty Git repository in /tmp/lost/.git/
$ echo "foo" >> file
$ git add file
$ git commit -m "Add some foo"
[main (root-commit) 1adf46e] Add some foo
 1 files changed, 1 insertions(+), 0 deletions(-)
 create mode 100644 file

$ git fsck
Checking object directories: 100% (256/256), done.

$ ls -R .git/objects
.git/objects/:
25  2d  4a  info  pack

.git/objects/25:
7cc5642cb1a054f08cc83f2d943e56fd3ebe99

.git/objects/2d:
491f5bbeed7c7e28290e93b5695ce4dd7401f1

.git/objects/4a:
1c03029e7407c0afe9fc0320b3258e188b115e


.git/objects/info:

.git/objects/pack:
```

Notice that there are only three objects, and none of them are dangling. In fact, starting from the `main` ref, which is the `2d491f5` commit object, the traversal points to the tree object `4a1c0302` and then the blob `257cc564`.

 The command `git cat-file -t SHA1 ID` can be used to determine an object's type.

Now let's make a second commit and then hard-reset back to the first commit:

```
$ echo bar >> file
$ git add file
$ git commit -m "Add some bar"
[main 66919fa] Add some bar
 1 files changed, 1 insertions(+), 0 deletions(-)
```

And now the "accident" that causes us to lose a commit:

```
$ git reset --hard HEAD^
HEAD is now at 2d491f5 Add some foo

$ git fsck
Checking object directories: 100% (256/256), done.
```

But wait! `git fsck` doesn't report any dangling object. It doesn't seem to be lost after all. This is exactly what the reflog is designed to do: prevent you from accidentally losing commits. (See "The Reflog" on page 232.) So let's try again after brutally eliminating the reflog:

```
# Not recommended; this is for purposes of exposition only!
$ rm -rf .git/logs
$ git fsck
Checking object directories: 100% (256/256), done.
dangling commit 66919fae5a5f62afc0a349cc216bb0c59ffe37d0

$ ls -R .git/objects
.git/objects/:
25   2d   3b   41   4a   66   info pack

.git/objects/25:
7cc5642cb1a054f08cc83f2d943e56fd3ebe99

.git/objects/2d:
491f5bbeed7c7e28290e93b5695ce4dd7401f1

.git/objects/3b:
d1f0e29744a1f32b08d5650e62e2e62afb177c

.git/objects/41:
31fe4d33cd85da805ac9a6697c2251c913881c

.git/objects/4a:
1c03029e7407c0afe9fc0320b3258e188b115e

.git/objects/66:
919fae5a5f62afc0a349cc216bb0c59ffe37d0


.git/objects/info:

.git/objects/pack:
```

You can use the `git fsck --no-reflog` command to find dangling objects as if the reflog were not available to reference commits. That is, objects that are reachable only from the reflog will be considered unreachable.

Now we can see that only the reflog was referencing the second commit `66919fae` in which the "bar" content was added.

But how would we even know what that dangling commit is?

```
$ git show 66919fae
commit 66919fae5a5f62afc0a349cc216bb0c59ffe37d0
Author: Jon Loeliger <jdl@example.com>
Date:   Sun Jul 10 17:16:28 2022 +0200

Add some bar

diff --git a/file b/file
index 257cc56..3bd1f0e 100644
--- a/file
+++ b/file
@@ -1 +1,2 @@
 foo
+bar

# The "index" line above named blob 3bd1f0e

$ git show 3bd1f0e
foo
bar
```

Note that the blob `3bd1f0e` is not considered dangling because it is actually referenced by the commit `66919fae`, even though the commit itself is unreferenced.

Sometimes, though, `git fsck` will find blobs that are unreferenced. Remember, every time you `git add` a file to the index, its blob is added to the object store. If you subsequently change that content and re-add it, no commit will have captured the intermediate blob that was added to the object store. Thus, it will be unreferenced:

```
$ echo baz >> file
$ git add file
$ git fsck
Checking object directories: 100% (256/256), done.
dangling commit 66919fae5a5f62afc0a349cc216bb0c59ffe37d0

$ echo quux >> file
$ git add file
$ git fsck
Checking object directories: 100% (256/256), done.
dangling blob 0c071e1d07528f124e31f1b6c71348ec13f21a7a
dangling commit 66919fae5a5f62afc0a349cc216bb0c59ffe37d0
```

The reason the first `git fsck` didn't show a dangling blob was because that blob was still referenced directly by the index. Only after the content associated with the pathname *file* was changed again and re-added did that blob become dangling:

```
$ git show 0c071e1d
foo
baz
```

If you find you have a very cluttered `git fsck` report consisting entirely of unnecessary blobs and commits and want to clean it up, consider running garbage collection as described in "Garbage Collection" on page 404.

Reconnecting a Lost Commit

Although using `git fsck` is a handy way to discover the SHA1 of lost commits and blobs, we mentioned the reflog earlier as another mechanism. In fact, you could cut and paste it from some lingering line of output found by scrolling back over your terminal output log. Ultimately, it doesn't matter how you discover the SHA1 of a lost blob or commit. The question remains: once you know it, how do you reconnect it or otherwise incorporate it into your project?

By definition, blobs are nameless file content. All you really have to do to reestablish a blob is place that content into a file and `git add` it again. As we showed in the previous section, `git show` can be used on the blob SHA1 to obtain the full object content. Just redirect that to your desired file:

```
$ git show 0c071e1d > file2
```

On the other hand, reconnecting a commit might depend on what you want to do with it. The simple example from the previous section is only one commit. But it could just as well have been the first commit in an entire sequence of commits that was lost. Maybe even an entire branch was accidentally lost! Consequently, a usual practice would reintroduce a lost commit as a branch.

Here, the previously lost commit that introduced the bar content, `11e0dc9c`, is re-introduced on the new branch called `recovered`:

```
$ git branch recovered 66919fae
$ git show-branch
* [main] Add some foo
 ! [recovered] Add some bar
--
 + [recovered] Add some bar
*+ [main] Add some foo
```

From there it can be manipulated (kept as is, merged, etc.) as you wish.

Using git filter-repo

The command `git filter-repo` (*https://oreil.ly/tW4qJ*) was designed and developed by Elijah Newren. Its source code is hosted in a public repository on GitHub. The `git-filter-repo` command facilitates the rewrite of an entire repository commit history using a wide range of available filter options. Some of these filters work on commits, and some work on tree or blob objects and directory structures, and other advanced filters allow for a function to be defined as generic callbacks.

Prior to the `git filter-repo` command, the command `git filter-branch` was the generic branch processing command allowing you to arbitrarily rewrite the commits of a branch using custom commands that operate on different objects within the repository. However, in the manual pages of `git filter-branch`, the *warning* section (*https://oreil.ly/H7vGj*) calls out the command as having a plethora of pitfalls that can lead to nonobvious muddling of an explicit repo history rewrite. It also recommends that you use `git filter-repo` as an alternative history filtering tool.

> If you still need to use the `git filter-branch` command, you are able to do so, but you need to be aware of its performance issues, and we highly advise that you read the *safety* section of the manual pages for the command.

The `git filter-repo` command is both useful and dangerous!

As you might have guessed, with great power comes great responsibility.[2] The power and purpose of `git filter-repo` is also the source of our warning: since it rewrites the entire repository's commit history, executing this command on a repository that has already been published for others to clone and use will likely cause them endless grief later. As with all rebasing operations, commit history will change. After this command, you should consider any repositories cloned from it earlier as obsolete.

With that warning about rewriting repository history behind us, let's find out what the command can do, when and why it might be useful, and how to use it responsibly.

Examples Using git filter-repo

Now that we know what `git filter-repo` can do, let's look at a few cases where it can be used productively. One of the most useful situations occurs when you have a private repository and want to clean it up or do a large-scale alteration on it prior to making it available for cloning and general use by others.

We built these explanations from the examples listed in the manual pages for the command. The manual describes the intent and how to use the code very clearly, so we decided to build a use case walking you through the following scenarios.

> These use case examples are published with the permission of the tool's author, Elijah Newren.

Before we start, you can clone the following repository to help you follow along in the exercises:

---

2 François-Marie Arouet, of course!

```
$ git clone https://github.com/ppremk/analyze-this.git
Cloning into 'analyze-this'...
remote: Enumerating objects: 22, done.
remote: Counting objects: 100% (22/22), done.
remote: Compressing objects: 100% (9/9), done.
remote: Total 22 (delta 7), reused 22 (delta 7), pack-reused 0
Receiving objects: 100% (22/22), 36.25 KiB | 337.00 KiB/s, done.
Resolving deltas: 100% (7/7), done.

$ cd analyze-this
```

Installing git-filter-repo

Since *git-filter-repo* is a single-file Python script, the simplest method to install it is via a package manager of choice based on your operating system:

```
$ [PACKAGE_MANAGER] install git-filter-repo
```

> Instructions on manual installation as well as other options for installing the *git-filter-repo* script (*https://oreil.ly/ey8Jd*) are online.

Analyzing a repository

The `--analyze` option when passed to the `git filter-repo` command will run an analysis on your repository commit history and produce a report that you can reference before deciding on what possible steps you can take to alter the repository. It can also be used post alteration to verify the intended outcome. Running this command will not update the repository:

```
$ git filter-repo --analyze
Processed 9 blob sizes
Processed 5 commits
Writing reports to .git/filter-repo/analysis...done.

$ tree .git/filter-repo/analysis
.git/filter-repo/analysis
├── README
├── blob-shas-and-paths.txt
├── directories-all-sizes.txt
├── directories-deleted-sizes.txt
├── extensions-all-sizes.txt
├── extensions-deleted-sizes.txt
├── path-all-sizes.txt
├── path-deleted-sizes.txt
└── renames.txt
```

The *README* file explains how to understand the contents of these files. For our use case, we will be altering this newly cloned repository to remove some huge files, rename some directories, and remove some unwanted files. We will start by looking at the various files and their sizes first:

```
$ cat .git/filter-repo/analysis/blob-shas-and-paths.txt
=== Files by sha and associated pathnames in reverse size ===
Format: sha, unpacked size, packed size, filename(s) object stored as
    04b334ff842a8ce96abd1d16b7904eacb649839f   35000000   34042 bigfile3.exe
    6f2bb1c9e846f0546416e8ec33bc007f353aeeff   30000000     797 bigfile2.exe
    d38148a863256f6af5aee0edb6020c4e87c2c24b   25000000     667 bigfile1.exe
    31204afb3d72e8c0f95fde7add90e3893421f422    2000000      77 file6.md
    7c2624a6b9687e88178638cd95b609c329177ade    1000000      50 [file4.md, file5.md]
    08869d950c7543382974f936596e462c1dcc0eaa         24      34 README-v0.md
    861761f28976d55103acf61e8423cd32779d7174         20      30 README.md
    99cf872931885fa266f3dc4d998092f087dc120a         14      23 scripts/env.config
    e69de29bb2d1d6434b8b29ae775ad8c2e48c5391          0       9 [logs/client.log, logs/server....
```

We can verify that there are some big files that clearly should not be tracked in this Git repository. There are also a few other nitpicks that stand out that we will clean up in the subsections that follow.

Path-based filtering

In this example, we will be removing a file and a directory and renaming two folders. Before we start altering this repository, let's take note of the commit history of the repository and its content first:

```
$ git log --oneline
* e2a20a2 (HEAD -> main, origin/main, origin/HEAD) add folders
* 19263cb add remaining files
* 9ea727a add bigfiles
* 1d07224 add udated readme
* cd654e0 intial commit

$ ls -al
total 7896
drwxr-xr-x  14 ppremk  stax       448 Mar 19 22:10 .
drwxr-xr-x   5 ppremk  stax       160 Mar 19 22:10 ..
drwxr-xr-x  13 ppremk  stax       416 Mar 19 22:19 .git
-rw-r--r--   1 ppremk  stax        24 Mar 19 22:10 README-v0.md
-rw-r--r--   1 ppremk  stax        20 Mar 19 22:10 README.md
-rw-r--r--   1 ppremk  stax  25000000 Mar 19 22:10 bigfile1.exe
-rw-r--r--   1 ppremk  stax  30000000 Mar 19 22:10 bigfile2.exe
-rw-r--r--   1 ppremk  stax  35000000 Mar 19 22:10 bigfile3.exe
-rw-r--r--   1 ppremk  stax   1000000 Mar 19 22:10 file4.md
-rw-r--r--   1 ppremk  stax   1000000 Mar 19 22:10 file5.md
-rw-r--r--   1 ppremk  stax   2000000 Mar 19 22:10 file6.md
drwxr-xr-x   4 ppremk  stax       128 Mar 19 22:10 logs
drwxr-xr-x   3 ppremk  stax        96 Mar 19 22:10 scripts
drwxr-xr-x   4 ppremk  stax       128 Mar 19 22:10 toolkit
```

Now let's remove the unwanted *README-v0.md* file:

```
$ git filter-repo --path README-v0.md --invert-paths
Parsed 5 commits
New history written in 0.20 seconds; now repacking/cleaning...
Repacking your repo and cleaning out old unneeded objects
HEAD is now at afd2aa7 add folders
Enumerating objects: 19, done.
```

```
Counting objects: 100% (19/19), done.
Delta compression using up to 8 threads
Compressing objects: 100% (10/10), done.
Writing objects: 100% (19/19), done.
Total 19 (delta 6), reused 11 (delta 4), pack-reused 0
Completely finished after 0.40 seconds.

# Note the new commit history after the file is removed

$ git log --oneline
* afd2aa7 (HEAD -> main) add folders
* bb4ce63 add remaining files
* 2f3721a add bigfiles
* 3f9bd4a add udated readme
```

When using the --path filter, you are able to remove one or more files or directories. It is important to note that when you do not specify the --invert-paths option when specifying the --path filter, the git filter-repo command will remove all files and directories except for the specified file or directory name.

Also, if you look closely at the git log output, the remote tracking information for the repository post alteration is removed. This is to prevent you from accidentally pushing the new changes of the repository to the upstream and causing unwanted consequences when force-overriding the old version of the repository with the new version of the commit history.

Next, let's remove the unwanted *logs* directory:

```
$ git filter-repo --path logs/ --invert-paths
Parsed 4 commits
New history written in 0.08 seconds; now repacking/cleaning...
Repacking your repo and cleaning out old unneeded objects
HEAD is now at ceacc4b add folders
Enumerating objects: 18, done.
Counting objects: 100% (18/18), done.
Delta compression using up to 8 threads
Compressing objects: 100% (9/9), done.
Writing objects: 100% (18/18), done.
Total 18 (delta 6), reused 14 (delta 4), pack-reused 0
Completely finished after 0.31 seconds.

# Note the new commit history after the directory is removed

$ git log --oneline
* ceacc4b (HEAD -> main) add folders
* bb4ce63 add remaining files
* 2f3721a add bigfiles
* 3f9bd4a add udated readme
```

Now we will rename the *scripts* folder to *configs* to better reflect its purpose; we will also rename the *toolkit* folder to *scripts*. To achieve this, we will use the --path-rename filter:

```
$ git filter-repo --path-rename scripts:configs --path-rename toolkit:scripts
Parsed 4 commits
New history written in 0.08 seconds; now repacking/cleaning...
```

```
Repacking your repo and cleaning out old unneeded objects
HEAD is now at ba656b4 add folders
Enumerating objects: 18, done.
Counting objects: 100% (18/18), done.
Delta compression using up to 8 threads
Compressing objects: 100% (9/9), done.
Writing objects: 100% (18/18), done.
Total 18 (delta 6), reused 14 (delta 4), pack-reused 0
Completely finished after 0.27 seconds.

# Note the new commit history after the directories are renamed

$ git log --oneline
* ba656b4 (HEAD -> main) add folders
* bb4ce63 add remaining files
* 2f3721a add bigfiles
* 3f9bd4a add udated readme

$ ls -l
total 7888
-rw-r--r--  1 ppremk  stax    20B Mar 19 22:10 README.md
-rw-r--r--  1 ppremk  stax    24M Mar 19 22:10 bigfile1.exe
-rw-r--r--  1 ppremk  stax    29M Mar 19 22:10 bigfile2.exe
-rw-r--r--  1 ppremk  stax    33M Mar 19 22:10 bigfile3.exe
drwxr-xr-x  3 ppremk  stax    96B Mar 19 22:30 configs
-rw-r--r--  1 ppremk  stax   977K Mar 19 22:10 file4.md
-rw-r--r--  1 ppremk  stax   977K Mar 19 22:10 file5.md
-rw-r--r--  1 ppremk  stax   1.9M Mar 19 22:10 file6.md
drwxr-xr-x  4 ppremk  stax   128B Mar 19 22:30 scripts
```

Great! Our alteration is taking shape. However, it looks like we still need to remove some big files that should not be part of the repository. A neat way to do this is by taking advantage of the `--strip-blobs-bigger-than` option when using the `git filter-repo` command.

We'll start by removing files exceeding a certain size:

```
# Remove files that are bigger than 5 MB

$ git filter-repo --strip-blobs-bigger-than 5M
Processed 8 blob sizes
Parsed 4 commits
New history written in 0.10 seconds; now repacking/cleaning...
Repacking your repo and cleaning out old unneeded objects
HEAD is now at eea637d add folders
Enumerating objects: 13, done.
Counting objects: 100% (13/13), done.
Delta compression using up to 8 threads
Compressing objects: 100% (7/7), done.
Writing objects: 100% (13/13), done.
Total 13 (delta 2), reused 8 (delta 1), pack-reused 0
Completely finished after 0.37 seconds.

# Note the new commit history after the directories are renamed

$ git log --oneline
* eea637d (HEAD -> main) add folders
* 21e1028 add remaining files
* 3f9bd4a add udated readme

# Verify the big files are removed
```

```
$ ls -l
total 7840
-rw-r--r--  1 ppremk  stax    20B Mar 19 22:10 README.md
drwxr-xr-x  3 ppremk  stax    96B Mar 19 22:30 configs
-rw-r--r--  1 ppremk  stax   977K Mar 19 22:10 file4.md
-rw-r--r--  1 ppremk  stax   977K Mar 19 22:10 file5.md
-rw-r--r--  1 ppremk  stax   1.9M Mar 19 22:10 file6.md
drwxr-xr-x  4 ppremk  stax   128B Mar 19 22:30 scripts
```

So far we have demonstrated operations that work on files and directories using
the `git filter-repo` command. We recommend that you spend time reading the
command's manual pages to understand all the possible options and variations on
using the path filters, given how flexible and powerful they are. In the next section,
we'll explore how you can change the content of a file.

Content-based filtering

Suppose you are reviewing the content of the *config* folder and learn that the *env.config*
stores some sensitive information that should not have been committed in the first
place. This is how you would go about redacting the sensitive information:

```
$ cat configs/env.config
PAT=S0m3T0k3n
```

To remove the sensitive information, `git filter-repo` digests a list of expressions
you specify in a file when passed in using the `--replace-text` filter:

```
# Create the expression file containing sensitive data you want to remove
$ echo "S0m3T0k3n" >> sensitive-data.txt

$ git filter-repo --replace-text sensitive-data.txt
Parsed 3 commits
New history written in 0.10 seconds; now repacking/cleaning...
Repacking your repo and cleaning out old unneeded objects
HEAD is now at 7a67e7e add folders
Enumerating objects: 13, done.
Counting objects: 100% (13/13), done.
Delta compression using up to 8 threads
Compressing objects: 100% (7/7), done.
Writing objects: 100% (13/13), done.
Total 13 (delta 2), reused 8 (delta 1), pack-reused 0
Completely finished after 0.30 seconds.

$ git log --oneline
* 7a67e7e (HEAD -> main) add folders
* 21e1028 add remaining files
* 3f9bd4a add udated readme

$ cat configs/env.config
PAT=***REMOVED***
```

Since we did not specify explicit replacement text, `git-filter-repo` by default replaces the matching results with ***REMOVED***. You can use string literals, glob pattern matching, and even regular expressions to find and match words you want to replace when creating the expression file.

 You can replace existing text with new text like so: old===⇒new. This expression will replace the word *old* with the word *new*.

Commit message filtering

We are almost done with our alteration of the repository. It is only fair to ensure that the commit messages representing the newly written history of our repository are updated to reflect the new version of the repository.

While inspecting the new history of the repository, you might notice that the first commit in the history series has a typo, and it also does not do what we wanted it to do: that is, to pick the latest version of the *README.md* file. Let's correct this:

```
$ git log --oneline
* 7a67e7e (HEAD -> main) add folders
* 21e1028 add remaining files
* 3f9bd4a add udated readme
```

To be able to change the commit message, `git filter-repo` again needs a list of expressions you specify in a file when passed in using the `--replace-message` filter:

```
# Create the expression file containing the new commit message you want to fix
# Note we are adding the old commit message as pointed out in the TIP above

$ echo "add udated readme==>add latest readme" >> fix-commit-msgs.txt

$ git filter-repo --replace-message fix-commit-msgs.txt
Parsed 3 commits
New history written in 0.08 seconds; now repacking/cleaning...
Repacking your repo and cleaning out old unneeded objects
HEAD is now at fbf574b add folders
Enumerating objects: 13, done.
Counting objects: 100% (13/13), done.
Delta compression using up to 8 threads
Compressing objects: 100% (6/6), done.
Writing objects: 100% (13/13), done.
Total 13 (delta 2), reused 10 (delta 2), pack-reused 0
Completely finished after 0.28 seconds.

$ git log --oneline
* fbf574b (HEAD -> main) add folders
* c13ca61 add remaining files
* 06f04cd add latest readme
```

As a final step, with this new altered version of the repository, you have the option to push this to a new upstream repository or to follow steps to ensure that the older version of the repository is prudently replaced with this new version. As with any type of collaborative development, the important aspect here is to ensure that every collaborator is going to be working with the new copy of the repository.

The filter options for `git-filter-repo` are just the tip of the iceberg. There are many advanced use cases and techniques one could leverage to overhaul and fix a repository. You have the ability to replace user and email details, rename tag names, replace a commit object's parent, and even do partial history rewrites targeting one specific branch or targeting changes for a range of commits. If such a need arises, we strongly recommend that you consult the manual pages!

 If you are interested in learning more about the inner workings of `git-filter-repo`, we recommend that you consult the *Internals* section of the command's manual page. The section lists at a high level how `git-filter-repo` works:

```
$ git filter-repo --help
```

Summary

In this chapter, we expanded our knowledge on how to manipulate commits in specific ways, beyond what was discussed in Chapter 9. We looked at a very powerful technique—using `git add -p`—to interactively stage hunks of changes for a specified file to help craft our commits, learned the benefits of using the `git rev-list` command, and learned methods to retrieve older versions of files. If you need to pick any one of these methods to build your git-manipulation-fu, we suggest putting in the time to learn the `git-filter-repo` and `git fsck` commands. They will be your Git Army knife when the need arises.

## PART V

Tips and Tricks

This final part of the book consists of two chapters that cover the practical aspects of working with Git repositories day in, day out.

Chapter 17 explains interactive rebasing concepts and offers techniques for migrating projects that are version-controlled (in either legacy systems or an existing Git-ready repository) to a new Git-hosted platform. It is important that you understand these concepts and techniques because, once you get the hang of performing a successful migration for one type of version control system, you'll be able to repeat the steps (or even skip some) when migrating other types of projects. We also talk about how to properly version-control large files or binaries in your repositories to avoid bloating the size of your repository, which can have undesired consequences when working in a shared environment.

In Chapter 18, we discuss GitHub, a popular Git hosting platform used by millions of developers. We cover features that allow you to execute standard Git operations beyond the Git command-line tool. We also discuss various client tools from GitHub before rounding out the chapter by sharing methods for extending the platform to fit your custom development workflows.

## CHAPTER 17

Tips, Tricks, and Techniques

With a plethora of commands and options, Git is a rich resource for performing varied and powerful changes to a repository. Sometimes, though, the actual steps to accomplish a particular task are a bit elusive. Sometimes the purpose of a particular command and option isn't really clear or becomes lost in a technical description.

This chapter provides a collection of tips, tricks, and techniques that highlight Git's ability to do interesting transformations.

Interactive Rebase with a Dirty Working Directory

Frequently, when developing a multicommit change sequence on a local branch, we realize we need to make an additional modification to a commit we made earlier in the sequence. Rather than scribbling a note about it on the side and coming back to it later, as an option we can immediately edit and introduce that change directly into a new commit and add a note in the commit log entry reminding us that it should be squashed into a previous commit.

However, when we eventually get around to cleaning up our commit sequence and want to use `git rebase -i`, we might find ourselves with a dirty working directory. In this case, Git will refuse to do the rebase:

```
$ git show-branch --more=10
[main] Tinker bar
[main^] Squash into 'More foo and bar'
[main~2] Modify bar
[main~3] More foo and bar
[main~4] Initial foo and bar.

$ git rebase -i main~4
error: cannot rebase: You have unstaged changes.
error: Please commit or stash them.
```

If this happens, simply clean out your dirty working directory with `git stash` first!

```
$ git stash
Saved working directory and index state WIP on main: ed6e906 Tinker bar

$ git rebase -i main~4

# In the editor, move main^ next to main~3
# and mark it for squashing.

pick 1a4be28 More foo and bar
squash 6195b3d Squash into 'more foo and bar'
pick 488b893 Modify bar
pick ed6e906 Tinker bar

# Follow instructions in your text editor

[detached HEAD e3c46b8] More foo and bar with additional stuff.
 Date: Sun Mar 27 16:18:02 2022 +0200
 2 files changed, 0 insertions(+), 0 deletions(-)
 create mode 100644 file2
 create mode 100644 file4
Successfully rebased and updated refs/heads/main.
```

Naturally, you will want to recover your working directory changes now:

```
$ git stash pop
# On branch main
# Changes not staged for commit:
#   (use "git add <file>..." to update what will be committed)
#   (use "git checkout -- <file>..." to discard changes in working directory)
#
#       modified:   foo
#
no changes added to commit (use "git add" and/or "git commit -a")
Dropped refs/stash@{0} (71b4655668e49ce88686fc9eda8432430b276470)
```

Garbage Collection

In "The git fsck Command" on page 387, we expanded on the concept of reachability. We explained how the Git object store and its commit graph might leave unreferenced or dangling objects within the object store, and gave a few examples of how some commands might leave these unreferenced objects in your repository.

Having dangling commits or unreachable objects is not necessarily bad; you may have moved away from a particular commit intentionally or added a blob file and then changed it before actually committing it. What is bad is that over a long period of time, manipulating the repository can leave many unreferenced objects in your object store.

Historically, within the computer science industry, such unreferenced objects are cleaned up through a process called *garbage collection*. It is the job of the `git gc` command to perform periodic garbage collection and keep your repository object stores neat and tidy.

Git's garbage collection has one other very important task: optimizing the size of the repository by locating unpacked objects (loose objects) and creating packfiles for them. We briefly discussed packfiles in "Packfiles" on page 32.

Packfile Heuristics

Unfortunately, there is a lack of documentation explaining the packing heuristics of Git's objects in detail, apart from the source code implementation. However, an excerpt from Git's technical documentation (*https://oreil.ly/uRXwS*) on this topic sheds some light. Following is a synopsis of how Git compresses objects.

When Git creates a packfile, it first locates files whose content is very similar and stores the complete content for one of them. It then computes the differences, or *deltas*, between similar files and stores just the differences. For example, if you were to change or add only one line to a file, Git might store the complete, newer version of the file and then note the one line that changed as a delta and store it in the pack too.

Git does the file packing very cleverly, though. Since Git is driven by *content*, it doesn't really care if the deltas it computes between two files actually pertain to two versions of the same file or not. That is, Git can take any two files from anywhere within the repository and compute deltas between them if it thinks they might be similar enough to yield good data compression. Thus Git has a fairly elaborate algorithm to locate and match potential delta candidates globally within a repository. Furthermore, Git is able to construct a series of deltas from one version of a file to another version, and another, and so on.

Git also maintains the content of the original blob SHA1 for each complete file (either the complete content or as a reconstruction after the deltas are applied) within the packed representation. This provides the basis for an index mechanism to locate objects within a pack.

So when does garbage collection happen, and how often? Is it done automatically, or does it need to be done manually? When it runs, does it remove everything it can? Pack everything it can?

All of these are good questions, and as usual, all of the answers are "It depends."

For starters, Git runs garbage collection automatically at strategic times:

- If there are too many loose objects in the repository
- When a push to a remote repository occurs
- After some commands that might introduce many loose objects
- When some commands, such as `git reflog expire`, explicitly request it

You can also explicitly request that Git run garbage collection by using `git gc`. There are a few situations when you should consider running `git gc` manually:

- If you have just completed a `git filter-repo`. Recall that `filter-repo` rewrites many commits, introduces new ones, and leaves the old ones on a `ref` that should be removed when you are satisfied with the results. All those dead objects that are no longer referenced, since you just removed the one `ref` pointing to them, should be removed via garbage collection.
- After some commands that might introduce many loose objects. This might be a large rebase effort, for example.

You should be wary of garbage collection in the following scenarios:

- If there are orphaned refs that you might want to recover
- If you have used `git rerere`[1] and you do not need to save the resolutions forever
- If only tags and branches are sufficient to cause Git to retain a commit permanently
- If you have used `FETCH_HEAD` retrievals (URL-direct retrievals via `git fetch`) because they are immediately subject to garbage collection

Git doesn't spontaneously jump to life and carry out garbage collection of its own free will, not even automatically. Instead, certain commands that you run cause Git to consider running garbage collection and packing. But just because you run those commands and Git runs `git gc` doesn't mean that Git *acts* on this trigger. Rather, Git takes that opportunity to inspect a whole series of configuration parameters that guide the inner workings of both the removal of unreferenced objects and the creation of packfiles. Some of the more important `git config` parameters include the following:

---

1 No, that's not a typo. See "Have You Been Here Before?" on page 415.

`gc.auto`
> The number of loose objects allowed to exist in a repository before garbage collection causes them to be packed. The default is 6,700.

`gc.autopacklimit`
> The number of packfiles that may exist in a repository before they are repacked into larger, more efficient packfiles. The default is 50.

`gc.pruneexpire`
> The period of time unreachable objects may linger in an object store. The default is two weeks.

`gc.reflogexpire`
> The time period when the `git reflog expire` command will start to remove `reflog` entries. The default is 90 days.

`gc.reflogexpireunreachable`
> The time period when the `git reflog expire` command will start to remove `reflog` entries, but only if they are unreachable from the current branch. The default is 30 days.

Most of the garbage collection config parameters have a value that means either "do it now" or "never do it."

Tips for Recovering Commits

Time is the enemy of lost commits. Eventually, Git's garbage collection will run and clean out any dangling or unreferenced commits and blobs. Garbage collection will eventually retire reflog refs as well. At that point, lost commits are lost, and `git fsck` will no longer be able to find them. If you know you are slow to realize a commit has been lost, you may want to adjust the default timeouts for reflog expiration and retire unreferenced commits during garbage collection:

```
# default is 90 days
$ git config --global gc.reflogExpire "6 months"

# default is 30 days
$ git config --global gc.reflogExpireUnreachable "60 days"

# default is 2 weeks
$ git config --global gc.pruneexpire="1 month"
```

Recovering from an Upstream Rebase

Sometimes when working in a distributed environment where you don't necessarily control the upstream repository from which you derived your current development clone, the upstream version of the branch on which you have developed your work will undergo a non-fast-forward change or a rebase. That change destroys the basis of your branch, and prevents you from directly sending your changes upstream.

Unfortunately, Git doesn't provide a way for an upstream repository maintainer to state how its branches will be treated. That is, there is no flag that says, "This branch will be rebased at will" or "Don't expect this branch to fast-forward." You, the downstream developer, just have to know, intuit its intended behavior, or ask the upstream maintainer. For the most part, other than that, branches are expected to fast-forward and not be rebased.

Sure, that can be bad. We've explained before how changing published history is bad. Nevertheless, it happens sometimes. Furthermore, there are some very good development models that even encourage the occasional rebasing of a branch during the normal course of development.

So when it happens, what do you do? How do you recover so that your work *can* be sent upstream again?

First, ask yourself whether the rebased branch is really the right branch on which you should have been basing your work in the first place. Branches are often intended to be read-only. For example, maybe a collection of branches is being gathered and merged together for testing purposes into a read-only branch, but the branches are otherwise available individually and should form the basis of development work. In this case, you likely shouldn't have been developing on the merged collection branch. (The Linux next branches tend to operate like this.)

Depending on the extent of the rebase that occurred upstream, you may get off easy and be able to recover with a simple `git pull --rebase`. Give it a try; if it works, you win. But we wouldn't count on it. You should be prepared to recover an ensuing mess with a judicious use of `reflog`.

The real, more reliable approach is to methodically transfer your developed and orphaned commit sequence from your now defunct branch to the new upstream branch. The basic sequence is as follows:

1. Rename your old upstream branch. It is important to do this before you fetch because it allows a clean fetch of the new upstream history. Try something like `git branch save-origin-main origin/main`.

2. Fetch from upstream to recover the current upstream content. A simple `git fetch` should be sufficient.

3. Rebase your commits from the renamed branch onto the new upstream branch using a command like `cherry-pick` or `rebase`. This should be the command `git rebase --onto origin/main save-origin-main main`.

4. Clean up and remove the temporary branch. Try using the command `git branch -D save-origin-main`.

It seems easy enough, but the key can often be in locating the point back in the history of the upstream branch where the original history and the new history begin to diverge. It's possible that everything between that point and your first commit isn't needed at all; that is, the rewritten commit history changes nothing that intersects with your work. In this case, you win because a rebase should happen readily. On the other hand, it is also possible that the rewritten history touches the same ground that you were developing. In this case, you likely have a tough rebase road ahead of you and will need to fully understand the semantics of the original and changed histories in order to figure out how to resolve your desired development changes.

Quick Overview of Changes

If you need to keep a repository up to date by continually fetching from an upstream source, you may find yourself frequently asking a question similar to "So, what changed in the past week?"

The answer might be found through the `git whatchanged` command. Like many commands, it accepts a plethora of options centered on `git rev-parse` for selecting commits, and formatting options typical of, say, `git log`, such as the `--pretty=` options.

Notably, you might want to use the `--since=` option:

```
# The Git source repository
$ cd ~/Repos/git
$ git whatchanged --since="three days ago" --oneline
745950c p4000: use -3000 when promising -3000
:100755 100755 d6e505c... 7e00c9d... M  t/perf/p4000-diff-algorithms.sh
42e52e3 Update draft release notes to 1.7.10
:100644 100644 ae446e0... a8fd0ac... M  Documentation/RelNotes/1.7.10.txt
561ae06 perf: export some important test-lib variables
:100755 100755 f8dd536... cf8e1ef... M  t/perf/p0000-perf-lib-sanity.sh
:100644 100644 bcc0131... 5580c22... M  t/perf/perf-lib.sh
1cbc324 perf: load test-lib-functions from the correct directory
:100755 100755 2ca4aac... f8dd536... M  t/perf/p0000-perf-lib-sanity.sh
:100644 100644 2a5e1f3... bcc0131... M  t/perf/perf-lib.sh
```

That's dense. But we did ask for `--oneline`! So the commit log has been summarized in single lines, like this:

```
561ae06 perf: export some important test-lib variables
```

And each of those is followed by the list of files that changed with each commit:

```
:100755 100755 f8dd536... cf8e1ef... M  t/perf/p0000-perf-lib-sanity.sh
:100644 100644 bcc0131... 5580c22... M  t/perf/perf-lib.sh
```

The preceding code includes the file mode bits before and after the commit, the SHA1s of each blob before and after the commit, a status letter (M here means *modified content* or *mode bits*), and finally, the path of the blob that changed.

Although the previous example defaulted the branch reference to main, you could pick anything of interest or explicitly request the set of changes that were just fetched:

```
$ git whatchanged ORIG_HEAD..HEAD
```

You can also limit the output to the set of changes that affect a named file:

```
$ cd /usr/src/linux
$ git pull

$ git whatchanged ORIG_HEAD..HEAD --oneline Makefile
fde7d90 Linux 3.3-rc7
:100644 100644 66d13c9... 56d4817... M  Makefile
192cfd5 Linux 3.3-rc6
:100644 100644 b61a963... 66d13c9... M  Makefile
```

The workhorse behind this output is git diff-tree. Grab yourself a caffeinated beverage prior to reading that manual page.

Cleaning Up

Everyone enjoys a clean and tidy directory structure. To help you achieve repository directory nirvana, you can use the git clean command to remove untracked files from your working tree.

Why should you bother to do this, you ask? Perhaps cleaning is part of an iterative build process that reuses the same directory for repeated builds but needs to have generated files cleaned out each time. (Think make clean.)

By default, git clean just removes all files that are *not* under version control from the current directory and down through your directory structure. Untracked directories are considered slightly more valuable than plain files and are left in place unless you supply the -d option.

Furthermore, for the purposes of this command, Git uses a slightly more conservative concept of "under version control." Specifically, the manual page uses the phrase "files that are unknown to Git," and for good reason: even files that are mentioned in the *.gitignore* and *.git/info/exclude* files are actually known to Git. They represent files that are not version-controlled, but Git does *know* about them. And because those files are called out in the *.gitignore* files, they must have some known (to you) behavior that shouldn't be disturbed by Git. So Git won't clean out the ignored files unless you explicitly request it with the -x option.

Naturally, the -X option causes the inverse behavior: namely, only files explicitly ignored by Git are removed. So be careful when choosing the files that are important to you.

If you are skittish, do a --dry-run first.

Using git-grep to Search a Repository

You may recall from "Using Pickaxe" on page 184 that we introduced the pickaxe option (spelled -Sstring) for the git log command, and then in "git diff with Path Limiting" on page 171, we showed it in use with the git diff command. The pickaxe option searches back through a branch's history of commit changes for commits that introduce or remove occurrences of a given string or regular expression.

Another command that can be used to search a repository is git grep. Rather than searching each commit's changes to a branch, the git grep command searches the content of files within a repository. Because git grep is really a generic Swiss Army knife with a multitude of options, it is more accurate to say that git grep searches for text patterns in tracked blobs (i.e., files) of the work tree, blobs cached in the index, or blobs in specified trees. By default, it just searches the tracked files of the work tree.

Thus pickaxe can be used to search a series of commit differences, whereas git grep can be used to search the repository tree at a specific point in that history.

Let's get the Git source repository and find out how git grep works![2]

```
$ cd /tmp
$ https://github.com/git/git.git

Cloning into 'git'...
remote: Counting objects: 129630, done.
remote: Compressing objects: 100% (42078/42078), done.
Receiving objects: 100% (129630/129630), 28.51 MiB | 1.20 MiB/s, done.
remote: Total 129630 (delta 95231), reused 119366 (delta 85847)
Resolving deltas: 100% (95231/95231), done.

$ cd git

$ git grep -i loeliger
.mailmap:Jon Loeliger <jdl@jdl.com> <jdl@freescale.com>
.mailmap:Jon Loeliger <jdl@jdl.com> <jdl@freescale.org>
Documentation/gitcore-tutorial.txt:Here is an ASCII art by Jon Loeliger that illustrates how
Documentation/revisions.txt:Here is an illustration, by Jon Loeliger.  Both commit nodes B
Documentation/revisions.txt:Here are a handful of examples using the Loeliger illustration above,

$ git grep jdl
.mailmap:Jon Loeliger <jdl@jdl.com> <jdl@freescale.com>
```

---

2 We elided an obsolete name reference and shortened the actual output lines for this example.

```
.mailmap:Jon Loeliger <jdl@jdl.com> <jdl@freescale.org>
Documentation/technical/pack-heuristics.txt:    <jdl> What is a "thin" pack?
```

Ever wonder where the documentation for the `git-grep` command itself is located? What files in the *git.git* even mention `git-grep` by name? Here's how you can find out:

```
# Still in the /tmp/git repository

$ git grep -l git-grep
.gitignore
Documentation/RelNotes/1.5.3.6.txt
Documentation/RelNotes/1.5.3.8.txt
Documentation/RelNotes/1.6.3.txt
Documentation/config/grep.txt
Documentation/git-grep.txt
Documentation/gitweb.conf.txt
command-list.txt
gitweb/gitweb.perl
grep.c
t/README
t/perf/p4220-log-grep-engines.sh
t/perf/p4221-log-grep-engines-fixed.sh
t/perf/p7810-grep.sh
t/perf/p7820-grep-engines.sh
t/perf/p7821-grep-engines-fixed.sh
```

There are a few things to note here. First, `git-grep` supports many of the normal command-line options to the traditional `grep` tool, such as `-i` for case-insensitive searches, `-l` for a list of just the matching filenames, and `-w` for word matching. Using the `--` separator option, you can limit the paths or directories that Git will search. To limit the search to the occurrence within the *Documentation/* directory, do something like this:

```
# Still in the /tmp/git repository

$ git grep -l git-grep -- Documentation
Documentation/RelNotes/1.5.3.6.txt
Documentation/RelNotes/1.5.3.8.txt
Documentation/RelNotes/1.6.3.txt
Documentation/config/grep.txt
Documentation/git-grep.txt
Documentation/gitweb.conf.txt
```

Using the `--untracked` option, you can also search for patterns in untracked (but not ignored) files that have neither been added to the cache nor committed as part of the repository history. This option may come in handy if you are developing some feature and have started adding new files but haven't yet committed them. A default `git grep` wouldn't search there, even though your past experience with the traditional `grep` command might lead you to believe that all files in your working directory (and possibly its subdirectories) would otherwise be searched.

So why even bother introducing `git grep` in the first place? Isn't the traditional shell tool sufficient? Yes and no.

There are several benefits to building the `git grep` command directly into the Git toolset. The first is speed and simplicity. Git doesn't have to completely check out a branch in order to do the search; it can operate directly on the objects from the object store. This means you don't have to write some script to check out a commit from way back in time, then search those files, then restore your original checked-out state. Second, Git can offer enhanced features and options by being an integrated tool. Notably, it offers searches that are limited to tracked files, untracked files, files cached in the index, ignored or excluded files, variations on searching snapshots from the repository history, and repository-specific pathspec limiters. You can learn more about the `git grep` command by typing **git grep --help** and reading the help pages.

Updating and Deleting refs

Way back in "Refs and Symrefs" on page 83, we introduced the concept of a ref and mentioned that Git also has several symbolic refs that it maintains. By now, you should be familiar with branches as refs, how they are maintained under the *.git* directory, and that the symbolic refs are also maintained there. Somewhere in there a bunch of SHA1 values exist and get updated, shuffled around, deleted, and referenced by other refs.

Occasionally, it is nice or even necessary to directly change or delete a ref. If you know what you are doing, you could manipulate all of those files by hand. But if you don't do it correctly, it is easy to mess things up.

To ensure that the basic ref manipulations are done properly, Git supplies the command `git update-ref`. This command understands all of the nuances of refs, symbolic refs, branches, SHA1 values, logging changes, the reflog, and so on. If you need to directly change a ref's value, you should use a command like this:

```
$ git update-ref someref SHA1
```

where *someref* is the name of a branch or ref to be updated to the new value, *SHA1*. If you want to delete a ref, the proper way to do so is as follows:

```
$ git update-ref -d someref
```

Of course, the normal branch operations might be more appropriate, but if you find yourself directly changing a ref, using `git update-ref` ensures that all of the bookkeeping for Git's infrastructure is done properly too.

Following Files That Moved

If, over the history of a file, the file is moved from one place to another within your repository directory structure, Git will usually only trace back over its history using its current name.

To see the complete history of the file, even across moves, use the `--follow` command. For example, the following command shows the commit log for a file currently named *file* but includes the log for its prior names as well:

```
$ git log --follow file
```

Add the `--name-only` option to have Git also state the name of that file as it changes:

```
$ git log --follow --name-only file
```

In the following example, file *a* is first added in the directory *foo* and then moved to the directory *bar*:

```
$ git init -b main
Initialized empty Git repository in /tmp/tips-tricks/moved-file/.git/

$ mkdir foo
$ touch foo/a
$ git add foo/a
$ git commit -m "First a in foo"
[main (root-commit) 1b4fbff] First a in foo
 1 file changed, 0 insertions(+), 0 deletions(-)
 create mode 100644 foo/a

$ mkdir bar
$ git mv foo/a bar/a
$ git commit -m "Move foo/a to bar/a"
[main 00229c3] Move foo/a to bar/a
 1 file changed, 0 insertions(+), 0 deletions(-)
 rename {foo => bar}/a (100%)
```

At this point, a simple `git log bar/a` will show only the commit that created the file *bar/a*, but adding the option `--follow` will trace back through its name changes too:

```
$ git log --oneline bar/a
00229c3 (HEAD -> main) Move foo/a to bar/a

$ git log --oneline --follow bar/a
00229c3 (HEAD -> main) Move foo/a to bar/a
1b4fbff First a in foo
```

If you want to use its original name, you have to work harder because only the current name of the file, *bar/a*, can be referenced normally. Adding the option - - and then any of its current or former names will work. And adding --all will produce a comprehensive search as if all refs were searched too:

```
$ git log --oneline foo/a
fatal: ambiguous argument 'foo/a': unknown revision or path not in the working tree.
Use '--' to separate paths from revisions, like this:
'git <command> [<revision>...] -- [<file>...]'

$ git log --oneline -- foo/a
00229c3 (HEAD -> main) Move foo/a to bar/a
1b4fbff First a in foo
```

Have You Been Here Before?

Ever have that feeling you've worked through a complex merge or rebase over and over again? Are you getting tired of it yet? Do you wish there was some way to automate it?

We thought so. And so did the Git developers!

Git has a feature named *rerere* that automates the chore of solving the same merge or rebase conflicts repeatedly. The seemingly alliterative name is a shortening of *reuse recorded resolution*. Sometimes long development cycles that use a branch to hold a line of development that undergoes many development iterations before finally being merged into a mainline development will have to be rebased or moved through the same set of conflicts and resolutions many times.

To enable and use the git rerere command, you must first set the Boolean rerere.enabled option to true:

```
$ git config --global rerere.enabled true
```

Once enabled, this feature records the right and left sides of a merge conflict in the *.git/rr-cache* directory and, if resolved, also records the manual resolution to that conflict. If the same conflict is seen again, the automatic resolution engages and preemptively solves the conflict.

When rerere is enabled and participates in a merge, it will prevent autocommitting of the merge. The developer who is performing the merge action will need to review the automatic conflict resolution before making it a part of the commit history.

Rerere has only one prominent shortcoming: the nonportability of the *.rr-cache* directory. Conflict and resolution recording happens on a per-clone basis and is not transmitted in push or pull operations.

Migrating to Git

When porting over an existing project to be version-controlled with Git, we advise you to plan on doing all of your importing, converting, and cleaning up once up front, before ever publishing the first Git version of your repository. There are several steps in a well-planned conversion that you really should take before anyone else has a chance to clone the first version of your Git repository. For example, all of your global changes, such as directory renaming, author and email address cleanup, large-file removal, branch fiddling, and tag construction, will be significantly more difficult for both you and your downstream consumers if they happen after your consumers have cloned the conversion repository.

When migrating to Git, two high-level scenarios are possible. The first occurs when you are migrating from one Git hosting platform to another. The second is when you're porting from a non-Git version control system to a Git version control system. The first scenario is relatively straightforward, especially when you focus on the Git-ready codebase ported between popular Git hosting platforms. The second scenario will require some forethought (transforming a non-Git codebase to a Git repository) before making the transition.

Migrating from a Git Version Control System

Suppose you have been hosting your project repositories in your local Git server and you decide to move those repositories to one of the many popular Git hosting platforms. The migration process can be as straightforward as adding a new remote origin path and removing the older value. It will help to consolidate all of the latest changes from every contributor to the repository before performing the migration. Technically, downstream collaborators are able to update their copy of the repository's version to the new remote origin path, but from an administrative point of view, coordinating the move from a central source of authority is highly recommended.

In the following example, we will be migrating one of our local repositories to GitHub. The following code is an example of how you can migrate your local repository to GitHub:

```
# path to your local repository
$ pwd
/tmp/active-projects/my-super-project

# Get existing remote origin path
$ git remote -v
origin      /tmp/bare-repositories/my-super-project (fetch)
origin      /tmp/bare-repositories/my-super-project (push)
```

 If you do not have an existing local repository, you can simulate the migration process by creating and initializing a new repository in your local machine. The only difference is that you will not have a remote origin value for your repository.

First, create a blank placeholder repository in your personal account on the GitHub platform (*https://github.com*). You can do this by clicking the New button on the Dashboard page (Figure 17-1).

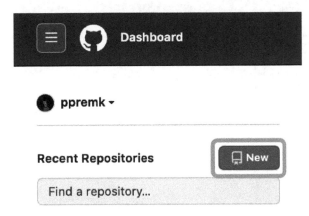

Figure 17-1. Clicking New on the Dashboard page

Next, on the "Create a new repository" page, provide the same name for your existing repository (Figure 17-2). It is important that you *do not* initialize the repository at this step!

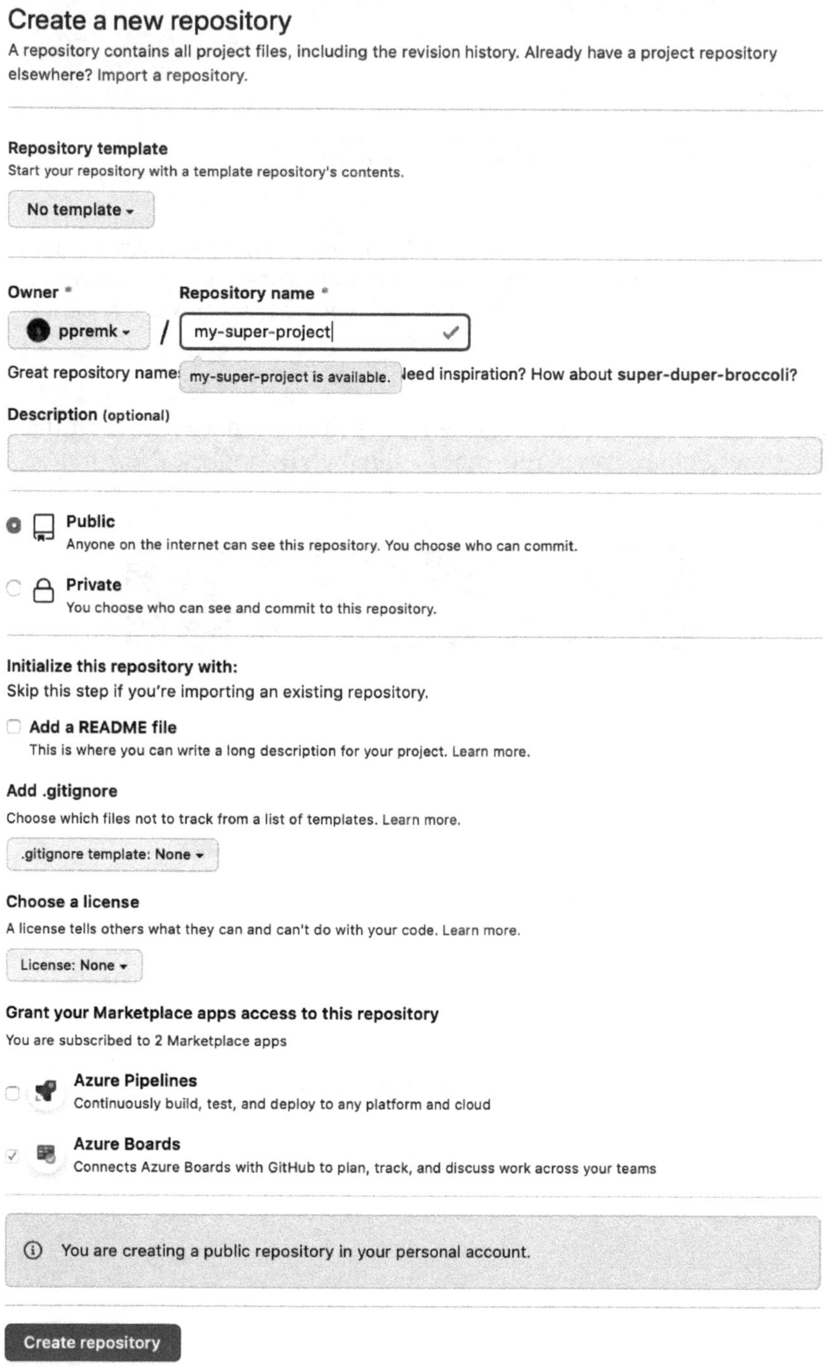

Create a new repository

A repository contains all project files, including the revision history. Already have a project repository elsewhere? Import a repository.

Repository template

Start your repository with a template repository's contents.

[No template ▾]

Owner *   **Repository name** *

[🔵 ppremk ▾] / [my-super-project| ✓]

Great repository name! [my-super-project is available.] Need inspiration? How about **super-duper-broccoli**?

Description (optional)

[   ]

● 🖥 **Public**
   Anyone on the internet can see this repository. You choose who can commit.

○ 🔒 **Private**
   You choose who can see and commit to this repository.

Initialize this repository with:

Skip this step if you're importing an existing repository.

☐ **Add a README file**
   This is where you can write a long description for your project. Learn more.

Add .gitignore

Choose which files not to track from a list of templates. Learn more.

[.gitignore template: None ▾]

Choose a license

A license tells others what they can and can't do with your code. Learn more.

[License: None ▾]

Grant your Marketplace apps access to this repository

You are subscribed to 2 Marketplace apps

☐ 🚀 **Azure Pipelines**
      Continuously build, test, and deploy to any platform and cloud

☑ 🔲 **Azure Boards**
      Connects Azure Boards with GitHub to plan, track, and discuss work across your teams

---

> ⓘ   You are creating a public repository in your personal account.

[Create repository]

Figure 17-2. Creating the placeholder repository

On the next page, follow the instruction that says "...*or push an existing repository from the command line*" (Figure 17-3).

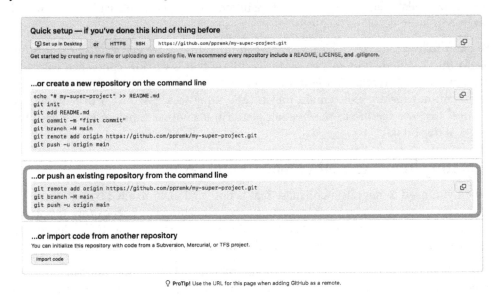

Figure 17-3. Update new remote origin and push

Since we are working with an existing repository, we will need to either remove the old remote origin value or specify the `git remote set-url` command to update the new URL path. We chose to remove the old remote origin because we want to publish our repository to the newly created upstream remote on GitHub:

```
$ git remote remove origin

# returns blank
$ git remote -v

# add the new remote origin url
$ git remote add origin https://github.com/ppremk/my-super-project.git

# push the local repository to the new upstream
# we can skip the 'git branch -M main'
since our default branch is already named main
$ git push -u origin main
Enumerating objects: 8, done.
Counting objects: 100% (8/8), done.
Delta compression using up to 8 threads
Compressing objects: 100% (6/6), done.
Writing objects: 100% (8/8), 917 bytes | 917.00 KiB/s, done.
Total 8 (delta 0), reused 0 (delta 0), pack-reused 0
To https://github.com/ppremk/my-super-project.git
 * [new branch]      main -> main
Branch 'main' set up to track remote branch 'main' from 'origin'.
```

Your local repository is now available on the new remote, which is hosted on GitHub. From this point on, you can leverage features of the platform that can help you and your team collaboratively develop and maintain your project. We will cover Git and GitHub in more detail in Chapter 18.

You can follow these same basic steps when migrating between popular Git hosting platforms. If you are only migrating the codebase that is version-controlled with Git, you simply need to remove the old remote and add a new remote since the repository's commit history will remain intact. (Migrating to a new platform metadata or features that are specific to the hosting platform is another topic and is beyond the scope of this book.)

Migrating from a Non-Git Version Control System

When you need to migrate a codebase that is not version controlled by Git, there are some additional steps you need to take prior to publishing your repository for others to consume. The amount of work and planning you need to do may differ depending on the source system, but you can group the common tasks into four steps.

The first step is to create a Git author data mapping file (this step may be required depending on the bridge tool used; see the next paragraph). This is to ensure that existing author information from the source project is correctly mapped to match the Git author data format when you successfully convert the project into a Git-ready repository. For instance, the git svn tool is able to consume an author mapping file containing a list of mapped SVN usernames to match the Git author format. Bear in mind that you may need to write some scripts to extract the required list of commit author details from the source project prior to creating the mapping file.

The second step is to use a bridge tool to convert your source project to a Git-ready repository. Several bridge tools are available that are specific to the source project's version control system. Some examples include git svn (*https://oreil.ly/N8cr5*) and git-p4 (*https://oreil.ly/pvoM1*). When performing a conversion, you will need to know the size of the project, the number of branches, how the binaries are stored, how far back you want to retain the version history, and whether the bridge tool you're using has any known limitations. Only then can you plan your conversion steps and communicate the transition to your collaborators accordingly.

 Depending on the tool you use, you can combine the first two steps into one. You can provide an author's mapping file as an option when performing the conversion via supported commands.

The third step is to perform some housekeeping and prepare the repository prior to publishing it for your collaborators. This can be a clean-up operation that may include removing unwanted files or directories, deciding how to manage large objects or binaries to be version-controlled, and adding relevant files such as *.gitignore*, along with any other tasks deemed necessary to ensure that your migrated repository is ready for consumption.

The fourth step is to publish your repository by creating a new remote origin URL for contributors to clone and push to. In short, you need to create a placeholder repository and push the newly migrated repository to a Git hosting platform of your choosing.

In the following example, we will convert an SVN repository into a Git repository. We will use *https://svnbook.red-bean.com* as our source.

First, we extract the author information and create a mapping file:

```
# Checkout an svn repository
$ svn checkout https://svn.code.sf.net/p/svnbook/source/trunk/
A    trunk/en
A    trunk/en/book
A    trunk/en/book/sample-repositories
...
...


# Get author information
# run the following in the "trunk" directory
$ svn log --xml --quiet | grep author | sort -u | perl -pe 's/.*>(.*?)<.*/$1 = /' > authors.txt

# Edit the authors.txt file content to match the following format
# Providing a correct Author Name and Email

$ cat authors.txt
FLamY = FLamY <FLamY@email.com>
Imaged = Imaged <Imaged@email.com>
```

> The script to generate SVN author information is referenced from the git-scm online book (*https://oreil.ly/NPkhh*). The shared link also contains examples and tips on how to migrate from various non-Git version control systems.

If you have not completed the *authors.txt* mapping file, you can save some time by downloading (*https://oreil.ly/1nDT5*) the content of a completed, mapped *authors.txt* file.

Since we will be using the `git svn` bridge, we will be able to provide the author mapping file as an option when cloning the source. The svnbook has 6,055 revisions, so this can take a while to clone. Thus we will be limiting the revisions using the `-r` option. Note that you may need to install the `git svn` tool via supported package managers if the tool is not available in your development environment:

```
# Limit the revision to be cloned
$ git svn clone -r1:100 https://svn.code.sf.net/p/svnbook/source/trunk/ --authors-file=authors.txt
...
...

$ cd trunk
$ pwd
/tmp/migrations/trunk

$ git log -2
commit c0e1e3844c8e54d1d5887b0c0adc9b761de7fd8e (HEAD -> master, git-svn)
Author: fitz <fitz@email.com>
Date:   Fri Nov 29 15:27:48 2002 +0000

    * ch03.xml:  port broken-book changes to trunk.

    git-svn-id: https://svn.code.sf.net/p/svnbook/source/trunk@100
        b70f5e92-ccc6-4167-9ab2-d027528d294b

commit 82f925a9b5a165c4abbcbe4381b4e6fb50950f3a
Author: cmpilato <cmpilato@email.com>
Date:   Wed Nov 27 18:31:51 2002 +0000

    * doc/book/book/ch05.xml
      Little spelling and grammar fixes and such.  Thanks to my beautiful
      wife Amy for trudging through a full reading of this chapter to
      help me find these things.  Sweetie, you wanna be a repository
      administrator now?

    git-svn-id: https://svn.code.sf.net/p/svnbook/source/trunk@99
        b70f5e92-ccc6-4167-9ab2-d027528d294b
```

 `git svn` also imports the subversion metadata when cloning the repository. This helps preserve the original `git-svn-id` that introduced the revision. If you do not need this metadata for reference, you can provide the `--no-metadata` option to skip importing the metadata.

Now we'll perform any required housekeeping operations and record those changes as new commits in the project's newly converted Git repository.

We will add a *README.md* file in the root of the directory to provide some context for the repository:

```
# execute in /tmp/migrations/trunk
$ echo "This repo was converted from SVN" >> README.md

# add and commit new changes to the repository
$ git status
[main cee31bf] Add README.md in project root
 1 file changed, 1 insertion(+)
 create mode 100644 README.md
```

Next, we'll add a new remote to the newly converted repository and push it upstream for collaborators to continue working on it in its new version-controlled format. The steps for this are similar to what we described in "Migrating from a Git Version Control System" on page 416.

 Since git svn creates the default branch name using Git's defaults, you can rename the branch from master to main using the git branch -M master main command.

Now let's push the converted repository to a placeholder repository of the same name:

```
# create placeholder repository on GitHub

# execute in /tmp/migrations/trunk
# add new remote origin
$ git remote add origin https://github.com/ppremk/svnbook.git

$ git push -u origin main
Enumerating objects: 561, done.
Counting objects: 100% (561/561), done.
Delta compression using up to 8 threads
Compressing objects: 100% (510/510), done.
Writing objects: 100% (561/561), 871.80 KiB | 7.45 MiB/s, done.
Total 561 (delta 255), reused 0 (delta 0), pack-reused 0
remote: Resolving deltas: 100% (255/255), done.
To https://github.com/ppremk/svnbook.git
 * [new branch]      main -> main
branch 'main' set up to track 'origin/main'.
```

Now we can navigate to the Git hosting platform to view the migrated repository (Figure 17-4).

If your migration requirements are not complex and you do not need the project's legacy commit history since it will be archived, you can simply perform a clean cut migration.

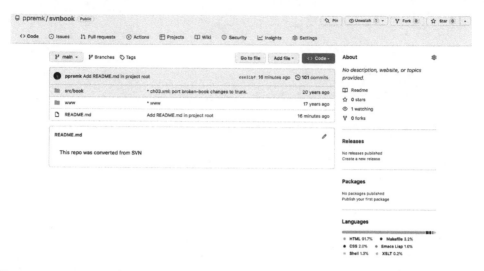

Figure 17-4. Migrated svnbook repository on GitHub

A *clean cut migration* is when you convert your most recent and updated version of the project as a new Git repository by initializing the new Git repository from the source project, continuing to add all the files, and committing them as your initial commit before pushing the repository to a new remote. Just ensure that you have performed all the necessary housekeeping on the source copy before making it available to your collaborators:

```
# Existing source project post housekeeping

$ pwd
/tmp/migrations/svn-repo/trunk

$ git init -b main
Initialized empty Git repository in /tmp/migrations/svn-repo/trunk/.git/

$ git status
On branch main

No commits yet

Untracked files:
  (use "git add <file>..." to include in what will be committed)
    .svn/
    en/
    tools/

nothing added to commit but untracked files present (use "git add" to track)

$ git add .
warning: CRLF will be replaced by LF in .svn/pristine/6d/6dab3fba2...
The file will have its original line endings in your working directory
warning: CRLF will be replaced by LF in en/book/sample-repositories/ch04-sample-repos.dump.
The file will have its original line endings in your working directory

$ git commit -m "Initial commit"
```

```
[main (root-commit) 7c09122] Initial commit
 182 files changed, 1573706 insertions(+)
 create mode 100644 .svn/entries
 create mode 100644 .svn/format
 ...
 ...

# Add new remote and push to upstream to conclude migration
```

A Note on Working with Large Repositories

A large repository at the highest level can be categorized as a repository with a commit history spanning years of development or a repository that is huge in size due to stored large binaries or files. It can also be a combination of both categories, which would usually be the result of a legacy migration operation. To be precise, such a repository can either be a monolith (*https://oreil.ly/sKxsv*) or a monorepo (*https://oreil.ly/izQUT*), depending on the type of project you are developing.

The techniques we are about to share when working with such a repository revolve around working with a range of Git objects that you need for your local development. These techniques each have their own trade-offs, ranging from performance to the output behavior of certain Git commands. You should consider whether the trade-offs are worth the effort when you decide to apply these techniques when working with your large repositories.

Following are brief explanations of the techniques:

Partial clone
> Git's *partial clone* feature optimizes the clone performance of your repository. It allows you to clone a repository without needing to transfer a copy of the entire Git object store during the clone operation. Git objects that are missing from the initial clone can later be fetched on demand when you need to work on them.
>
> You can specify a partial clone using the `--filter=<filter-spec>` option together with the `clone` command.
>
> For instance, the `git clone --filter=blob:none repo_url` command will only clone tree objects and reachable commits. Only blobs that are reachable from the tip commit are fetched.
>
> The `git clone --filter=tree:0 repo_url` command will clone only reachable commits. Only trees and blobs that are reachable from the tip commit are fetched.

Shallow clone
> Git's *shallow clone* feature enables you to clone your repository with a truncated commit history to the specified number of commits. Typically, this implies the most recent commit or the latest revision of your repository.

You can specify a shallow clone using the `--depth <depth>` option together with the `clone` command.

For instance, when you specify the `git clone --depth=1 repo_url` command, the clone will fetch only the tip commit along with its reachable tree and blob objects. You can also perform a shallow clone based on a date. The command `git clone --shallow-since=[date] repo_url` will clone a repository with a truncated history of commits after the supplied date.

Sparse checkout

Git's *sparse-checkout* command was introduced in Git version 2.25.0. It simplifies the process required to initialize and configure working with a restricted set of directories within your repository. The command is also designed to significantly improve performance when you are working on a large repository.

When you use `sparse-checkout` with your existing repository, you need to initialize the necessary Git configuration option, then specify which directories you will be working with in the local repository:

```
# initialize git configurations to support sparse-checkout
$ git sparse-checkout init --cone

# specify which directories to work with sparse-checkout
$ git sparse-checkout set <dir1> <di2> <dir3>
```

We highly recommend that you read the GitHub blog posts "Get Up to Speed with Partial Clone and Shallow Clone" (*https://oreil.ly/sI1B9*) and "Bring Your Monorepo Down to Size with Sparse-Checkout" (*https://oreil.ly/EHvxv*) to learn how you can use `sparse-checkout` when working with a monorepo. These blog posts are published by Derrick Stolee, a Git contributor since 2017 who focuses on performance. Derrick has also contributed to speeding up the performance of the `git log --graph` and the `git push` commands for large repositories.

In the next section, we'll explore another technique that focuses on version controlling large files or objects in your Git repository.

Git LFS

Git Large File Storage, or Git LFS, is an open source Git extension developed to track large files or objects in a Git repository. Generally, Git is able to version control large files, but this becomes an issue when the size of the repository grows rapidly, slowing the performance of your regular Git operations.

If you predominantly work with large, text-based files, this may not be a big issue because the compression library used by Git (*https://www.zlib.net*) is able to handle an effective compression of those files, optimizing them for transport and storage in your Git repository. For files that do not compress well and need to be version-controlled, such as video files, audio files, game graphics texture files, and datasets used for data science projects, Git LFS is an ideal tool.

It's fairly easy to use Git LFS. This is because, as it is an extension, much of the plumbing work is already hidden from you when you start using it in your repository. Upon installation and initial configuration, you can continue to track any large files as you would any other files via the standard Git operations and commands. Also, mainstream Git hosting platforms readily provide support for working with Git LFS on their servers, allowing you to leverage the feature seamlessly.

Repository Before Git LFS and After Git LFS

Let's look at how a repository grows in size when you version control a large file.

For our example, we will use a video file since video files do not compress well. The initial repository we create will contain a 1 MB code file and a 100 MB video file. Figure 17-5 depicts how we would edit the initial video file and track those changes as new commits for every change we make; this could be changes to the saturation setting or even some fancy animation we may add to the video.

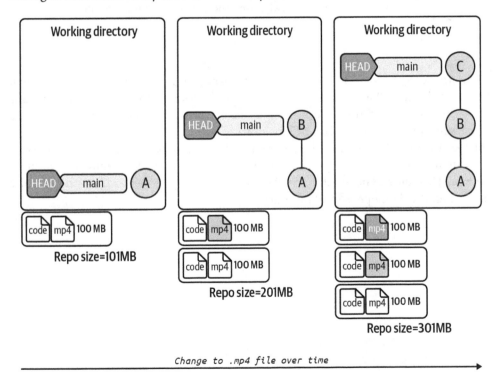

Figure 17-5. Repository size over time without Git LFS

Notice how the size of the repository grows with every commit we add. This will also be the total size that a developer will be cloning from a remote server when they need to work on the repository.

Although in our example the size of the repo is 300 MB, imagine if the project you are working on tracks video game files or datasets, which can cause a repository to approach several gigabytes in size. This can significantly impact the bandwidth of your remote server when you have multiple developers cloning, pushing, and pulling changes concurrently, resulting in sluggish network performance.

Now let's examine the same repository when using Git LFS.

The big difference here is that when you use Git LFS in your repository, the extension will store the large file in an LFS server instead of storing it directly in the Git object store. Git LFS will store a pointer file in place of the large file you are tracking, allowing for the size of the repository to remain small while you make continuous changes to those huge files. Simple yet efficient!

 The dotted box and the repo size illustrate the actual size of the repository when you newly clone and check out to the repository.

In Figure 17-6, notice that the size of the repository remains small because you will be checked out to the current version of a specific commit in time. This also means that when you clone the repository and check out to the default branch, you are essentially downloading a 101 MB repository, which is the version with the latest changes to the video file. Developers wanting to work on older versions of the video file can always get the specific version when they check out to a known commit or branch. This allows Git to fetch the video file from the LFS server if it is not already present on the developer's local machine.

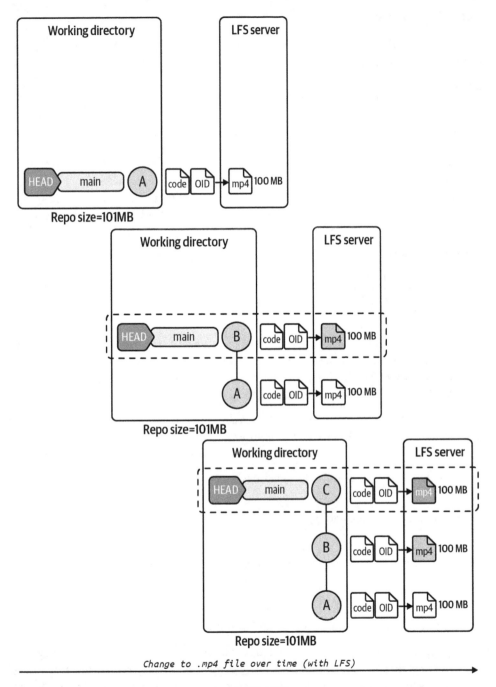

Figure 17-6. Repository size over time with Git LFS

Installing Git LFS

You can install the Git LFS command-line extension via popular package managers or directly from GitHub (*https://oreil.ly/OUpOT*):

```
# Linux-based systems
$ sudo apt-get install git-lfs=3.1.4

# MacOS
$ brew install git-lfs
```

Installing the Git LFS extension will also add two filters to your Git configuration file. These two filters (together with a configured *.gitattributes* file) are responsible for intercepting normal Git operations and will ensure that large tracked files are not directly stored in your repository's Git object store. Instead, they will be stored in your local directory in the path *.git/lfs/objects/*:

```
$ cat ~/.gitconfig
[filter "lfs"]
        smudge = git-lfs smudge -- %f
        process = git-lfs filter-process
        required = true
        clean = git-lfs clean -- %f
```

When you add an LFS-tracked file, the clean filter will intercept the git add command. It will generate an SHA-256 hash of the large file based on the file content, store it in the local *.git/lfs/objects/* folder, generate the pointer file containing an OID, and store it in the repository's Git object store.

A *pointer file* is a UTF-8–based text file. It adheres to a specific format and requires three fields: the version denoting the pointer file specification, the OID representing the tracked file's object ID, and the size of the file captured in bytes.

Running the following command generates a pointer file for a specified file in your local directory:

```
$ git lfs pointer --file=path/to/file
Git LFS pointer for file

version https://git-lfs.github.com/spec/v1
oid sha256:91104678a2b7598a4df9fd42e16baac8e8f695208e5990d47449b9c458ce7a47
size 35000000
```

In order to push the LFS-tracked file, you will still rely on the git push command; a pre-push hook will push the LFS file to the remote LFS server.

On the flip side, when you check out tracked LFS files from your repository into your working directory, the smudge filter is triggered. When the smudge filter runs, it intercepts the process that writes Git repo content to your working directory. For Git LFS, the smudge filter will intercept writing the Git LFS pointer file, parse the pointer file in memory, and read the Git LFS OID, using the OID to look into

---

the `.git/lfs/objects/{OID}` path. If the file is present, it will read the LFS object; otherwise, it will download it. Finally, the `smudge` filter will write the LFS content to the working directory.

 In-depth technical specifications for the Git LFS extension (*https:// oreil.ly/xJkTe*) are available online.

Tracking Large Objects with Git LFS

After installing the Git LFS extension, you can use it in your repositories.

First you need to configure Git LFS for your repository:

```
# initialize new repository
$ pwd
/tmp/git-lfs

# inspect .git directory before configuring git lfs
$ tree .git
.git
├── HEAD
├── config
├── description
├── hooks
│   ├── applypatch-msg.sample
│   ├── commit-msg.sample
│   ├── fsmonitor-watchman.sample
│   ├── post-update.sample
│   ├── pre-applypatch.sample
│   ├── pre-commit.sample
│   ├── pre-merge-commit.sample
│   ├── pre-push.sample
│   ├── pre-rebase.sample
│   ├── pre-receive.sample
│   ├── prepare-commit-msg.sample
│   ├── push-to-checkout.sample
│   └── update.sample
├── info
│   └── exclude
├── objects
│   ├── info
│   └── pack
└── refs
    ├── heads
    └── tags

8 directories, 17 files

# configure git lfs for this repository
$ git lfs install
Updated git hooks.
Git LFS initialized.

# inspect .git directory after configuring git lfs
$ tree .git
.git
```

```
├── HEAD
├── config
├── description
├── hooks
│   ├── applypatch-msg.sample
│   ├── commit-msg.sample
│   ├── fsmonitor-watchman.sample
│   ├── post-checkout
│   ├── post-commit
│   ├── post-merge
│   ├── post-update.sample
│   ├── pre-applypatch.sample
│   ├── pre-commit.sample
│   ├── pre-merge-commit.sample
│   ├── pre-push
│   ├── pre-push.sample
│   ├── pre-rebase.sample
│   ├── pre-receive.sample
│   ├── prepare-commit-msg.sample
│   ├── push-to-checkout.sample
│   └── update.sample
├── info
│   └── exclude
├── lfs
│   └── tmp
├── objects
│   ├── info
│   └── pack
└── refs
    ├── heads
    └── tags

10 directories, 21 files
```

Git LFS installs an additional folder, *.git/lfs/tmp*, along with the following commit hooks: `post-checkout`, `post-commit`, `post-merge`, and `pre-push`. This is in direct relation to the `clean` and `smudge` filters, which Git LFS uses when intercepting the standard `git add`, `git push`, and `git checkout` commands.

Now you can add some large files and start tracking them as a Git LFS file:

```
# create some large files
$ truncate -s 100M video1.mp4
$ truncate -s 100M video2.mp4
$ truncate -s 300M texture1.png
$ truncate -s 350M texture2.png

$ ls -al
total 0
drwxr-xr-x   7 ppremk  stax        224 Apr 24 16:36 .
drwxr-xr-x   6 ppremk  stax        192 Apr 24 16:15 ..
drwxr-xr-x  10 ppremk  stax        320 Apr 24 16:36 .git
-rw-r--r--   1 ppremk  stax  314572800 Apr 24 16:36 texture1.png
-rw-r--r--   1 ppremk  stax  367001600 Apr 24 16:36 texture2.png
-rw-r--r--   1 ppremk  stax  104857600 Apr 24 16:35 video1.mp4
-rw-r--r--   1 ppremk  stax  104857600 Apr 24 16:35 video2.mp4

$ git status
On branch main

No commits yet
```

```
Untracked files:
  (use "git add <file>..." to include in what will be committed)
    texture1.png
    texture2.png
    video1.mp4
    video2.mp4

nothing added to commit but untracked files present (use "git add" to track)
```

Since our example has a combination of video and image files, to track them we will need to specify the file types for Git LFS to manage. Running the following command will result in the creation of a *.gitattributes* file. We will need to track this file as well. Note that you can configure tracking for new file types at any time by running the same command with different parameters specifying the file type you plan to add:

```
$ git lfs track "*.mp4" "*.png"
Tracking "*.mp4"
Tracking "*.png"

$ cat .gitattributes
*.mp4 filter=lfs diff=lfs merge=lfs -text
*.png filter=lfs diff=lfs merge=lfs -text

# Important to track and commit the .gitattributes file
$ git add .gitattributes
...

# Continue to add remaining files as how you would normally
$ git add video1.mp4 video2.mp4 texture1.png texture2.png
$ git commit -m "Add video and texture files"

$ git log --oneline
0c88d26 (HEAD -> main) Add video and texture files
f134596 Add lfs tracking file

# show information of Git LFS files in the index and working tree
$ git lfs ls-files
17a88af837 * texture1.png
37e130c167 * texture2.png
20492a4d0d * video1.mp4
20492a4d0d * video2.mp4

$ tree .git/lfs
.git/lfs
├── objects
│   ├── 17
│   │   └── a8
│   │       └── 17a88af83717f68b8bd97873ffcf022c8aed703416fe9b08e0fa9e3287692bf0
│   ├── 20
│   │   └── 49
│   │       └── 20492a4d0d84f8beb1767f6616229f85d44c2827b64bdbfb260ee12fa1109e0e
│   └── 37
│       └── e1
│           └── 37e130c1679c21acfe85c2c2f30aba984c910d389c8df9340b5bc4455f809220
└── tmp

8 directories, 3 files
```

As you can see, the steps for working with Git LFS are fairly straightforward. Most of the internal work is already handled by the extension for you. All you need to do is install Git LFS on your machine, configure the repositories that will track large files, and continue to track those files as you would any normal file in Git.

Useful Git LFS Techniques

Listed are some recommended techniques for tracking files in Git LFS:

Tracking file types correctly
> When you supply a glob pattern to match a file type, as in the following command:

```
git lfs track "*.mp4"
```

> make sure you include the quotation marks, because otherwise your shell will expand the glob pattern. As a result, Git LFS will track all individual files matching the specified pattern, and any new *.mp4* files will not be tracked since only the individual file names will be listed in the *.gitattributes* files instead of the matching pattern.

Glob pattern matching
> Git LFS supports tracking patterns similar to those supported by the *.gitignore* file. This allows you to specify matching patterns to track directories or complex filenames. It is recommended that you execute the `git lfs track` command from the top-level directory of your repository since the patterns are matched relative to the directory in which it is executed. For example:

> - `git lfs track images/` tracks all files in the *images* directory and its subdirectories.
> - `git lfs track *-lfs*.png` tracks all *.png* files containing *-lfs* in their filename.

Matching files in case-sensitive platforms
> When working with developers in a cross-platform setting, case sensitivity plays an important role. For example, when you specify the following pattern on Windows or macOS:

```
git lfs track "*.png"
```

> both *image.PNG* and *image.png* files would be matched. However, on a Linux machine, only the *image.png* file would be matched. You can consider the following technique:

```
git lfs track "*.[pP][nN][gG]"
```

as a smart way to ensure that case-insensitive files are correctly matched to your glob patterns.

Untracking an LFS file

If you decide to untrack a file type, you can do so using the git lfs untrack command. Upon execution, you will need to add and commit the updated *.gitattributes* file again to reflect the changes:

```
$ git lfs untrack "*.png"
Untracking "*.png"

# git add and commit the updated .gitattributes file
```

Resolving binary merge conflicts

Resolving merge conflicts in a text-based file is fairly easy, but when dealing with large binaries, Git does not handle merge conflicts well. The best way to resolve a binary merge conflict is to avoid it. With the lock command, you can register a file as locked on the remote server. Locking a file will ensure that Git LFS makes the specified file *read-only* on your local machine, thus preventing any users from editing the file without having to lock it first. This enables you or another developer to exclusively make changes to a large tracked binary file and avoid the hassle of figuring out how to resolve a merge conflict in the event the file is concurrently modified.

To lock a tracked LFS file, the first step is to specify which file types support locking:

```
$ git lfs track "*.png" --lockable
```

Next, when you are about to edit the file, you will need to specify the lock command:

```
$ git lfs lock assets/image.png
Locked assets/image.png
```

Once you are done working on the file, you can unlock the file via the unlock command. When pushing changes from your local repository, Git LFS will validate that the file is not locked by another developer:

```
$ git lfs unlock assets/image.png
Unlocked assets/image.png
```

To get a list of files that are locked, you can run the git lfs locks command:

```
$ git lfs locks
assets/image.png    ppremk  ID:1401911
```

You can unlock an existing file by supplying the `--force` option with the command; for example, `git lfs unlock assets/image.png --force`.

Converting Existing Repositories to Use Git LFS

If your existing repository already has large files and it is not configured to use Git LFS, you can still install and track the known file types using LFS. However, from the time you start tracking those files, Git LFS does not automatically convert older versions of the files as a Git LFS object.

In short, those older versions are already part of the commit history. If you need to convert the older files to use LFS, that will require a commit history rewrite. If the trade-off for migrating an existing repository to use Git LFS over losing the commit history is something you can live with, the `git lfs migrate` command is the tool you need.

Let's examine this:

```
# clone an existing repository
$ git clone https://github.com/ppremk/analyze-this.git
Cloning into 'analyze-this'...
remote: Enumerating objects: 22, done.
remote: Counting objects: 100% (22/22), done.
remote: Compressing objects: 100% (9/9), done.
remote: Total 22 (delta 7), reused 22 (delta 7), pack-reused 0
Receiving objects: 100% (22/22), 36.25 KiB | 331.00 KiB/s, done.
Resolving deltas: 100% (7/7), done.

# inspect files
$ ls -al
total 7896
-rw-r--r--  1 ppremk  stax        24 Apr 28 00:47 README-v0.md
-rw-r--r--  1 ppremk  stax        20 Apr 28 00:47 README.md
-rw-r--r--  1 ppremk  stax  25000000 Apr 28 00:47 bigfile1.exe
-rw-r--r--  1 ppremk  stax  30000000 Apr 28 00:47 bigfile2.exe
-rw-r--r--  1 ppremk  stax  35000000 Apr 28 00:47 bigfile3.exe
-rw-r--r--  1 ppremk  stax   1000000 Apr 28 00:47 file4.md
-rw-r--r--  1 ppremk  stax   1000000 Apr 28 00:47 file5.md
-rw-r--r--  1 ppremk  stax   2000000 Apr 28 00:47 file6.md
drwxr-xr-x  4 ppremk  stax       128 Apr 28 00:47 logs
drwxr-xr-x  3 ppremk  stax        96 Apr 28 00:47 scripts
drwxr-xr-x  4 ppremk  stax       128 Apr 28 00:47 toolkit

$ git log --oneline
e2a20a2 (HEAD -> main, origin/main, origin/HEAD) add folders
19263cb add remaining files
9ea727a add bigfiles
1d07224 add udated readme
cd654e0 intial commit
```

By default, the `git lfs migrate` command will only work on your currently checked-out branch. You can use the `--everything` option to include every branch in your repository.

Next, we will examine which file types are taking up space in your repository:

```
# check for large files in the cloned local repository
$ git lfs migrate info --everything
migrate: Sorting commits: ..., done.
migrate: Examining commits: 100% (5/5), done.
*.exe      90 MB   3/3 files(s)   100%
*.md       4.0 MB  5/5 files(s)   100%
*.config   14 B    1/1 files(s)   100%

LFS Objects 0 B    0/4 files(s)     0%
```

Now we will migrate the files to use Git LFS. Keep in mind that the `git lfs migrate` command will perform the conversions only in your local repository. You will need to force-push or create a new remote to push the migrated repository after executing the LFS conversion:

```
# The ".exe" file is a good candidate to migrate over to use Git LFS
$ git lfs migrate import --everything --include="*.exe"
migrate: Sorting commits: ..., done.
migrate: Rewriting commits: 100% (5/5), done.
  main      e2a20a2db7916f1efc5430a9a15bc5c0a8c41860 -> 7e08e949e76653c8f008a65aa42cea9d48b8b473
migrate: Updating refs: ..., done.
migrate: checkout: ..., done.

# check for the new commit history
$ git log --oneline
7e08e94 (HEAD -> main) add folders
293ff49 add remaining files
9fab33c add bigfiles
bdd78fa add udated readme
b682340 intial commit

# Force push to existing remote or create a new remote to push the LFS migrated repo
```

The `git lfs migrate` command will examine, create, and modify *.gitattributes* files as necessary.

Summary

Some of the tips we shared in this chapter can help you quickly navigate your day-to-day Git requirements, especially when you need to know what has changed recently in your repository and when you need to do a direct search on objects in the Git object store using the `git grep` command. In this chapter, we also discussed ways you can successfully plan and migrate your repository to be a full-fledged Git repo. We ended the chapter by explaining how large files can be version-controlled using Git LFS—something we highly recommend when you need to work with files that Git does not compress well, to avoid inflating the size of your repository unnecessarily.

## CHAPTER 18

Git and GitHub

Since the inception of Git in 2005, we've seen the growth of a community of Git-based tools. Today those tools number in the hundreds and come in many forms, from desktop GUIs (*https://oreil.ly/f9gaX*) to Git extensions in popular IDEs. But one stands out in the minds of many developers and even nondevelopers: GitHub (*https://github.com*).

Many regard the emergence of GitHub in a way that many of us now consider working under the phrase *social coding*. This concept of working was first applied to open source enterprises, but over the years we have seen this idea of code as a point of geographically distributed collaboration grow even in closed source enterprises. It is not surprising that this trend has led to a transformation in which developers maintain and build software by way of *innersource* these days.

In this chapter, we focus on how GitHub leverages native Git functionalities, mainly, what to expect when you host your repository on the platform. We start by providing an overview of GitHub as a hosting platform for personal and business accounts. Then we elaborate on how GitHub fits within the Git ecosystem. Next, we dive into specifics around working with your repository in GitHub and navigating its available functionalities, combined with learning how to apply a simple branching strategy and resolving merge conflicts. Before summarizing the chapter, we briefly discuss available methods for extending and integrating with the GitHub platform and how you can practice modern software development using GitHub.

With that, let's take a look at what GitHub has to offer.

About GitHub

GitHub is, in a nutshell, a Git hosting platform. It is regarded as one of the most popular platforms, rich in features that facilitate disciplines such as collaborative coding, automation and CI/CD, security, project management, team administration, and a set of client apps. These functionalities have been a catalyst for building a community of developers who thrive on building and releasing software products on the platform, be it for personal or business use.

At the time of this writing, GitHub has 83+ million developers, 4+ million organizations, and 200+ million repositories and is present in about 90% of Fortune 100 companies, making it the largest and most advanced development platform in the world (*https://oreil.ly/B6tLd*) (Figure 18-1).

Figure 18-1. GitHub home page

Types of GitHub Accounts

To start using GitHub, first you need to create an account on the platform. Your GitHub.com personal account is your identity on the platform, and it represents you as an individual. Having an active account allows you to collaborate on code stored on the platform. It also enables you to organize and control access to the code or repository stored on GitHub.

You can create three types of accounts on GitHub:

Personal accounts

Everyone's personal account has a username and profile. Figure 18-2 shows an example of a user profile. With an active personal account, you can own repositories, GitHub Packages, and projects. Any actions you take on the platform will be attributed to your personal account.

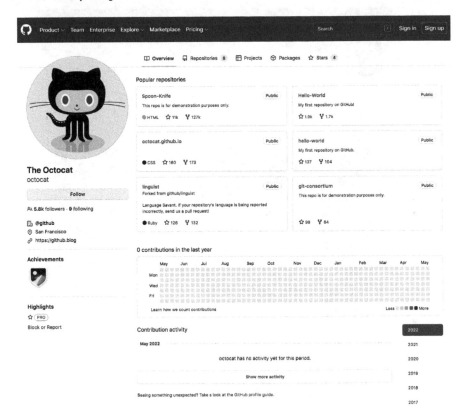

Figure 18-2. Octocat's account profile

There are two types of personal accounts: GitHub Free and GitHub Pro. Neither type has a limit imposed on the number of public or private repositories an account can own. They also allow for an unlimited number of collaborators on those repositories owned by the account. The difference between the types is that with a GitHub Free account, you will have access only to limited feature sets for private repositories.

Organization accounts

Organization accounts are shared accounts. An organization account allows for an unlimited number of persons to collaborate on resources owned by the organization. Similar to a personal account, an organization account can own repositories, GitHub packages, and projects. Figure 18-3 shows the option to display a *README.md* view in the profile page.

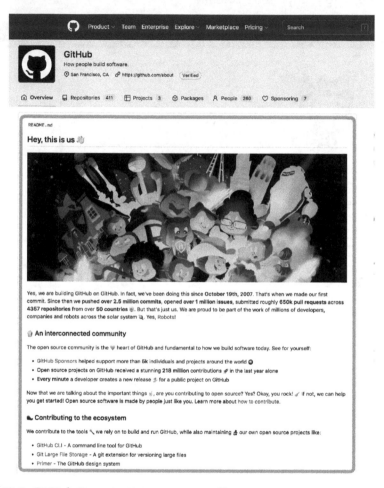

Figure 18-3. GitHub Organization account profile

As a person who has granted access to an organization, you will not be able to directly sign in to an organization account. Instead, you will need to sign in to your own personal account. Then, actions you perform on resources owned by the organization will be attributed to your personal account. Your personal account can be associated with multiple organizations.

With an organization account, a hierarchy of roles are introduced for each personal account that is granted access. The three types of roles are *owner*, *member*, and *outside collaborators*. An owner is also regarded as an organization admin. These roles are introduced to gate different levels of access to the organization and its resources. Figure 18-4, referenced from the official GitHub documentation page (*https://oreil.ly/QD7xC*), helps illustrate this concept.

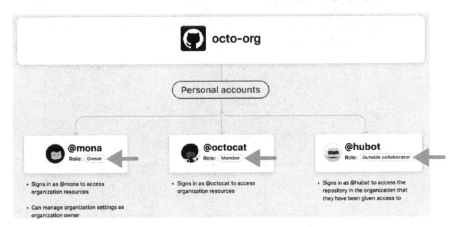

Figure 18-4. Roles in an organization account

Enterprise accounts

An enterprise account is very similar to an organization account. With an enterprise account, you can manage multiple organizations.

The GitHub Enterprise Cloud and GitHub Enterprise Server are variations of enterprise accounts that enable you to enforce and centrally manage any policies or billing information for one or more organizations owned by the enterprise account. They also allow for specific enforcement options for various settings, and they support delegation of policy configuration and enforcement to organization owners to provide flexibility when administering the account.

With a GitHub enterprise account, you also have two deployment options to choose from: GitHub Enterprise Cloud, which is cloud-hosted on a GitHub-operated data center, and self-hosted, where you can deploy a GitHub Enterprise Server in your own data center or on supported cloud providers.

It is important to understand that, when you use GitHub, you sign in using your personal account. An organization account helps enhance the collaboration between multiple personal accounts, and with an enterprise account, it becomes easier to centrally manage multiple organizations under one roof.

For pricing information and a high-level overview of the features provided by each account, visit the GitHub website (*https://oreil.ly/YiH5i*). An in-depth comparison of the features (*https://oreil.ly/m4rvL*) is available online as well.

GitHub in the Git Ecosystem

In "Git Components" on page 3, we provided an overview of Git components. Figure 18-5 revisits that figure here in the context of GitHub.

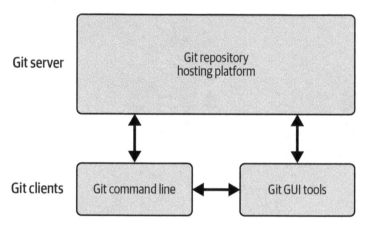

Figure 18-5. Overview of Git components

Building on Figure 18-5, GitHub is a *Git repository hosting platform*, which technically also makes it a *Git server*. Beyond supporting native Git functionality, GitHub also has features that enable social coding by lowering the barrier to collaborate. Features such as GitHub issues, pull request, protected branches, codeowners, organizations, teams, and projects are some examples.

As a Git Client, GitHub over the years has developed and made freely available some great tools to help support adoption of the platform. They include the following:

GitHub Desktop
> With GitHub Desktop, you can work in your familiar Git workflow via a visual interface. It is an open source, Electron-based GitHub app that allows you to make and amend your commits interactively, check out branches from pull requests, create new branches, easily switch between repositories, and even add coauthors to your commits. Figure 18-6 shows that Git Desktop is a GUI *Git Client*.

Figure 18-6. GitHub Desktop

If you're interested in contributing to the development of GitHub Desktop, you can fork the repository (*https://oreil.ly/ 5pOEm*).

GitHub CLI

The GitHub CLI is a command-line tool that brings GitHub's features into your development environment (either run as a system process that is not connected to any terminal or run as terminal emulators). You can interact with a GitHub repository's issues, pull requests, and a variety of GitHub features right from your development environment. This tool aims to reduce context switching between your development environment and the GitHub UI to perform tasks in your typical development workflow.

The GitHub CLI can be installed using popular package managers for supported operating systems. It is also freely available and supports extension of its standard functionality. Once it's installed, you can use the gh command to query and work with any GitHub repositories directly from your local terminal:

```
# install GitHub CLI

$ gh repo
Work with GitHub repositories

USAGE
```

```
gh repo <command> [flags]

CORE COMMANDS
  clone:      Clone a repository locally
  create:     Create a new repository
  fork:       Create a fork of a repository
  list:       List repositories owned by user or organization
  sync:       Sync a repository
  view:       View a repository

INHERITED FLAGS
  --help   Show help for command

ARGUMENTS
  A repository can be supplied as an argument in any of the following formats:
  - "OWNER/REPO"
  - by URL, e.g. "https://github.com/OWNER/REPO"

EXAMPLES
  $ gh repo create
  $ gh repo clone cli/cli
  $ gh repo view --web

LEARN MORE
  Use 'gh <command> <subcommand> --help' for more information about a command.
  Read the manual at https://cli.github.com/manual
```

GitHub CLI complements but does not replace the native Git commands. However, it does bring GitHub features to your command line. You can learn more about installation and potentially contribute to GitHub CLI (*https://oreil.ly/XB9bG*).

GitHub Mobile

GitHub Mobile is a client application aimed at helping you manage your work on GitHub from your mobile and smartphone devices. With the mobile application, you are limited to only GitHub features. You can triage and manage notifications, collaborate on issues, and pull requests. It also allows you to secure your GitHub.com account with two-factor authentication.

GitHub codespaces

A GitHub codespace is a development environment hosted in the cloud. The development environment spins up a Visual Studio code that you can access from your browser.

You can create a codespace from any branch or commit in your GitHub repository. All development work you do will use cloud-based compute resources. Generally, a codespace runs on a variety of VM-based compute options hosted by GitHub; you can pick compute options ranging from 2 to 32 core machines.

An advantage of using a codespace is that it provides a consistent development environment. All you need to do is commit a configuration file to your repository in order to create reusable codespace configurations for every allowed collaborator of your repository.

To learn more about GitHub codespaces, we recommend that you read the official documentation (*https://oreil.ly/uTvwd*).

Figure 18-7 shows how easy it is to start a new codespace from within your browser. This is one step closer to getting away from the "works on my machine" conundrum developers have been facing over the years.

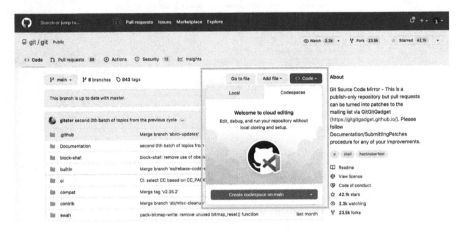

Figure 18-7. Launching a codespaces

 Your organization admin can manage billing costs when using codespaces by setting a spending limit to avoid surprise overspending.

Hosting a Repository in GitHub

When you have successfully created an account on GitHub, you can easily create a repository and start collaborating with your peers. After logging in from the Sign In page, you are directed to the GitHub Dashboard, shown in Figure 18-8. Here you are presented with some useful information in a unified view; you can quickly jump to repositories that were worked on recently, keep track of recent activity, get a feed of the latest changes from GitHub, and discover new projects or activities of people you follow via your personal news feed.

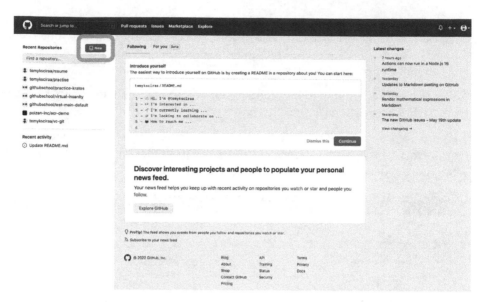

Figure 18-8. GitHub Dashboard

To create a new repository, click the New button on the upper left of the page. This will bring you to the "Create a new repository" page (Figure 18-9). Here you can provide a new repository name under your personal account in the input field. If you are a member of an organization, you can choose the organization account from the Owner drop-down combo button.

You can also create a new repo by navigating directly to the New Repository page (*https://oreil.ly/LBZIr*).

Also on this page, you have the option to provide a description for the repository, followed by an option to make this repository either public or private (depending on the type of account, a third repository visibility type labeled Internal is also presented as an option). A public repository is discoverable and accessible to anyone who is on GitHub.com. A private repository will require the owner of the project to invite collaborators, making it less discoverable. A repository owner can convert the visibility of a repository at any point in time. However, bear in mind the consequences of switching visibilities of a repository, especially if your project already has a thriving community of active contributors. If you plan to make your project freely available, we recommend that you set your repository visibility to public from the start.

Once you have decided on your repository's visibility, you have the option to initialize the repository. This simply means creating a new bare repository with a *README.md* file. You also have the option to add some additional files: a *.gitignore* file based on a list of templates for popular programming languages, and a *license* file offering a list of templates to choose from.

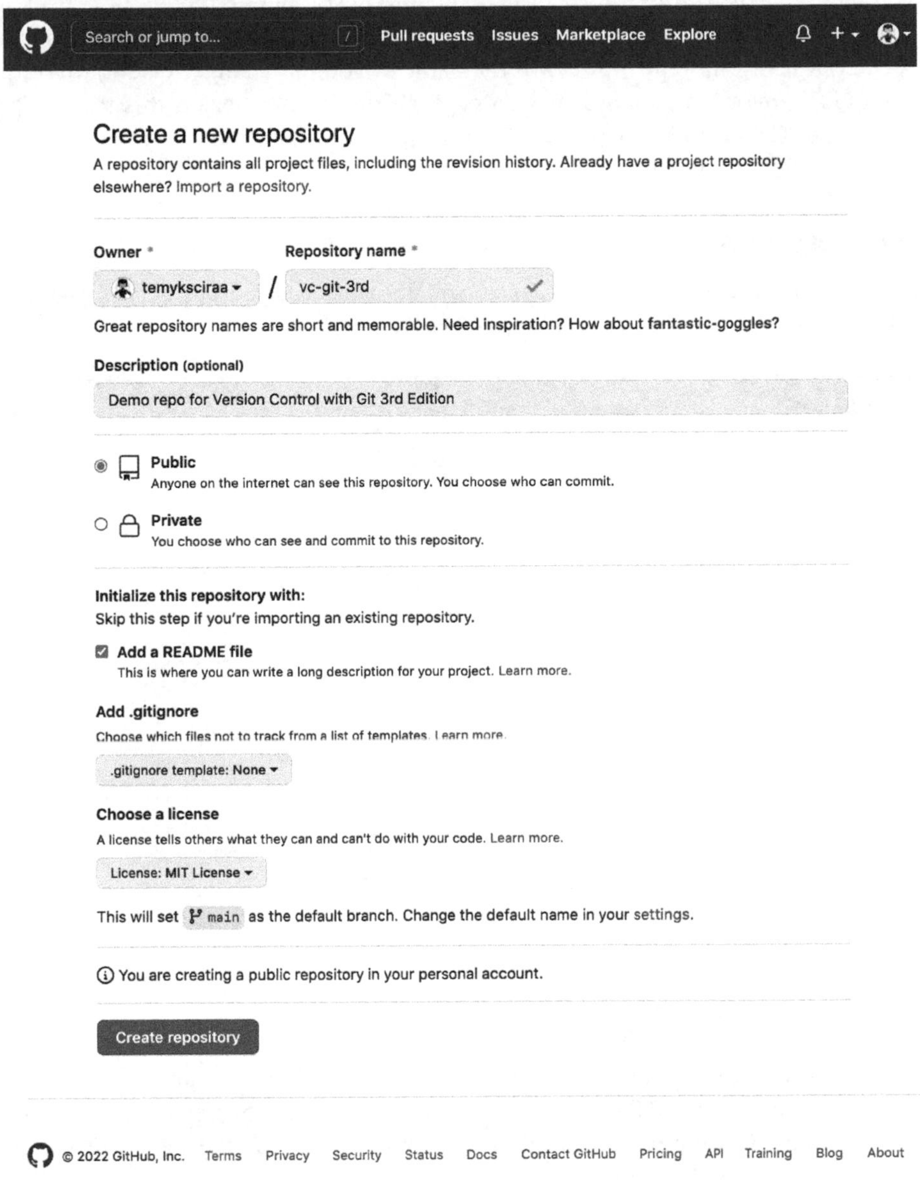

Figure 18-9. Creating a new repository

If you are not sure which type of license to choose for your project, a high-level overview of license types (*https://oreil.ly/sI7U7*) is online.

If you have an existing repository and you plan to host it in GitHub, do not check the option to "Add a README file." By leaving this option unchecked, you will create a placeholder upstream repository with the name of your choosing. Review "Migrating from a Git Version Control System" on page 416 for a refresher on this topic. Upon clicking the "Create repository" button, your new repository will be created with the options you have provided

Repository View

Figure 18-10 shows the Repository page, which features tabs and links to frequently used features supporting your development needs.

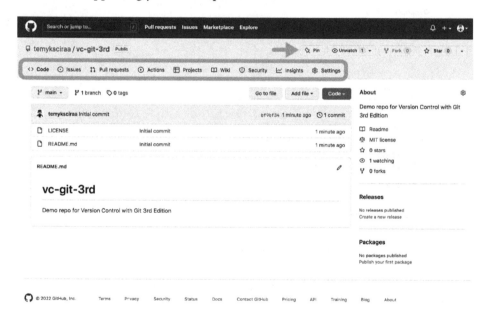

Figure 18-10. Repository view

The Repository view is your default view. This page displays the names of the owner and of the repository. In Figure 18-10, temyksciraa is the owner of the *vc-git-3rd* repository, and this repository is public. Toward the top of the page are the Pin, Watch, Fork, and Star buttons.

The Pin option pins the repository on your GitHub profile page (Figure 18-11).

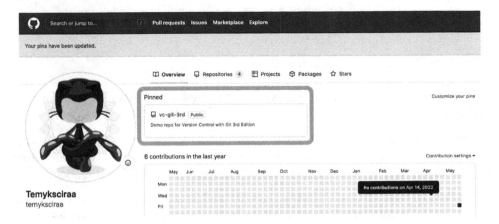

Figure 18-11. Pinned repository

As shown in Figure 18-12, you can control notifications you receive on activities in this repository. The options allow you to be granular regarding which activity is important to you. In an open source project, the watcher count can often be a signal of the usefulness or popularity of the project.

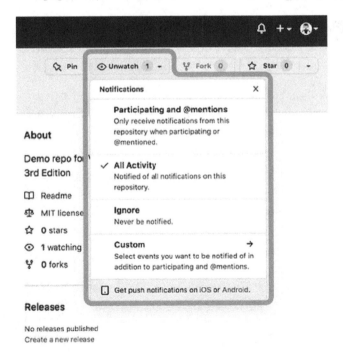

Figure 18-12. Watch options

In GitHub, *@mention* is an easy way to notify or include someone in a discussion on issues or pull requests. The *@mention* refers to a user or team account.

The Fork option allows you to create a copy of the repository in an account you have access to.

In the past, the term *forking* carried a negative connotation. In the coding landscape of yesteryear, forking often meant an aggressive parting of ways with the primary copy of the project, with the intent to take the program in a different direction.

GitHub's idea of forking is a positive one that enables a greater number of contributors to make a greater number of contributions in a controlled and highly visible way. This does not pose any risk to the core project because the changes are happening in the forked repository, not the original repository.

A primary benefit of this model is the transparency and public visibility of the community contributions, even before they are submitted back to the core project for discussion and potential incorporation. Figure 18-13 is a view of the mirror copy of the Git source code on GitHub and represents a great example of forking.

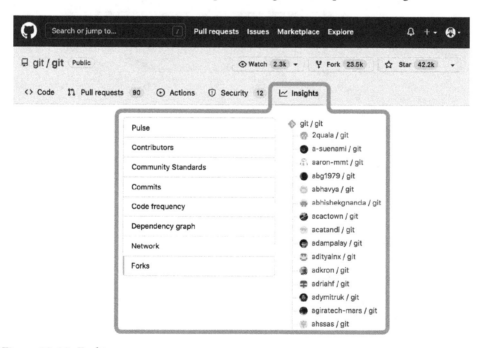

Figure 18-13. Forking

The Star button acts as a bookmark to repositories you are interested in or following. You can curate a list of categories for any repositories you would like to follow, as shown in Figure 18-14.

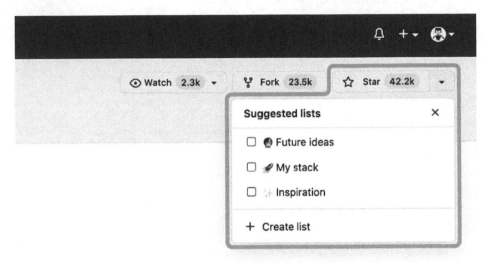

Figure 18-14. Creating Star lists

Code

Figure 18-15 shows the root view of your repository. Here, you can view the total number of branches and tags in the repository, along with an About section that displays a description of the repository and links to list the repository's README, License, Stars, Code of Conduct if available, Watching, and Forks. If the repository contains Releases or GitHub Packages, they will also be displayed here. This view also displays profile pictures of contributors to the project and a breakdown of programming languages used in the project repository.

You can search for a specific file in the repository using the "Go to file" button. In addition, you can quickly add a file to the repository without cloning the repo you are able to do so via the "Add file" button. Figure 18-16 shows how to get the remote URL of the repository for cloning using supported protocols. It is also where you can launch a codespace if codespaces are enabled.

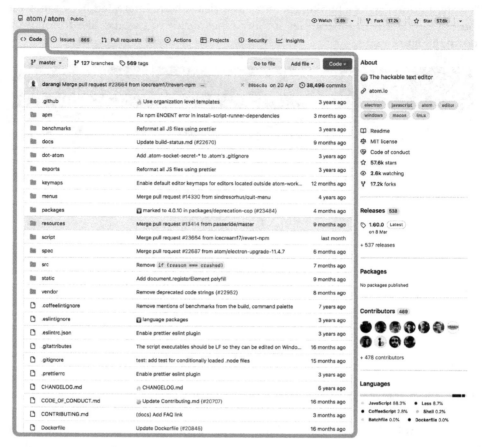

Figure 18-15. Code view

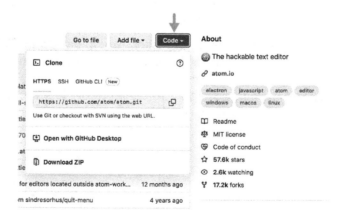

Figure 18-16. Code button

Figure 18-17 shows a header and information for the files within the repository. The header captures a summary of the commit message, the short commit SHA, and a timestamp of the commit. It also summarizes the total number of commits for the repository.

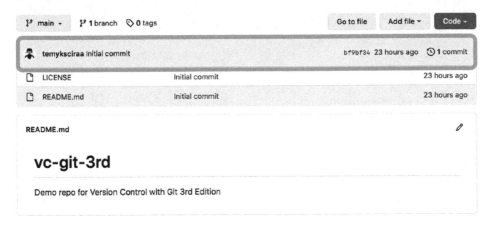

Figure 18-17. Repository file list

Clicking the commit details in the header will bring you to a contextual page displaying extended information about the specific commit. To view a visual commit history for the selected branch, you can click the total number of commits in the header (Figure 18-18).

The repository file list view is a 1:1 representation of your project files and structure. In other words, it is basically what you will see in your working directory when you clone your repository. The cool thing about this view from GitHub.com is that, if you have a markdown file named *README.md* in the directory, the UI will automatically render the content of the *README.md* file for you in the Code view. You can include README files in specific folders to improve async communication and assist in open source development.

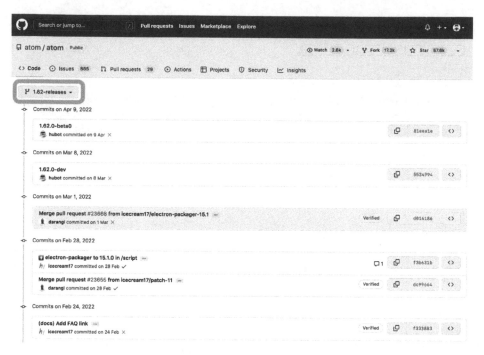

Figure 18-18. Visual commit history

Issues

GitHub issues help you manage and organize your work on GitHub. Although not a Git feature, issues allow you to track feedback, ideas, tasks, and even bugs for your project. When you create an issue, you can cross-reference related issues or pull requests and even *@mention* teams or users who collaborate on the repository. Figure 18-19 displays all related issues (either in a closed or open state) for a particular repository. This allows you to capture a historic context for how or why certain development decisions were made in the lifetime of the project. You can even pin popular issues in the same view.

In the Issues list view, you can sort, filter, and manage labels and milestones for your repository. You can also create a new issue from here by clicking the "New issue" button.

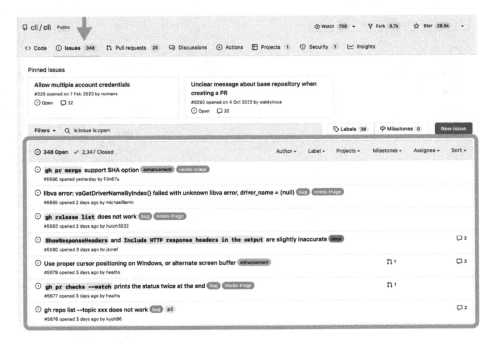

Figure 18-19. Issues list

The issues view in Figure 18-20 shows the main thread for an issue, followed by *issue-comment* replies. In the Comment field, you can write and format replies using a syntax for formatting text called *GitHub Flavored Markdown*. You can take advantage of the text formatting toolbar to help in using the correct syntax. All of the activities you do in an issue are reflected in the issue's timeline.

This includes activities such as adding an assignee, creating labels, and adding the issue to either a milestone or a project. You can also create a new branch for a specific issue to work on adding a feature or bug fix in isolation from the default branch, or to link an existing pull request to the issue referencing the changes you introduce to address the context discussed in the issue.

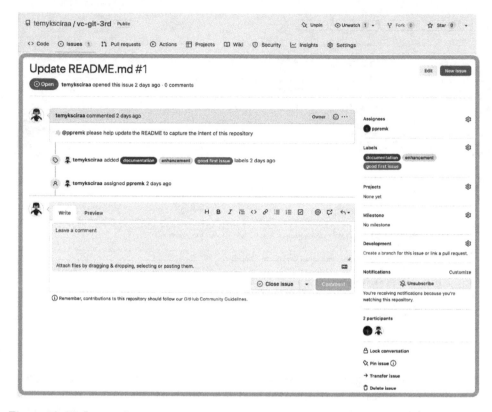

Figure 18-20. Issues view

You can keep up with the progress on the issue by subscribing or customizing the issue notification settings as shown in Figure 18-21.

Depending on the rights you have been assigned in the repository, when required you can lock the conversation of the issue, pin it, transfer it, or even delete it (we recommend closing the issue instead of deleting it, to help in capturing the history of the effort).

For more detail on how you can leverage GitHub issues to organize and track your work on GitHub, we recommend that you review the official documentation (*https:// oreil.ly/5iuAU*).

> You can find the specifications for the GitHub Flavored Markdown syntax online (*https://oreil.ly/ZXE7c*).

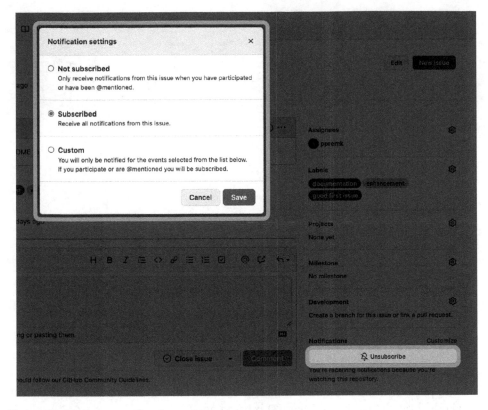

Figure 18-21. Issue notification settings

Pull Requests

A GitHub pull request allows you to inform changes you are proposing in a branch for a specific repository. You can facilitate code reviews and discussions on the potential changes you are proposing with collaborators of the repository, further prompting required changes or commits to address feedback from the process. Once all required criteria are met, you can then proceed to merge your pull request into the intended target branch of the repository.

Much like the view shown in Figure 18-19, a pull request (Figure 18-22) has a similar pull request list and shares the same functionality.

You can create a new pull request from here by clicking the "New pull request" button.

Figure 18-22. Pull request list

Figure 18-23 also shares many similarities with Figure 18-20, albeit with a few exceptions. For example, there is an extra Reviewers option. This option alerts assigned reviewers to any open pull requests. Just like the issues view, all activities you do in a pull request are reflected in the pull request's timeline, including the commits you add via the branch that the pull request is based on.

> Reviewers can be automatically assigned if there is a *CODEOWN-ERS* file (*https://oreil.ly/dHqJs*) defined in a branch in the repository.

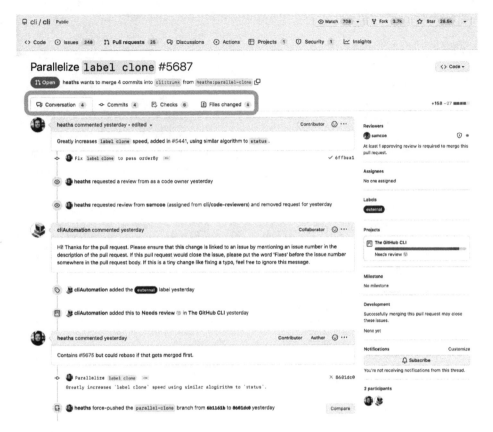

Figure 18-23. Pull request view

The pull request view shown in Figure 18-23 also includes a number of tabs. The Conversations tab is meant to facilitate review discussions for the changes you are introducing via a topic or feature branch. The conversations can be captured as an issue comment or inline review on the line of code that is committed.

Figure 18-24 is an example of an inline code comment conversation.

Figure 18-24. Inline code comment conversation

Within the Conversation tab, near the end of the page, there is a section that includes a list for one of the *Code quality features* in a pull request. (The other is the Checks tab.) The view shown in Figure 18-25 informs you whether your commits meet the required standards and conditions enforced by the owner of the repository.

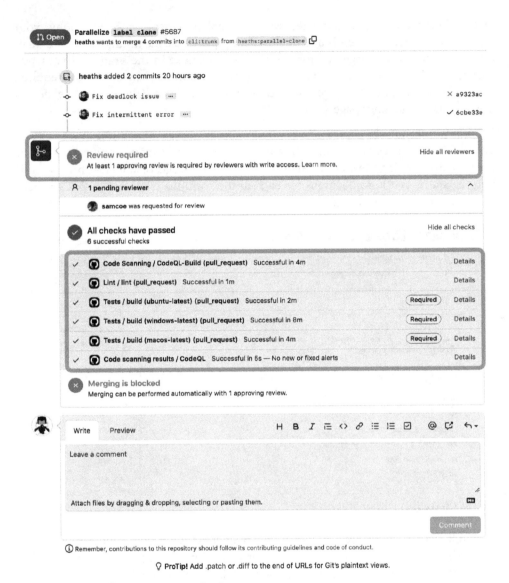

Figure 18-25. Pull request status check

Status checks are mostly associated with external processes, most commonly your continuous integration builds and deployment pipelines, code linting, and code quality checks, which are triggered for every push you make in the branch of your pull request in the repository. Repository owners and admins can configure required status checks via branch protection rules from the "Code and automation" section of the repository's settings page.

In the Commits tab, you are presented with the branch commit history (Figure 18-26) associated with your pull request. From this view you can jump to specific commits by clicking the commit SHA, the commit message, or the < > - browse code button. Status check notifications for each of the commits (shown as a tick or check mark) are also displayed in this view.

Figure 18-26. Branch commit history

In a pull request, there are two types of status checks. One is the pull request status check shown in Figure 18-25, and the other is the Checks page. Figure 18-27 differs from Figure 18-25 in that checks provide detailed line annotations and messaging and are available for use only with a GitHub app.

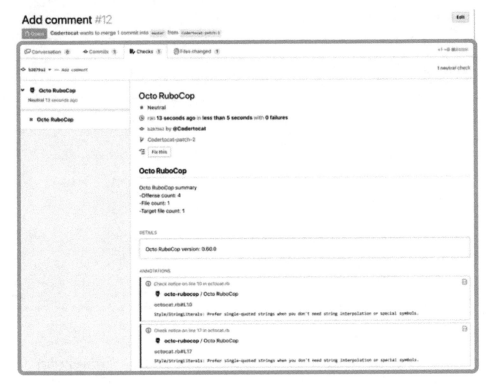

Add comment #12

Codertocat wants to merge 1 commit into master from Codertocat-patch-2

Conversation · Commits · Checks · Files changed

b287962 — Add comment

1 neutral check

Octo RuboCop
Neutral 13 seconds ago

Octo RuboCop

Octo RuboCop

* Neutral
* ran 13 seconds ago in less than 5 seconds with 0 failures
* b287962 by @Codertocat
* Codertocat-patch-2
* Fix this

Octo RuboCop

Octo RuboCop summary
-Offense count: 4
-File count: 1
-Target file count: 1

DETAILS

Octo RuboCop version: 0.60.0

ANNOTATIONS

Check notice on line 10 in octocat.rb

octo-rubocop / Octo RuboCop

octocat.rb#L10

Style/StringLiterals: Prefer single-quoted strings when you don't need string interpolation or special symbols.

Check notice on line 17 in octocat.rb

octo-rubocop / Octo RuboCop

octocat.rb#L17

Style/StringLiterals: Prefer single-quoted strings when you don't need string interpolation or special symbols.

Figure 18-27. Checks

As mentioned in the official GitHub documentation about checks (*https://oreil.ly/0jzxV*), the Checks tab will be populated for pull requests only if you set up checks.

When reviewing a pull request, any collaborators with read access to the repository can view and comment on the proposed changes. These reviews can include suggestions specific to lines of code in files being introduced or the overall batch of commits in the branch of the pull request. The "Files changed" tab is where the maintainer of the repository can review incoming changes and apply them directly from the pull request. Figure 18-28 shows a view after the "Files changed" tab.

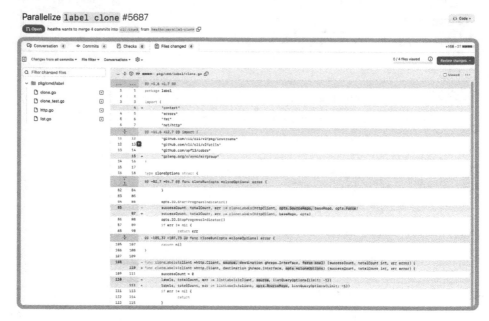

Figure 18-28. Files changed

As a reviewer, you can suggest changes by clicking on the blue plus sign when you hover over the lines in a file (see Figure 18-29).

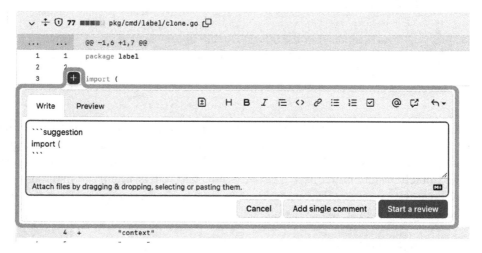

Figure 18-29. Suggesting changes

The files tree view allows for easy navigation between files that are edited in the pull request. You can compare changes from selected commits or all commits in the pull request (see Figure 18-30).

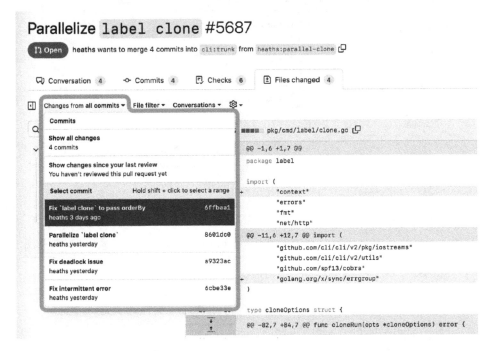

Figure 18-30. Comparing changes

When viewing introduced changes in a file, you can select how the diff view is presented by clicking the gear icon. You can select from a unified or a split view and also select to hide whitespace when necessary (see Figure 18-31).

Finally, as a maintainer or owner of the repository, you can approve a pull request (Figure 18-32) by clicking the "Review changes" button. Here you can comment on, approve, or request changes to the proposed contribution. Note that you will be able to approve or request changes only for pull requests of other collaborators!

Figure 18-31. Diff view

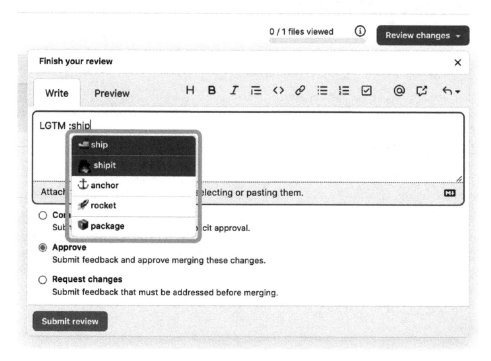

Figure 18-32. Approving a pull request

The *shipit* squirrel and the acronym LGTM (Looks Good To Me) go hand in hand when approving a pull request!

Figure 18-33 shows the end result of an approved pull request. If all status checks are passing and required approvals are in place, the pull request is ready to merge into a target branch! When deciding to merge, GitHub provides you with three merge options to choose from, as shown in Figure 18-34. The options are self-explanatory and build on the native Git merge strategies we discussed in Chapter 17.

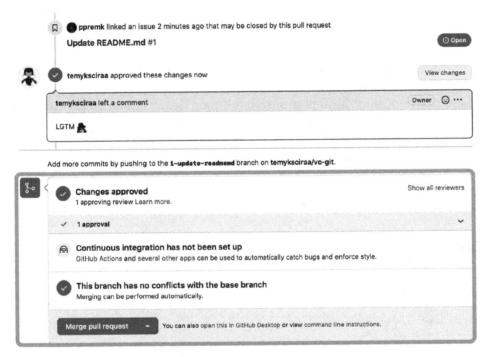

Figure 18-33. Approved pull request in a conversation

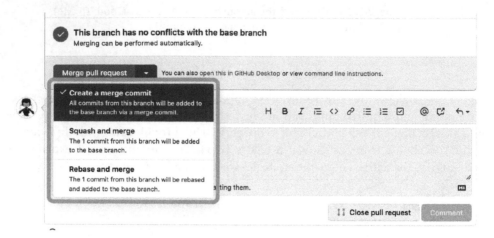

Figure 18-34. Three merge options

Once you have merged the pull request, it is a good housekeeping practice to choose the "Delete branch" option (Figure 18-35). The deleted branch can be restored at a later time if required, but bear in mind that you may run into conflicts given the development of the project over time.

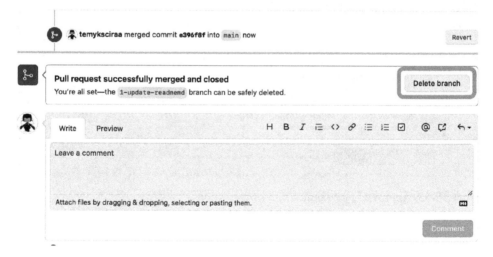

Figure 18-35. Delete branch

The GitHub Flow

The GitHub Flow is a lightweight branch-based workflow. From a pure Git implementation, the branching strategy for GitHub Flow consists of one long-lived branch and short-lived branches from which changes are merged.

Typically the long-lived branch is the *default* branch, commonly termed *main*, and the short-lived branches are the *feature* branches, representing changes that are being introduced.

The principle here is that you will be using short-lived branches to introduce changes to your repository that will be merged to the long-lived branch once the short-lived branches satisfy mandatory requirements. These changes can range from bug fixes to features and functionalities you add to your project.

When adopting the GitHub Flow, you can follow the steps directly through the GitHub web interface, standard Git command line, GitHub CLI, or GitHub Desktop or any IDEs that support Git as an extension.

Following are the steps for adopting the GitHub Flow:

Step 1: Create a branch

The first step is to create a branch in your repository (Figure 18-36). Pick a meaningful name for your branch; this will help your collaborators quickly grasp the intended changes being introduced. When working in a team, it's also best to stick to an agreed naming convention for a better development experience.

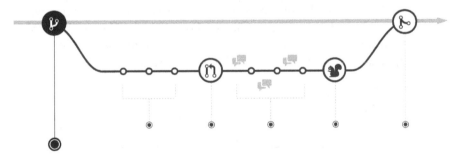

Figure 18-36. Creating a branch

Introducing changes via a branch also allows you to experiment and iterate on changes in isolation and away from the main branch, avoiding breaking anything in your main codebase.

Step 2: Make changes

The next step is to start introducing changes. This is done via commits (see Figure 18-37). Be sure to craft your commits to be atomic, capturing and grouping changes as a logical unit. By doing so, if you need to revert a specific change, you can select to revert a single commit instead of having to roll back a batch of changes.

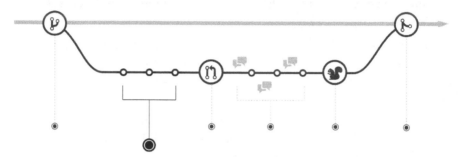

Figure 18-37. Making changes

A clear and succinct commit message will make life easier for you and your collaborators in future development efforts!

Step 3: Create a pull request

Once you are ready to share your changes and solicit reviews from your collaborators, you can open a pull request for your branch (see Figure 18-38). In your pull request, including context on changes you are introducing will provide valuable information for collaborators who will be conducting the review. This will allow for meaningful async discussions around the specifics of your changes, leading to a smooth and pleasant reviewing experience.

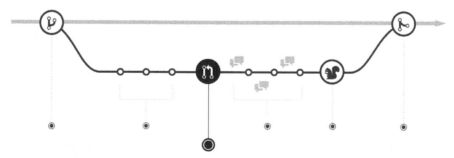

Figure 18-38. Creating a pull request

It is important to note that the pull request you open is on GitHub. For this to happen, you will need to propagate your changes to the remote repository hosted there. In short, if you have been working on your local machine, you will need to push your changes to the remote upstream repository on GitHub.com.

Step 4: Address review comments

After the pull request is opened, you and your collaborators can easily have conversations about the code and changes you are introducing (see Figure 18-39). If the repository already has code quality features set up, such as status checks, you will need to ensure that all criteria are met, all while the review process is ongoing.

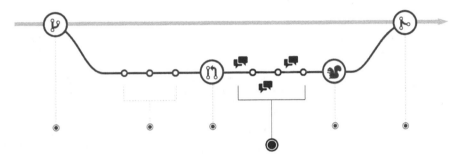

Figure 18-39. Addressing review comments

Reviewers can request changes, leave comments, and approve your changes, all of which you can access from the Conversation tab.

Step 5: Deploy your code

Once your pull request is approved, you have the option to deploy from your feature branch to a staging or even production environment (see Figure 18-40). This step is highly dependent on your workflow, specifically, the automation, continuous integration builds, and deployment pipelines adopted by teams as their development practice.

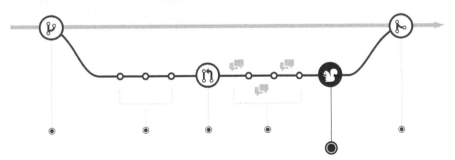

Figure 18-40. Deploying the code

At GitHub, *ChatOps* allow a pull request to be deployed to a production environment, making it self-serve for any contributor of a repository. As an industry-standard best practice, we've seen similar workflows but with deployment done to a staging rather than a production environment.

Step 6: Merge the pull request

The final step in the GitHub Flow is to merge your pull request into the main branch (see Figure 18-41). Depending on the branch protection rule configured for the repository, you may need to ensure that all checks, statuses, and approvals are in place prior to completing the merge.

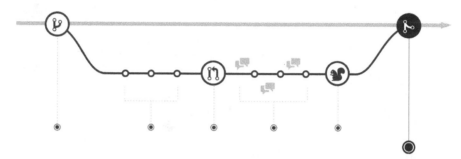

Figure 18-41. Merging the pull request

Upon successfully merging your feature branch into the main branch, as a good housekeeping practice you should delete the feature branch since all your changes will be part of the main line. This also helps prevent collaborators from accidentally working on a branch that may be outdated.

A comprehensive guide on the GitHub Flow, with substeps for each step we described here, is available on the official GitHub documentation page (*https://oreil.ly/VKZc9*).

In addition to the GitHub Flow, there are alternative workflows that you can adopt according to your development needs. You can learn about them in the Git documentation (*https://oreil.ly/siP25*).

One popular workflow that is commonly compared to the GitHub Flow is the *Git Flow*. We recommend reading this blog post by Vincent Driessen (*https://oreil.ly/Y6prx*) to learn more about the Git Flow branching model.

Resolving Merge Conflicts in GitHub

Merge conflicts are a natural by-product of working with a distributed version control system like Git. A merge conflict isn't necessarily a bad thing. As you already know, merge conflicts occur when branches have competing or conflicting changes.

When dealing with merge conflicts in your workflow, on the GitHub web interface, you have the ability to visually compare changes you intend to merge from your branch and the target base branch. You can view a list of conflicting changes or files during a merge conflict via the "Resolve conflicts" button (see Figure 18-42) on the "Pull request" page.

Figure 18-42. Resolving a merge conflict

Let's simulate a merge conflict and learn how to resolve it on the GitHub web interface.

We will use the GitHub Flow to introduce a change to the *README.md* file in our example repo. For simplicity, we will skip Step 4 and Step 5 from the previous exercise to help focus on key takeaways from this section:

Step 1: Create a branch

We will create a new branch from the GitHub web interface as user *temyksciraa* by clicking the branch selector menu. Provide a meaningful branch name and click the "Create: branch" option (Figure 18-43).

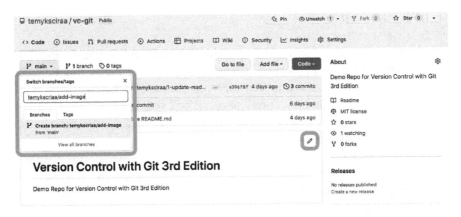

Figure 18-43. Adding a new feature branch

Step 2: Make changes

Next, we will start introducing changes to the *README.md* file. We can directly edit the file by clicking the pencil icon at the upper right of the file when in view mode. We'll provide a good commit message and commit directly to the branch created earlier (Figure 18-44).

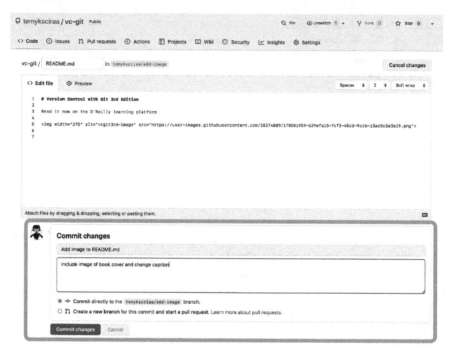

Figure 18-44. Adding new changes to README.md

Step 3: Create a pull request

When in the Code tab, GitHub provides a shortcut for you to quickly create a pull request from branches with changes that were pushed to the repository recently (it detects this automatically and proposes a banner with the branch name). Clicking "Compare & pull request" will redirect you to the "Create a pull request" page where you can verify the changes and open a new pull request (Figure 18-45).

 For this example to work, please do not immediately merge the pull request you just created!

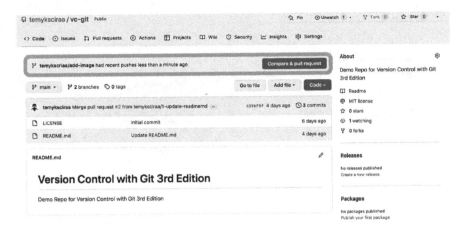

Figure 18-45. Creating a new pull request

Step 4: Address review comments

After the pull request is opened, you and your collaborators can easily have conversations about the code and changes you are introducing. If the repository already has code quality features set up, such as status checks, you will need to ensure that all criteria are met, all while the review process is ongoing.

Reviewers can request changes, leave comments, and approve your changes, all of which you can access from the Conversation tab.

Step 5: Deploy your code

Once your pull request is approved, you have the option to deploy from your feature branch to a staging or even production environment. This step is highly dependent on your workflow, specifically, the automation, continuous integration builds, and deployment pipelines adopted by teams as their development practice.

At GitHub, *ChatOps* allow a pull request to be deployed to a production environment, making it self-serve for any contributor of a repository. As an industry-standard best practice, we've seen similar workflows but with deployment done to a staging rather than a production environment.

Step 6: Merge the pull request

When you are ready, you can merge the pull request by clicking the "Merge pull request" button (Figure 18-46).

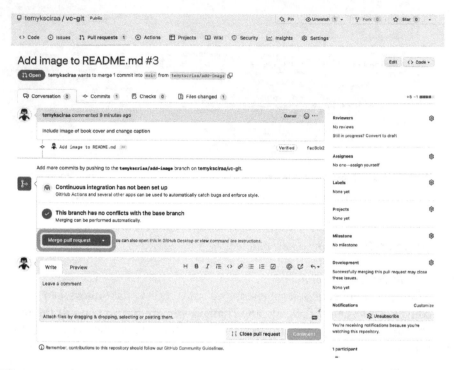

Figure 18-46. Merging changes

Now that we have prepared the first branch, we will introduce a new conflicting change via another new branch created from the main branch. Follow the steps we outlined initially for GitHub Flow to create this branch and introduce changes to it, and then open a pull request when you are ready, but do not merge the changes yet!

> We will simulate the user *ppremk* creating a new branch named *ppremk/update-readme* for this example.

In order to trigger the merge conflict, you should now merge the changes from the earlier pull request, that is, the changes introduced by user *temyksciraa* via the `temyksciraa/add-image` branch in Figure 18-46.

Upon merging, you will see the "Resolve conflicts" button shown in the pull request section of the newly created pull request by the second user, in this case the user logged in as *ppremk* (Figure 18-47).

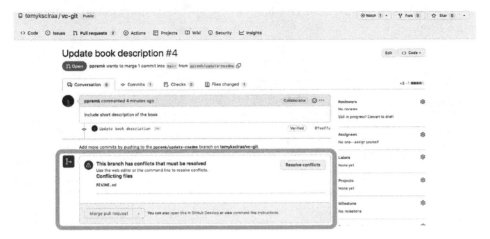

Figure 18-47. Resolving conflicts

In the "Conflict resolution" page shown in Figure 18-48, you can view the conflict resolution markers along with some information on the branches that are having the conflict. This is captured as a short description between the pull request title and the conflict resolution file list view. Resolve the conflict as you see fit. We discussed how to inspect and resolve conflicts in "Inspecting Conflicts" on page 132.

Figure 18-48. Conflict resolution page

When there is more than one conflicting change for a file, you can traverse through the conflicts by clicking the Prev and Next options in the file content view header component.

In our example, we have decided to combine both conflicting changes introduced via the separate branches. We have also cleaned up the conflict resolution markers.

As a final step to resolve the conflict, click the "Mark as resolved" button (see Figure 18-49).

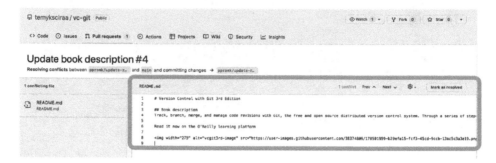

Figure 18-49. Marking a conflict as resolved

Once you have marked a conflict as resolved, the files with the conflict will display a green checkmark to denote the resolution and whether all conflicting files have been marked as resolved. By clicking the "Commit merge" button at the upper right of the page, you can continue with the next steps for merging the pull request (see Figure 18-50).

Figure 18-50. Committing a conflict resolution

On the "Pull request" page, you will notice that the "Merge pull request" button (see Figure 18-51) is visible again, and you can proceed to merge the changes to the target branch. Do note that your resolution will show up as an extra commit, with the default commit message "Merge branch *main* into…"

After completing the merge, you can navigate to the Code tab to view the new content of the *README.md* file, which combines changes from users *temyksciraa* and *ppremk* in the same file (Figure 18-52).

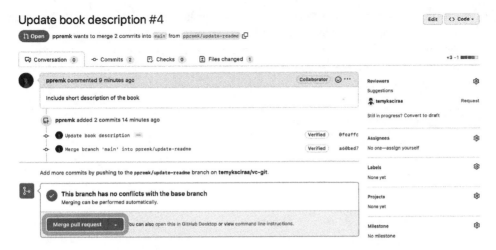

Figure 18-51. *Merging a resolved conflict*

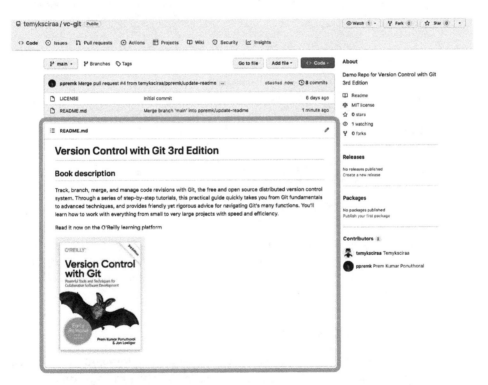

Figure 18-52. *Updated README.md*

In this example, we were able to resolve simple conflicts that can be directly resolved via the GitHub web interface. There will be situations where the merge conflict is complex, and it will not be intuitive to resolve the conflict from the web interface directly. For such scenarios, you will need to resolve the conflict from the command line (Figure 18-53).

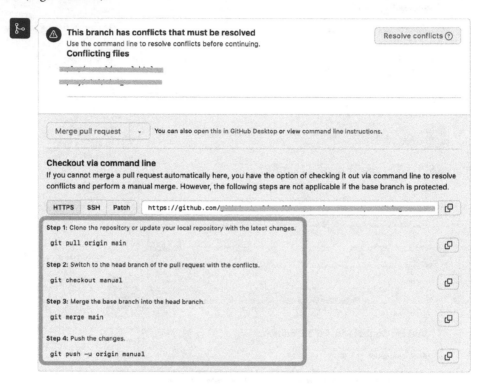

Figure 18-53. Resolving the conflict from the command line

GitHub provides you with some tips on how to do this. Clicking the link "command line instructions" will give you the steps you can take to resolve the conflict from your local machine. Upon resolving the conflict locally, you will need to push the changes back to the upstream repository to continue merging the change.

Development Workflows

The choice of Git as a development team's version control system and, more specifically, the choice of GitHub as the repository host facilitates dozens of unique usage patterns. Three of these usage styles are briefly described.

The centralized model, shown in Figure 18-54, while still offering the local commit insulation that isn't afforded by true centralized systems like SVN, is the simplest but least interesting of the models. It is an easy first step because developers push their local commits frequently so as to simulate the "everything is on the central server" state that was enforced by their version control tool of yesteryear. Although this can be a viable starting pattern with Git, it is a mere stepping stone toward unique and valuable leveraging of the distributed and collaborative model Git and GitHub have to offer.

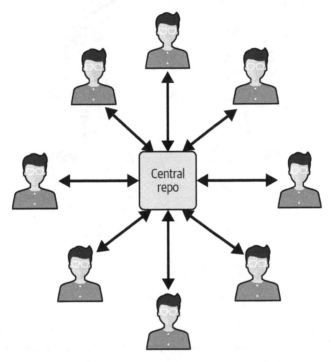

Figure 18-54. Centralized model

Next up is the lieutenant and commander model shown in Figure 18-55. You'll recognize it as very similar to that enabled by the pull request facilities of GitHub. It is important to note that Git projects in the absence of GitHub have a means of implementing this model through emails and links passed around as patches, but always with greater apparent friction and ceremony than real pull requests.

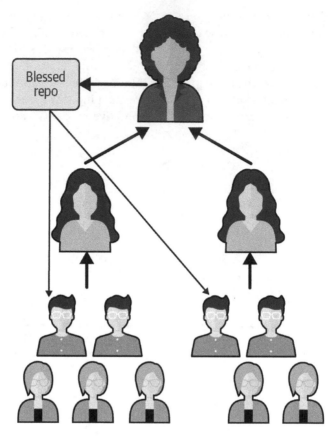

Figure 18-55. Linux lieutenant and commander model

Last, for companies that are leveraging open source and want to donate back their bug fixes but keep the innovations in-house, an arbitrator for the two repositories can be established. This arbitrator, as shown in Figure 18-56, picks and chooses which commits are cherry-picked and pushed back into the public domain to the open source version of the project. Although this is possible, as companies gain experience interfacing with the open source culture and community, this style of approach is becoming less common. Companies either hire open source developers as contractors or have dedicated teams enforcing proper policies and guidance on how a developer can contribute back to a project correctly, avoiding any unwanted legal issues.

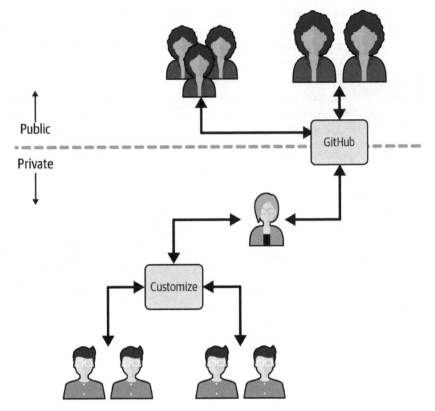

Figure 18-56. Partial open source model

Integrating with GitHub

GitHub as a Git hosting web application platform is a great starting point, but with its growing community of developers who are eager to use true services and not just features exposed through the web interface, GitHub can be seamlessly integrated in a variety of ways.

To facilitate the community construction of supporting tools, GitHub has built a full API available in two stable versions: the *REST API* and the *GraphQL API*. GitHub's REST API has gone through three major evolutions, and the current REST API v3 (*https://oreil.ly/J6UZg*), as it is known, offers almost all UI-accessible features in an equivalent API form. In some cases, advanced services are offered through the API that aren't even part of the GitHub UI yet. The GraphQL API (*https://oreil.ly/nQRXP*), on the other hand, offers different functionalities and provides a more precise and flexible method to query the exact data you need to fetch through supported clients.

Webhooks (*https://oreil.ly/1ISTX*) is another integration option that you can use to extend GitHub. Through webhooks, you can build a GitHub app or an OAuth app that can be triggered to execute certain business logic by listening to events subscribed at an organization or repository level. You can be very specific as to the list of events you can subscribe to since there will be a rate limit enforced by GitHub for the number of requests that are sent to the server. For instance, applying a label to or closing an issue is considered an event. The "Webhook events and payloads" (*https://oreil.ly/TH2uC*) page lists all available webhooks and their payloads.

Figure 18-57 shows code samples of a GitHub API call and its response.

Figure 18-57. REST API code sample

The API call's response will list all issues assigned to the authenticated user across all visible repositories.

Figure 18-58 shows a code sample of a GraphQL API call.

```
query {
  repository(owner:"octocat", name:"Hello-World") {
    issues(last:20, states:CLOSED) {
      edges {
        node {
          title
          url
          labels(first:5) {
            edges {
              node {
                name
              }
            }
          }
        }
      }
    }
  }
}
```

Figure 18-58. GraphQL API code sample

 The query in Figure 18-58 returns the 20 most recently closed issues (the issue's title and URL) and the first five labels in the repository octocat/Hello-World.

Note that a GitHub app (*https://oreil.ly/sVXBc*) is a first-class actor within GitHub, has more fine-grained control on permission, and uses its own identity to perform required actions when triggered. An OAuth app (*https://oreil.ly/TEFHl*) uses GitHub as an identity provider to authenticate as the user who needs to grant access to the requesting app.

The "Differences Between GitHub Apps and OAuth Apps" official documentation (*https://oreil.ly/Wrkso*) is a recommended read if you plan to build integrations using this model. Note that there is a possibility that by the time this book is published, legacy OAuth apps on GitHub may not be supported.

Summary

GitHub today has shaken the foundations of many traditional centralized version control systems by showing that high-performance, collaborative, and distributed version control can be found in open source solutions as well as in an enterprise setup that adopts a similar principle.

What we have elaborated on in this chapter barely scratches the surface of what you can achieve on the platform. We have not discussed useful GitHub features such as GitHub Actions, GitHub Packages, GitHub Pages, GitHub Repository Releases, or the GitHub Project Board, all of which you can leverage to suit your modern development needs! Discussing how you can leverage Git and GitHub in today's modern software development practices such as GitOps or even IssueOps would require a separate book; trying to cover it all in one chapter wouldn't do the topic justice.

Offset by only a short delay from Git's own development, GitHub has equally shown that a sharp web application as a Git hosting platform can reduce tool burden, facilitate quicker fixes, allow a greater number of contributors to further a project, and, most importantly, turn the act of coding into a truly social, collaborative activity, all while maintaining a high quality of work.

History of Git

No cautious, creative person starts a project nowadays without a backup strategy. Because data is ephemeral and can be lost easily—through an errant code change or a catastrophic disk crash, say—it is wise to maintain a living archive of all work.

For text and code projects, the backup strategy typically includes version control, or tracking and managing revisions. Each developer can make several revisions per day, and the ever-increasing corpus serves simultaneously as repository, project narrative, communication medium, and team and product management tool. Given its pivotal role, version control is most effective when tailored to the working habits and goals of the project team.

A tool that manages and tracks different versions of software or other content is referred to generically as a version control system (VCS), a source code manager (SCM), a revision control system (RCS), and several other permutations of the words *revision, version, code, content, control, management*, and *system*. Although the authors and users of each tool might debate esoterics, each system addresses the same issue: develop and maintain a repository of content, provide access to historical editions of each datum, and record all changes in a log. In this book, the term *version control system* is used to refer generically to any form of revision control system.

Git, a particularly powerful, flexible, and low-overhead version control tool that makes collaborative development a pleasure, was invented by Linus Torvalds to support the development of the Linux[1] kernel, but it has since proven valuable to a wide range of projects.

---

1 Linux® is the registered trademark of Linus Torvalds in the United States and other countries.

The Birth of Git

Often, when there is discord between a tool and a project, the developers simply create a new tool. Indeed, in the world of software, the temptation to create new tools can be deceptively easy and inviting. In the face of many existing version control systems, the decision to create another one shouldn't be made casually. However, given a critical need, a bit of insight, and a healthy dose of motivation, forging a new tool can be exactly the right course.

Git, affectionately termed "the information manager from hell" by its creator (Linus is known for both his irascibility and his dry wit), is such a tool. Although the precise circumstances and timing of its genesis are shrouded in political wrangling within the Linux kernel community, there is no doubt that what came from that fire is a well-engineered version control system capable of supporting the worldwide development of software on a large scale.

Prior to Git, the Linux kernel was developed using the commercial BitKeeper VCS, which provided sophisticated operations not available in then-current, free software VCSs such as RCS and the Concurrent Versions System (CVS). However, when the company that owned BitKeeper placed additional restrictions on its "free as in beer" version in the spring of 2005, the Linux community realized that BitKeeper was no longer a viable solution.

Linus looked for alternatives. Eschewing commercial solutions, he studied the free software packages but found the same limitations and flaws that led him to reject them previously. What was wrong with the existing VCSs? What were the elusive missing features or characteristics that Linus wanted and couldn't find?

Facilitate distributed development
> There are many facets to "distributed development," and Linus wanted a new VCS that would cover most of them. It had to allow parallel as well as independent and simultaneous development in private repositories without the need for constant synchronization with a central repository, which could form a development bottleneck. It had to allow multiple developers in multiple locations even if some of them were offline temporarily.

Scale to handle thousands of developers
> It isn't enough just to have a distributed development model. Linus knew that thousands of developers contribute to each Linux release. So any new VCS had to handle a very large number of developers whether they were working on the same or different parts of a common project. And the new VCS had to be able to integrate all of their work reliably.

Perform quickly and efficiently

Linus was determined to ensure that a new VCS was fast and efficient. In order to support the sheer volume of update operations that would be made on the Linux kernel alone, he knew that both individual update operations and network transfer operations would have to be very fast. To save space and thus transfer time, compression and "delta" techniques would be needed. Using a distributed model instead of a centralized model also ensured that network latency would not hinder daily development.

Maintain integrity and trust

Because Git is a distributed revision control system, it is vital to obtain absolute assurance that data integrity is maintained and is not somehow being altered. How do you know the data hasn't been altered in transition from one developer to the next? Or from one repository to the next? Or, for that matter, that the data in a Git repository is even what it purports to be?

Git uses a common cryptographic hash function, called Secure Hash Function (SHA1), to name and identify objects within its database. Though perhaps not absolute, in practice it has proven to be solid enough to ensure integrity and trust for all of Git's distributed repositories.

Enforce accountability

One of the key aspects of a version control system is knowing who changed files and, if at all possible, why. Git enforces a change log on every commit that changes a file. The information stored in that change log is left up to the developer, project requirements, management, convention, and so on. Git ensures that changes will not happen mysteriously to files under version control because there is an accountability trail for all changes.

Immutability

Git's repository database contains data objects that are *immutable*. That is, once they have been created and placed in the database, they cannot be modified. They can be re-created differently, of course, but the original data cannot be altered without consequences. The design of the Git database means that the entire history stored within the version control database is also immutable. Using immutable objects has several advantages, including quick comparison for equality.

Atomic transactions

With atomic transactions, a number of different but related changes are performed either all together or not at all. This property ensures that the version control database is not left in a partially changed or corrupted state while an update or commit is happening. Git implements atomic transactions by recording complete, discrete repository states that cannot be broken down into individual or smaller state changes.

Support and encourage branched development

Almost all VCSs can name different genealogies of development within a single project. For instance, one sequence of code changes could be called "development," while another is referred to as "test." Each version control system can also split a single line of development into multiple lines and then unify, or merge, the disparate threads. As with most VCSs, Git calls a line of development a *branch* and assigns each branch a name.

Along with branching comes merging. Just as Linus wanted easy branching to foster alternate lines of development, he also wanted to facilitate easy merging of those branches. Because branch merging has often been a painful and difficult operation in version control systems, it would be essential to support clean, fast, easy merging.

Complete repositories

So that individual developers needn't query a centralized repository server for historical revision information, it was essential that each repository have a complete copy of all historical revisions of every file.

A clean internal design

Even though end users might not be concerned about a clean internal design, it was important to Linus, and ultimately to other Git developers. Git's object model has simple structures that capture fundamental concepts for raw data, directory structure, the recording of changes, and so forth. Coupling the object model with a globally unique identifier technique allowed a very clean data model that could be managed in a distributed development environment.

Be free, as in freedom

'Nuff said.

Given a clean slate to create a new VCS, many talented software engineers collaborated and Git was born. Necessity was the mother of invention again!

Precedents

The complete history of VCSs is beyond the scope of this book. However, there are several landmark, innovative systems that set the stage for or directly led to the development of Git. (This section is selective, hoping to record when new features were introduced or became popular within the free software community.)

The Source Code Control System (SCCS) was one of the original systems on Unix[2] and was developed by M. J. Rochkind in the early 1970s.[3] This is arguably the first VCS available on any Unix system.

The central store that SCCS provided was called a repository, and that fundamental concept remains pertinent to this day. SCCS also provided a simple locking model to serialize development. If a developer needed files to run and test a program, they would check them out unlocked. However, to edit a file, they had to check it out with a lock (a convention enforced through the Unix filesystem). When finished, the developer would check the file back into the repository and unlock it.

The Revision Control System (RCS) was introduced by Walter F. Tichy in the early 1980s.[4] RCS introduced both forward and reverse delta concepts for the efficient storage of different file revisions.

The Concurrent Versions System (CVS), designed and originally implemented by Dick Grune in 1986 and then crafted anew some four years later by Berliner and colleagues, extended and modified the RCS model with great success. CVS became very popular and was the de facto standard within the open source community (*https://oreil.ly/rK76m*) for many years. CVS provided several advances over RCS, including distributed development and repository-wide changesets for entire "modules."

Furthermore, CVS introduced a new paradigm for the lock. Whereas earlier systems required a developer to lock each file before changing it and thus forced one developer to wait for another in serial fashion, CVS gave each developer write permission in their private working copy. Thus changes by different developers could be merged automatically by CVS unless two developers tried to change the same line. In that case, the conflict was flagged, and the developers were left to work out the solution. The new rules for the lock allowed different developers to write code concurrently.

As often occurs, perceived shortcomings and faults in CVS eventually led to a new VCS. Subversion (SVN), introduced in 2001, quickly became popular within the free software community. Unlike CVS, SVN committed changes atomically and had significantly better support for branches.

BitKeeper and Mercurial were radical departures from all the aforementioned solutions. Each eliminated the central repository; instead, the store was distributed, providing each developer with their own shareable copy. Git is derived from this peer-to-peer model.

---

2 UNIX® is a registered trademark of The Open Group in the United States and other countries.

3 "The Source Code Control System," *IEEE Transactions on Software Engineering* 1(4) (1975): 364–370.

4 "RCS: A System for Version Control," *Software Practice and Experience* 15(7) (1985): 637–654.

Finally, Mercurial and Monotone contrived a hash fingerprint to uniquely identify a file's content. The name assigned to the file is a moniker and a convenient handle for the user and nothing more. Git features this notion as well. Internally, the Git identifier is based on the file's contents, a concept known as a *content-addressable file store*. The concept is not new.[5] Git immediately borrowed the idea from Monotone, according to Linus.[6] Mercurial was implementing the concept simultaneously with Git.

Timeline

With the stage set, a bit of external impetus, and a dire VCS crisis imminent, Git sprang to life in April 2005.

Git became self-hosted on April 7 with this commit:

```
commit e83c5163316f89bfbde7d9ab23ca2e25604af29
Author: Linus Torvalds <torvalds@ppc970.osdl.org>
Date:   Thu Apr 7 15:13:13 2005 -0700

Initial revision of "git", the information manager from hell
```

Shortly thereafter, the first Linux commit was made:

```
commit 1da177e4c3f41524e886b7f1b8a0c1fc7321cac2
Author: Linus Torvalds <torvalds@ppc970.osdl.org>
Date:   Sat Apr 16 15:20:36 2005 -0700

Linux-2.6.12-rc2

Initial git repository build. I'm not bothering with the full history,
even though we have it. We can create a separate "historical" git
archive of that later if we want to, and in the meantime it's about
3.2GB when imported into git - space that would just make the early
git days unnecessarily complicated, when we don't have a lot of good
infrastructure for it.

Let it rip!
```

That one commit introduced the bulk of the entire Linux kernel into a Git repository.[7] It consisted of the following:

```
17291 files changed, 6718755 insertions(+), 0 deletions(-)
```

Yes, that's an introduction of 6.7 million lines of code!

It was just three minutes later when the first patch using Git was applied to the kernel. Convinced that it was working, Linus announced it on April 20, 2005, to the Linux Kernel Mailing List.

---

5 See "Venti: A New Approach to Archival Storage" (*https://oreil.ly/A5ljM*), Plan 9, Bell Labs.

6 Private email.

7 See this starting point (*https://oreil.ly/fj0nf*) on how the old BitKeeper logs were imported into a Git repository for older history (pre-2.5).

Knowing full well that he wanted to return to the task of developing the kernel, Linus handed the maintenance of the Git source code to Junio Hamano on July 25, 2005, announcing that "Junio was the obvious choice."

About two months later, version 2.6.12 of the Linux kernel was released using Git.

What's in a Name?

Linus himself rationalizes the name "Git" by claiming, "I'm an egotistical @$%&, and I name all my projects after myself. First Linux, now git." Granted, the name "Linux" for the kernel was sort of a hybrid of Linus and Minix. The irony of using a British term for a silly or worthless person was not missed, either.

Since then, others have suggested some alternative and perhaps more palatable interpretations: the Global Information Tracker seems to be the most popular.

Installing Git

So, before you can use Git, you must install it. The steps to install Git depend greatly on the vendor and version of your operating system. This appendix describes how to install Git on Linux, macOS, and Microsoft Windows. We also share how you can obtain the Git source code and then build and install from it.

Using Linux Binary Distributions

Many Linux vendors provide precompiled, binary packages to make the installation of new applications, tools, and utilities easy. Each package specifies its dependencies, and the distribution's package manager typically installs the prerequisites and the desired package in one (well-orchestrated and automated) fell swoop.

Debian/Ubuntu

On most Debian and Ubuntu systems, Git is offered as a collection of packages, where each package can be installed independently depending on your needs. Prior to the 12.04 release, the primary Git package was called `git-core`. As of the 12.04 release, it is simply called `git`. Examples of other git packages include `git-gui`, `gitk`, `gitweb`, and `git-svn`.

Because distributions vary greatly, it's best to search your distribution's package depot for a complete list of Git-related packages.

This command installs the latest (stable) version of Git on your Debian/Ubuntu operating system:

```
$ apt-get install git
```

Other Binary Distributions

To install Git on other Linux distributions, find the appropriate package or packages, and use the distribution's native package manager to install the software:

On Gentoo systems
```
$ emerge --ask --verbose dev-vcs/git
```

On Arch Linux systems
```
$ pacman -S git
```

On Fedora systems
```
# For up to Fedora version 21
$ yum install git

# For Fedora version 22 and above
$ dnf install git
```

On other distributions
> For other popular Linux distributions, the git-scm download documentation (*https://oreil.ly/eods1*) lists all the commands you need.

Again, be mindful that some distributions may split the Git release among many different packages. If your system lacks a particular Git command, you may need to install an additional package.

Be sure to verify that your distribution's Git packages are sufficiently up to date. After Git is installed on your system, run `git --version` to verify the latest version of Git. At the time of this writing, the latest version is Git 2.37.0.

Installing Git on macOS

On macOS, the approach is similar. You have various options for installing Git via popular package manager and binary installers:

Homebrew
```
$ brew install git
```

MacPorts
```
# Requires MacPorts to be installed prior to installing Git
$ sudo port install git
```

Other installers
> The git-scm download documentation (*https://oreil.ly/8QlHq*) lists popular installers.

Installing Git on Windows

On Windows, you have the option to install Git from a standalone installer, from a portable installer, or by using the Windows Package Manager, winget (*https://oreil.ly/OfzUG*), or the community maintained package manager, chocolatey (*https://oreil.ly/h5NLj*):

Git for Windows
> Download the installer (*https://oreil.ly/RsWSY*), and follow the instructions to configure and select options when installing it via the standalone installer.

winget
```
# Execute from Powershell or Command Prompt
PS C:\>winget install --id Git.Git -e --source winget
```

Chocolatey
```
# Execute from Powershell or Command Prompt
PS C:\>choco install git.install
```

Obtaining a Source Release

If you prefer, you can download (*https://mirrors.edge.kernel.org/pub/software/scm/git*) the Git code from its canonical source or download a specific version of Git. You can find various versions available as tarballs. As mentioned earlier, the version we are using in this book is Git 2.37.0:

```
$ wget https://mirrors.edge.kernel.org/pub/software/scm/git/git-2.37.0.tar.gz
$ tar xzf git-2.37.0.tar.gz
$ cd git-2.37.0
```

Building and Installing from Source Release

Git is similar to other pieces of open source software. Just configure it, type **make**, and install it. Small matter of software, right? Perhaps.

If your system has the proper libraries and a robust build environment, and if you do not need to customize Git, then building the code can be a snap. On the other hand, if your machine lacks a compiler or a suite of server and software development libraries, or if you've never built a complex application from source, then you should consider building Git from scratch only as a last resort. Git is highly configurable, and building it shouldn't be taken lightly.

To continue the build, consult the *INSTALL* file (*https://oreil.ly/dCEy3*) in the Git source bundle. The file lists several external dependencies, including the *zlib*, *ssh*, and *libcurl* libraries, to name a few.

Note that some of the requisite libraries and packages may belong to larger packages.

Once your system and build options are ready, the rest is easy. These commands build and install Git in your home directory (we added the `--prefix=/usr/local` flag to install Git for all users):

```
$ cd git-2.37.0
$ ./configure --prefix=/usr/local
$ sudo make all
$ sudo make install

# refresh the shell
$ exec bash

$ git --version
git version 2.37.0

$ which git
/usr/local/bin/git
```

To install the Git documentation, add the doc and install-doc targets to the make and make install commands, respectively:

```
$ cd git-2.37.0
$ make all doc
$ sudo make install install-doc
```

A build from source includes all the Git subpackages and commands. There is no need to build or install those utilities independently.

Index

Symbols

! (exclamation point)
  feature branch indicator, 63
  .gitignore file, 119
\# (pound sign)
  comments for merge commits, 130
  comments in .gitignore file, 118
* (asterisk)
  REMOVED replacement text, 398
  active branch indicator, 63
  git show-branch commits, 64
  refspec syntax, 249
\+ (plus sign)
  git diff command output, 18, 158, 168
    --word-diff= mode, 162
  git show-branch commits, 64
  refspec syntax, 249
+++ (triple plus sign) in git diff output, 18, 158,
  168
- (dash)
  bare double dash, 9
    filename indication, 9, 70, 415
    git grep path limiting, 412
  git diff command output, 18, 158, 168
    merge conflicts, 128, 133-136
    --word-diff= mode, 162
  git show-branch commits, 64
  git show-branch separator, 63, 64
  short (-) and long (--) options, 8
--- (triple minus sign) in git diff output, 18, 158,
  168
. (dot)
  current directory in Unix, 12
  double-dot syntax (..)

    commit ranges, 97, 280, 322
    commit ranges for patches, 319, 322-325
    git diff command ranges, 168-171
    ranges as set operation, 97
  triple-dot syntax (...)
    commit ranges, 100, 171, 280
    git diff path... command, 163
    git log graph of merge structure, 218
    qualifiers for refs, 235
.. (double-dot syntax)
  commit ranges, 97, 322
    main and origin/main, 280
    patch generation, 319, 322-325
  git diff command ranges, 168-171
  ranges as set operation, 97
... (triple-dot syntax)
  commit ranges, 100, 171, 280
  git diff path... command, 163
  git log graph of merge structure, 218
  qualifiers for refs, 235
/ (slash)
  branch names, 57
  directory parameter when trailing, 353
: (colon)
  commit:path options, 386
  pushes with just destination ref, 281
  refspec syntax, 249
< > (angle brackets) as git log commit indica-
  tors, 137
<<<===>>> (conflict resolution markers), 71
  git diff command for conflict, 128, 133-136
    --check option to highlight markers, 132
  inspecting conflicted files, 132-138
  text merge driver, 152

501

N

names of branches, 57
  ambiguous name handling, 277
  default branch name, 57
  git branch command introducing, 62
  hierarchical branch names, 57
  pointer to most recent commit, 59, 64
  rules for names, 57
  tag with same name, 60
names of repositories, 246-251
namespaces
  refs, 83
  SHA1 hashes, 38
  tracking branches, 244-246
Newren, Elijah, 391, 392
nonbare repositories (see development repositories)
normal merges strategies
  applying, 151
  merge-org strategy, 148
  octopus strategy, 148, 149
  recursive strategy, 148, 149
  resolve strategy, 148

O

object IDs, 29, 82
  (see also SHA1 hash values)
object store, 26, 33-35
  about object creation, 49-54
  content tracking, 29-31
  content-addressable database, 29
    git commit --amend command regenerating, 194
  files and trees, 39
  git show command to display objects, 90
  listing objects in, 387
  object type via git cat-file command, 388
  packfiles, 27, 32
  refs and symrefs, 83-85
  repository internal workings, 36-47, 49-54
    blob objects and hashes, 38
    commit objects, 43-45
    .git hidden directory, 36-38
    tag objects, 46
    tree hierarchies, 42
  unreachable objects, 387
    garbage collection, 75, 404-407
    unreachable commits, 75
octopus merge strategy, 148, 149

applying, 151
  largest to date, 150
online resources (see resources online)
origin remote, 243
  creating for example depot, 253-255
  origin/main, 83
ORIG_HEAD, 83-84
  git reset --hard ORIG_HEAD to discard merge, 141
  git reset command saving HEAD to, 141, 199
ours merge strategy, 150
  applying, 151

P

packfiles, 27, 32
  garbage collection creating, 405
  packing heuristics, 405
  SHA1 for each object in pack, 405
parent commits, 85, 94
parent repository as upstream, 299
partial clones, 425
  GitHub blog post on tips, 426
patches
  about, 315
  about transfer protocols, 315
  applying, 330-337
    git diff output extra information, 334
    resetting or aborting, 333
    show patch and files affected, 332
    three-way merge, 334
  bad patches, 337
  generating patches, 317
    commit ranges, 319, 322-325
    -n option for most recent n commits, 318
    topological sorts and patches, 325
  history of Git, 494
  hooks for patch actions, 347
  interactive hunk staging, 371-381
    hunk definition, 374
    splitting hunks, 375
  mailing patches, 326-329
    bad patches, 337
  merging versus patching, 338
  upstream versus downstream role duality, 301
  why use patches, 316
path limiting options, 385

About the Author

Prem Kumar Ponuthorai is responsible for strategizing and enabling GitHub's offerings for the Expert Services Delivery organization. Having built on his software engineering background by becoming a Git convert, Prem has given Git workshops at conferences and provided training in Git for enterprise customers across diverse industries.

Jon Loeliger is a freelance software engineer who contributes to open source projects such as Linux, U-Boot, and Git. He has given tutorial presentations on Git at many conferences, including Linux World, and has written several papers on Git for *Linux Magazine*.

Colophon

The animal on the cover of *Version Control with Git* is a long-eared bat. It is a fairly large bat that is common and widespread throughout Great Britain and Ireland. It can also be found in Japan. Often seen in colonies of 50 to 100 or more, it lives in open woodlands, as well as in parks and gardens and in spaces under houses and church roofs. It also hibernates in caves, where it is more solitary in habit.

The long-eared bat is a medium-sized bat with a broad wingspan of about 25 cm. Its ears are very long and have a very distinctive fold. Their inner edges meet each other on the top of the head, and their outer edges end just behind the angle of the mouth. When the bat sleeps, it folds its ears under its wings. During flight, the ears are pointing forward. Its fur is long, fluffy, and silky, extending a short way onto the surface of its wings. It is dusky brown in color on top and light or dirty brown in color below. Juveniles are pale gray, lacking the brown tinges of the adults. Its diet consists of flies, moths, and beetles. It glides among foliage, frequently hovering to scour for insects. When traveling to another tree, its flight is swift, strong, and close to the ground.

Long-eared bats breed in autumn and spring. Pregnant females form nursery colonies of 100 or more in early summer, and the single young or twins are born in June and July. Bats are the only true flying mammals. Contrary to popular misconception, they are not blind, and many can actually see very well. All British bats use echolocation to orient themselves at night; they emit bursts of sound that are of such high frequencies they are beyond the human range of hearing and are therefore called *ultrasound*. The bats then listen to and interpret the echoes bounced back from objects around them (including prey), which allows them to build a "sound picture" of their surroundings.

Like all bats, this species is vulnerable to a number of threats, including the loss of roost sites, as hollow trees are often cut down if thought unsafe. Pesticide use has devastating effects, causing severe declines in insect abundance and contaminating food with potentially fatal toxins. Insecticides applied to timbers inside buildings where roosts occur are a particular danger. The initial treatment can wipe out whole colonies (spraying timber where bats are roosting is now illegal), but the effects of these chemicals can be lethal to bats for up to 20 years. In Britain, under the Wildlife and Countryside Act, it is illegal to intentionally kill, injure, take, or sell a bat; to possess a live bat or part of a bat; and to intentionally, recklessly damage, obstruct, or destroy access to bat roosts. Under the conservation regulations, it is an offense to damage or destroy breeding sites or resting places. Offenders can be charged up to 5,000 pounds per bat affected and be sentenced to six months of imprisonment.

Many of the animals on O'Reilly covers are endangered; all of them are important to the world.

The cover illustration is by Karen Montgomery, based on an antique line engraving from *Dover Animals*. The cover fonts are Gilroy Semibold and Guardian Sans. The text font is Adobe Minion Pro; the heading font is Adobe Myriad Condensed; and the code font is Dalton Maag's Ubuntu Mono.

O'REILLY®

Learn from experts.
Become one yourself.

Books | Live online courses
Instant Answers | Virtual events
Videos | Interactive learning

Get started at oreilly.com.

Printed in the USA
CPSIA information can be obtained
at www.ICGtesting.com
JSHW050246090424
60798JS00010B/181